DOMESTIC
ECONOMIES

Engendering
Latin America

EDITORS:

Donna J. Guy
Ohio State University

Mary Karasch
Oakland University

Asunción Lavrin
Arizona State University

DOMESTIC ECONOMIES

Family, Work, and Welfare
in Mexico City, 1884–1943

Ann S. Blum

UNIVERSITY OF NEBRASKA PRESS § LINCOLN AND LONDON

Publication of this book was assisted by a grant from the Andrew
W. Mellon Foundation.

Portions of chapter 5 previously appeared as "Dying of Sadness:
Hospitalism and Child Welfare, Mexico City, 1920–1940," in
*Disease in the History of Modern Latin America: From Malaria
to AIDS*, ed. Diego Armus (Durham NC: Duke University Press,
2003), 209–36; portions of chapter 6 previously appeared as
"Cleaning the Revolutionary Household: Domestic Servants and
Public Welfare in Mexico City, 1900–1935," in *Journal of Women's
History* 15, no. 4 (Winter 2004): 67–90; and chapter 7 previously
appeared as "Breaking and Making Families: Adoption and Public
Welfare, Mexico City, 1938–1942," in *Sex in Revolution: Gender,
Politics, and Power in Modern Mexico*, ed. Jocelyn Olcott, Mary
Kay Vaughan, and Gabriela Cano (Durham NC: Duke University
Press, 2006), 127–44.

Library of Congress Cataloging-in-Publication Data

Blum, Ann Shelby, 1950–
Domestic economies: family, work, and welfare in Mexico City,
1884–1943 / Ann S. Blum.
p. cm.
Includes bibliographical references and index.
ISBN 978-0-8032-1359-3 (paper : alk. paper)
1. Family—Mexico—Mexico City—History—19th century.
2. Family—Mexico—Mexico City—History—20th century.
3. Child welfare—Mexico—Mexico City—History. 4. Child
labor—Mexico—Mexico City—History. 5. Labor—Mexico—
Mexico City—History. 6. Mexico City (Mexico)—Social conditions—20th century. 7. Mexico—Politics and government—
1867–1910. 8. Mexico—Politics and government—1910–1946.
9. Díaz, Porfirio, 1830–1915—Political and social views. 10. Díaz,
Porfirio, 1830–1915—Influence. I. Title.
HQ562.15.M49B55 2009
306.850972'53—dc22
2009023607

Set in Monotype Bulmer. Designed by A. Shahan.

Contents

Illustrations

Selective Chronology

1767   Casa de Niños Expósitos (Foundling Home) was founded in Mexico City, capital of New Spain.

1774   Hospicio de Pobres (Poorhouse) was founded in Mexico City.

1821   Mexico won independence from Spain.

1856–61   La Reforma (The Reform): the Constitution of 1857 established the separation of church and state and brought the life cycle under state authority. A series of laws and decrees on marriage and the family followed. New laws also brought primary education and welfare institutions under federal authority, but owing to lack of funds, welfare administration was soon handed over to the Mexico City Ayuntamiento (City Council).

1862–67   Segundo Imperio (Second Empire): Mexican conservatives installed Maximilian as emperor.

1867   Maximilian was defeated and the republic restored. Benito Juárez became president.

1871   Liberal civil code was issued, omitting formal adoption.

1876–1911   Porfiriato: politics during this era were dominated by perennial president General Porfirio Díaz.

1877   Mexico City's public welfare institutions came under federal administration.

1883   Concepción Gimeno de Flaquer launched *El Álbum de la Mujer*.

1884   Revised civil code was issued.

1884   Hospicio de Pobres was restricted to children and renamed the Hospicio de Niños.

1898   Dr. Miguel Domínguez was appointed director of the Mexico City foundling home and began implementing new wet nurse regulations.

1905   New Hospicio de Niños opened on the *calzada* San Antonio Abad.

1910   Centennial of Mexico's independence movement was celebrated.

1910   Francisco I. Madero challenged the reelection of Porfirio Díaz and called for revolution.

1911   Díaz resigned and went into exile. Madero entered Mexico City and took up presidency.

1913   Decena Trágica (Tragic Ten Days), Mexico City: In the February coup against Madero, he and his vice president were killed.

1913–14   Constitutionalist forces, led by Venustiano Carranza, fought federal forces, led by Victoriano Huerta.

1914   Francisco (Pancho) Villa broke with the Constitutionalists, who then retreated to Veracruz. Villistas and Zapatistas occupied Mexico City.

1914   First Constitutionalist decree on divorce was issued.

1916   First Pan-American Congress on the Child was held in Montevideo, Uruguay.

1916   Convención Constitucional (Constitutional Convention) was held in Querétaro.

1917   Constitution and Ley sobre Relaciones Familiares (Law of Family Relations) were issued. Constitutional Article 123 limited child labor. Family law instituted formal adoption.

1920–24   Alvaro Obregón served as president.

1921   Primer Congreso Mexicano del Niño (First Mexican Congress on the Child) was organized by Félix Palvicini, director of the Mexico City newspaper *El Universal*.

1921   La Semana del Niño (Week of the Child) was held in conjunction with the centennial celebration of Mexican independence.

1922   First of the Centros de Higiene Infantil (Child Health Centers) opened in Mexico City. First Mother's Day celebrated in Mexico.

1923   Second Congreso Mexicano del Niño took place.

1924–28   Plutarco Elías Calles served as president.

1926   Mexico City Tribunal para Menores (Juvenile Court) was established.

1926–29   La Cristiada (Cristero Rebellion) pitted the Catholic Church against the secular revolutionary state over the anticlerical provisions of the 1917 constitution.

1928–34   The Maximato: Politics were dominated by political boss Plutarco Elías Calles, called the "Jefe Máximo."

1929   Partido Nacional Revolucionario (PNR) was founded.

1928   New civil code was issued, effective 1932.

1931   Federal labor code was issued.

1933   New foundling home, officially renamed the Casa de Cuna, opened in suburban Coyoacán. Dr. Federico Gómez became director.

1934–40 Lázaro Cárdenas served as president.

1935 VII Pan-American Congress on the Child was held in Mexico City.

1938 Secretaría de Asistencia Pública (Ministry of Public Assistance) was created.

1938 President Cárdenas expropriated and nationalized U.S.-owned oil companies.

1940–46 Manuel Ávila Camacho served as president.

1943 Código del Seguridad Social (Social Security Code) was passed, effective 1945.

Acknowledgments

My brother Tom once characterized the academic life this way: "Read, read, read. Talk, talk, talk. Write, write, write." He is not an academic but he got it right. This book developed through conversations with my colleagues and engagement with their written work, and it is a great pleasure to thank those who have been most closely involved in its development.

The germ of this study first emerged from informal conversations with friends about the different meanings of family in the United States and Mexico. Those conversations persuaded me that studying the family was a good place for an outsider to begin delving more deeply into the dynamics of Mexican society. Those preliminary ideas and commitments acquired an intellectual framework and became a dissertation at the University of California, Berkeley. I am indebted to dissertation advisors, Tulio Halperín-

Donghi, chair, Margaret Chowning, and Francine Masiello for their guidance and encouragement. At Berkeley, Linda Lewin's rigorous research modeled the intriguing possibilities for exploring the social history of the family through the study of law. And during a visiting year at Cornell, conversations with Mary Beth Norton shaped my early questions about the lives of children outside of their families of origin.

The circle of intellectual support for this project included Sylvia Arrom and Donna Guy. I owe both of them special thanks. Silvia was working on her history of the Mexico City poorhouse and Donna had begun her study of childhood in Argentina when I was in the early stages of research on Mexican child welfare institutions. Both Silvia and Donna were extraordinarily generous in sharing their own work in progress. Both have read and offered extensive comments at different phases of this study, and I continue to learn from their work.

Two colleagues whose research focuses on Mexico City have been especially important to the development of this book. John Lear's contributions date back to student days when he gave me invaluable tips on Mexico City archives. His enthusiasm for the archival treasure hunt and his commitment to the history of the city were infectious. The depth and integrity of his work continue to be inspiring. As a colleague, he sets the standard for generosity. Thank you, John. Similarly, conversations with Katherine Bliss began in the archives and often continued over *comida corrida* in Mexico City's downtown cafeterias. In later years, we talked shop over tea or beer in Cambridge. Those conversations culminated in our collaboration on an article on adolescence in Mexico City. My admiration for Katherine's historical thinking is immeasurable and so are my thanks.

The Oaxaca Summer Institute in Mexican History has provided a stimulating venue for developing work related to this project. I owe special thanks to the seminar's director, William Beezley, for creating those memorable opportunities. Working in the seminar with William French has been a high point of my academic calendar. It has been a privilege and a pleasure to sustain a conversation with such a thoughtful and widely read colleague. Bill's insights, questions, and friendly challenges have sparked many of the ideas that I explore in this book and in related work, and I am greatly indebted to him. My warmest thanks also to the many students and visiting scholars who have made the seminar such a rich experience.

Parts of this book, differently configured, have appeared as journal articles and chapters in anthologies. I would like to thank the anonymous readers who commented on drafts of that work. It is a great pleasure to thank the editors by name for their confidence, patience, and feedback: Diego Armus, Katherine Bliss, Eileen Boris, Gabriela Cano, Claudia Fonseca, William French, Donna Guy, Jessaca Leinaweaver, Sonya Lipsett-Rivera, Jocelyn Olcott, Donald Stevens, Mary Kay Vaughan, and Mark Wasserman. I also want to thank colleagues who have invited me to present conference and workshop papers or have commented on them. They include Katherine Bliss, Laura Briggs, Donna Guy, Elizabeth Q. Hutchison, John Lear, Sonya Lipsett-Rivera, Teresa Meade, Nara Milanich, Jocelyn Olcott, Jadwiga Pieper, Julia Rodriguez, and Adam Warren.

Institutional support has also been crucial for developing this study. I am grateful for funding from the University of California, Berkeley's Center for Latin American Studies, the Graduate Humanities Fellowship Program, and the History Department Heller Fund, and from the President's Council on Cornell Women, of Cornell University. Since joining the faculty of the University of Massachusetts, Boston, I have been especially appreciative of the university's support for my research. In 2001 a grant from the Endowed Faculty Development Research Fund, established by the retired faculty and designated for junior faculty, supported a summer of research. I am grateful also for the 2004 grant from the Joseph P. Healey Fund, which supported another extended research stint. My colleagues in the Hispanic Studies Department, especially Reyes Coll-Tellechea and Clara Estow, provided additional administrative and financial support and plenty of encouragement.

This book's editorial phase has incurred other kinds of debts. My brother's summary of academic life predated the digital revolution. Dereck Mangus has been the skillful photo editor for this project. As we pored over photographs, our conversations ranged far and wide. Helen Snively's astute comments and encouragement helped reshape the final manuscript. At the University of Nebraska Press, Heather Lundine guided the project through the editorial process.

Then there are personal debts. During my many sojourns in Mexico City, Herzonia Yáñez Chávez's friendship and generous hospitality have provided a home away from home. Our visits to her Wednesday *mercado sobre ruedas* and the delicious meals that follow have become an entirely new area of informal research. Over the years, Raúl García Barrios and Emma León have frequently lured me out of Mexico City to Cuernavaca to explore other Mexicos. The warmth of their friendship is a great gift. And, of course, my love and boundless thanks to Ruthie Gilmore, Cheryl Springer, and Sheila Tully. Their intellectual acuity always inspires me, their encouragement lifts me over the hard spots, and their friendship makes the whole enterprise worthwhile.

Mere thank you's don't begin to express my gratitude to my immediate family. They have been patient with my frequent and sometimes prolonged research trips and my preoccupation with writing, and that has not always been easy. They have also found creative ways to help. I am especially grateful to Peter Taylor and Pam Blum for a new desk chair—the best kind of material support. My sister, Pamela Blum, hosted my family for weeks at a time to give me precious uninterrupted time to write. More than once, Peter rescued chapters from electronic oblivion. But there is no adequate way to thank Peter for his contributions to this book or, more important, for his part in the minutiae and transcendence of everyday life.

Finally, I am profoundly thankful for the many ways my extended family has inspired this study. I dedicate this book to Vicki and Alison and to our children. You don't have to read another word, but all of you are in every keystroke.

Introduction

Childhood, Class, and Family in Mexico City

In the spring of 1906 officials at the federal agency overseeing Mexico City's public welfare system wrote to government lawyers requesting a precise legal definition of a foundling (*expósito*).[1] Since the late 1870s the federal government had administered the city's public orphanages, including the foundling home named the Casa de Niños Expósitos. But apparently government officials were no longer satisfied with the definition of a foundling in the home's 1898 regulations: a child without known parents. Those regulations perpetuated a definition based on abandonment practices that reached back to the late eighteenth century when the foundling home first opened under religious auspices and when infants borne by unmarried women were abandoned as a strategy for preserving family honor.[2] By 1906 times had changed. Single mothers still brought their children to the foundling home, but poverty motivated them, not shame. The 1906 request for this definition indicates that officials at the highest levels of the Mexican government sought to clarify the statutory foundations of the state's responsibility for children of the urban poor. The lawyer who responded to the officials' inquiry defined a foundling as an abandoned child "who by his age is incapable of providing for his own subsistence, or, a child under the age of seven."[3]

This correspondence between welfare officials and the government lawyer deserves close scrutiny because it invokes a complex of interrelated ideas and practices that reflect some of the profound differences between today's understandings of family, childhood, and social responsibility and those prevalent in 1906. Two such practices, child abandonment and child labor, are central themes of this book. A large social and economic gulf separated the welfare officials involved in this exchange from the families most likely to abandon their children or put them to work. Given that gulf, the public welfare system served as an arena for encounters between the poor and the powerful over the fate of those children. Their cross-class interactions are another central concern of this study. The lawyer's answer also rested on social and cultural assumptions about the intersection of family, work, and welfare that by 1906 were undergoing profound transformations. In this book I trace changing concepts of family, childhood, and social responsibility to assess the roles they played in class and state formation in Mexico in the late nineteenth and early twentieth centuries. This bureaucratic exchange, therefore, provides an apt point of departure for introducing these themes and arguments.

The very term "foundling" invokes a long history of ideas about sex, gender, and social status: having a child outside of marriage tarnished a woman's and her family's reputation, and she passed on to her children the stain of her sexual transgression. During the eighteenth and nineteenth centuries, foundling homes proliferated in cities throughout Europe and the Americas to provide a humane alternative for desperate single mothers considering infanticide. The opening of the Casa de Niños Expósitos in Mexico City in 1767 marked growing concerns about women's chastity, the fate of illegitimate children, and the issue of social responsibility for those children.[4]

The historical practice of abandoning infants, even to a charitable institution, contradicts the core values that most twenty-first century readers associate with the mother-child relationship, as do other earlier childrearing practices, such as the widespread use of wet nurses as a substitute for maternal breast-feeding. Indeed, foundling homes and wet-nursing were closely connected. Like many other institutions of its kind, the Casa de Niños Expósitos placed abandoned babies in the homes of village nurses; some stayed there as long as six years before returning to the orphanage. This enduring policy tied abandonment and wet-nursing to wider networks of child circulation, that is, the movement of children out of their families of origin and into other households or institutions.[5] By 1906 decades of criticism of wet-nursing by Mexican doctors had not put an end to the widespread use of wet nurses, but it had influenced a change in foundling home policy: now wet nurses lived and worked inside the institution under doctors' supervision.[6]

Just as the interrelated practices of infant abandonment, wet-nursing, and child circulation are fundamentally at odds with modern ideas of motherhood, childhood, and the family, so also is the government lawyer's assumption that children as young as seven were capable of working to support themselves. His statement calls for explanation. Many of the lawyer's class peers routinely employed young children in their own homes and enterprises, while many parents among the urban poor put their children to work out of need. Working in a respectable household, for example, supposedly offered girls from poor families a mix of protection and education, and many lived with wealthier families and worked without pay as nannies or domestics. This blend of fostering and labor, which also took place within family networks, fell under the rubric of informal adoption, especially of girls. For boys, unpaid apprenticeships were considered education: work taught boys the productive skills they needed to support themselves and their dependents in later life.[7] Such arrangements rested on the deeply rooted understanding that informed the asymmetrical relations between patron and client: those who received protection and assistance owed labor in return.

The same expectations had long shaped the policies organizing public child welfare institutions.[8] Like their late-colonial predecessors who founded the Mexico City poorhouse in 1774, welfare officials in the nineteenth and early twentieth centuries were convinced that the habits and discipline of labor and productivity underlay citizenship and the construction of a modern polity. They strove to craft welfare policies that distinguished deserving recipients of public aid from the urban poor whose misery, they believed, resulted from laziness or vice. The education offered at the Casa de Niños Expósitos and the Hospicio de Niños (Children's Hospice), the former poorhouse officially converted to an orphanage in 1884, emphasized training for labor. Both establishments frequently released boys into apprenticeships with artisans and used loosely regulated informal adoptions to place girls in domestic service. Parents who placed their children in the Hospicio to receive an education and learn a trade often withdrew them when they were old enough to work to help support or care for younger siblings. Thus, when the government lawyer asserted that seven-year-olds could work to support themselves, he referred to long-standing labor practices connecting patronage, welfare, and informal adoption—practices that shaped the experiences of many children of the urban poor.

In the broader context of early twentieth-century Mexico, the lawyer's definition of a foundling is as significant for the understandings of childhood that he omitted as for those he invoked. By 1906 a very different concept of childhood, closely tied to gender roles defining respectability and class status, had consolidated among those in Mexico's middle and upper social strata.[9] They believed children should have the opportunity for play and other innocent pastimes—the antithesis of labor—and their education should be prolonged. Writers addressing privileged audiences stressed children's vulnerability and purity, qualities also associated with elite ideals of femininity. Applied to childhood, these ideals infused the gender division of parental duties with even greater importance. Mothers were supposed to devote themselves exclusively to the oversight of infancy and early childhood within the confines of the home. Privileged women could focus on the emotional aspects of mothering and delegate the more arduous tasks to their domestics, including live-in wet nurses, nannies, and servants, some of whom were scarcely older than the employers' own children. Fathers, in turn, were expected to model responsibility and productivity and take a more active role in the education and discipline of older children. Generations of legal codes on the family attested to the long history of those intergenerational obligations and divisions of parental roles along gender lines.[10]

But in late nineteenth-century Mexico and throughout Europe and the Americas, new ideas about health and hygiene influenced concepts of childhood as a special life stage and also inflected parents' roles in significant ways. In a context of high rates of infant mortality among all social classes, the Mexican government committed substantial funds to develop children's medicine in the capital. Middle- and upper-class parents sought the most up-to-date medical care to protect and enhance their children's health.[11] Long-established practices like wet-nursing came under attack for medical and moral reasons, influencing ideas of motherhood as much as infant care. Concerns about family health also prompted homemakers to maintain higher standards of domestic and personal hygiene, thus transforming the physical environments and routines of childrearing.[12]

The new childrearing routines and housekeeping standards that were attached to late nineteenth-century bourgeois family ideologies had a profound impact on wet nurses, nannies, and domestics: poorly paid girls and women of the working classes. The public child welfare system played an important role in mediating between employers and domestics. Employers preferred to hire domestics without children who could focus exclusively on their work and charges. But domestics with children sometimes had nowhere to place their children except in welfare institutions. Others received such meager pay that they were forced to intern their children in the foundling home or the Hospicio. Likewise, in training girls for domestic work and releasing them into service through informal adoption, the public welfare system supplied workers for the capital's domestic labor force and helped shape the ways that domestic labor connected families across class lines. In the process, public welfare policy and institutions fostered interlocking, or mutually constituted, family forms and class identities founded on the labor of girls and women.[13]

From the perspective of privileged Mexicans—including welfare officials and government lawyers—the ideals and practices of protected childhood and related gender roles distinguished their own childrearing and values from the families of Mexico City's working poor, where fathers were often absent, mothers often worked outside the home, and children often left school to work.[14] Many children who entered orphanages had living parents too poor to maintain them. Mothers who abandoned their infants to foundling homes often did so anonymously, so that the babies' parentage would remain a secret: that is why foundlings — of unknown parents — were considered orphans. In this book, I argue that concepts of childhood, inextricably tied to adult gender and labor roles, were fundamental to the evolution of Mexican class identities during the late nineteenth and early twentieth century. The lawyer's definition of a foundling pointed clearly to the class-specific concepts of childhood, family, and work that shaped the Mexican government's welfare policies. It also measured the distance separating middle- and upper-class concepts of protected childhood and of ideals about parental roles from the labor practices and household formations that reflected the urgent needs and limited options of poor families. Yet as different as these class-based family forms were, they were founded on an exchange of reproductive labor across class lines and formed interlocking domestic economies.

Through its child welfare policies the government maintained the material and symbolic distinctions between protected and working childhoods and thereby played an important role in shaping the family forms and practices on which class identities were founded. Indeed, the distinctions between protected and working childhoods, along with domestic service and other markers of bourgeois or plebian family status, contributed actively to class formation. These distinctions were also in flux, like much else in Mexico at the time. In this book I trace and explain both changes and continuities in the assumptions grounding concepts of the family and childhood in Mexico, as well as the class and labor relations that flowed from them from the mid-1880s to the early 1940s.

The decades in question span the later years of the Porfiriato, the period from 1876 to 1911 dominated by Mexico's perennial president General Porfirio Díaz. They also include the military phase of Mexico's revolution from 1911 through 1917 and extend through the 1920s and 1930s, the era of national reconstruction and consolidation of the revolutionary state. At either end of this span, the two dates 1884 and 1943 represent milestones in Mexican public policy based on concepts of childhood and social responsibility for children. The first milestone was little noticed except by the families of the capital's working poor: in 1884, Mexico City's poorhouse, renamed the Hospicio de Niños, officially restricted admission to children. The new policy responded to the ways that Mexico City residents used the institution: for some time, children had made up the majority of the asylum's internal population. This move also reflected the belief that children were a special social category and the assumption that poor children were more deserving of public assistance than their elders. Even so, the assistance provided at the Hospicio emphasized training for early entry into the workforce.[15] Almost sixty years later, in 1943, Mexico's first social security legislation reflected profound transformations in social understandings of childhood as a life stage, children's social roles, and especially children's relationship to work. The revolutionary Constitution of 1917 had committed the Mexican state to providing social security to workers. When the law was finally issued twenty-five years later, it defined children as dependents, not workers, and further defined the shared responsibility between parents and the state to provide for children's support.[16]

The concept of protected childhood entailed one safeguarded by hygienic nurture and medical supervision, devoted to innocent pastimes and education and, above all, freedom from work. Yet in Mexico, the process of expanding that protection to include all children regardless of class was scarcely smooth on an ideological level and, in practice, was incomplete. During the Porfiriato, conflict over competing concepts of childhood came to light through the welfare system's involvement with abandonment, wet-nursing, child labor, and adoption. Indeed, the clash between ideals and realities of childhood revealed the uneven and contested process of change in beliefs shaping families and linking them to Mexico's political sphere. Along with other highly charged social issues such as prostitution and crime, which social analysts considered inherent attributes of the lower classes, topics related to childhood touched sensitive nerves in public debate.[17] In the capital city's print press, for example, passions ran high on the subjects of breast-feeding and maternal responsibility. Critics attacked wet-nursing in the name of improving the health and survival of all infants. But the importance of applying those goals to children across the social spectrum cannot fully explain the overwrought depictions of wet nurses as corrupt, diseased, and immoral, or of their female employers as vain and frivolous to the point of endangering their children's lives. Rather, the exaggerated and gendered sentiments of the anti–wet nurse campaign reveal how highly charged the politics of reproduction and class had become in the broader context of the Díaz government's push to develop industry and modernize society.[18]

Similarly, Porfirian welfare policies exposed elite sensitivities about contradictory concepts of childhood. As happened with wet-nursing, inconsistencies between welfare policies on abandonment and their actual implementation point to the volatile class politics of the family. At the turn of the century, for example, a new rule at the foundling home made it possible for parents to intern their children but still retain legal authority over them. But when single mothers deposited and then retrieved their children at unprecedented rates, officials had second thoughts and restricted those options, making family reunification more difficult for the urban poor. By rescinding the option to use the foundling home as a temporary resource, officials revealed their discomfort with poor mothers' sense of entitlement to family life.

Conflicted class-based concepts of childhood also emerged in the welfare policy on adoption. After the mid-nineteenth century, Mexican civil law did not permit formal adoption, but public orphanages allowed two kinds of informal adoption: for family formation and for labor. Welfare administrators claimed that both practices were in children's best interests. Even without the support of the law, a growing number of childless couples applied to the foundling home to adopt babies.[19] Concurrently, brokers rounded up groups of older children from the Hospicio de Niños and the Casa de Niños Expósitos to send as workers to regions undergoing an economic boom. These jarring contradictions illuminate the high interpersonal and material stakes in the class politics of childhood or, more broadly, of social reproduction.

The Politics of Family and Childhood

Family and childhood may seem remote from the issues that provoked Mexico's political revolution of 1910. Mexicans who answered the first calls for revolution took up arms to support a more inclusive political system, to gain access to land, and to secure labor rights. But the Porfirian facade of social and cultural certainties founded on class-based family differences would crumble in the face of revolution. Well before the fighting subsided, revolutionaries began debating the implications of the struggle for the Mexican family—the primary building block of Mexican society—and began planning the social revolution. Thus the concepts and practices of protected childhood, originally confined to privileged families, evolved within the context of conflict and discontinuity that characterized the military phase of the revolution and the decades of national reconstruction that followed.

Focusing on family and childhood during this tumultuous period illuminates new ways that the Mexican Revolution reconfigured the compact between state and citizen, as children moved to the center of the political stage and came to represent the national future. Officials of the defeated Díaz regime had asserted repeatedly that the state bore no responsibility for the poor: that was the role of private philanthropy.[20] Rejecting this attitude, Mexican revolutionaries and reformers conceived of a state that would take the lead in social change. In this, they emulated the founding fathers of modern Mexico: the Liberals who authored the Constitution of 1857 had separated church from state and then had crafted the series of laws known as La Reforma (the Reform), which brought the family and its life cycles, as well as welfare and education, under secular state oversight.

The blueprint for the twentieth-century revolutionary state, the Constitution of 1917, is best known for mandating land reform, severely restricting the power of the Catholic Church, and expanding the state's role in socializing future citizens through universal secular education. The document also significantly limited child labor, thereby making a strong statement about the model of childhood that was appropriate for Mexico's revolutionary society.[21] The victorious faction then demonstrated the centrality of family in the revolutionary political and social project by quickly issuing a new law regulating family relations. The law's innovations included strengthening mothers' legal authority over their children, allowing definitive divorce (rather than mere separation) and remarriage, and legalizing formal adoption.[22] In these ways, two of the founding documents of Mexico's revolutionary order set out the terms that established the state's power to intervene in family life and set the stage for making the family — and childhood — key sites of state-led social change.

These measures indicate both the scope and limits of Mexico's revolutionary project for social change focused on the family. Although the 1917 Constitution's article on labor relations was advanced for its time and other Latin American nations would wait decades to legalize divorce, the authors of the 1917 Constitution and Ley sobre Relaciones Familiares (Law of Family Relations) did not propose radical reconfigurations of relations within the family. In contrast, only one year later revolutionary Russia issued a family code that many of its authors believed would soon be unnecessary: with capitalism eliminated, all family functions would be socialized and the bourgeois family would disappear.[23] In Mexico the social trends and public programs that would extend the ideal of protection to all children adhered closely to the more moderate currents of reform that swept Europe and the Americas in the years following World War I; those measures focused on education and child health and, as in Mexico, limited child labor. Nor did Mexico necessarily lead the way in public services for families and children compared to other nations of the Americas. Child-centered movements throughout the continent prompted the formation of organizations such as the Pan-American Child Congresses. Starting in 1916 those meetings brought together specialists in child development, medicine, and pedagogy—which were combined in a new field called puericulture that integrated children's health with their family and social environments. Congress proceedings prompted governments throughout the region to implement the delegates' expert recommendations, and the resulting reforms often equaled and sometimes exceeded Mexico's public programs for families and children.[24] Historian Mary Kay Vaughan has described the Mexican revolutionary state's growing role in social life as a public appropriation of social reproduction, but this process occurred on a relatively moderate and middle-class model.[25] Even so, the changes that the state-led reform program brought had profound implications for the ways that families lived their lives and their children grew up.

Recently, historians focusing on Mexico City during this era have assessed the impact of the revolution on urban education, labor relations, moral reform, and public health.[26] They have found that reform-minded professionals saw the revolution as an unprecedented opportunity to renovate existing public services and introduce new programs aimed at raising the levels of health and education among the lower classes. Proposals for family-focused reform juxtaposed deeply held beliefs among more conservative Mexicans; innovative ideas about social responsibility, family, and gender roles; and demands for even more radical change from Mexicans on the political left. These conflicting agendas provoked lively and frequently polarized public debate about the meanings and responsibilities of being a parent or child and about the state's role in family life.

At the same time, the experience of revolution strengthened the sense of political and social rights among the capital's working classes. New public services in maternal-child medicine, child welfare, and youth corrections created additional resources for the families of Mexico City's working poor. These new services also created myriad sites of intervention and interaction between poor families and their children, and state officials and their representatives. In complex and sometimes contradictory ways, this mix molded the constellation of public services for children that emerged from Mexico's social and political ferment, accelerated the pace of change in ideas about children's social roles, and elevated children in national life.

Several of the Mexican public programs that were directed at children and youth in the capital city come into focus in this book, in particular, those concerning maternal-child health and child labor. For example, because so many Mexicans had died from war and disease, the nation placed a high priority on fighting infant mortality and improving reproductive health. The government took a leading role in those campaigns by establishing a network of maternal-child health clinics located in Mexico City's working-class neighborhoods.[27] The mission of the public clinics mirrored the growing role of medicine in middle-class child-rearing practice. Like their Porfirian predecessors, however, physicians at the foundling home encountered unexpected obstacles to matching the successes of private and outpatient medicine with their infant inmates. Their path toward a solution led them to better appreciate working-class families, especially the mothers' role.

I approach the question of child labor during the reform period from two angles. First, the public welfare system had the task of implementing the law on formal adoption. Although adopters were required to view adoptees as their own children, people continued to expect them to be servants. The welfare system's adoption program sheds light on the gradual acceptance of formal adoption, which opened discussion about the parent-child relationship and was also an important strand in the growing consensus against child labor. But the process of protecting adoptees from work put the spotlight on women's work: frequently, paid work disqualified women from state-approved motherhood.

Second, the Mexico City juvenile court, founded in 1926, provided a program of reform and social reintegration tailored to the intellectual and physical development of adolescents, a relatively new social category. The vast majority of the children and youths who came before the court were from poor families, and officials became deeply implicated in the complex dynamics of families that depended on underage labor. The dilemmas that those families faced and the inability of court officials to solve them delineate the limits to social reform initiatives aimed at the changing family dynamics that were, in fact, founded on economic realities.

Despite these contradictions, between 1920 and 1940 Mexico's new public services for children and youth, and the public debate about them helped narrow the ideological, if not the material, divide between protected and working childhoods. In contrast to the government lawyer who asserted in 1906 that a seven-year-old child could work for his or her own living, by the 1930s physicians, educators, and social analysts agreed that child labor was the root cause of multiple problems: poor physical and intellectual development, juvenile delinquency, and the dissolution of families and even of society. An official writing in 1937 stated that child labor might meet immediate economic needs but that work harmed children because it rarely helped prepare them for the future.[28] To him, his fellow officials, and his class peers, child labor and its negative consequences highlighted Mexico's deficient social progress, and all of Mexican society—led by the state—should work together to correct it.

In 1943 Mexico's new social security law demonstrated that such ideas enjoyed wide acceptance. The law's authors wrote children out of the equation of family obligations founded on work: that relationship now lay between the Mexican state and working parents, who together shared responsibility for the well-being of the nation's dependent children.[29] Indeed, by that time, public policies and public cultures of childhood demonstrated that Mexico had become a significantly more child-centered society than during the Porfiriato. Children and youth of all social classes had come to represent the shared promise and future of the Mexican nation, which politicians and social analysts often described as a family.[30]

The metaphor of Mexico's revolutionary family is usually taken to mean a historical consensus in which former revolutionary rivals were joined in a single pantheon of national heroes symbolizing the institutionalized revolutionary state. I believe it is time to reassess this family metaphor, to explore the ways that actual children as well as representations of childhood came to embody revolutionary goals and values and helped cement a social and political consensus based on largely middle-class family identities. The family metaphor, moreover, naturalized gender relations premised on biological reproduction and then projected them onto the nation at large.[31] The family ideal—productive and protective fathers, nurturing mothers, and healthy children—offered the paternalistic state powerful justifications for its authority over its fractious constituents. Within the family model, children represented continuity and renewal, and both supporters and critics of government policies frequently invoked children to validate or attack competing visions of the Mexican national project. In these ways, children came to occupy a pivotal place in national life and nationalistic discourse, becoming at once the locus for debates over Mexican identities and the embodiment of the future.

Historical Perspectives on Family, Child Circulation, and Social Reproduction

I consider this a work of family history, that is, a study of relationships founded on kinship and social reproduction and their change over time. Within the frame of the family, I take a special interest in children's experiences and in the labor of childrearing. I also find that changing conceptions of childhood cannot be detached from conceptions of women's reproductive labor, and so I pay close attention to the interplay between those two trajectories. My focus on the labor of social reproduction, including domestic service and wet-nursing, breaches the conventional boundaries between families defined strictly by kinship: that is why I examine families connected by work and by adoption. To capture the dynamics of urban, working-class families, I include within my analytical framework some of the principal public institutions that substituted for families, as well as the government officials whose decisions influenced the experiences of children born into poor families in Mexico City.

Although this book covers a pivotal sixty-year period, it is a mere snapshot of long-term historical change. It also cuts across a number of historical subdisciplines, including the histories of women, gender, law, labor, and medicine, and an emerging history of childhood.[32] The rich secondary literatures that inform and inspire this book have demonstrated that many of the family and labor relations I describe have had long histories that transcend standard political periods and national boundaries. The histories of family relations and labor that scholars have teased out from the archival record merit some introduction, as do a number of terms and concepts that ground my analysis.

Historians Elizabeth Kuznesof and Robert Oppenheimer have described the Latin American family as a "central complex of relationships" that can serve as a lens "to make societal sense out of seemingly impersonal relations" in the realms of politics and the economy. They propose that studying the family can provide historical insights into the formal and informal socioeconomic institutions of class relations, such as "labor unions, slavery, domestic service, and patron-client relations."[33] Addressing the same set of questions from a different angle, anthropologist Rayna Rapp has argued that family identities are central to production and consumption. She observes that it is "because people accept" the family as meaningful and have a "commitment to the concept of family" that "they enter into relations of production, reproduction, and consumption with one another—they marry, beget children, work to support dependents, transmit and inherit cultural and material resources."[34]

In this book, I analyze the family from both perspectives. I use family as a lens to gain insight into politics and class relations. And I hope to bring into focus the interlocking domestic economies of urban, working-class families and the more privileged families that employed them and adopted their children, along with the child welfare system that often mediated those family interactions across class lines. By approaching the history of the family along these vectors, I aspire to reveal the meanings that mothers, fathers, and children invested in those interactions and the identities they derived from them during a period of dramatic social change.

To "make societal sense" of family relationships and their connections across class lines and with political institutions, I have drawn questions, methods, and terminology from an array of historical subdisciplines and from the social sciences. To begin with, my approach to family history has been enriched by questions that have been central to women's history, especially the project of recovering women's perspectives, decisions, and the ways they contributed both to the fabric of everyday life and to broad historical events.[35] A significant body of new research in women's history has shown, for example, that concepts of motherhood pervaded Mexican political discourse during the period of social reconstruction that followed the military phase of the revolution.[36] In this book I seek to illuminate some of the ways that the rhetorical importance placed on motherhood not only influenced social policy but also shaped the experiences of urban, working-class mothers and their children.

My approach to understanding family relations has also been shaped by work in gender history. Indeed, in recent years attention to gender—akin to other socially constructed and historically contingent categories like race and class—has transformed the practice of history and the social sciences. Gender, as distinct from biological sex, comprises social norms based on ideas about masculinity and femininity, the complementarity of those attributes, and the actions, social hierarchies, and systems of power that ideas about masculinity and femininity seem to legitimate and thus reinforce.[37] Through the lens of gender, the family can be seen as a set of relationships that are premised on men's and women's different roles in the biological reproduction and nurture of the next generation, and also as a set of social norms that are made to seem natural by biological reproduction. These norms organize and legitimate the distribution of power within the family and are then projected onto society at large.[38]

This study also incorporates the insights into changing concepts of the family and childhood that can be gained from a close examination of laws regulating families. Before and after the revolution, Mexican lawmakers saw the family as the fundamental social unit and wrote family laws that expressed ideals about social and political relationships. In this book, I pay particular attention to the ways that evolving family law reflected ideas about class differences and trends in thinking about the social roles and responsibilities of parents and children, and the ways that family law mirrored state-society relations. Revolutionary laws to regulate child labor, create formal adoption, and establish a special court for juveniles, for example, strengthened the definition of childhood as a special stage of life and reflected a growing social consensus about the state's responsibility to protect children from exploitation. Those laws also influenced the experience of growing up poor in Mexico City from one generation to the next.

Similarly, I approach the history of medicine from the perspective of the family. During the period analyzed in this book, children's medicine developed rapidly in Mexico, thanks largely to state support. Medical research introduced new ideas about infection and disease and about children's physical and intellectual development and thus contributed significantly to defining modern childhood. Medical findings and recommendations informed expert and lay opinion about how infants should be cared for and children raised.[39] Because mothers bore primary responsibility for raising children, medicine influenced their roles, both the physical work involved and the meanings attached to motherhood. New standards of personal and domestic hygiene impinged on the work that wet nurses, nannies, and domestics performed, and, in that regard, I approach medicine as a kind of labor discipline. This approach reveals that medicine had different impacts on poor and privileged families. Moreover, public welfare institutions serving the children of the urban poor had difficulty reproducing the successes of medical child care regimens that doctors recommended to their well-to-do patients. This persistent failure challenged physician reformers who sincerely believed that medicine could cure social ills and compelled them to view families of the urban poor in a different light.[40]

These strands of analysis converge in the concept of social reproduction, which encompasses the creation, sustenance, and socialization of new generations. Social reproduction entails childbearing and child care, household labor, and work outside the home that sustains the family.[41] Like other labor historians, I am interested in work and the ways it shapes class position and class identities. It is through the dynamics of social reproduction, and thus through the family, that I approach the question of labor, social class, and class formation. To support their families, many of the parents and children who are the focus of this book worked in low-paying jobs on the margins of the capital city's economy. Ironically, those economic margins were often located in the heart of more privileged families: domestic work required girls and women to leave their own families to work for others. Unpacking the interlocking, cross-class "domestic economies" of social reproduction reveals the ways that urban Mexicans understood and acted on their position in the class hierarchies of the capital city and how their options shaped their household composition and family life. Thus, this approach helps bring into focus the material and symbolic consequences of the work of social reproduction.

Ancestors and Precedents

My interests in family, labor, and childhood are founded on a rich historical literature that raises a multitude of questions and suggests a variety of approaches to answer them. Historians of Latin America have long noted that family forms diverged from legal and ecclesiastical norms and have studied the ways that these differences map onto class and labor. A variety of factors produced and accentuated the differences in family and household composition between Latin America's laboring classes and the families that were organized to command the labor of others and to transmit property and status from one generation to the next. Over Latin America's long history, such factors included colonial labor drafts exacted from indigenous households, the transport and enslavement of Africans and their descendants, the eviction of peasant producers from their land or absorption of entire villages by expanding estates, and trans-Atlantic, transnational, and internal labor migrations.

At the pinnacle of the social hierarchy stood the patriarchal patronage household extending employment and relations of ritual kinship (*compadrazgo*) to tenants, clients, slaves, servants, and their children.[42] These families conformed to legal and ecclesiastical norms of marriage, legitimate birth, and property transmission. But in Latin America the majority of families did not conform to those norms and were by default defined as defective or dependent.[43] Moreover, such families, many of which were composed of unmarried mothers and their illegitimate children, were often stranded outside the legal protections that sanctioned families enjoyed. Ann Twinam has illuminated the ways that, during Latin America's late colonial period, the relationship between legitimate birth and family honor — social reputation — reinforced class distinctions in an increasingly fluid social context.[44] In turn, the legal family model not only established and reinforced boundaries between families but also demarcated private from public social spheres: families without legal sanction lived less private lives and experienced more frequent interventions by public authorities.[45]

Like their colonial counterparts, families of the working poor in Mexico City during the late nineteenth and early twentieth centuries were often informal in the eyes of the law and had fluid patterns of work and residence. But they also had a diverse range of resources for meeting personal and economic challenges. These resources included networks of relatives, neighbors, and coworkers, networks that sometimes extended outside the city. Families in crisis also turned to employers, patrons, and ritual kin (*compadres*), with greater means and social resources. In addition, urban institutions of public child welfare, maternal-child health, and juvenile correction increasingly provided crucial support for solving short- and long-term domestic problems.[46]

The involvement of public authorities in family disputes and in disciplining urban youth had a long history of clear class, race, and gender patterns. Bianca Premo discovered that in eighteenth-century Lima, Peru, children of mixed race, who were more likely to be born outside of marriage and to reside in a mother-headed household, appeared before city authorities more frequently than children from households with a present father or father substitute wielding private authority. Moreover, Premo found that the daughters of mother-headed households were more vulnerable to sexual assault, and mothers, more frequently than fathers, appealed to the courts for legal redress.[47] Scholars have identified similar patterns of recourse to public authority in cities throughout Latin America.[48] Historically, appeals to and interventions by public authority in the Mexican capital reflected the economically and socially weaker position of households that lacked a paternal authority or an adult male income.

Likewise, children circulated out of such families. The movement was often lateral—into similar households of relatives or neighbors. As Claudia Fonseca has observed of child circulation in twentieth-century Brazilian urban squatter communities, over time the practices of child circulation comprise more than strategies for family survival; they acquire meanings, sometimes contradictory, and become the foundation of complex relationships and identities.[49] But throughout Latin American history, children have frequently circulated across class lines. When they entered the protection of wealthier households, they usually did not become socially equal with their benefactors. Earlier, in the colonial period, Latin American children were placed out to fulfill service obligations. Wealthy households also absorbed both parentless children and children of servants as working dependents (*criados* or *hijos de familia*), a practice that encompassed both protection and service.[50] As John Boswell demonstrates, in Europe these practices had premodern roots and a complex history that combined piety and labor exploitation.[51] In nineteenth- and twentieth-century Mexico, the movement of children under such terms reinforced the class and status differentials between their families of origin and their new patrons and caretakers.

Orphans formed another category of circulating children. Mexican social practice considered children who had lost a mother or a father orphans, like those who had lost both parents. Alive or dead, the parents' race and social and marital status shaped the treatment the orphan would receive.[52] At one extreme, documents from the colonial Yucatán mention a quasi slave trade in orphans.[53] At the other extreme, during the colonial period, orphans also inspired the wealthy to undertake pious works and make donations or bequests to convents for orphans' maintenance, education, and dowries. Many such asylums accepted orphans only of legitimate birth: many rejected those of mixed race.[54] Significantly, when the Mexico City foundling home opened in 1767, it differed from other hospices in accepting children of illegitimate birth belonging to every racial category.[55]

Not all orphans, however, entered institutions. Within the system of ritual or spiritual kinship the care of orphans was an important element in the mutual obligations between compadres.[56] But even caretakers who had committed to those obligations might later reconsider and consign their charges to orphanages. In late nineteenth-century Mexico City, children whose fathers had died or abandoned the family were more likely to enter orphanages because of their mother's poverty. Children whose mothers had died were likely to enter orphanages because no one else would care for them.

In Mexico, the multiple forms of child circulation and the class identities attached to them became part of a distinctive national ethos. Foreign and native commentators frequently praised the inclusiveness of the Mexican family, noted a characteristic tenderness for children and charity toward orphans, and insisted that servants were considered family members.[57] In 1876, enumerating the virtues of Mexicans of Spanish descent, geographer Antonio García Cubas invoked a suite of closely linked relationships: "I must mention, particularly, the respect paid by children to their parents; their hospitality; their humane treatment toward their servants, who are considered as belonging to the family, and their protection of orphans. As soon as a child loses its parents, it is adopted by its godfathers, and if these should be wanting, a rivalry is excited between other families to shelter the abandoned creature."[58] The informal adoption that García Cubas referred to remained a well-established Mexican practice: it provided the satisfaction of a young child's affection and labor, neither necessarily exclusive of the other in the context of the patronage household. The importance of this ethos, which even today many Mexicans consider a defining characteristic of their national family practice, makes the historical records all the more valuable for their documentation of its protections and of its limits.[59]

Adoption also had a long legal tradition. In Spanish law, drawing from Roman law, formal adoption was a means to create an heir. In the mid-nineteenth century Mexican reformers wrote that option out of civil law. With legal adoption precluded, informal adoptions continued to flourish—and most were probably for labor.[60] Foundling home records reveal, however, that a steady stream of couples sought to adopt to form their families. This trend, otherwise difficult to detect, was clearly influential: this was the version of adoption that would be written back into revolutionary family law in 1917.

By the early twentieth century, mounting sentiments against child labor contributed to changes in adoption law and practice. Viviana Zelizer has argued, for example, that in the late nineteenth-century United States, as expectations of and tolerance for child labor declined, children lost their economic value, that is, the value derived from their ability to earn a wage and contribute to domestic maintenance. Instead, children acquired sentimental value, becoming "priceless."[61] In Mexico, protected or "sentimental" childhood, closely tied to the construction of maternal roles focused on the home and dedicated to child nurture, fed the trend of adoption to form families rather than for labor. Adoption's evolution in Mexican law and practice thus exposes the ways that new meanings became attached to the social relationships of family and household, and especially to the concept of childhood. This process of change also carries a new set of contradictions bearing on social reproduction. Domestic servants and women in related occupations continued to be the core clientele of Mexico City public welfare institutions, the same institutions that supplied their children for adoption to petitioners of means. In this way, changes in Mexican adoption law and practice reveal how class position shaped women's reproductive labor: child nurture for the middle and upper classes and domestic service for the poor.[62]

Like other feminist scholars who have examined the gender relations of social reproduction, Rayna Rapp observes that the concepts and meanings of family mask "the realities of household formation and sustenance" and gloss over the different experiences of household members.[63] Feminist analyses of housework highlight the ways that unpaid domestic labor benefits male workers and ultimately provides a free service to capital by reproducing the next generation of workers.[64] Barbara Nelson, a historian of welfare in the United States, has shown how twentieth-century government entitlement programs imposed and institutionalized this gender division of labor. Nelson describes the "two-channel welfare state": men benefited from policies that shored up the "family" wage, while protective labor legislation and welfare benefits were founded on the assumption that women's principal work was unpaid: child rearing and housekeeping.[65] Throughout the period of this study, Mexican public assistance compensated for the needs of families without an adult male wage earner. Nelson's model, developed from her study of welfare in the United States, lacks an additional dynamic that was important in Mexico, where the middle class viewed the movement of women and children into nonkin households as a form of private charity: those interactions were an important factor in the social reproduction of Mexico City's working class as well as in the middle and upper classes.

Private patronage continued to be a central element of assistance, and, indeed, much Mexican public welfare policy was designed to serve the preferences of the middle and upper classes. In particular, Mexico City's public welfare institutions for children played a key role in reproducing the urban labor force of social reproduction. They took in the children of women employed in domestic service and related work, effectively subsidizing employers, and trained the majority of those female inmates as domestics. They also funneled inmates into unpaid domestic work through informal adoptions. And, when adoptions for labor declined, welfare agencies used domestic service as assistance for mothers in need and the juvenile court used domestic service as probation for girls. In all these ways, public welfare mediated and reinforced class entitlements to family based on the labor of working-class women and girls.

As Porfirian moralists and revolutionary reformers raised the rhetorical and social value of motherhood and domesticity, low wages for domestic service widened the gap—not only in income and but also in social capital—between employers and servants. In cross-class exchanges over domestic labor, value flowed out of poor families and into more privileged ones. Women who worked as domestics transferred labor and child care away from their own homes and children to benefit their employers' households and families, while their own families experienced instability and separation.[66] Daughters of domestics often sacrificed both schooling and paid work to take over housework and child care so their mothers could take paid work. Meanwhile, this process enhanced the social position of employers' families, because they could maintain higher standards of hygiene and consumption. Similarly, middle-class families that employed wet nurses or adopted children from public welfare institutions benefited from other women's reproductive labor, literally—in the form of breast-feeding or childbearing. In the late 1930s these reproductive exchanges—or economies—across class lines, along with the role that public welfare played, were fully exposed in the adoption review process: an applicant's ability to employ a domestic became a key criterion in her qualifying to adopt through Mexican public welfare. In this context, the enduring role of child welfare services in forming and institutionalizing the urban domestic labor sector offers valuable insights into historical constructions of gendered class identities tied to social reproduction and to the meanings that people invested in their family relationships.[67]

Did Mexico City's trends in family ideology and class-based forms of the family represent the situation elsewhere in Mexico? The often-cited expression "many Mexicos" sums up the country's cultural diversity, which was compounded by enduring regional political cultures and the notoriously uneven pace of economic development. In this sense, Mexico City stands somewhat apart from the rest of the country. In the late nineteenth century, international investment and cosmopolitan cultural currents converged on the capital and influenced the formation of class identities at both ends of the social spectrum: the elite and professional classes were influenced by European and U.S. culture, fashions, and intellectual trends, and a cohesive working class based its identity on shared experiences of work and residential life. Importantly, Mexico City was also the seat of a rapidly expanding and increasingly centralized state bureaucracy: public health and welfare services for children and families were pioneered in the capital and concentrated there.[68]

At the same time, the social, cultural, and economic boundaries demarcating the capital from neighboring states and distant regions were porous. Throughout Mexico, expanding estates pushed rural people off their land and into growing centers of mining and manufacturing. The national railroad system that was the pride of the Díaz regime converged on Mexico City, bringing migrants of all social classes from every part of the country: these new arrivals, like long-term residents, often maintained links with family networks in the provinces. The rising pace of internal migration also blurred distinctions between *capitalino* and provincial family practices. Indeed, applicants came from all over the country to adopt children from the institutions of the Mexico City welfare system. In time, many of the public health and welfare services initiated in the capital served as templates for federal agencies with a national scope. In these ways, the city represented a centralized version of national developments. The capital's print press reflected these connections. Newspapers and magazines presented readers with a mix of city news, national politics, and international events, juxtaposed with articles on family morality, household economics, and childrearing by authors from Europe, the United States, and Latin America, including Mexico, and interspersed with advertisements for both Mexican products and imported goods for personal and household use. Thus, the domestic practices and public cultures of family and childhood described and analyzed in this study embrace a distinct urban milieu as well as broad national and transnational trends.

Sources and Methods

This study is based on primary sources that have long served as tools for historians of the family in Latin America. These sources include Mexico's extensive body of legal codes and decrees defining family relations, population censuses, court cases adjudicating family relations, manuscript records and published reports of the public welfare system, and articles in the print press.[69] Those sources usually privilege the views of the educated and powerful and can seem frustratingly silent on the perspectives of single mothers, orphanage inmates, wet nurses, domestics, and child workers. Still, their perspectives do emerge from the historical record.

The nineteenth-century sources on which this study is founded range from the bare-bones notations of the foundling home registers and wet nurse account books to the flowery rhetoric of neoromantic poets. Even schematic sources, however, provide the grist for analyzing patterns of agency and experience among the urban poor. For example, for over a century the foundling home administrators used the same formulas for keeping the registers of admission and release. If the Hospicio kept similar registers, they no longer exist, and the fluctuating size and composition of the Hospicio's internal population has to be extracted from a diverse range of documents.

In contrast, the consistency of foundling home record keeping facilitates several types of quantitative analysis. One is of the motives or circumstances behind children's admission, reasons for release, and patterns of adoption. Continuity and change in these factors illuminate class-distinct entitlements to family life. Small alterations in the formulas of institutional record keeping also reveal a great deal about changing administrative priorities. Additionally, almost daily, welfare officials confronted desperate parents, whose emotions worked their way into the formulaic notations of the registers as well as official correspondence. Even in their official capacity, moreover, welfare administrators such as Dr. Manuel Domínguez, physician and foundling home director from 1898 to 1905, and his twentieth-century counterpart, Dr. Federico Gómez, emerge from official correspondence and reports as individuals who brought particular strengths and limitations to their work.

Journalistic sources provide a spectrum of views on the family and childhood. The upper classes may have dominated the nineteenth-century mainstream press as well as specialist medical journals and women's magazines, but they did not control the full spectrum of public opinion. Journalists, physicians, and poets applied fashionable rhetorical flourishes to depict their own social sphere in idealized terms. With equal eloquence, engravers like José Guadalupe Posada and popular bards of the penny press challenged elite worldviews when they depicted the urban social landscape from street level. Members of the capital city's working classes were also quick to report to the mainstream press when government officials failed to fulfill the "paternal" responsibilities that legitimated their authority. When the press served as a court of public opinion, officials were sensitive about possible scandal, showing that even mainstream newspapers were not entirely an elite-controlled medium. During the 1920s and 1930s Mexico City newspapers and magazines staked out positions on the family and childhood that resonated with the polarizing issues of national politics. The importance of the print arena and the high political stakes in the politics of family prompted government agencies to create their own publications to promote the official line on child health and child welfare.

In this study I use two principal kinds of legal sources: statutes that convey ideals about family relations and regulate them, and sources that document Mexicans from all walks of life, putting the long-standing principles of family law into practice and sometimes struggling to understand legal innovations. The formal language of legal codes and decrees illuminates the thinking of jurists and legislators of different political generations—virtually all members of the privileged classes—about parent-child relationships, gender, and the government's role in family life. Uneducated members of the urban working classes, however, often had a firm grasp of the fundamental legal principles that defined paternal and maternal responsibilities and filial obedience. Mothers and fathers unable to read or write hired scribes to help them frame requests for public assistance for themselves or their children. The structured language of these petitions based claims for aid on legally defined parental responsibilities and rights. Thus, illiteracy and economic marginality did not preclude the ability to contribute to the written record or to the process of constructing the social meanings of the law.[70] Adoption application and review documents of the 1920s and 1930s, on the other hand, reveal educated Mexicans and welfare officials wrestling with the implications of legal adoption for ideas about gender roles and social class, the ways that formal adoption challenged the practice of adopting servants and opened to question the meanings of the parent-child relationship.

The marked changes in volume and density of twentieth-century official sources reflect the expanding roles of government agencies and the proliferation of bureaucratic interventions into working- and middle-class family life. The records of the juvenile court and of the adoption review process, in particular, present new possibilities for investigating and analyzing family relations. The depth of these sources derives in part from the establishment and expansion of the new profession of social work in Mexico. The visiting nurses of the maternal-child health clinics, the inspectors of the juvenile court, and the social workers of the welfare system overseeing adoptions conducted extensive interviews and sometimes became primary actors in the family dramas they were sent to investigate. Whether it was owing to their class backgrounds or to their training, their reports filtered the statements of their clients through a mesh of middle-class bias. Other scholars have noted the challenges of interpreting records about the poor created by their self-described betters.[71] It is therefore important to approach social workers' reports with an eye for negatively biased assumptions about morals, hygiene, and family dysfunction. It is equally important to read the family testimonies elicited by social workers with an awareness that the class differences and the high stakes riding on the interviews could place the interviewees on the defensive, perhaps prompting them to say what they believed the social workers, as representatives of public authority, wanted to hear. Even so, juvenile court records clearly expose the strategies and values that organized the domestic economies of the urban working poor and often convey a sense of the meanings that parents and children invested in those strategies. Similarly, many would-be adopters spoke to social workers with extraordinary frankness about their innermost feelings, as did, occasionally, children and adolescents up for adoption. These records, then, provide a rich body of testimony for careful analysis of ideas about family relationships, work, and childhood across the social spectrum.[72]

Although many of the primary sources that inform this study are common tools for family historians, they have been mined less often as sources for labor history. Labor historians have long noted the ubiquity of domestics in Mexican society but have also often expressed frustration over the lack of documentation on domestic service.[73] Some have asserted that this major labor sector could not be studied, because most domestic service took place in private homes; women moved in and out of domestic work over their life course, and in Mexico City domestics rarely joined formal labor organizations.[74] A now extensive body of research on social reproduction, however, has demonstrated that families and households are important sites of labor. Additionally, some recent historical studies have carried the concept of social reproduction beyond the confines of the home, to address all the paid and unpaid work that sustains families and produces the next generation.[75] I analyze public institutions of child welfare as another kind of household where the labor of social reproduction takes place.

Applying these insights to the records of the child welfare system, the juvenile court, and public health services for mothers and babies opens new perspectives on domestic service and the work of social reproduction more broadly. Even though the records of public welfare and the juvenile court were created for other reasons, they show that domestic service remained a central component of child circulation well into the twentieth century. The same records reveal changing social attitudes toward child labor. Adult domestics emerge from these sources in several guises. Domestics made up the core clientele of public welfare; during the 1930s the ability to hire a domestic was a deciding factor in adoption approvals. Similarly, these records illuminate another subset of the domestic labor force, wet nurses, workers whose labor was documented almost entirely by their critics. The foundling home was the largest single employer of wet nurses in the capital region and the locus of attempts to reform the practice in the late 1890s. At that time reformers were most concerned with persuading privileged parents to stop using wet nurses. But in the 1920s the public health campaign to reduce infant mortality reached into thousands of urban, working-class households, as administrators and doctors sought to replace established practices of personal and domestic hygiene and childrearing with medically approved methods. Using the records of public health and welfare and the juvenile court to document and analyze paid and unpaid housework and childrearing, then, sheds light on the practices and meanings of domestic service and of reproductive labor more broadly during a period of rapid and often wrenching political, social, and economic change.

Organization and Sequence of Chapters

Two watershed events—the overthrow of Porfirio Díaz and the Mexican Revolution—shaped my decisions about the overall organization of this book. It is divided into two broad chronological parts, the first focusing on the Porfiriato and the second on the years of revolution and reform. The nature of my sources and their analytical possibilities, however, influenced my decision to organize the chapters thematically rather than strictly by chronology—which would have created a disorienting zigzag among themes. A thematic approach supports an in-depth examination, from multiple perspectives, of the dynamics and discourses of particular aspects of welfare, work, and family in Mexico City.

Within the book's two parts, chapter topics are roughly parallel: each part has a chapter devoted to child circulation, infant health, and adoption. Part 1 is entitled "The Porfirian Family: Child Welfare, Child Labor, and Child Nurture, 1884–1912." Porfirian policies impacting the families and children of the urban poor centered on Mexico City's public orphanages, the Casa de Niños Expósitos and the Hospicio de Niños. The three chapters in this part, therefore, have a close institutional focus. Chapter 1, "Porfirian Patterns and Meanings of Child Circulation: Child Labor and Child Welfare in the Capital City," establishes the urban context, with its high rates of migration and low-paid work. The chapter examines patterns of use of the public orphanages and analyzes the ideology and practices of child labor and child circulation at different social levels. Chapter 2, "Labor or Love: Trends in Porfirian Adoption Practice," explores informal adoption from the perspectives of law, practice, and ideology. Chapter 3, "Moral and Medical Economies of Motherhood: Infant Feeding at the Mexico City Foundling Home," examines the anti-wet nurse campaign of the late nineteenth century to elucidate its differential effects on childrearing and maternal roles among the poor and the well-to-do, as well as at the foundling home, the vortex of attempted reforms to infant feeding.

Part 2, "Reworking the Family: Family Relations and Revolutionary Reform, 1913–1943" examines ideologies and practices of family and childhood in Mexico's revolutionary order. The chapters in part 2 explore the multiple ways that revolutionary principles informed new laws and reform initiatives in maternal-child health, the concepts and practices of child labor and adoption, and the formation of collective identities based on changing concepts of family and childhood. The institutional basis of this section moves beyond the capital's two principal orphanages because the reform period saw an explosion of public agencies focused on families and children. Chapter 4, "The Family in the Revolutionary Order: Conceptual Foundations," sets the stage for later developments by analyzing the revolutionary debates over the family and resulting legislation. Chapter 5, "The Revolutionary Family: Children's Health and Collective Identities," examines the ways that the high-priority campaign to reduce infant mortality and improve children's health in the capital prompted a massive outreach program aimed at altering not only family hygiene but also family relations. The child health campaign also supported the construction of collective identities based on family and childhood and helped forge the concept of Mexico's "revolutionary family." The nature of my sources for chapters 6 and 7 opens up a diverse urban landscape of neighborhoods and homes. Chapter 6, "Domestic Economies: Family Dynamics, Child Labor, and Child Circulation," revisits the questions of child labor and child circulation from the institutional perspective of the juvenile court and from the point of view of families that depended on child labor. The final chapter, "Breaking and Making Families: Adoption, Child Labor, and Women's Work," examines the uneven process of adjustment after adoption became legal, and the implications of that process for attitudes toward child labor and reproductive labor, more broadly. Finally, the conclusion reviews trends in concepts of family, work, childhood, and social responsibility for children through the lens of Mexico's 1943 Ley de Seguridad Social (Law of Social Security), which defined children as nonworking dependents of their working parents and of the state.

Throughout, translations from Spanish into English are my own unless otherwise indicated. In part 2, the names of all welfare and juvenile court clients—adults and children—have been changed.

 **THE PORFIRIAN FAMILY**

Child Welfare, Child Labor,
and Child Nurture, 1884–1912

1 Porfirian Patterns and Meanings of Child Circulation

Child Labor and Child Welfare in the Capital City

Two contradictory constructions of childhood emerged from nineteenth-century patterns of reform and stasis at Mexico City's two principal orphanages. The first, less charitable, version held that the children of the urban poor who entered public welfare institutions had to earn their own keep. This depiction was reinforced by the recurrent interventions into the administration of the poor house, the Hospicio de Pobres (Poorhouse), which was originally founded in 1774 as a hybrid religious and civic institution to reform beggars through religious instruction and work. Mexico's liberal reform of the late 1850s and early 1860s had secularized education and placed welfare institutions under public administration: subsequent reorganizations at the Hospicio aimed to develop a productive, civic-minded working class through primary education and vocational training. In 1884 a major restructuring of the Hospicio restricted admission to children and renamed the institution the Hospicio de Niños (Children's Hospice), thus defining children as the deserving recipients of public welfare. Still, its regulations and internal regimen fortified the expectation that its young residents, both because of their class origin and because they received public aid, would start working at an early age.

A contrasting concept of childhood painted young welfare wards as the favored objects of the state's paternal protection. This version was most readily apparent at the public Casa de Niños Expósitos (Foundling Home), where decades of stasis did little to alter governing policies and internal regimen. This orphanage, popularly known as the Casa de Cuna, was founded by Archbishop Francisco Antonio Lorenzana y Buitrón in 1767 to receive infants born out of wedlock, both to protect their families from the stain of illegitimacy and to save the children from the taint of their mothers' sexual transgressions. By the middle of the nineteenth century, the foundling home was under a civil administration and poverty rather than honor motivated most admissions. Still, the home retained its reputation as pious protector of the innocent, and during the late nineteenth century, its administrators and patrons infused older ideas about charity and piety with a sentimental view of infancy and early childhood.

Meanwhile, outside the walls of the two establishments, Mexico City underwent dramatic transformations as rural migrants poured into the capital region. By the end of the nineteenth century newcomers outnumbered residents born in the capital by two to one. The constant stream of arrivals held wages low and also swelled the population of new slum neighborhoods. Planners and developers reconfigured the city's residential landscapes as elegant mansions sprang up along the new boulevards and downtown high real estate values pushed the poor to the urban periphery.

In this context, the dual construction of childhood had significant material consequences for thousands of working-class families and their children: it shaped the roles that the two orphanages played in cross-class interactions within the welfare institutions for children as well as in urban patterns of child circulation, that is, the movement of children out of their families of origin.

Institutional Stasis and Change

For over a century after its foundation in 1767, employees and administrators who kept the registers of the Casa de Niños Expósitos preserved the same formulaic notations for recording admission, death, and release from the orphanage. The registers sketched entire life histories in a few lines, beginning with the babies' dates of entry and baptism. Next to most entries, a small cross and date in the margin signaled the child's death, often shortly after arrival or before the child reached the age of one. In the institution's early decades, the registrars recorded whether the parents bringing the children were Spanish, Indian, or of mixed descent (mestizo). After Mexico's independence from Spain in 1821, race-based designations fell out of use but indications of social class or respectability persisted. For most of the nineteenth century, admission to the foundling home usually involved a face-to-face interview between the adult bringing in the child and an administrator, who recorded the social status of clients of distinction by affixing the respectful titles don and doña before their names. By the 1860s the number of adults meriting such notations had dwindled to a minority among the institution's clientele but they continued to come, either to intern their own illegitimate infants and thus protect their own honor or to intern the babies of their spiritual kin (compadres) and thus preserve their reputation by concealing their identity. Through the year 1893, the respectful forms of address appeared regularly in the admissions records. But in the early months of 1894 only a few appeared and by the end of the year they had disappeared completely from the registers. Thereafter, employees of the establishment reserved honorific titles for correspondence with the families and guardians of paying pensioners, mostly from other states; with immediate peers; or with members of the elite Círculo de Amigos de Porfirio Díaz (Circle of Friends of Porfirio Díaz) who took an interest in orphanage affairs.[1]

Why in the mid-1890s did the administrators suddenly stop the century-long tradition of using honorific titles for local clients? For some time recognizably respectable families had constituted a small fraction among clients and it seems that by the mid-1890s they simply ceased to entrust their children to the home. Moreover, from the 1870s onward a flood of recent migrants undermined the stable sense of neighborhood that had characterized the foundling home's operations in earlier decades, when perennial volunteers sponsored newly admitted infants in baptism at the Sagrario Metropolitano, the chapel of the cathedral, and a visiting committee of elite ladies adopted their favorites.[2] Now staff and administrators probably recognized few of the people who brought their children.

The capital's social geography was also in flux. Public transportation integrated the capital's outskirts more closely with the city center. Toward the end of the century, planners inspired by Hausmann's Paris dramatically redesigned Mexico City in anticipation of celebrations for the 1910 centennial of the independence movement. Rising real estate values in the city center accentuated residential patterns of class segregation.[3] In stark contrast to the elegant mansions and monuments rising along the axis of the Paseo de la Reforma that transected the city center, slums mushroomed around the railroad stations and the construction site of the new penitentiary. Similar neighborhoods developed toward the south, around the new hospitals, public works facilities, hog slaughterhouse, and textile factories along San Antonio Abad, which was later the site of a new compound to house the Hospicio de Niños.[4] In the crowded plebian *colonias* of Morelos, La Bolsa, and Díaz de León, the lack of city services resulted in poor sanitation and widespread health problems. The foundling home's immediate area, La Merced, only a few blocks from the *zócalo* (central plaza), became notorious for having some of the city's worst living conditions. The orphanage's increasingly disreputable location and immediate neighbors may have tarnished its long-time associations with family honor and elite patronage, and respectable families may have avoided venturing into the area.

Whatever the causes underlying this seemingly minor point of institutional record keeping, the disappearance of dons and doñas from the admissions registers marked the culmination of long-term trends in public use of the foundling home and signaled a watershed in administrative practices. Until the late 1890s operations had remained virtually unchanged since its foundation despite frequent shifts of external oversight after 1861 and a steady rise in admissions beginning in the mid-1870s. Yet only a few years after respectable local clients vanished from the institution's admissions registers, the orphanage's policies and patterns of use underwent dramatic changes. In 1898 the federal welfare administration installed a well-known

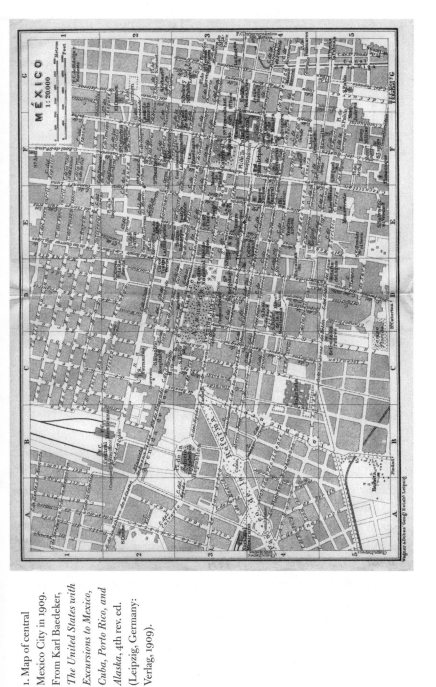

1. Map of central
Mexico City in 1909.
From Karl Baedeker,
*The United States with
Excursions to Mexico,
Cuba, Porto Rico, and
Alaska*, 4th rev. ed.
(Leipzig, Germany:
Verlag, 1909).

physician as the new director and instituted policies that would expand the use of the home by a broad urban public. In response, struggling families of the capital transformed the foundling home from an institutional vestige of an ancient system of family honor and a dead end in child circulation, into a crucial resource providing short-term solutions to domestic crises. The increasingly heavy traffic through the orphanage's gates marked a profound shift in its role in the patterns and practices of child circulation in the capital city.

At the Hospicio de Pobres, in contrast, city and federal officials frequently intervened into the regulations and daily regimen before restricting the institution to children in 1884. Founded in 1774 to confine and reform vagrants and beggars, the Hospicio had evolved into the capital city's flagship institution of public assistance. Because of its importance, the Hospicio drew the attention of leading philanthropists and its rambling compound absorbed a series of their charitable projects. In 1806 a school for orphans opened in the establishment. A department where women could give birth to their illegitimate children in secret opened the same year. A department of juvenile correction opened in 1841. And a clinic for diseases of the eye was endowed in 1848.[5] Over time, the makeup of the Hospicio's residents shifted from adults to children.

Mexico's liberal reform of the late 1850s and early 1860s heightened the Hospicio's importance and simultaneously reduced its resources. The reform laws divested all corporations of their property; although the laws were aimed at the church, they included civil corporations like the Hospicio. The new legislation also mandated secular primary education and brought welfare establishments under government oversight.[6] These mandates, with their ideological charge, positioned the Hospicio as the showcase of government policy toward the poor, and subsequent political regimes pointedly refashioned the Hospicio to reflect their social and civic priorities.

For feuding liberals and conservatives alike, however, precepts of order, efficiency, and discipline transcended political divisions and drove every cycle of reorganization at the poor house. Liberal supporters of Benito Juárez sought to federalize the capital's welfare institutions. Lacking sufficient operating funds, the federal government quickly handed welfare back to city oversight but not before divesting the Hospicio of its income-producing properties. During the short-lived Segundo Imperio (Second Empire), Austrian monarchs Maximilian and Charlotte reversed the secular mandates and installed the charitable order, the Hermanas de la Caridad (Sisters of Charity), to administer the establishment. Charlotte also patronized a maternity hospital located adjacent to the Hospicio compound. In 1867, with the return of Juárez and the restoration of the republic, another round of reforms began by evicting the charitable order and refocusing the regulations and regimen on instilling the habits of labor and civic responsibility in Hospicio's young charges—"sons of society"—and integrating their manual instruction with federally mandated public education.[7]

In 1877, shortly after coming to power, General Porfirio Díaz transferred welfare administration from the city to the federal government. In doing so he fulfilled a primary goal of the liberal reform. Even though he elevated the level of welfare administration and created a new body to oversee operations, the Dirección de Beneficencia Pública (Directorate of Public Welfare), Díaz placed public welfare low on the scale of government priorities. Instead, his officials reiterated that public assistance was neither a state prerogative nor a duty. Private philanthropy had to play a significant role. "Public welfare alone cannot satisfy the more pressing needs of the indigent and weak," states an 1885 circular extending the legal scope of private philanthropy in Mexico. Rather, continues the document, private charity is "recognized in all the civilized countries as the surest and most natural means to tend to the pains and miseries of humanity."[8]

Decades later in 1905, speeches opening the new Hospital General echoed those sentiments. The state provided social and medical services only because private charity was insufficient to the task. Moreover, public assistance would receive only funds leftover from the state's basic functions: maintaining order and defending the national territory.[9] Despite these disclaimers, by 1900 the federal government had begun constructing a new Hospicio de Niños located to the south of the city center on the calzada San Antonio Abad, costing 1.3 million pesos, and capable of housing more than a thousand children.[10] The opening ceremonies in September 1905 gave orators a fresh occasion to celebrate public benevolence with great fanfare while simultaneously reiterating the government's limited responsibility to assist the poor.[11]

Indeed, the Hospicio's 1884 reorganization made children the exception to the Díaz administration's rule limiting government responsibility for the poor. The move to restrict the establishment to children defined them as the worthy poor and the government as their beneficent patron. This shift was not purely ideological. The 1884 reorganization acknowledged that Mexico City residents had gradually changed their use of the institution. Over the decades the number of adults housed in the Hospicio had declined steadily: by 1881 the institution's population totaled 741, with 698 of them children.[12] During the late years of the Díaz era, when girls and young women predominated in the Hospicio's population, they became favored tokens for displaying Porfirian public beneficence. Thus, reorganizing the Hospicio in 1884 accomplished more than affirming Díaz's commitments to core liberal precepts or clarifying the establishment's mission. In limiting Hospicio access to children, mostly to girls, the Díaz administration reinforced concepts of state paternalism and feminine dependence, reflecting Porfirian ideals of family structure.[13]

Child Circulation in the Porfirian Capital

As the increasing number of children housed in the Hospicio revealed, over the decades the foundling home and the Hospicio had become inextricably integrated with the capital city's networks and practices of child circulation. The two establishments played distinct roles linked to family cycles of reproduction and to adults' and children's labor roles. Some children entered the foundling home and the Hospicio because their parents had died and no relatives or neighbors would take them in, but the majority had at least one living parent. The roles the institutions played in child circulation depended on which parent had responsibility for the child. In working-class households headed by women or dependent on women's incomes, childbirth and infant care made the family highly vulnerable to separation. Although the Casa de Niños Expósitos had originally been founded to accept children born outside of marriage, honor admissions diminished steadily; by the late 1800s the vast majority of admissions were motivated by poverty. The Hospicio admitted children at age seven. Girls could remain in the Hospicio until age fourteen to continue their education and training, usually as domestics. After 1884, however, girls' vocational training included mechanized production of low-cost consumer goods. Boys over ten were transferred to a separate institution, the trade school. Renamed the Escuela

Industrial de Huérfanos (Industrial School for Orphans) in 1880, the trade school provided primary education and vocational training for boys to age eighteen. Also in 1880 welfare administrators transferred the corrections department for boys from the trade school to the rancho Momoluco in the southern suburb of Coyoacán, where the new facility soon housed more than three hundred delinquents.[14] Even after the trade school and reform school had been separated, however, Mexico City residents continued to conflate vocational training with discipline. When parents petitioned to have boys admitted to the Escuela Industrial, they expressed their concerns about their ability to control their sons and about the boys' need to learn a trade and good work habits.[15]

Additionally, the terms of release from these institutions reflected contemporary understandings of child development and gendered expectations of child labor. Historically, many surviving foundlings, particularly girls, had remained in the Casa de Niños Expósitos indefinitely, some into old age. The few families who withdrew their children from the orphanage did so after weaning, when they required less maternal attention. Families frequently withdrew their daughters from the Hospicio as soon as they could responsibly perform housework and child care; the number of female residents dropped sharply after age fourteen. In contrast, girls who were completely orphaned and had no relatives willing to care for them remained in the Hospicio into their late teens, some into adulthood. And parents often petitioned to keep their sons in the trade school and off the streets for as long as possible.[16]

During the final decades of the nineteenth century, these established patterns of child circulation linked to welfare practice changed dramatically. A significant number of families mobilized their resources and withdrew their children from the foundling home as quickly as possible. Despite public pieties about protecting girls without families, welfare administrators evicted long-term female residents from both orphanages. The trajectories of minors who passed through these institutions as well as interventions by families, spiritual kin, and public officials, suggest significant shifts in the underlying conceptions of familial and public responsibility for children.

Overall, discrepancies between the regulations and the actual use of public child welfare institutions under Díaz reveal a tension between the expectations of labor based on children's class of origin and evolving concepts of childhood as a life stage characterized by innocence and requiring protection. Placing the emergence of new patterns of child circulation into the larger urban context raises challenging questions about the ways that shifting social configurations stemming from migration, urbanization, and changing labor markets may have prompted parents of the city's working poor to think differently about their children.

Urban Landscapes of Migration and Labor

When Díaz raised the administration of Mexico City's principal public institutions of child welfare to the federal level, he integrated policies affecting families and children more closely with other national priorities. Descriptions of his regime's development program often emphasize expansion of public primary education, the extended rail system, and large-scale public works, along with laws that supported the concentration of land ownership for commercial agriculture. The government also encouraged foreigners to invest in mining and in manufacturing consumer goods. These large-scale economic priorities had a significant impact on family life throughout the country: land concentration displaced rural families and manufacturing destabilized the household economies of artisans. These disruptions, in turn, underlay changing patterns of use of Mexico City's child welfare establishments.

Outside the walls of the orphanages, the capital region experienced rapid growth driven by migration. Between 1877 and 1900 the Federal District's population grew by two-thirds, to more than half a million, and the trend kept accelerating: by 1910 it was 120 percent of the 1877 baseline.[17] As they had in earlier migrations, women predominated among young urban migrants: censuses show that between 1895 and 1910 women outnumbered men in every age category between fifteen and thirty.[18]

Although women predominated in age groups likely to be having children, many unions were unstable, holding down the birthrate in the Federal District. Many children lived in female-headed households: single women and widows outnumbered married women. In 1900 for every 1000 women aged twelve to fifty, official statistics recorded fewer than 150 children under a year old.[19] In 1895 the Federal District registered well under 4,000 births, over half of them to married parents. This number seems low, given that the same year the district recorded more than 8,000 deaths of infants,

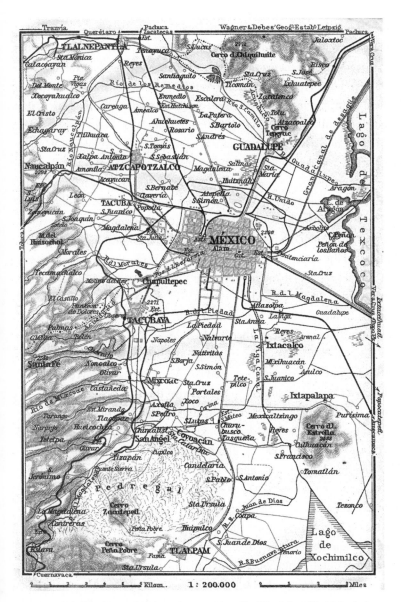

2. Map of Mexico City and environs in 1909. From Karl Baedeker, *The United States with Excursions to Mexico, Cuba, Porto Rico, and Alaska*, 4th rev. ed. (Leipzig, Germany: Verlag, 1909).

that is, children under one year old. In 1900 improved enforcement of birth registration reversed the proportions of legitimate births to births outside of marriage; of more than 29,000 registered births, fewer than 10,000 children were born to married parents.[20] But while the birthrate within the Federal District remained low compared to that of the nation at large, the constant arrival of migrants swelled the population of children and youth. In the Federal District, official statistics for 1900 put juveniles at 25 percent of the population, and by 1900 roughly two-thirds of all residents were migrants.[21]

For new arrivals and long-term residents alike, the economy of Mexico City and its environs presented steep obstacles to keeping a family together. The stream of migrants fed a glut in unskilled labor and held wages low. Families on the economic margins mobilized several strategies to compensate: families separated and regrouped at key life-cycle junctures and many women and children worked.[22]

Statistics on school attendance and child labor reveal how much children contributed to sustain their households. The 1867 Ley de Instrucción Pública (Law of Public Instruction) made primary school attendance mandatory, but enforcement remained lax. An industrial census of the Federal District for 1879 counted more than two thousand children working throughout the city in a broad range of jobs, including tobacco and textile manufacturing and metal work. In bookbinding and pottery, children made up half the recorded workforce; they constituted a third of the carpenters.[23] These figures, however, accounted only for formal workplaces and missed children working at home, in markets, and on the streets. During the 1890s and early 1900s official figures showed rising school attendance in the Federal District: by 1910, 60 percent of children were reported as attending school. A significant number of those children attended classes sporadically or dropped out, but officials admitted that many of the parents of truants were too poor to pay the fines or were homeless and therefore difficult to locate. Contemporary observers noted that children who did not attend school were likely to be working.[24]

Households without an adult male wage earner faced a particular disadvantage. Women's wages were lower than men's to begin with. The twin forces of child labor and increasing mechanization further undermined the value of women's work. As of 1879 some of the nontextile occupations, such as shoemaking, that were not exclusively male preserves employed more children than women.[25] In food production women lost jobs to mechanization, especially with the introduction of automated corn-grinding and tortilla-making machines.[26] On the other hand, mechanization drove the expansion of the garment industry and pulled many women into the needle trades. A few seamstresses commanded wages recognizing their skilled work, but many others worked at home for centavos per piece and suffered from periodic unemployment. And while the expanding garment industry provided more jobs, the introduction of sewing machines gave rise to sweatshops and placed independent workers at a disadvantage. Wages for sewing declined throughout the 1890s; many workers earned less than half a peso for a twelve-hour workday.[27] Meanwhile, as of 1910 domestic service employed about 43 percent of women in the workforce, a figure that had remained constant for more than one hundred years, and many domestic positions were unpaid.[28]

Generations of welfare officials and philanthropists emphasized that work would raise the urban poor from their misery; welfare administrators, therefore, organized public assistance around training and inculcation of a work ethic.[29] At times these understandings dovetailed with other politically inflected agendas for public welfare, as when officials of the Restored Republic sought to develop a republican artisan class or Porfirian philanthropists gestured toward the liberal ideal of realizing individual talent. Underlying official statements through the decades and across the political spectrum sounded the persistent theme that "allocating work to those who live at the public expense is a necessity recognized by all the countries of the civilized world."[30]

After the reform laws forced the Hospicio to sell off its income-producing properties, administrators increasingly relied on its residents to perform internal maintenance. Officials claimed that housekeeping work was training. Juan de Dios Peza, a journalist, playwright, and society poet of the Porfiriato, wrote this for an 1881 prize day ceremony at the trade school: "If you work you will come / To see yourself free and triumphant: / The loving Fatherland saved you: / You will save the Fatherland."[31] Officials also fulfilled their own pronouncements that "the majority of the girls have no other future than domestic service, sad as this may be," by delivering domestic servants to urban employers through loosely supervised informal adoptions.[32]

In his 1881 report on Mexico City's welfare system, Peza waxed sentimental: "If the charity that one practices for adults honors and gratifies, that which one engages in for children redeems and glorifies."[33] When the Hospicio was restricted to children in 1884, the redefinition of the worthy poor as children drew on sentimental views of childhood but simultaneously charged the historical link between assistance and labor with contradictory meanings: children who received welfare in the name of the paternal and protective government were nevertheless expected to work.

Networks of Circulation

In 1896 a five-year-old boy was admitted to the Hospicio because his father had abandoned him soon after his mother died.[34] Likewise in 1912 Roberto Castellanos was admitted to the Hospicio at age seven when Agustina Armenda, a neighbor who had taken him in after his mother's death, could no longer care for him and no one could locate his father.[35] Underscoring the central role of women in the care of children and the fragility of family coherence in a mother's absence, a late nineteenth-century broadside illustrated an orphan's lament for his mother with a picture of a boy mourning at her grave. A motherless child was condemned to wander weeping through the world, to sleep in doorways: "All is suffering and tears."[36] Some children were indeed thrust onto the city streets to fend for themselves: in 1897 the beggars' asylum reported that it had served 104 boys and 79 girls over the course of the year.[37]

Most of the institution's inmates (asilados) had a living parent: they were considered half-orphans, either huérfanos de padre or huérfanos de madre. But in fact a father's absence and mother's low wages accounted for most children's admission to the Hospicio. In 1905 when a migrant mother from the state of Puebla petitioned to have her six-year-old son admitted to the Hospicio, she emphasized that the boy's father had abandoned the family. She also invoked the responsibility of the state to serve as a father substitute, arguing that if not admitted, her son would be "exposed to abandonment given that I have to serve to gain the means to subsist." With her petition, she submitted testimonials attesting that she was "a poor and honorable woman, hardworking, who . . . supports herself on the little she earns doing ironing."[38] As a recent arrival to the capital, she may have had to seek admission for her son because she had no nearby relatives who could care for him while she worked.

Profiles of Hospicio inmates' families derived from surviving records of the late Porfiriato reveal the preponderance of girls from women-headed families under severe economic duress.[39] Indeed, male residents were more likely than females to come from economically viable households. According to the Hospicio's director, in 1886, 25 percent of the male residents had relatives or guardians with sufficient means to support them, compared to only 9 percent of females. Far more girls than boys had living parents, 55 and 32 percent respectively. But more girls than boys had only a mother to support them: 44 percent of the girls, compared to 38 percent of the boys.[40] Statistics from December 1906 again show how many of the residents depended on women for support. Among the hundred older girls and young women aged fourteen to twenty, all but twelve had at least one parent but only nine of them had a male relative. Similarly, of the seventy-four boys over twelve, fourteen were orphans and only four of the others had male relatives.[41] In a 1912 list of sixty-six older female residents whom administrators judged capable of leaving to fend for themselves, the majority depended on female relatives, usually their mothers, most of whom were servants, washed laundry, or worked in the garment industry or in poorly paid food production.[42]

The narratives in admission petitions flesh out these statistics. Teodora Ceja, a widow petitioning to admit her two young sons to the Hospicio in 1890, wrote that she could not support them "owing to my poverty . . . and having to submit myself to service."[43] In 1912 Felicitas Casteñeda, petitioning to have her five-year-old daughter Rosa admitted to the Hospicio, stated that she found herself "in very critical circumstances, since for my subsistence I count only on the earnings that my work grinding corn and making tortillas provides me, and those wages are the insignificant quantity of ten centavos a day."[44] Contrary to the broadside bewailing the fate of motherless children, the Hospicio's inmate lists indicate that children of single or abandoned mothers and widows had the greatest need for assistance. In other words, such children stood the greatest risk of separation from their families or familiar caregivers.

Families' petitions to admit their children to public institutions highlight the gendered nature of need and use of the public welfare system: the Hospicio, like the foundling home, represented protections and authority that substituted for those of absent biological fathers or live-in paternal substitutes. Petitioners to the Hospicio and the trade school testified to the welfare system's paternal role when they invoked a father's responsibility to provide education and training in a trade, as defined in the civil code.[45] The law also invited parents to call on the state for assistance in disciplining their children.[46] In 1885 when Luis Castellanos petitioned the trade school to admit his two sons, aged ten and eleven, he asserted that owing to his poverty he lacked the "indispensable elements" for their education, which the law defined as his responsibility. But Castellanos also noted that his sons had shown little application to their studies and had "bad tendencies."[47] Thus, he made clear that he understood his legal paternal obligation to educate his sons and prepare them to earn a living, testified that poverty prevented him from doing so, and also invoked the joint role of the state in assisting with discipline.

Petitions from mothers of older boys played on the assumption that they had outgrown a mother's influence and needed paternal vigilance; indeed, the transition from a woman's care to that of a father substitute often marked the end of childhood for both boys and girls. A widow petitioned to have her thirteen-year-old son admitted to the trade school. Illiterate herself, she had a scribe frame and shape her predicament into a petition that established her honor, her parental authority, and her legal right to make the request, testifying that "I am the legitimate mother of the youth . . . under whose authority he lives." Her petition also invoked both the work ethic and the danger that her son might become a threat to society: "At present it is necessary for my son, owing to his age, to learn a trade that answers to his needs or rather to his subsistence in the future, so that he may not become a dissolute person, something I do not want to see." She also asked to have the fee for stamping the petition waived owing to her "well-known poverty." Her son was admitted, but, unfortunately, he and some other boys assigned to train in the soap-making workshop were expelled for bad behavior.[48]

The disciplinary role of the city's child welfare institutions shows how little protection was available for children and how it differed by gender. Public officials and welfare administrators could discipline boys by expel-ling them from welfare institutions or they could send boys to the juvenile corrections facility. Disagreement reigned among judicial officials and welfare administrators, however, over public disciplinary measures for girls, and for most of the nineteenth century the public system lacked any corrections facility for them. In 1878 in a document calling for the creation of a department for female "deposits," the governor of the Federal District noted that young girls, abandoned or without family, presented themselves at his office and to the police and requested asylum.[49] Public welfare officials jealously guarded their authority over Hospicio admissions. Without the authority to send homeless girls to the Hospicio, the governor complained that he was obliged to return them to the street and "into prostitution."[50] Similarly, criminal judges complained that they had no authority to refer girls to the Hospicio and so were forced to send them to jail, where they would become corrupted by contact with adult prisoners.[51] Both concerns reflected officials' belief that girls and young women outside of a family context and paternal control would inevitably succumb to vice and engage in sexual commerce.

Conversely, the recruitment of young women into prostitution, a legal and regulated trade in Mexico, was fed largely by the limited and low-wage employment options for women in the capital.[52] Officials may have abetted their own worst expectations for unsupervised girls. In 1895 the Hospicio turned away two young women arrested for unlicensed prostitution because they admitted to the crime.[53] The institution categorically refused entry to underage female delinquents. Girls who left home because of conflicts with parents and fell afoul of the law did not have the same access to a special facility afforded to boys and were cast into an adult world of enforced self-sufficiency. Despite the complaints of criminal judges indicating that the city needed a corrections facility for underage girls, the girls' correction department established in the Hospicio in 1878 soon fell into disuse. Writing in 1906 Martiniano Alfaro, author of a history of the Hospicio, claimed that under no conditions did the institution receive inmates—male or female—for correction.[54] Thus, as the Hospicio's inmate population became increasingly female over the decades, policy enforcement moralized about female virtue and vice while simultaneously widening the gap between protections for the worthy female poor and policies shunning young female transgressors.[55]

A combination of factors created the predominance of older girls in the Hospicio. Boys moved to the trade school to complete their education and vocational training, but for girls the Hospicio was the last stop on the welfare circuit and they tended to accumulate there. As the collective inmate profiles indicate, the feminization of the Hospicio's inmate population pointed to feminized poverty in the capital. The fate of homeless girls and girls who transgressed legal and moral codes also suggests that the Hospicio offered important protections. The Hospicio's 1884 regulations, like previous versions, allowed girls over twelve, "interned in the establishment for orphanhood or poverty," to continue their education and training in trades and skills for making "an honest living."[56] The establishment benefited from their presence by putting the older girls and women to work in housekeeping, supervising the younger children, and assisting in classes of *primeras letras* or in the embroidery and manufacturing workshops. Later policy statements claimed that the Hospicio accommodated older orphan girls, allowing them to "continue in the Establishment, as long as the Secretaría de Gobernación [ministry of the interior] did not dispose otherwise."[57]

In his 1906 history of the Hospicio, Martiniano Alfaro linked the feminization of the establishment's inmate population to the paternal generosity of the Díaz administration: "How gratifying it will have been for many of those poor girls, disinherited by fortune . . . to feel protected and sheltered by the solicitous care of a paternal government. . . . This will spontaneously awaken in their souls feelings of gratitude toward their benefactors, and especially, toward the Supreme Being."[58] Despite these official pieties about protecting girls, after 1884 most attempts to limit the institutional population focused on removing older girls and young women, whose age disqualified them for the protections granted to children.

Eviction and exclusion, however, were only two of the channels that led child welfare clients back into circulation as laborers. Terms of release from the public system reflected families' labor expectations as well as institutional disciplinary policies. A December 1903 list of girl inmates aged fifteen and over indicates that the vast majority who remained did so because they were complete orphans; girls with family were more likely to be withdrawn earlier, usually by age fourteen.[59] From the first of January to the middle of February 1904, 26 boys left the Hospicio: 1 died, 1 was adopted,

12 rejoined their families, and 12 were dismissed for absence without leave. The statistics for girls' release during the same period were similar, with one striking exception. The families of 11 girls petitioned for their release, and 10 girls were dismissed for absence without permission. But officials dismissed 46 girls, all over the age of fifteen, because they were considered capable of supporting themselves.[60] Boys in the same age group would have been transferred to the trade school, not evicted onto the street.

Administrators had another way to relieve overcrowding or to make way for new admissions. When inmates failed to return by the appointed time from their Sunday paseo or their visits home, the institution could expel them "for abuse of license." In January 1893 the trade school dismissed 60 boys for unapproved absence and a few weeks later expelled an additional 25 for absence and insubordination. Even with these dismissals the school remained crowded, with an inmate population of 322. Perhaps the need to reduce the numbers led officials to enforce the rules more strictly than usual.[61] The dismissal policy also allowed administrators to pass minors back to their families without carefully reviewing the merits of the case. In 1911 a mother pleaded to have her son readmitted to the trade school after he had been dismissed along with 45 others for unauthorized absence. The woman insisted that he had simply stayed with her because he was ill. After she produced a doctor's testimonial, the director, Félix Palavicini (who became a leading advocate for children in the early 1920s) permitted the boy to return on the condition that any future infractions would result in his permanent expulsion.[62]

In other instances, the motives for dismissing inmates revealed administrators' expectations that welfare beneficiaries adhere to approved behavior, which excluded occupations associated with the city's bustling street commerce. In 1907 when the interim director of the trade school wrote to his superiors requesting permission to expel Alfonso Castillo, he observed that in addition to the boy's "bad conduct" and failure to present himself for the weekly review during the vacation period, Alfonso had been seen "in the street shining shoes." The trade of *bolero* was considered the equivalent of vagrancy. The director was particularly incensed that Alfonso had been wearing his school uniform, bringing discredit to the school.[63] Expulsion from welfare institutions, then, was a significant factor in the urban pathways of child circulation and child labor, given that expelled minors returned to households that may have still have been economically unstable, were thrown onto their own resources, or sought employment in exchange for shelter and a low wage.

Although Porfirian welfare officials and moralists invoked the ethos of self-improvement in their formal policy statements, not many children who passed through the chain of welfare institutions did so on those terms. The few individuals who did live up to administrators' standards were held up as models of behavior for all others. Juan de Dios Peza, urging administrators to grant trade school student Arturo del Castillo a scholarship to continue his studies, called him a "lad with prospects and a future." Moreover, Peza suggested that the scholarship would "encourage the aspirations of his comrades to whom the prize will serve as a stimulus." That President Porfirio Díaz himself authorized Arturo's scholarship reflects the significance of the youth's behavior and example in justifying Porfirian concepts of public beneficence — and working-class obedience.[64] Without the Hospicio, speculated its chronicler Martiniano Alfaro, "how many minds might be lost or perhaps badly used, and instead of bearing the best fruits, would have been the cause of iniquity or of dishonor?" But, he continued, "fortunately, the innumerable benefits of that most noble institution have been palpable and can be eloquently represented by all the professionals, artisans, mechanics, in sum, all who grew up there."[65] This kind of official rhetoric suggested that passage through welfare institutions raised children from the city's most marginal families to membership in the productive working classes or even to professional status. In practice, however, Alfaro exaggerated the "innumerable benefits" of welfare institutions: the professions that he listed were not open to girls or young women. Moreover, the records attest that many residents' careers in the institutions were truncated by expulsion or by return to families that needed another working hand.

Urban Systems of Infant and Child Abandonment

In March 1899 Dr. Manuel Domínguez wrote to his supervisors at the federal secretariat overseeing public welfare to express his satisfaction with the changes he had introduced since becoming director of the Casa de Niños Expósitos the previous year and to describe his aspirations for expanding the institution's role in the city's social life: "To my way of thinking, perhaps the scant number of children who come to us is owing to the fact that the public is not aware of the advantageous conditions in which, under our current regulations, the little inmates stay here. The directorate could spread the word, bringing all classes of people to visit the house, and circulate the regulations among them. I have the impression that . . . after a short time we will have achieved the resuscitation of this useful institution."[66]

Dr. Manuel Domínguez brought the experience of a long career that combined medicine, public service, and private philanthropy to his position at the foundling home. A native of Querétaro, Domínguez went to Mexico City to study medicine. Under Maximilian, he held political posts outside the capital, but with the restoration of the republic, he returned to Mexico City to practice medicine. There he developed a successful practice while teaching legal medicine, among other subjects, at the Escuela Nacional de Medicina, where he became director. His political career resumed when Díaz took power. Positions on the Mexico City Ayuntamiento (City Council), including council president, acquainted him with the workings of local political networks. Twice elected to Congress, Domínguez also fraternized in high political circles. With leading philanthropists such as Francisco Díaz de León, Domínguez founded the beggars' asylum in Mexico City as well as the Sociedad Filantrópica Mexicana (Mexican Philanthropic Society)—patronized by the First Lady. He frequently wrote for *El Bien Social*, the philanthropic society's magazine, which was devoted to promoting the work ethic, thrift, and moral uplift among the literate urban working class. His appointment to the foundling home followed eight years of directing the state asylum for the blind.[67] With this background, Domínguez was eminently prepared to carry out a major reorganization of the foundling home, but probably ill-prepared for his encounters with real, rather than idealized or stereotyped, families of the urban poor.

As soon as he assumed his new duties, Domínguez had ample opportunity to meet the poor firsthand. During the mid-and late 1890s, annual admissions to the foundling home had averaged well below 200. In contrast, shortly after Domínguez wrote of his hopes—as if in answer to his wishes—admissions soared: 520 children entered in the twenty-two months between April 1899 and January 1901.[68] This heavy traffic, however, brought changes in family behavior contradictory to those Domínguez intended. Decades of markedly low admissions and the extended tenure of Fr. Francisco Higareda as director had perhaps obscured the slow but steady changes in the public's use of the institution. Higareda's well-known piety and the fact that a few families of distinction continued to intern their infants or adopt inmates helped prolong the establishment's reputation for providing baptism and salvation to foundlings, helping preserve family honor, and providing an arena for elite charitable practice.[69]

But the era of low annual admissions—in the low sixties—had ended in 1884, just as Higareda retired and Dr. Angel Carpio arrived as director. Families now brought their children at a pace unmatched since a century earlier. Between 1885 and 1894, 1,255 children entered the foundling home: 651 boys and 604 girls. Rates of admission rose in steps. From 1885 to 1887 the home averaged 87 admissions per year. From 1888 through 1891, it averaged about 128. During 1893, a year of world economic crisis compounded by drought in Mexico, admissions spiked to 180, while during 1892 and 1894 more than 140 children entered. Between 1885 and 1894 families retrieved only 23 percent of children admitted, about the same proportion as in previous eras. On the other hand, over the decade, 222 children, or 18 percent of those admitted, left in adoption, a far higher proportion than before.[70] While more families were forced to relinquish their children to the state, more households were in a position to take them in, illustrating the growing disparity between families in poverty and households of means.

While the rise in admissions between 1884 and 1895 had been significant, the spike in admissions after 1898 brought a significant change in the practice of abandonment and in relations between the families needing assistance and the home's administrators. As the century turned, families brought children in unprecedented numbers but they also retrieved them at a record rate. It was an assertive new poor that confronted welfare administrators over the fate of their children and transformed the involvement of spiritual kin, from supporting abandonment to playing an activist role in family reunification. Subsequent administrative attempts to tighten the foundling home's policy responded to the soaring rates of admission and retrieval but also to administrators' inability to control the terms of admission. Moreover, the urban poor were reluctant to relinquish their children permanently to state custody at a time when more people were seeking infants and toddlers for adoption. Thus, although it might seem that increased admissions to the foundling home at the turn of the century reflected parents' increasing indifference to their babies and toddlers, in fact the change in use of the foundling home reflected new meanings attached to the parent-child relationship.

From the reform of the late 1850s through 1876, the end of the República Restaurada (Restored Republic), the government had rarely intervened in the home, reflecting a persistent and deeply rooted consensus on concepts of class-based entitlements to family life. Low numbers of foundling home admissions, in turn, reflected the relative stability of the urban environment. But Porfirian economic policies prompted high rates of migration and undercut urban living standards and thus had an impact on these assumptions, on abandonment practices, and on the foundling home itself. After decades of stasis, the rise in admissions that began in the early years of the Díaz administration and peaked just after the turn of the century pointed to profound disruptions to family life in the city and illuminated the shifting meanings attached to family stability and child circulation in the politics of class formation. The hectic pace of admissions and retrievals at the turn of the century revealed that economically stressed parents of young children, no longer able to sustain family life, reshaped the only public aid available to them—interning their children—into a short-term service for managing immediate crises. The new activism among the parents who retrieved their children revealed a strong feeling of entitlement to a coherent family. Thus, the new patterns of use suggested important changes in the value that families invested in their children, even in infants requiring intensive maternal care. In response, administrators, who never intended to provide such a service, reassessed the role that the foundling home played in the capital's welfare system and in urban social life.

In 1898 the appointment of Domínguez as director prompted new regulations that centered on clarifying class distinctions among entering children by creating three categories. These were the *expósito*, or foundling, whose parent forfeited legal authority over the child; the *amparado*, supported by the state with the parent retaining authority; and the *pensionista*, whose parent or guardian paid room and board to retain authority. In the past, children entered as either foundlings or pensioners: the status of amparado was an innovation. Reflecting historical usage, children entering in the status of expósito were considered "legitimate children of the house" and were still given the surname Lorenzana after the home's eighteenth-century clerical founder. The director, in his role of legal guardian, had the right to place expósitos in adoption.[71] Parents seeking the status of amparado for a child had to petition the supervising federal agency and prove that they could not work to support the child or pay a pension to the foundling home. Parents or guardians of pensionistas paid monthly fees of five pesos for nursing babies sent to the country and ten pesos for weaned children housed in the establishment. For the few pensioners entering the special *departamento de distinguidos*, the institution charged twenty pesos a month.[72] Once inscribed, a child "belonged" to the house. Parents and guardians of pensionistas could retrieve their children at will if they had kept up their pension payments. When parents of amparados wished to retrieve their children, they had to provide evidence that they were now in a position to support and educate them. Parents and guardians of amparados and pensionistas who wished to stay in touch with children were permitted a weekly visit. If they failed to pay the monthly fees or failed to visit for two years—without an acceptable excuse—the child would be considered abandoned and become available for adoption.[73]

Other innovations in the 1898 regulations included changes in the medical management of infant care, especially the reorganization of infant feeding. As the Hospicio's regulations allowed, the new regulations for the foundling home allowed administrators to evict long-term inmates over twenty-one. Finally, the administrative regime initiated in 1898 ensured that the welfare office, the Dirección General de Beneficencia Pública (General Directorate of Public Welfare), housed within the Secretaría de Gobernación, paid close attention to the home's affairs.

The foundling home's 1898 regulations went even further than the earlier reorganization of the Hospicio in establishing an explicit state commitment to children. The 1898 document extended the right (*el derecho*) to public shelter, support, and medical assistance to children from birth to age four, coming from a broad range of circumstances: "The right to the asylum belongs to all abandoned children; orphans without father or mother who have no guardian or person who wishes to take them in; those who cannot be supported and educated by their parents, because of their lack of resources owing to a *proven* impossibility of working; and those who, by means of a monthly pension, are presented to the house by their parents or relatives."[74]

This statement omitted any mention of social stigma resulting from birth outside of marriage, acknowledged the right to state aid for children of poor or disabled parents, and offered boarding services for young children from families of means. But, strikingly, the document grounded state assistance on a nascent concept of children's rights. As such, the foundling home's 1898 regulations marked an extraordinary innovation, especially in contrast to sentimental views of charity toward children or to elite prejudice against the capital's lower classes. At one pole, that of sentiment, poet Juan de Dios Peza used religious imagery to celebrate a ceremonial visit to the foundling home in 1899 by the president's wife, Carmen Romero Rubio de Díaz:

> To the angel, whose hand
> Gives shelter to the orphan,
> And bread to the beggar . . .
> And the abandoned child
> With holy love embraces,
> And lightens in this house
> The weight of his cross.[75]

But while children safely interned under government vigilance were deemed to deserve pious sentiments, the same individuals fell into the category of the dangerous poor once they reached maturity. In 1882 the urban chronicler Manuel Rivera Cambas recorded local elite opinion when he wrote, "Foundlings who reach their majority leave to dedicate themselves to various kinds of work or stay in the establishment . . . or are sent to the country to work. It bears noting that in the suburbs of the capital, the villages in which there are more of them are considered places full of delinquents and those individuals are always a real danger to society."[76] In contrast to both sentimental and censorious views, the foundling home regulations established a rights-based compact between children and the state, while also reaffirming that the institution served as a major intersection in the city's pathways of child circulation.

The 1898 regulations, especially the newly created status of amparado, as well as subsequent adjustments in operations, opened a period of dynamic interaction between upper-level manipulations of policy and the urban public's use of foundling home services in shifting systems of child circulation. Only to a limited extent did the rise in admissions reflect the city's swelling migrant population; rather, admissions reflected the impact of a glut of unskilled laborers on the survival strategies of established urban families. Indeed, migrants were underrepresented among the parents bringing children: the 1899–1900 admissions register records only twenty-four migrant parents at a time when two-thirds of the residents of the Federal District were born elsewhere. The relative absence of obvious migrants among the home's admissions suggests that newcomers may not have been familiar with urban institutions, although some migrants may have been hidden among the admissions from suburban communities, where so many new arrivals congregated. Information on baptisms in the 1899–1900 admissions register shows that the city center was strongly represented and that outlying communities were closely integrated with the urban center.[77] Transportation was clearly a factor: the well-developed system of public transport could carry parents and their children from the city outskirts into No. 3 Puente de la Merced, where the foundling home still occupied its crumbling colonial-era compound.[78]

Maternal Tenacity

In May 1899, when a single mother named Luz Godines brought her month-old son Felipe to the foundling home, she joined the unprecedented number of parents who placed their children there at the turn of the twentieth century. Although the foundling home's new regulations allowed Luz to retain parental authority if she petitioned the state to cover his board in the orphanage, the fact that she entered Felipe as a foundling and thereby relinquished her parental rights speaks to the urgency of her situation. However desperate she may have felt on that day, Luz had social resources. With the support of her baby's compadres she had Felipe baptized in the chapel of the capital's cathedral. Their sponsorship of Felipe also created a relationship of mutual obligation, which encompassed more than religious duties. In the days after she legally relinquished her baby, Luz mobilized her support networks to bring him home. Only a week later, accompanied by her *comadre*, Luz returned to the foundling home to reclaim him. Director Domínguez noted in the margin next to Felipe's admission record: "In view of the mother's entreaties and because the godmother . . . is the guarantor, this child was handed back."[79]

In early July of the same year, Margarita García relinquished her parental rights over her three-year-old daughter, María del Carmen, when she entered the girl as a foundling at the Casa de Niños Expósitos. Three years before, when Margarita had María baptized in a downtown parish church, two comadres had stood as sponsors. Less than a month after abandoning her daughter, Margarita resolved to retrieve her and turned to her community for support. Instead of the two comadres who had assisted at the child's baptism, she took the precaution of enlisting the extra leverage of masculine authority for her return trip to the foundling home. Camilo Ramírez, a mattress maker, accompanied her and served as guarantor so that she could reclaim her child.[80]

These two cases point to both continuity and change in the profiles of families who brought children to the foundling home in the late 1890s. Luz's case exhibits many continuities with past abandonment practice. She was a single mother; her son had been baptized; and she left him as a foundling, relinquishing her rights. On the other hand, in contrast to earlier patterns of use of the foundling home, Luz mobilized her support network to retrieve her child, and her comadre played a key role in reuniting mother and son. Margarita's case points to other important factors in the new patterns of use that emerged at the turn of the century. First, her daughter's age and place of baptism show that Margarita was not a recent arrival to Mexico City but instead had established social networks in the capital. Something had recently disrupted Margarita's life and forced her to abandon her three-year-old to the state institution. At the time of her child's baptism and in the crisis that precipitated the child's abandonment, Margarita turned for support to members of her own community. One of her comadres at her daughter's baptism had the same surname as she did and could well have been a relative. When she needed to retrieve her child from the foundling home, she persuaded a local artisan to help her. Importantly, as in the release of Felipe to Luz, orphanage staff overlooked the finality of legal abandonment and facilitated reunification of mother and child.

Administrators recorded no information about the family circumstances of a significant number of children, but a few indicators sketch in the story for the remainder. As they had for decades, women bore the burden of seeking their children's admission to the foundling home. Between 1899 and 1901, women brought 405 out of the 520 entries, with mothers bringing 249 children and women with an unidentified connection to the family counting for another 83. But fathers brought 37 children, testifying to their family context. Children's surnames (*apellidos*) also provide evidence: 212 children in this register, or 40 percent, had surnames different from their mothers, meaning that they were either legitimate and their parents married, or *natural*, that is, their parents were not married but their fathers had legally recognized them. In contrast, the register recorded only 86 children, or about 16 percent, who were clearly born outside of marriage, as they shared their mothers' surnames. Another indication that economic motives drove foundling home admissions was the increase in the number of older children and children with siblings.[81] Taken together, these two indicators—the number of children whose parents were married or whose fathers acknowledged some family responsibility, and the entrance of older children and siblings—point to sudden crises disrupting formerly stable households. Indeed, parents often stated poverty (*falta de recursos*) as the reason they brought their children to the foundling home.

Certainly honor abandonments, that is, admissions motivated by the stigma of illegitimate birth, had been on the decline for decades. In the early 1860s, a government welfare inspector had observed that unmarried mothers wanted to keep their babies; he commented on the cruelty of the policy that separated mothers from the babies they gave birth to in the Departamento de Partos Ocultos (Department of Concealed Births) located in the Hospicio compound. There, unmarried mothers could come to give birth in secret, and policy had at one time mandated that babies born in the department be sent directly to the foundling home.[82] Not long after the inspector observed that even single mothers wished to keep their babies, the old department closed. After that, however, a steady stream of abandonments had flowed from the public Hospital de Maternidad e Infancia (Maternity and Children's Hospital) during its early years of operation.[83] These, too, had dwindled by the mid-1880s, suggesting a continued weakening of the stigma attached to bearing children outside marriage. By 1899 the majority of infants admitted to the foundling home directly from the public maternity hospital came because their mothers had died in childbirth.[84] Moreover, despite the high rate of foundling home admissions at the turn of the century, the institution admitted only twenty-eight children who had been abandoned or lost in the streets, proportionally not many more than in the late 1870s before the surge in migration.[85]

Indeed, mothers went to great lengths to keep their children even under duress. Homeless women with babies found ways to use the foundling home without abandoning their infants. In one early twentieth-century register of employees holding low-ranking positions in the home, the vast majority was female and virtually every one had a child.[86] Other mothers applied to the ministry for aid or opted to pay the lowest possible pension that would let them retain their parental rights. Mothers, not fathers, retained authority over the majority of children admitted as amparados. Between 1898 and early 1901, parents of 204 entering children were able to pay the pension to send their children to the countryside for nursing and 43 children were pensioned at a higher rate for maintenance in the home. Often, once the mothers could move without hindrance, they found alternatives to the foundling home and returned to retrieve their children; some came back as soon as the next day.[87]

Indeed, the high rate of retrievals clearly differentiates the patterns of use for 1899–1900 from earlier practices. Out of the turn-of-the-century cohort of 520, 214 children, or 41 percent of the total, returned to their families. The high number of retrievals constituted a marked change from the 23 percent of children whose families reclaimed them during the decade from 1884 to 1895.[88]

Retrievals reflected a strong sense of entitlement to family coherence. As the stories of Luz Godines and Margarita García illustrate, mothers mobilized their community support networks to help reclaim their children. Godparents played a key role, but godmothers were crucial. At the turn of the century, it was the support of compadres, especially that of comadres, that predicted a mother's ability to reunite her family. Among the 1898 to 1901 admissions, only 32 percent of the children who lacked *madrinas* (godmothers) eventually left the institution.[89] Only 28 percent of children who had only a *padrino* (godfather) were able to leave.[90] But children with a madrina or both a madrina and padrino had a substantially greater chance of going home: 52 and 56 percent respectively. Together with the underrepresentation of migrants and the importance of madrinas as an instrumental resource of support in family reunification, the patterns of children's entry and exit from the foundling home portray a new role for the institution. It was becoming a place of last resort for mothers who had lived in the Federal District long enough to establish community networks and who knew about urban institutions and their regulations and used them creatively to solve temporary personal crises.

The new role of madrinas in family reunification represented a significant development. Previously, the way spiritual kin participated in abandonment had demonstrated continuities in constructs of family honor: to protect parental anonymity, godparents carried the child to the foundling home and petitioned for its admission. In the mid-1890s, madrinas had made no difference in family reunification. At the turn of the century, however, madrinas undertook an active role in reconstituting families separated by crisis. These patterns reveal networks of solidarity supporting a strong sense of entitlement to family life among the urban poor.[91] Such networks may have existed for a long time: the foundling home's low annual admissions throughout most of the nineteenth century hint as much. But by 1899 elevated rates of admission and the overall profile of the children's families of origin suggest that an increasing number of families previously able to rely on support networks to avoid abandoning their children were now forced by poverty to place them in the institution, at least briefly. At the same time, community supports, especially spiritual kin, supported more parents in overcoming the crisis and retrieving their children. The unprecedented rate of retrieval, moreover, spoke to mothers' strong attachment to their children and determination to reconstitute their families.

Maternal tenacity and support from compadres, however, could not entirely forestall the effects of urban change and economic pressure. During the first years of the new century, admissions to the foundling home reached unprecedented heights, rising to 409 children in 1901, 421 in 1902, and peaking at 455 in 1903.[92] The following year admissions dropped significantly, to 315. After Domínguez resigned in September 1905, admissions declined steadily. Under his replacement, Dr. Francisco de Paulo Carral, and for the rest of the decade, annual admissions more or less stabilized at under 200. The spike in admissions between 1900 and 1903 reflected Domínguez's vision for expanding the institution's social role, as well as the acute needs of urban families and—importantly—the relative flexibility of orphanage policy and enforcement. Admissions dropped after 1903 as the federal ministry imposed stricter conditions for admitting and retrieving children. Indeed, the interaction between welfare policy and urban family practice in the early 1900s played out the economic and social stresses of the moment through the politics of child circulation.

Many of the children admitted to the foundling home between 1900 and 1903 were transients, but ministry officials objected to such comings and goings for several reasons. First, overcrowding might provoke an epidemic among the inmates or force the government to make a major capital investment in the orphanage, such as constructing new dormitories, rather than continue its crisis-management approach to the structure's chronic disrepair. Moreover, the new parental activism in child retrieval challenged the established norms and proprieties of abandonment. Additionally, high rates of retrieval reduced the number of children available to meet the rising demand for adoptions. To reinforce class distinctions based on family entitlements, officials in the central welfare administration reacted to parental assertiveness by raising the fees for maintaining a child.[93] These measures reflected the ministry's attempt to reinforce the historical patterns of abandonment that had become institutionalized in charitable practice in prior decades.

Whatever the ministry's policy, the foundling home's administrators found themselves involved in daily confrontations and negotiations with parents relinquishing their children. As Domínguez indicated in his marginal note when he released Felipe Godines, these encounters could be emotional. Such experiences tempered the directors' approach to hardline policy enforcement. Despite the penal law and the 1898 regulations insisting that parents leaving children as expósitos lost legal authority, administrators sometimes released expósitos to parents who came to reclaim them—at least five times between 1899 and 1900.[94] In one situation, mitigating circumstances involving acute family tensions prompted the director to waive the finality of the expósito designation. A man placed his newborn granddaughter in the foundling home, saying that he refused to accept the baby—his daughter's illegitimate child—into the family. About ten days later, the baby's mother came to ask that the baby's status be changed to amparada, with a pension paid by the state. The director supported her wishes to retain her parental rights.[95] On other occasions, the staff seemed to prefer that children return to their families rather than remain hostage to an unpaid pension.[96]

But officials at the Dirección General de Beneficencia Pública did not share such flexible attitudes and in September 1904 they ordered that rules about payments be strictly enforced.[97] Many parents opted to pay the pension to preserve their legal authority even when they knew that maintaining regular payments would be difficult or impossible; entering a child as a pensioner was a gesture of optimism that the family would be reunited. Families and guardians had also become accustomed to missing payments and making up the debt in sporadic lump sums. Sometimes sufficient pleading at the time they sought a child's release persuaded the director to excuse the pension debt. Other parents simply deferred the moment when they would have to admit to relinquishing the child; over time they drifted away from their pension obligations.

To discourage these behaviors, indeed, to enforce the old policy about outright abandonment, officials at the Dirección increased the basic monthly pension to ten pesos.[98] Domínguez wrote sheepishly to his supervisors that he did not have the heart to make the new rate retroactive and he warned that parents did not respond to threats.[99] In May 1905, however, the newly appointed director of Beneficencia Pública, Alberto Robles Gil, ordered that any parent or guardian of a pensioner who failed to pay for two consecutive months forfeited parental authority; the child would become a ward of the system and available for adoption.[100] Domínguez obediently forwarded a list of sixteen children whose pensions had fallen into arrears.[101]

Soon after the May directive on pension payments, Domínguez sent warnings to parents and guardians in danger of losing legal authority over their children. In June an offer came to adopt one of the girls whose pension had gone unpaid since 1902. Unable to locate her father, who was reported to have left the country, Domínguez had no choice but to allow the adoption.[102] Shortly afterward, he made inquiries in suburban Tacuba to locate the father of another girl requested for adoption; by the end of the month she too had been given in adoption.[103] In another instance Domínguez kept up his inquiries until he located an acquaintance of the child's father and urged him to inform the man that he was about to lose his daughter. The foundling home's administrative clerk wrote, "Because the girl in question is very *simpática* [appealing] and because since February the man has not presented himself to see her or to pay her pension, she must now be considered a daughter of the house and for that her family may lose all rights over her to the point that if someone wants to adopt her they can take her."[104]

Once the immediate enforcement crisis had passed, however, Domínguez and his successors tended to wait longer than the stipulated two months before altering the status of the child and to wait again before permitting the child to be adopted. One volume of pension accounts indicates that only 7 of the 290 children admitted as pensioners between the end of November 1902 and late March 1904 had changed status to foundling because of a pension debt. One of them, a boy named Juan, did not become officially expósito until July 1907. And a girl whose pension was last paid in May 1905 was given in adoption in September 1905 but recalled when her mother paid her debt. Although the mother again fell behind in her pension payments, the child did not officially reenter the category of foundling until the end of October 1908.[105]

From the perspective of upper-ranking officials at the Dirección General, however, the state should not tolerate any irregularity: better that a child become a public ward. Ministry officials imposed stern conditions that forced uncomfortable decisions. And the behavior of the inmates' parents not only thwarted the carefully defined client categories but also exhibited what some officials viewed as lack of gratitude.

As the first decade of the twentieth century advanced, patterns of admission and release testified to the impact of the more rigid policies on the city's families; retrievals dropped as abandonments rose. Between September 1901 and December 1902, 537 children entered: 260, or 48 percent, went back home. Compadres may have played a more significant role in retrieval than the records indicate. Changes in record keeping in this period somewhat obscured the role of compadres in retrieval because the foundling home staff became lax in recording the names of godparents. From September 1901 through December 1902, however, 206 out of the 537 children who entered the foundling home were baptized at the time of admission, and so presumably they had at least one godparent. Of the baptized children, 66 died and 99 went home, constituting 48 percent of baptized admissions and 41 percent of the total retrievals among that admissions cohort. In 1904 only 22 percent of children were admitted as expósitos and the level of retrievals remained high: 315 were admitted in total and over 50 percent eventually went home. Expósitos constituted only 22 percent of 1904 admissions.[106]

But the pattern of high retrievals and low abandonments did not last long. By 1905 only 32 percent of the 173 children who entered were retrieved by their families. Outright abandonments kept rising: 21 percent in 1905 and 39 percent in 1906. In that year, the percentage of children left as expósitos overtook the 33 percent of children whose families were able to retrieve them. That trend continued through 1909 and can be explained in part by the increasing reluctance of welfare officials to grant children the status of amparado, which allowed parents to retain rights and have support paid by the state. In 1906, 31 percent of admitted children received state support and the numbers kept dropping: 14 percent received state support in 1907 and only 10 percent in 1909. By then 47 percent of admissions entered as expósitos, and only 27 percent went home.[107]

The significant drop in the number of annual admissions after 1905 probably reflected public response to the tighter pension policy. Despite economic stress, few families wanted to risk losing their children. In December 1905 Director Francisco de Paulo Carral responded to an inquiry from his supervisors in the Dirección about the high number of applications for amparado status: "What is happening is that there are people, who, when informed of the ways their children can enter, want to keep authority over them; and since once the children are considered among the foundlings they lose their parental authority over them, they prefer to leave them as amparados."[108] After 1905 the parents who brought their children to the foundling home were mostly urban families whose marginal economic circumstances left them no other options.

In early 1906 officials at the Dirección General, perhaps hoping to find grounds to control admissions more strictly, sought a precise legal definition of the term expósito—not to be found in either the civil or the criminal code. Only eight years earlier the foundling home's 1898 regulations had affirmed and perpetuated usage based in historical abandonment practice, one that emphasized preserving family honor in defining expósito as a child without known parents. The 1898 regulations had also extended the right to public shelter to children in a range of social and economic circumstances and had placed the burden of proving indigence on the parents, not the child. In 1906, however, the Dirección consulted a lawyer who showed no such sentimentality. He defined an expósito as an abandoned child "who by his age is incapable of providing for his own subsistence, or, a child under the age of seven."[109]

Sentiment and Discipline

The celebrated painting *Orphans at Their Mother's Grave*, by the Mexican artist Luis Monroy, depicts a cemetery scene. An adolescent girl and her younger brother are dressed in mourning and rest against the pedestal of an elegant marble tomb as they gaze tearfully at the humble wooden cross that marks the resting place of their departed mother. An article about the artist and his oeuvre published in a women's magazine singled out this painting as one of Monroy's best and noted approvingly that "the tears of his characters evoke our tears."[110] Similar elevated sentiments toward unfortunate children animated Porfirian ceremonial philanthropy. But the interwoven themes developed in the occasional poetry of Juan de Dios Peza pointed to fundamental contradictions between rhetorical celebrations of piety and charity and class-based concepts of childhood. Mexico's First Lady prompted angelic comparisons when she performed charitable acts at the foundling home; meanwhile, the young inmates of the trade school were exhorted to work to earn their salvation. When asked for a definition of an expósito, a lawyer for the welfare administration implied that children as young as seven were capable of their own support. Thus he demonstrated that elite sympathy for motherless children did not preclude the expectation that even the youngest child welfare clients should work to earn their keep.

Welfare policy based on these contradictions positioned the public orphanages of the capital in the mainstream of urban circuits of child circulation and also gave the institutions a central role in reinforcing family forms based on the low-wage or unpaid labor of children and women. The Hospicio's core clientele consisted of families dependent on women's labor in domestic service and related occupations where wages were too low to keep families intact. But families that placed their children in the Hospicio or the trade school actually sought to delay the moment when their children had to work to contribute to the family economy. Welfare spokespersons such as Martiniano Alfaro celebrated the paternal role of the Hospicio in protecting and educating the daughters of such families, many of them

Los huérfanos en el sepulcro de la madre.

3. *Los Huérfanos en el Sepulcro de la Madre* (*Orphans at Their Mother's Grave*). Lithograph of a painting by Luis Monroy. From *Álbum de la Mujer* 3, no. 4 (27 July 1884): 50. Secretaría de Hacienda y Crédito Público, Biblioteca Miguel Lerdo de Tejada, Fondo Reservado.

headed by women, while highlighting the overlapping concepts of family and assistance that kept women dependent.

In contrast, when mothers acted assertively to keep their families together, they met with resistance from welfare officials. By the late 1890s urban families that had once been able to stay together faced economic crises forcing them to intern their children in the foundling home, however briefly. At the turn of the century, urban, working-class mothers took advantage of a policy innovation—the status of amparado—and made an unprecedented effort to retrieve their children from the foundling home, calling on their networks of support for assistance in doing so. When mothers attempted to preserve legal authority over their children and reunify their families, the retrieval of their children created unacceptable ambiguities for upper-ranking welfare officials, who aimed for the opposite goal. They wanted to expand the institution's social role by increasing the number of children entrusted to the home but, at the same time, maintain definitive policies on relinquishment. Above all, they wished to enforce the elite understanding that the working poor, especially single mothers, were less entitled to family life. These contradictory expectations were nowhere more evident than in welfare officials' enactment of adoption policy.

Labor or Love

Trends in Porfirian Adoption Practice

In 1905, shortly after the old poor house in the city's center was closed, demolished, and replaced by the new Hospicio de Niños on the calzada San Antonio Abad, Martiniano Alfaro, the Hospicio's secretary and historian, expressed his satisfaction at the establishment's success in placing welfare wards in adoptions. "One cannot determine exactly how many boys and girls have left the Hospicio under adoption," he wrote, explaining that records had not been kept, but he estimated that "on average, 3 percent of inmates" were adopted every year.[1] Alfaro noted with enthusiasm the growing but unknown number of children from the Hospicio who had been adopted by prominent members of society from the states of Yucatán, Campeche, and Tabasco, the states that bordered the Gulf of Mexico. He also claimed that many other children had been adopted in the capital. In some cases the adoptee had become an integral member of the family, to the point of inheriting from the adoptive parents.[2]

Such good fortune seemed certain for Ricardo A. Lorenzana, adopted from the Casa de Niños Expósitos, Mexico City's other major home for orphans. After Ricardo's mother died, his grandmother placed him there in the status of expósito in February 1910. In May of 1912 a customs official from Tamaulipas submitted testimonials from the director of the customs service and a member of Congress in support of his petition to adopt Ricardo. Six months after signing the adoption contract, the adoptive father wrote to the director of Beneficencia Pública to report on the well-being of the little boy. His letter, radiant with love and pride, recounted that the new parents had baptized the child with their own names, that the boy was thriving, and that he would grow to be a useful member of society.[3]

But Mexico City's working poor were more suspicious about the conditions under which their children passed into the hands of others. Kidnapping rings operated in the capital, and families of the victims believed that their children had been abducted to exploit their labor. A broadside of November 1907 states that within a two-month period forty-nine children between the ages of two and thirteen had disappeared, and notes that other kidnappings had occurred in the recent past. The broadside describes the kidnappers as "without morality," and raises fears that some of the children could already have perished from the punishments the thieves meted out to make them learn their work. Although the broadside points to parents' lack of vigilance as one reason why children disappeared, it emphasizes the pain of the affected families: "Poor mothers and fathers full of limitless anguish search without rest for the whereabouts of their little children."[4]

Administrators of child welfare institutions also had sufficient reasons to be cautious in their oversight of adoption. Some adoption petitioners were not what they seemed. In January 1901 the widely read daily newspaper, *El Imparcial*, reported that a man who had adopted a baby girl from the foundling home had been arrested for attempting to pass her off as the child of a millionaire.[5]

The circulation of rumors about kidnapping in working-class neighborhoods, the eruption of occasional scandals involving adoptions of welfare wards, and the conflicting views of adoption at the different social strata

Los Roba-Chicos en México

Desaparición Misteriosa de 49 Niños, en el tiempo trascurrido del 24 de Septiembre al 24 de Noviembre del año actual.

Hace próximamente como dos meses que han comenzado de nueva cuenta lo mismo que en una época anterior, la desaparición de chiquillos. Las pobres madres y padres llenos de angustias sin límites indagan sin descanso el paradero de sus pequeños hijos, ignorando si viven ó han muerto tal vez de hambre ó de alguna enfermedad ó á fuerza de los castigos que esos infames robadores de chicos les impondrán probablemente: para que aprendan á hacer cualquier trabajo por el que sus hurtadores traten de explotar

¿Y por qué motivo se pierden tanto los niños yendo á manos de esos explotadores sin moralidad que les nombran roba chicos? Por el descuido de sus padres, es caro: Asombra la cifra que poco más ó menos se ha registrado en México, en cuanto á niños extraviados. Desde el 24 de Septiembre pasado al 24 del mes actual de Noviembre se han perdido cuarenta y nueve chicuelos entre hombres y mujeres. Cruelísima resulta la susodicha cantidad, cuarenta y nueve niños significan cuarenta y nue-

ve dramas familiares, cuarenta y nueve víctimas que han sufrido sed y hambre y tal vez malos tratos cuarenta y nueve procesos judiciales que han comenzado á tramitarse por las autoridades de esta capital

Del sexo masculino. Son: Angel Muñoz 4 años 3 meses Elías Benítez 8 años 5 meses, J Concepción Hernández 5 años 6 meses, Teófilo Refugio, 4 años, 9 meses Atenógenes Pérez 7 años, 2 meses, Faustino Pichardo 3 años un mes, Esteban Carrillo 10 años 2 meses. Macario Guzmán 6 años 5 meses Francisco Estebez, 12 años, Conrrado Peña 8 años, un mes Emeterio Telléz 6 años 2 meses Candelario Rendón 5 años, 8 meses, Higinio Aguirre 5 años 4 meses Agapito López, 4 años 3 meses, Fidencio Gónzalez 3 años, un mes, Laureano Estrada, 2 años 6 meses, Edmundo Lorenzo, 2 años, 7 meses Florencio Pacheco 4 años 5 meses Elpidio Muro, 11 años un mes Luis Flores, 7 años, 4 meses. Macario Espinosa, 5 años, 9 meses, Silvestre Anjolín, 6 años un mes Ernesto Bustos 8 años 2 meses. Jacobo Lima, 13 años 4

4. "Los roba-chicos en México: Desaparación misteriosa de 49 niños, en el tiempo transcurrido del 24 de septiembre al 24 de noviembre del año actual" (Kidnappers in Mexico City: Mysterious disappearance of 49 children, from September 24 to November 24 of the present year). José Guadalupe Posada, Broadside, 1907. Colorado Springs Fine Arts Center, Taylor Museum.

in the capital city illuminate clashing conceptions of the value of children at the turn of the century: a market in child labor fed a demand for under-age workers, while families at both ends of the social spectrum valued having children to nurture and protect. During the late Porfiriato both views prompted a growing number of individuals to find new ways to use adoption from the public orphanages, conduits in Mexico City's established systems of child circulation. Welfare administrators acted as intermediaries between adopters and client families in the increasingly complex social transaction of adoption. Hospicio administrators, however, kept no precise tally of the children placed in adoptions, which speaks to their ambivalence about the fate of those children. Although some adoptions were solemnized by contract and the Hospicio charged a fee to process adoption requests, the lack of documentation shows how informal that transaction apparently was to officials and to many adopting adults.

Surviving records of the late Porfiriato contextualize Martiniano Alfaro's happy gloss on adoptions through the welfare system; they also indicate that welfare administrators and adoption petitioners varied in their interpretations of the meaning and uses of adoption, as did other players within urban systems of child circulation. Mexicans adopted for love and for labor: neither motive could be said to predominate. Rather, as the century turned and Mexico approached the centennial of its independence movement, emerging trends in adoption revealed that children's social value, the meanings of childhood, and the nature of the relationships created by adoption were in flux. Most importantly, because adopted children came from poor families and entered households of means, often as working dependents, turn-of-the-century adoption practices illuminated a fundamental conflict over class-based concepts of childhood and entitlements to family life.

Adoption Law and Practice

Adoption in Mexico had a long legal and social history that over time created layered and overlapping meanings for the practice, sometimes based on family relationships and sometimes on the obligation of charity recipients to work for their benefactors. Historically, legal definitions emphasized family relationships, but in practice most adoptions were informal and based on the unequal social positions of adopter and adoptee. By the late nineteenth century, however, a growing number of Mexicans of means informally adopted babies and young children to form families. At the same time, adoptions for labor not only continued but also appeared to be linked to a brisk market in child labor.

Adoption had entered Spanish law through Roman law, and Spanish legal codes originating in the thirteenth century considered the relationships established by adoption to be similar to those created by birth or spiritual kinship. Thus, the law forbade marriage not only between adopted parents and children but also between the adopted child and the birth children of the adoptive father.[6] Adopted children could inherit from an adoptive parent who died without leaving a will but only if that parent had no other heirs, legitimate or *natural*—that is, illegitimate but legally recognized. Under Spanish law, however, if the king approved the adoption, then the adoptive father had full legal paternal authority (*patria potestad*) over the adopted child, and the adopted child had the same inheritance rights as the father's legitimate children.[7]

Eighteenth-century regulations of the Casa de Niños Expósitos permitted adoptions, most of which were likely to fall within the informal category rather than the formal variety approved by the king. The regulations urged only that adopting adults (*adoptantes*) be respectable, have sufficient means, and not engage in low or disreputable occupations.[8] Eighteenth-century adoptions of foundlings spanned the social spectrum: foundling home documents from the 1790s include the adoption of a mestiza baby by an indigenous couple.[9] Early nineteenth-century censuses of Mexico City reveal a considerable amount of infertility, and childless couples adopted infants and toddlers from the foundling home.[10] Widows also adopted small children and older girls as companions.[11]

Adoptions from the foundling home were closely linked to women's charitable works. In the early 1840s Fanny Calderón de la Barca, the Scottish-born wife of a Spanish diplomat, made several visits to the orphanage in the company of the establishment's elite benefactors. She described the babies as "belonging" to the ladies and described the ladies' role probably as they themselves defined it: "The child . . . remains under the charge of the society for life; but, of the hundreds and tens of hundreds that have passed through their hands, scarcely one has been left to grow up in the Cuna. They are constantly adopted by respectable persons, who, according to their inclination or abilities, bring them up either as favoured servants or as their own children; and the condition of a huérfano, an orphan—as a child from the hospital is always called—is perfectly on a level with that of the most petted child of the house."[12] On a later visit, Calderón de la Barca was surprised when "one little girl sidled up to me and said in a most insinuating voice, 'Me llevas tú? Will you take me away with you?'—for even at this early age they begin to have a glimmering idea that those whom the ladies choose from amongst them are peculiarly favored."[13]

As Calderón de la Barca's account suggests, elite patronage of the orphanages tinged adoption practice with charitable meanings, which did not preclude "petted" and "peculiarly favored" children from working as servants in their adopted households. Some children, however, were adopted by relatives, like a boy from the Hospicio whose uncle, a general, decided to take charge of his education.[14] Still, the majority of the children in the orphanages came from poor families, and most adoption petitioners came from the middle and upper classes. Moreover, for the greater part of the nineteenth century, most adoption petitioners were residents of Mexico City and adoption constituted one aspect of local circuits of child circulation. The geography of adoption began to change during the Porfiriato, however, as rail transportation improved. Not only did parents and guardians from outside the Federal District board their children and wards at the foundling home and the Hospicio, but also a significant number of applicants from other states requested children for adoption.[15]

In the mid-nineteenth century, the ascendance of liberal doctrine, with its emphasis on the individual and on the free movement of property, introduced a new legal regime affecting adoption. The initial 1857 cycle of reform laws bearing on the family gave adoption full civil status; subsequent laws quickly narrowed the legal definition and finally eliminated adoption as a formal legal instrument for creating an heir.[16] The distinguished liberal jurist Justo Sierra considered adoption a vestige of Mexico's old regime and outside of custom, and he pointedly omitted it from his 1859 draft civil code.[17] Sierra rejected adoption partly for its absolutist connotations: only the monarch had possessed the authority to grant full adoptions because they created paternal authority. But Sierra may also have disliked informal adoption because of its close association with the informal practices of godparenthood.[18] Compadrazgo, interwoven with religious rituals like baptism and with the social relations of patronage, stood in opposition to the liberal ideal of contractual social relations between individuals.[19]

In 1861, when the reform laws nationalized charitable institutions, the regulations on adoption from the Hospicio and foundling home remained unchanged.[20] Yet the reform had whittled away the legal foundation of adoption and left it open to multiple interpretations. The 1866 adoption of two girls from the Hospicio illustrates the ambiguities. In February of that year, don Lucio Ortiz Nava and his mother, doña Inés Merino de Nava, petitioned the Hospicio to adopt María Granados and Soledad Moreno, both residents in the orphanage. (Although the records do not indicate the girls' ages, subsequent events suggest that they were both in their teens.) Hospicio administrators forwarded the request to city officials, before whom the petitioners made a formal declaration. Invoking the law, the Navas pledged to adopt the girls "as daughters" and committed themselves to "all the obligations of parents by nature to give them a Christian and civil education." City officials, in turn, agreed to the adoption on conditions designed to protect the girls: if at any time María or Soledad were exposed to immoral examples or suffered harm the city would intervene and bring them back under its authority.[21]

The arrangement quickly soured. By April the Navas asked the city to take their adoptive "daughters" back. The Navas complained that the girls persisted in socializing with each other, and perhaps with friends outside the home, and resisted the education that the adopters attempted to impart. Indeed, one night while the family was at prayers the girls ran away. Once they were apprehended, they were returned to the Hospicio.[22]

This case points to the contradictions between the legacy of legal adoption, which had established family relationships, and informal practice. The Navas's adoption application invoked the relationships and obligations of birth parent and child. In this instance, however, the "parents" were not a couple, but mother and son. Indeed, if the girls had been considered full members of the family they would surely have been included in evening prayers. Despite their pledge to adopt María Granados and Soledad Moreno "as daughters," the Navas had almost certainly adopted the girls as servants and their "education" probably consisted of household work. The girls made their perspective clear by fleeing the house.

The 1866 adoption of María and Soledad took place during the Segundo Imperio (Second Empire), under Austrian monarchs Maximilian and Charlotte, who were soon deposed by Mexico's resurgent liberals, led by Benito Juárez. The triumphant officials of the restored republic quickly turned their attention to reorganizing welfare establishments on the liberal principles delineated in the laws of the reform.[23] The Hospicio's 1868 regulations reflected the elimination of formal adoption from the reform laws and the views of liberals such as Justo Sierra and pushed adoption from public welfare institutions further away from ideas of family and further toward labor, specifically domestic labor.

The new regulations explicitly favored the adoption of girls as servants; indeed, the document explicitly provided only for the adoption of girls. Given that the regulations elaborated the guidelines for adoptions in the context of defining labor arrangements for the release of inmates, administrators clearly anticipated that girls would be adopted as servants. Even so, the regulations drew on past experience to warn that adoption contracts must be made with caution to avoid abuses.[24] The regulations also called on the Hospicio's women's visiting committee—wives of political officials and leading citizens—to look out for suitable positions for the girls. In this, the regulations echoed Fanny Calderón de la Barca's report on the foundling home and pointed to the interlocking networks of private and public patronage, child circulation, and labor.[25] Although older boys were occasionally adopted, this was less common, in part because orphanage regulations provided for their placement in apprenticeships, which, like domestic service positions, were usually unpaid.[26] Thus the terms of the orphanage's regulations construed adoption as a gendered relationship, tying girls' trajectories along circuits of child circulation to domestic service. Likewise, instead of creating fatherhood and an heir, as the old regime of legal adoption had done, the informal adoptions for labor delineated by the 1868 regulations emphasized elite women's roles in charitable work and anticipated that the adoptee's primary relationship would be with her female employer.

While the Hospicio's regulations tied informal adoption to domestic work, the authors of the civil codes of 1870 and 1884 followed Justo Sierra's draft code in omitting formal adoption and denying that it had a place in Mexican society. Referring to adoption for the creation of heirs, the commission that wrote the 1870 code asserted that in Mexican society adoption had purely "theoretical" origins and that usually it created family discord. The code's authors argued that there was no need to enter into artificial relations like those created by adoption, which only "opened the door to all kinds of vexations, could be the cause of crimes, . . . and usually sowed the most complete disagreement within families."[27] The "complete disagreement" was an oblique reference to disputes over inheritance caused by bringing an adoptee into the family. On the other hand, the code's authors gestured to the charitable meanings of adoption by asserting that Mexicans could help orphans without resorting to formal adoptions, and in this they clearly meant adoptions like those of María Granados and Soledad Moreno. Despite its omission from the civil codes, however, adoption survived in the fee schedules of the 1872 law of civil registry: registering an adoption cost five pesos for the rich but was free for the poor.[28]

Several legal issues suggest why formal adoption to create an heir was eliminated from nineteenth-century civil law. First, the civil code of 1870 expressed liberal doctrine in terms of strengthening the inheritance regime of the legitimate family. During the colonial period, adoption had been used to bring illegitimate children into the legitimate household and also to create legal heirs: both motives no doubt caused vexation and family disagreements.[29] In contrast, the 1870 code favored marriage of the parents as the means to legitimate children. But efforts to fortify the legitimate family and its mechanisms for inheritance by legitimate children weakened the claims of family members linked by informal relations, especially any claims that illegitimate children might make on their fathers. This had been precisely the goal of the French Code Napoleon of 1804, the model for many Latin American nineteenth-century civil codes.[30]

Moreover, the authors of the 1870 code also tacitly approved of the informal adoption of minors as laborers or as unequal dependents. Notably, both the 1870 code and its 1884 revision granted employers the same rights as guardians in disciplining their underage domestic servants.[31] The codes also granted orphanage administrators two powers: to serve as the guardians of abandoned children and to regulate adoption "in accordance with the law, and the terms of the regulations of the establishment."[32] Now that legal formal adoption had been abolished, the regulations of welfare institutions and the predilections of their administrators established the parameters for adopting children in their care.

Within this loose framework, the thirty-seven adoptions overseen by the foundling home from 1877 through 1879 spanned the spectrum of possible motives. Couples and single women favored children between the ages of one and five, and some, who presumably could afford to hire a wet nurse, sought infants. Those who adopted babies preferred boys, although robust health and skin color could have been additional factors. Adopters of toddlers and older children preferred girls.[33] Only two children between the ages of six and ten were adopted, perhaps because they provided neither the satisfactions of nurturing a baby nor had the capacity for sustained work. Older inmates capable of productive work were adopted in fairly substantial numbers: seven aged eleven to fifteen and five others aged seventeen to twenty-five. Those adopting the twelve older inmates included eight couples, two single men, and two single women. One of the married couples possibly acting out of charitable motives was the poet and philanthropist Juan de Dios Peza and his wife.[34]

Eliminated from the law, adoption nevertheless remained the umbrella term for a wide spectrum of family and labor practices. Adoptions from Mexico City's orphanages continued to flourish and illuminated the class relations embedded in the structure of the welfare system. Broadly interpreted by Mexicans of diverse social standing, adoption could mean fostering, charity, affection, family formation, or the child's obligation to work.[35] At the extremes, for every story of a child adopted and accepted as a member of the family, like Ricardo A. Lorenzana, there was a story of exploitation and abuse. But in the intermediate area of practice, the Hospicio facilitated the adoption of mostly female minors as servants into middle-and upper-class households. At the same time, a rise in the number of group adoptions of Hospicio inmates and older foundling home wards of both sexes pointed to a surge in demand for labor adoptions. Yet labor was not the only motive for adoption. At the Casa de Niños Expósitos a growing number of adoptions of babies and toddlers reflected motives of family formation despite the lack of a legal framework. As Porfirian economic policies increased the divide between rich and poor, however, both kinds of adoptions—labor and family formation—accentuated class differences based on entitlements to family stability and access to the labor necessary to sustain it.

The Ambiguities of Uncodified Practice

"¡Pobre Ernestina!" a serialized tale written and published in 1886 by Federico Carlos Jens in the women's magazine *La Familia*, traced the tragic life of its heroine, orphaned young when her parents died in a cholera epidemic: poor Ernestina was "born to weep." Still too young to appreciate the gravity of her loss, the girl was taken into the home of her godfather, don Anselmo, "more from a sentiment of holy charity than from a sense of duty." As Ernestina grew, her benefactor, a "rich merchant . . . lavished her with attentions and affection to lessen the pain that afflicted her." But not all members of the family welcomed the unfortunate girl into the household: don Anselmo's daughter, Emma, jealous of the affection bestowed on Ernestina, never ceased to remind her rival that she was only "a sad orphan, alone in the world." In addition to Emma's jealousy, Ernestina's thwarted love for Javier, her padrino's son, pointed to the problematic position of the adoptee within her godfather's household. Ernestina understood that she owed "what I am to charity," whereas the wealthy object of her love had "a title that honors him, a future."[36] The couple finally surmounted separation and misunderstanding and married, something they could not have done if Ernestina had been formally adopted. But Jens did not permit Ernestina to enjoy happiness for long. The story ended with her early death, Javier at her side.[37]

Jens's tale provides one interpretation of what the authors of the 1870 civil code meant by helping orphans. The story is founded on elite understandings that relationships of compadrazgo obliged compadres to provide protection and support for their *ahijados* (godchildren). Yet even when cast as an act of "holy charity," this variant of informal adoption could not overcome the inequality embedded in the relationship: the child who received charity from her padrino was not an equal member of her benefactor's family. Indeed, the death of Ernestina's parents in a cholera epidemic obliquely suggests that they were of a lower social class than their compadre, don Anselmo, whose family was sufficiently well nourished and sheltered to avoid the scourge. The class dimension of Ernestina's adoption made her marriage with Javier all the more problematic. Significantly, Ernestina's creator did not allow her to live to bear heirs to Javier. In addition to the issue of social inequality based on class, the melodramatic tale also reveals that informal adoption was a nexus of gender and power relations where concepts of charity and dependence converged. As imagined by Jens, the protected and dependent lower-class orphan was female and her fate rested on decisions and actions taken by her godfather and his son.[38]

Although fictional, Ernestina's story suggests some of the contradictory concepts of family embedded in the practice of informal adoption. In late nineteenth-century Mexico, the refusal to legally codify adoption meant that the individuals involved could draw on different interpretations of the relationships of power and intimacy implied by adoption's historical precedents. Such was the case for María de Jesús Benita Lorenzana, an orphan raised in the foundling home until she was transferred to the Hospicio to begin her primary education. In January 1888 Dr. Francisco de P. Tagle and his wife María Leal adopted María de Jesús "as a daughter." The experience was disastrous for her. The adoption terminated eight months later when a judge remanded the girl to the Hospital Juárez for treatment of her "injuries" and she brought a formal complaint against the adopting couple for mistreating her. Despite her experience of abuse, when María de Jesús reentered the Hospicio she informed the director that she wanted to leave again "as soon as some family that wanted to adopt her as a daughter presented itself." Indeed, she had a candidate in mind. To hasten her departure from the Hospicio, she wrote to María Pliego and her husband, who submitted a petition to adopt her "as a daughter" and promised "to stand in for true parents." Based on three letters of recommendation testifying to the couple's honorable reputation and secure economic position, the adoption was approved.[39]

The two adoptions of María de Jesús Benita point to implicit understandings that adoption created familial relationships. Like the Nava family over twenty years earlier, both adopting couples ostensibly adopted the girl "as a daughter." Although the law provided no legal definition of the relationships created by adoption, in this instance all parties concurred in treating the transaction as one creating familial bonds and responsibilities. As such, María's first adopters violated that understanding by abusing her. Yet the promise of living in a family clearly held a strong attraction for María, who had spent her entire childhood in public institutions. The records indicate neither how she met María Pliego nor whether she was treated as a daughter in her new home. But perhaps María's distrust for Hospicio administrators who had placed her in an abusive situation led her to take matters into her own hands and select her own candidates to "stand in as true parents." María's activism on her own behalf—her complaint against her abusers and her determined pursuit of a better placement—were sufficiently unusual to highlight both the power and the potential for abuse that welfare officials and administrators wielded in the informal adoption process, especially when they conflated labor with adoption's implied family relations.

As guardians (*tutores*) of welfare wards, the directors of Mexico City's public orphanages could interpret adoption in ways that served institutional interests as well as the moralizing family discourses of the upper classes. Thus, in 1887, when the foundling home director Dr. Angel Carpio found that seven of the older female inmates presented disciplinary challenges, he sought to place them in service in private households. The problem came to a head in February 1887 when Carpio, trying to save money, cut two cleaners' positions and attempted to fill them with some of young women who had grown to maturity within the establishment. Echoing the implications of Navas' 1866 declaration, Carpio insisted that the work of cleaning, arranging the wards for younger children, and supervising the little ones not only was beneficial for the institution but also served as education for the older residents. The young women involved, however, "responded badly, saying that they were not maids nor had they been so."[40] Their insistence shows that they construed their status as "daughters of the house" to be above that of the institution's *servidumbre*, the extensive staff of nannies, cleaners, and laundry workers. Carpio complained to his superiors that the women displayed a lack of respect and subordination in front of the younger children, set a bad example, and disrupted the harmony and morality of the house. He admonished the offenders several times and pointed out how much harm they would face if they did not obey and perform their assigned tasks with good will. Although the women finally agreed "to serve," Carpio said they maintained their attitude of disrespect and insubordination.

They also took their complaint to the press. Two city newspapers, *Voz de México* and *El Monitor Republicano*, ran the story and decried the threat of "expulsion" of life-long "daughters of the house." The bad publicity prompted Carpio to write for support from officials in the Secretaría de Gobernación, the ministry that oversaw public welfare. In his letter he asked them to endorse his interpretation of his role as guardian and the use of domestic service placements as a disciplinary measure. He proposed that the inmates who had reached age twenty-one should agree to seek positions that would allow them to live honorably and independently. If they did so, he would assist them and write letters of recommendation to prospective employers. Pending official approval, Carpio would give the inmates who were still underage to anyone offering them honorable work. If they refused to leave the institution voluntarily, the welfare directorate would be obliged to punish them for their behavior, even with expulsion.

Carpio searched the foundling home archives for rationales and precedents for his course of action. The first document he drew on dated from the liberal reform and authorized the foundling home's director to release minor children to persons who solicited them as long as the petitioners enjoyed an honorable reputation and sufficient means, the same terms and qualifications as for adoption. Carpio dug even more deeply into historical precedent and established practice and consulted the original eighteenth-century constitution and regulations of the establishment. These mandated the release of female inmates aged twelve and males aged fourteen to serve in private houses of respectable families.[41]

Carpio's search for historical justifications showed how cautiously he was approaching the issue in the wake of negative publicity. In fact, he might have turned to the Hospicio's current regulations instead of antique foundling home documents. By 1884 Hospicio regulations dropped references to adoption and stated merely that it was the director's responsibility to "grant to the girl inmates over fourteen permission to take service positions outside the establishment, after affirming that the persons wishing to hire them had the necessary morality and could make the necessary arrangements."[42]

In endorsing Carpio's proposal, officials at the Secretaría de Gobernación drew on concepts of paternal authority and responsibility: "Supposing that the state substitutes itself completely for the parents, in regard to the inmates of that establishment, doubtless it has the same rights and duties as all prudent fathers, even one with ample resources to feed his children, to procure them suitable and proper employment to subsist independently, especially when they reach their majority, and even more so when special circumstances make it necessary for them to leave home."[43]

The official statement on paternal authority and protection contrasts markedly with the perspectives expressed by the press, which probably represented broad public opinion. The press reports on the incident construed the episode as a violation of the paternal protection that the institution owed to the "daughters of the house," while the welfare officials involved construed the women's release from the foundling home into service as an exercise in paternal wisdom. This instance illustrates the complex and contradictory ways that ideas of family became attached to public assistance as well as to domestic service and discipline, all of which converged in the practice of informal adoption. Carpio's interpretation of his rights and responsibilities, seconded by his supervisors in the ministry, throws some light onto the probable fate of the older inmates who had been adopted from the foundling home in the late 1870s: Carpio's predecessor and the young people's adopters almost certainly understood that adoption meant labor. The young women's resistance to seeing themselves as servants echoes that of María Granados and Soledad Moreno twenty years before and suggests that adoptions of adolescents and young adults did not last long.

Under Carpio's administration, the same principles of service and discipline that he had applied to the placement of the young women applied to the adoption placements of some of the younger children. In 1886, soon after seven-year-old Librado Lorenzana had been adopted, he behaved badly enough that his adopter decided he no longer wanted the boy. Perhaps Librado was hoping to be sent back to the familiar environment of the foundling home. Instead of accepting the boy and seeking a more compatible arrangement for him, however, Director Carpio had him placed in the Escuela Correccional (Reform School) for punishment. After about three months there, Librado returned to his adopter.[44]

While welfare administrators deliberately used adoption as service placements, a significant number of adopters sought infants and very young children to raise as their own. Over 70 percent, or 163, of the adoptions between 1884 and 1895, while Carpio was directing the foundling home, were of children younger than five years old; they outnumbered adoptions of older children for labor during the same period. Babies under one year had become the most popular age group for adoption: 90 were adopted, 30 of them infants under a month old. Children aged one to five were the next most popular group, amounting to a total of 73 adoptions: 62 of them were adopted by couples, probably to form families. Women, many of them single, petitioned to adopt 64 of the children under the age of five. They may have been motivated by a combination of traditional charitable practices and a desire to nurture young children.[45] From April 1896 to April 1898 the percentage of adoptions of children under age five rose even higher, to over 80 percent of the total.[46]

Although foundling home documents do not record the motives of couples and single women adopting babies and young children, literature directed at middle- and upper-class female readers idealized the mother-child relationship and glorified elite feminine charity toward children. Magazines such as *El Álbum de la Mujer*, launched in 1883, and *La Familia*, first published in 1884, offered poetry, fiction, and essays by Mexican and foreign authors devoted to childhood, motherhood, and women's domestic roles. In an 1883 editorial entitled "Wife and Mother," Concepción Gimeno de Flaquer, the editor of *El Álbum*, wrote, "The mother is the greatest influence of the universe because on her lap society is formed. The mother is the soul of humanity . . . the angel who keeps vigil over our childhood dreams. . . . Sacrifice! Abnegation! . . . The mother expresses the ideal of divine love descended to the heart of women."[47] An essay in *La Familia*, entitled "The Woman of the Home," began: "To speak worthily of that angel on earth, a man must doff his hat and almost prostrate himself on his knees: such is the respect that her virtue inspires. The woman of the home, the immaculate wife, the sublime mother, is the most noble, the most tender, the being most worthy of respect and admiration that exists under heaven."[48]

Other essayists moralized that women's public roles should be dedicated to "love of the unfortunate" and to the formation of associations to "do good . . . and offer counsel to wretchedness and succor to poverty."[49] In 1883 an article in *El Álbum* celebrated the recent foundation of a private orphans' asylum called "La Buena Madre" by an association of elite women: "Only from a woman could that idea spring forth. . . . In all feminine hearts is found the well developed fiber of maternity."[50] According to this body of literature, which sanctified motherhood and defined the home as a woman's temple, the nurture of children became the reason for a woman's existence. And with charity seen as the extension of women's maternal instincts, the adoption of young welfare wards not only combined the most sublime feminine attributes but also offered childless women the means to exercise their sacred maternal role.

In contrast, writers for the feminine press looked down on mothers who were forced by poverty to place their children in the orphanages and considered them defective in their lack of maternal feeling. "Is it true that there are mothers who abandon their children?" inquired a Spanish author in an essay on motherhood reprinted in *La Familia* in 1883. "They exist," affirmed the writer, but "those mothers cannot be put together like the rest of mortals." Moreover, the moralist continued, "One crime leads to another," implying that the women who abandoned their children conceived them outside of marriage.[51] These same timeworn tropes had originally justified establishing the foundling home in the eighteenth century: admission would save illegitimate children from the corruption of their mothers' sin and shame and possibly from the fate of infanticide.

On the other side of this exchange, adoptions from the foundling home that were tinged with the ideals of charity or a glorified image of maternity saved the children from their origins and reinforced the virtue and social position of individuals who could afford to incorporate new dependents into their households. Such adoptions bolstered definitions of family bonds based on affection. They also underscored the principles defining protected childhood, including the notion that infancy and early childhood were malleable life stages. Even children of lower-class and possibly illegitimate origin were open to the beneficial environmental influences of virtuous maternal nurture and bourgeois values, while elite concepts of class, family, and childhood supported welfare administrators' contention that adoptions were in the best interests of state wards. The adoptions for family formation and charity that predominated at the foundling home, however, also masked adoptions like that of Librado Lorenzana, whose case reveals the harsh, disciplinary side of adoption and shows how vulnerable to abuse were the young public wards released into informal adoptions.

Love or Labor?

From 1898 to 1905, the years when Dr. Manuel Domínguez directed the foundling home, the patterns of admission, retrieval, and adoption illuminate the class tensions inherent in the role that the orphanages played as a conduit for urban child circulation and the role that adoption played in enforcing class-based family forms. Initially, Domínguez not only favored but also sought to enforce adoptions for family formation, a use of adoption consistent with concepts of protected childhood. His best intentions, however, would be frustrated and he would oversee a spike in adoptions of older children as laborers.

On assuming his position as director in 1898, Domínguez rewrote the institutional regulations with two views of parental authority in mind. On the one hand, when he introduced the new status of amparado, he showed his concern that even the poorest parents be able to retain their legal authority over their children. He also shaped the new regulations to facilitate permanent transfers of children away from their families of origin. These regulations contained provisions to make adoptions easier and, at the same time, make the transaction more formal. Although the civil code of 1884 omitted any mention of adoption as a legal procedure, Domínguez wrote into the regulations the requirement that adopting adults (adoptantes) sign a contract before a trustee (*fiador*) and two witnesses. They had to promise to keep the child always with them (*a su lado*) and "fulfill toward the child the sacred role that corresponds to paternal authority."[52] Despite this new formality, the regulations outlined no standardized screening process for adoption applicants.

Domínguez also wanted adopters to make adoptees their legal heirs. The 1884 civil code had introduced testamentary freedom, meaning that people were free to leave their property to whomever they wished.[53] These provisions seem to have prompted Domínguez to propose that adopters pass their property to their adoptees. A new adoption contract printed in 1899 for the Casa de Niños Expósitos stated that the adopters agreed to make the adoptees "the legitimate heir of their property" and, having adopted the children "freely and spontaneously," the adopters "renounced, now and forever," any law that allowed them to violate the terms they had agreed to.[54]

But after the contracts had been printed and were in use, someone — perhaps one of Domínguez's supervisors, or perhaps a disgruntled adopter — became aware that the agreement was not consistent with the 1884 civil code, which omitted adoption. A revised printed contract in use at the foundling home by 1900 redefined the adoptive relationship as guardianship (*tutela*) and eliminated any mention of adoptees becoming the legitimate children or heirs of the adopters. The 1884 civil code had granted the status of guardian to employers of underage servants, however, so the wording of the 1900 adoption contract reflected an attempt to differentiate adoption from domestic service. It stated that the adopters were obliged to keep the adoptees "not as a servant" but as a member of the family. The adopters further agreed to feed, clothe, and educate the adopted children, "being careful of their morality and securing a place that ensured their future," so that the adoptees became "useful to the family to which they entered and to their country, on the same terms and conditions that, according to my abilities, I would wish and procure for the members of my family."[55] Perhaps Domínguez hoped that signing the contract would commit adopters to terms and conditions that favored family sentiments over exploitative labor.

Domínguez seems to have been pursuing conflicting goals concerning adoption. On the one hand, his first version of the adoption contract expressed the intention that adoptions from the foundling home build on the pattern established under his predecessor, Dr. Angel Carpio. During that period, as mentioned earlier, over 80 percent of the children adopted were under the age of five, a trend pointing to motives of family formation.[56] But despite these good initial intentions, Domínguez, like Carpio, began using adoption as one way to divest the establishment of unwanted older inmates.

As adults sought children for adoption, their range of options was shaped by the combination of Domínguez's conflicting goals, the new regulations, and the revised adoption contracts. Within this range, applicants actively sought every possibility. At the turn of the century, the ages of the children being adopted showed patterns similar to those in Carpio's time. Some infants entering the foundling home were adopted immediately, suggesting that some couples and single women had a standing request with the administration for suitable babies.[57] Although the home's admission and adoption records give no indication of the children's features or adopters' preferences, criteria probably included good health and possibly lighter skin. Of course, adopters of recently admitted infants could have been adopting their own illegitimate children or those of a relative. At any rate, children adopted for family formation, especially babies and toddlers, may actually have stood a good chance of inheriting from their adoptive parents.[58]

A significant number of people sought children for other purposes. The years 1899 and 1900 saw a rising incidence of multiple or group adoptions, especially of older children. Most of the children selected in such situations were over five, pointing to motives other than family formation. Although forty-four children admitted in 1899 and 1900 went alone to adoptive households or families, twenty-one minors from that cohort were adopted in groups, and more than twenty older minors admitted between 1884 and 1895 were adopted between 1899 and 1904, many of them in groups.[59] The spike in adoptions of older inmates and the increase of multiple adoptions together pointed to an increase in the use of adoption as a source of labor, either overtly or under cover of charitable works.

Some adopters returned repeatedly seeking children. Among them were the brothers José and Alfredo Domínguez Peón, prominent players in the economic development in the state of Yucatán.[60] Within a two-year period, José Domínguez Peón adopted fourteen children: three girls and eleven boys. All the boys were five or older. He returned seven of them. A number of the children he rejected were subsequently taken by Alfredo Domínguez Peón, who in 1899 and 1900 also adopted three sisters ranging in age from almost five to almost eight, as well as one more child in 1902. Others also played this game of adopt-and-return, even with the same children. Natalia Díaz Vda. de Cámara adopted several of the children discarded by José Domínguez Peón, plus two others. She also found some children unsatisfactory, notably Lorenza, aged two years and two months, whom she returned after only ten days. A few months later, Lorenza was adopted by Carmela Ortiz de Cárdenas, who also adopted an older boy. Ramón Ortega Cárdenas adopted two boys returned by José Domínguez Peón, but he also returned one. He adopted three other children: a five-year-old boy and two girls, ages four and ten.[61] As these cases illustrate, children as young as two were adopted for motives other than family formation.

Adoption contracts dating from before Domínguez's arrival explicitly forbade the return of children for any reason.[62] The 1898 regulations, however, offered several justifications for terminating an adoption; a mere change of heart sufficed.[63] The first contract form printed in 1899 made no mention of returning the adopted child, but the 1900 revision defined the conditions for termination. The adopter agreed that if for some reason he or she "did not find it convenient to keep" the adoptee, or if the adoptee "refused to stay" under the protection of the adopter, the child was to be returned to the orphanage.[64]

In previous decades, adopted girls had sometimes been returned when they reached adolescence. But once the door had opened to returns, the pace of adoption turnovers quickened. Felipa's history illustrates the point: "By order of the director, the girl Felipa, thirteen years old, entered for the third time, returned by Sra. Rafaela Gómez, who adopted her on the 30th of December 1898. She entered for the second time on the 17th of May 1898."[65] In August 1899 she was adopted by Leocadio Duarte García, who had also adopted three boys, aged eleven, eighteen, and nineteen.[66]

Domínguez may have believed that permitting returns protected minors from abuse. Certainly, returns pointed to conflict between the minors and the adopting adults. On the one hand, middle-and upper-class adopters may now have expected the children they brought into their households, whether for labor or for charity, to meet higher standards of behavior in speech and cleanliness—and obedience. So, while some adopters may in fact have had charitable motives, they were demonstrably conditional. On the other hand, some of the children probably resisted adoption, whether actively or passively, perhaps hoping to return to the foundling home where they had friends, siblings, or familiar caretakers. In some instances, their rapid return points to overt resistance to a strange or possibly abusive environment. At age six, a boy named Manuel had been adopted and returned twice. His first adopter returned him for being too young to be useful, revealing that even quite young adoptees were expected to work. José Domínguez Peón, his second adopter, returned him after only one day; perhaps the boy had made a dramatic display of his objections. Another boy named Ramón was first adopted at age eight, returned for bad behavior, adopted a second time at the age of nine and a half, and returned shortly afterward.[67]

Whatever the reasons that led adopters to take out and return children of various ages, such cases make it abundantly clear that adopters of older children did not consider the minors their heirs. Nor could Domínguez insist on it. He may have fashioned his first adoption contract with its injunctions on heirship to encourage the patterns of adoption that had emerged under his predecessor, when the majority of adopters sought babies and young children. The revised contract forms indicate, however, that Dominguez's idealistic intentions for the state's underage wards were quickly brought in line with the letter of the law, which in turn served the preferences of adopters who sought children for labor.

Neither foundling home administrators nor upper-ranking welfare officials raised any objection to the potentially abusive patterns evident in the demand for children. And even though the revised contract contained a proviso against adopting to acquire servants, welfare administrators never inquired into adopters' motives, even in flagrant cases like that of José Domínguez Peón, or of Ramon Axtle Sierra, who adopted seven minors, ages five to eleven, between September 1901 and December 1902.[68] Administrators overseeing adoptions continued to assess the petitioners entirely on the basis of social position and connections. A girl named Guadalupe, who entered the foundling home in late May 1902, was adopted in August by someone whom Domínguez described as "a person perfectly suited by his social position and sufficient resources to defray the expense of maintaining the little one."[69]

In 1901, when *El Imparcial* exposed a swindler, the case revealed how loosely Domínguez and his staff screened applicants. In June 1900 the man in question met all the requirements for adopting a baby girl. Although he gave the child a new name, a month later he brought her back and had her admitted as a pensioner. His wife retrieved the child, but again the man returned the baby, this time paying to have her board with a wet nurse in the countryside. The couple's erratic behavior might have raised suspicions about their intentions. A few months later, however, the man took the baby out again and tried to pass her off as the child of a millionaire. Whether he was trying to sell the baby or extort money is not clear, but the newspaper soon revealed his scheme.[70]

In August 1905 another report in the press illuminated the darker side of adoptions. A married woman, aged twenty-eight and childless, had been visiting the orphanage for some time, seeking an available baby. She finally selected an infant girl, Loreto, "because of not having children of my own."[71] Scarcely a week before, the baby girl had been brought in by her parents, who claimed that they lacked the resources to keep her. The police officer who accompanied the parents signed the form that admitted the child as a foundling; therefore, the parents relinquished their legal authority over her. This seemed to be a straightforward admission, giving

Domínguez guardianship and an adoption of the kind he favored. The adoption contract was completed on August 20. But the child did not remain in the hands of the original adopter. A few days later *El Imparcial*, in a note entitled "A Sensational Intrigue," reported that the baby Loreto had been taken from the foundling home, not by the ostensible adopter, but by a different woman who also claimed to be the baby's mother. Welfare officials ordered an investigation, and the presiding judge ordered that the baby, who had by then passed into the possession of a third party, be returned to the foundling home.[72]

These instances reveal that even petitioners seeking infants did not necessarily intend to raise them as their own. Some adopters seem to have acted as brokers, passing the children to others. The rapid pace of group adoptions and stories of urban kidnapping rings suggest as much. Indeed, there is sufficient evidence of a market in children to throw into question the operating assumptions of orphanage administrators and upper-ranking welfare officials. Whether or not they were complicit in this human traffic, public officials considered the children who passed through the foundling home to be eminently transferable. In their eyes, they served the children's best interests by shifting them from their family and class of origin regardless of the motives behind the adoption or the adoptive environment.

Although a loose adoption policy opened the door to abuse and exploitation, the federal government claimed only limited authority to prosecute abusers. In early 1904 a woman wrote to Domínguez from Mérida, Yucatán, to report that a man who had adopted a girl from the Hospicio was abusing her. The man she accused had also adopted a ten-year-old boy from the foundling home.[73] The woman requested that the Secretaría de Gobernación allow the girl to name a guardian or to return to the Hospicio. Welfare officials, however, asserted that the girl would have to file her complaint with the competent judicial authority in the state of Yucatán. Although the welfare system ignored her, the girl at least had a concerned adult looking out for her well-being. Indeed, the woman who had written to complain had herself adopted a girl from the foundling home and may have pursued the case of the abused girl in the local courts. Officials at the secretariat, however, conveniently invoked the principles of federalism to wash their hands of adoptees who passed out of the capital district.[74]

Still, this case may have prompted officials to impose one limiting criterion: forbidding adoptions to the several states bordering the Gulf of Mexico. Until about 1904 petitioners from those states had accounted for the largest single group of out-of-state adoptions, although petitioners came from almost every region of Mexico. The Yucatán was a region experiencing a feverish economic boom based on the export of henequen fiber to the United States. The number of adoptions to Yucatán residents presents persuasive evidence that many adopters from those areas did indeed intend to put to work the children they took from Mexico City's orphanages. To compensate for the region's severe labor shortage, employers imported workers from other parts of the country, including densely populated central Mexico. Few of the workers, however, went willingly or with full knowledge of the conditions that awaited them, and some among them were convicts and jailed political dissidents. Many transported workers were *enganchados* (coerced), promised jobs, or simply abducted, only to find themselves forced to labor in abusive conditions. A substantial number of workers in Yucatán were kidnapped children, affirming the rumors about kidnapping rings that circulated in the capital and supporting the suspicions raised by the broadside of 1907. John Kenneth Turner, a U.S. journalist posing as an investor, revealed that in Mérida, Yucatán's capital, labor brokers fulfilled commissions for men, women, and child workers; he saw their fate as equal to slavery. Economic leaders like the Domínguez Peón brothers, members of an extensive family with investments in henequen, railroads, banking, and other enterprises, may have been adopting children to work in their own households and businesses or to pass along to other employers. The social prominence of adopters, their influential role in one of Mexico's most important economic sectors, and their access to the highest levels of state and federal government no doubt would have deterred low-ranking government officials from bringing any accusations of wrongdoing against them.[75]

Even after adoption to the Gulf states was prohibited, the assumed social position of adoption petitioners created the expectation that the rule would be stretched. Nor is it clear whether the ban on adoptions to the Gulf ever extended to the Hospicio. Certainly, in his 1906 report on the Hospicio, Martiniano Alfaro boasted of an increasing number of adoption placements to the states in question and asserted that adoption applicants from the region enjoyed high social standing.[76] At the foundling home, Domínguez was disappointed that officials refused to waive the restriction in the case of a would-be adopter from Orizaba. Addressing the applicant as an "esteemed friend and associate," the director conveyed the negative decision and added, "Believe me that the resolution causes me great displeasure, because I am certain that the girl . . . would have a resounding future with you."[77] Domínguez's successor, Dr. Francisco de P. Carral, also attempted to have adoptions to the Yucatán approved, and like Domínguez tried to convince officials to override the restriction.[78]

It is difficult to reconcile the contradictory attitudes that welfare administrators held about adoption throughout this period. While Carpio was director of the foundling home, most adopters sought babies, probably for family formation. Yet Carpio also used adoption to discipline some young inmates. Domínguez, director from 1898 to 1905, clearly had his wards' best interests in mind when he tried to enforce adoptions for heirship and then used a contract that explicitly distinguished between adoption as a member of the family and adoption as a servant. Yet he turned a blind eye to the possible implications of group adoptions, especially those to the Gulf region.

Similarly, competing trends in the adoption of welfare wards at the turn of the century point to diametrically opposed concepts of the practice and of childhood itself. A relatively few high-profile individuals clearly sought young workers from a vulnerable and defenseless welfare population. Many other adopters, however, like the customs official and his wife who adopted Ricardo A. Lorenzana, sought the fulfillment of raising an adopted child as their own. In these seemingly irreconcilable ways, adoptions from Mexico City's public orphanages shed light on a moment of profound but demonstrably uneven transformation in concepts of childhood and family and on the growing role of state institutions in shaping class-based family forms.

The Class Politics of Adoption

The social and economic disruptions that led to rising rates of admission at the foundling home at the turn of the century pointed to the class tensions implicit in the welfare system's role in redistributing children. While economic circumstances were forcing more parents to intern their children, even if briefly, more individuals sought to adopt children. Parents who left their children at the home and then fell behind in their pension payments ran a high risk of losing their children to others. Domínguez warned of the danger. "I am sorry to tell you," he wrote to one parent in 1904, "that since we have not received the pension for the boy Jesús, he has entered the category of foundling. I will do what I can so that the boy is not given away should someone wish to adopt him, but as it could happen at any moment that I cease to direct this establishment, I fulfill a duty in notifying you that the little one will run the risk of passing into the power of a stranger."[79] Domínguez and his successors also favored flexibility on the rule that parents who entered children as expósitos lost legal authority over them: they frequently allowed such parents to reclaim their children, perhaps out of sympathy or to avoid unfavorable publicity.[80] But the high number of admissions, the demand for adoptions, and the secretariat's impatience over flexible interpretations of the regulations created new tensions as the orphanage continued to circulate children through adoption.

The outbreak of revolution exacerbated those tensions. The political system that had shaped welfare policy for almost thirty years seemed indomitable during the centennial celebrations of 1910, but by 1911 Mexico was in turmoil. Francisco Madero, the idealistic reformer, had been elected president and Porfirio Díaz had departed into exile. These events, however, brought little stability. In the turmoil of revolution, the political character of the successive revolutionary regimes played out even at the level of welfare oversight of adoption.

During Madero's administration, directives on adoption from welfare officials in the upper levels of government began to reflect concern over appearances of impropriety. A circular advised Mexico City orphanage directors to conduct adoptions with the greatest prudence, to grant them only to persons meriting the utmost confidence, and to give in adoption only such children as stood no chance of being reclaimed.[81] These strictures proved difficult to implement in a context of political instability and violence. In February 1913 a coup ended in Madero's assassination and brought the strong-armed General Victoriano Huerta to power, inflicting ten days of intense fighting on residents of the city center. One woman, hearing that her child's father had been killed during the Decena Trágica (Tragic Ten Days), brought her infant daughter to the Casa de Niños Expósitos and left her as a foundling. Shortly afterward, the baby was given in adoption to a man who presented her to his wife as his own.[82]

When the baby's mother discovered that her partner was still alive, she returned to the foundling home to reclaim her child. The orphanage sent for the baby, but the adoptive father refused to give her back and the administration supported his position, claiming that the mother had relinquished her rights to the child in accordance to penal code Article 625, which terminated parental authority for reasons of abandonment. Administrators rarely enforced Article 625 so strictly: at the time, they were almost routinely allowing children admitted as foundlings to leave with their parents. Perhaps the social position of the adopter intimidated the administrators: he had family connections who could put up the two hundred pesos surety for an adoption and sufficient property to support and educate the child to be a useful member of society. The mother did not.[83] But perhaps the political character of Huerta's reactionary coup, which sought to reinstate the status quo of the Díaz regime, influenced the outcome of this adoption.

This incident seems to have prompted an administrative effort to close loopholes in a manner that emphasized intolerance and rigidity. In April 1913, to remove any ambiguity about abandonment and to enforce its finality and legal penalties, the foundling home director developed a new form for parents to sign when they sought to admit a child as a foundling, "with the object that they ratify their resolution before authority." He hoped that "this formality will moralize little by little the women who almost daily, with the greatest cold blood, present themselves in this house with the intention to abandon."[84] Because the penal code regulated abandonment, the transaction had to be witnessed by a police officer, whose presence must have intimidated many parents. Officers often signed the forms for illiterate applicants.

With the country in the throes of revolution, political legitimacy rested on uncertain foundations. To reassert the historic legal mandate dating from the mid-nineteenth-century reform that permitted the foundling home to authorize adoptions, the Secretaría de Gobernación requested that the director produce a copy of the legislation. He wrote back that he had failed to locate the document in the archives or to obtain a copy of the reform laws of which the 1861 directive was presumably a part.[85] In the chaos of the moment, but as a precaution against scandal, the best that secretariat officials could do was to reissue two earlier stipulations: only minors who had no one who might reclaim them should be given in adoption and, then, only to applicants who "merited absolute confidence."[86]

The earlier prohibition against adoptions to the Gulf states was forgotten. Even in the midst of revolution the demand for adoptions remained high, especially from that region. Many of the minors who went to the Gulf in group adoptions were named Lorenzana, meaning they had entered the foundling home as wards of the welfare system and, indeed, had no one who might reclaim them. In 1914 Carlos Albert traveled from Mérida to Mexico City and asked to adopt eight children. The Hospicio's director wrote to the director general of Beneficencia Pública indicating that he was well aware that such adoptions were for labor and that, although Albert would sign the contract, the children would very likely pass from his charge to other "people of the same morality and education."[87] One girl refused to go. The others were brought before the director and asked if they agreed to go live in Mérida in the care of Albert. They were informed of the rigors of the tropical climate and of the obligations they owed their adopter in exchange for the benefits they would receive. The documents of their cases end there, so it appears they left for Mérida.

The same year, Agripino Díaz and Josefina Méndez Rivas de Díaz of Orizaba, Veracruz, adopted a group of six girls, ages five to ten. In return for the education the couple were to give the girls, the adoptees were obliged to "lend them submissive obedience" (*prestarles una obediencia sumisa*).[88] Also in 1914 don Pastor Campos from Mérida solicited permission to adopt a boy and three girls. He proposed to "give them education [and] instruction, cover their needs, and use their services as domestic servants . . . giving them equitable recompense." Despite his overt intentions, he signed a contract that stated he must consider them not as servants but as members of the family. The children all signed their consent, perhaps encouraged by the provision that they could return to the Hospicio if they wished.[89] Given that welfare officials had refused to intervene in the case of reported abuse in 1904, however, the option to return to the Hospicio likely existed on paper only, especially during the years of revolutionary upheaval.

Family Formation, Class Formation

For decades the foundling home had facilitated the preservation of family honor by absorbing the illegitimate offspring of Mexico City's *gente decente*, but that function had slowly died out over time. As poverty pressured more urban families to relinquish their children to the state, the foundling home facilitated their adoption by members of the same classes that used to conceal their children born outside of marriage. Whether adopters with means sought babies to nurture and claim as their own or wanted older children for labor, the public orphanages institutionalized extralegal practices that had operated informally for decades. Indeed, as orphanage administrators obeyed their mandate to place children in service and that practice blurred with informal adoption, government officials became involved in traffic in children. Notwithstanding the good intentions of individuals like Miguel Domínguez, who attempted to enforce adoption as a means of creating heirs, the behavior of other officials suggests cynicism rather than the widely publicized visions of a happy future for adopted state wards. Still, records from the foundling home do provide important evidence that infants and young children were adopted for other motives. The couples that adopted to form families led an otherwise invisible trend in family practice well in advance of legal trends. By 1910 the educator and writer Laura Méndez de Cuenca, addressing a middle-class readership, made no distinction between "maternity . . . by nature or by adoption," and many of those who adopted young foundling home inmates would have agreed.[90]

Trends in adoption practice during the late Porfiriato expose the foundations of class-based family entitlements. Sublime motherhood and protected childhood were the privileges of the adopting classes. Those privileges often rested on the performance of unpaid domestic labor by children separated from their families of origin, more often by economic duress than by parental death. In households of means where servants performed domestic labor, the demand to adopt babies and young children, and especially nursing infants, raises further questions concerning the class-based divisions of labor in their care. Mexican doctors specializing in infancy increasingly urged even elite mothers to breast-feed their own children, but many families of means employed wet nurses. At the foundling home, where abandonment and adoption marked a primary intersection in urban pathways of child circulation, the 1898 introduction of a new medical regime of infant feeding threw stark light on the increasing divide in class distinctions founded on the privileges of protected childhood.

Moral and Medical Economies
of Motherhood

Infant Feeding at the Mexico City Foundling Home

The year 1898 saw the close of an era: welfare officials brought the network of village wet nurses who worked for the Casa de Niños Expósitos inside the institution.[1] Since the eighteenth century, orphanage administrators had placed foundlings with rural wet nurses. The foundlings' sojourns with village families, like their passage through the orphanage, marked a significant node in the metropolitan networks of child circulation: children might remain with their nurses for up to six years before returning to the establishment for their education and preparation for employment. The village nursing system also linked the practices of urban abandonment to women's domestic economic roles: wet-nursing provided an important source of household income for childbearing women. This enduring arrangement between the foundling home and village nurses reflected an established practice among all social classes of hiring wet nurses to supplement or substitute for maternal breast-feeding.

By 1898, however, decades of attacks on wet-nursing prompted a sweeping reorganization of infant-feeding practices at the foundling home. Welfare administrators brought wet-nursing inside the institution where it could be medically supervised, established a wet nurse inspection service, and introduced bottle-feeding. The orphanage's new feeding regimen, however, presented unexpected difficulties: administrators faced a chronic shortage of wet nurses and formula feeding was disastrous for the babies' health. Because the reorganization of the foundling home's wet-nursing system was part of a broader regulation of infant-feeding practices, the problems that welfare officials encountered within the orphanage exposed a knot of contradictions at the convergence of social and economic trends affecting families across the social spectrum. These trends included class-based concepts of motherhood; medical influences on infant care; the changing economic roles of working-class women; and the centralization of child welfare institutions.

Mexican moralists had long criticized wet-nursing, but during the late nineteenth century the practice came under renewed attack for medical reasons.[2] The mounting anti-wet nurse campaign in the city's newspapers and feminine press sought primarily to influence infant-feeding practices among the middle and upper classes. Some of the arguments against wet-nursing were moral. Just as the foundling epitomized the antithesis of the protected child, the wet nurse played the foil to the ideal bourgeois mother, who devoted herself unstintingly to her offspring. Wet nurses, in contrast, were depicted as mercenary for abandoning their own babies to sell their breast milk to others. But while critics were hard on women who nursed for wages, they were also hard on their employers, calling them vain and selfish.[3] Other arguments targeting wet-nursing combined morality with medicine. Equating maternal virtue with physical purity, critics considered wet nurses not only morally defective but also diseased.

Leaders in Mexican obstetrics, the medical specialty that included pregnancy, childbirth, and infancy, blamed the nation's high rates of infant mortality in large part on wet-nursing. Such medical concerns shaped the reforms of infant feeding at the foundling home. Physicians believed that close medical supervision of all aspects of infant care, especially feeding, would improve infant survival.[4] Officials annexed a wet nurse inspection service to the orphanage to certify that women seeking positions in the orphanage and with private employers were free from disease and produced abundant milk.[5] In the interests of better hygiene, the new orphanage regime required wet nurses to board their own babies in the country with other wet nurses. Although medically motivated, this last aspect of the reforms compelled prospective nurses to choose between motherhood and paid work.

Moral and medical strictures against wet-nursing only partially masked the underlying class and economic dimensions of both the practice and the critique. Economic privilege on the one hand and poverty on the other shaped class-distinct reproductive practices. Middle-class respectability required a strict separation of maternity and domesticity from the masculine world of labor and production.[6] Critics of wet-nursing premised their model of ideal maternity on an exclusive relationship between the protected child and a mother free from all other social or economic responsibilities. Families of the urban poor could ill afford to maintain such strict divisions of labor. Wet-nursing transgressed the boundaries between motherhood and work by confounding breast-feeding with paid labor. The heightened attack on wet-nursing—labor performed exclusively by working-class women—reflected the rising ideological barriers between the social prestige attached to maternity and women's paid labor, considered a corrupting influence. Indeed, critiques of wet-nursing echoed the accusations of immorality leveled against women who worked in the capital's growing manufacturing sector, which represented the antithesis of protected domesticity.[7] Moreover, the intensifying campaign against wet-nursing that prompted the foundling home's 1898 reforms coincided with the increasing use of the institution by families under economic duress, who claimed poverty as their primary reason for relinquishing their children. Just as poverty drove the movement of children into public orphanages, wet-nursing was a career of necessity.

The foundling home's reorganized infant-feeding regime illustrated the ways that bourgeois family models influenced welfare services. Similarly, late nineteenth-century trends in adoption for family formation reflected the bourgeois ethos of protected childhood, closely tied to ideals of motherhood. Those paired pieties, however, masked the role that public welfare institutions played in facilitating adoption for labor. Like the divergent practices of informal adoption, infant-feeding reform at the orphanage clearly revealed the role of public welfare policy in defining and sometimes enforcing class-based family forms: family coherence and protection for the privileged, separation and discipline for the poor.

Except for bringing wet-nursing indoors, the foundling home's infant-feeding reforms achieved none of the stated goals and instead created a crisis. The new wet nurse regimen held little appeal for potential applicants. Separated from their children and strictly supervised by the foundling home medical staff, few women stayed long on the job. The inspection service, which was set up to identify the healthiest nurses for employment, failed to attract sufficient job seekers. Foundling home administrators had difficulty hiring and retaining enough nurses, especially when admissions surged after the turn of the century. To compensate, officials introduced and quickly expanded the use of bottle-fed formulas for public wards, with disastrous results: the majority of bottle-fed babies died. Physician director Manuel Domínguez, a long-time critic of wet-nursing, launched the infant-feeding reforms with enthusiasm but quickly became enmeshed in a web of contradictions that challenged his most deeply held convictions. And while it is difficult to discern the perspectives of the wet nurses from records created by their critics, it is still clear that they voted with their feet and walked off the job. Thus, they gave their own interpretation to the dictum that breast-feeding was the fundamental duty of motherhood.

Wet-Nursing and Child Circulation: Metropolitan Economies of Reproduction

For over a century, clerical and municipal administrators of the Casa de Niños Expósitos had followed the 1774 regulations and placed foundlings with rural wet nurses, described by a mid-nineteenth-century observer as Indian and mestiza.[8] The longevity of the placing-out system suggests that officials considered village women and rural community life beneficial to the foundling home's infant wards. Or, perhaps the system survived simply through official indifference. Despite the growing chorus of criticism against wet-nursing, evidence of stress on village nursing starting in the 1870s, and despite the 1884 appointment of physician Angel Carpio to direct the foundling home, welfare administrators initiated no reforms until 1898.

From the 1840s through the 1870s, the orphanage maintained about a hundred nurses on its payroll.[9] For generations the women of Tlalnepantla and Tacuba, communities located to the city's north and west, held a virtual monopoly on this important source of household income. Late eighteenth-century decrees established the wage for nursing foundlings at the level the poor paid for the service, considered high enough to ensure the child's well-being. The amount remained unchanged a century later: four pesos a month for nursing a baby and two pesos for boarding a child after weaning (*destete*). Indeed, the pay for wet-nursing was comparable to and reasonably competitive with wages for domestic servants, laundry workers, or those in the garment industry.[10] Moreover, the larger sum for nursing recognized the value of a woman's milk and the labor of breast-feeding while payment for the fostering of weaned children acknowledged that the relationship between nurse and nursling continued even after weaning.

In each community a supervisor (*fiadora*) oversaw and probably recruited the nurses for the foundling home, but women nursing for pay in their own homes were, in a sense, self-employed. The village system allowed childbearing women to incorporate an additional—or several additional—infants and weaned toddlers into their preexisting domestic routines and into other kinds of paid work. Women could combine nursing with economic activities like taking in laundry, producing food on a small scale, and buying and selling in the market. Foundling home nurses built considerable mobility into their routines. Once a month they carried their charges to the orphanage, located in the heart of the city and adjacent to the Merced market, to collect their wages and submit the babies for inspection.[11] In these ways wet-nursing linked the practices of urban abandonment and child circulation with women's participation in the service and market economies of the capital region.

Most importantly, nursing at home allowed a mother to keep her own children by her side. In contrast, many private employers of domestic servants, especially of nannies and wet nurses, did not let them bring their children to work. Additionally, nursing in a private home confined a woman in ways that village nursing did not. Private employment separated a nurse not only from her children but also from her partner, whereas nursing in her own home permitted a woman to maintain her intimate relationships and participate in community life. Like private employers, the foundling home originally forbade the *recibidoras*, nurses employed within the institution to receive new admissions, from having sexual relations with their husbands.[12]

Just as adoption brought foundlings into households of means, the village system integrated the nurslings into working-class households and village community life. At mid-century, foundlings frequently spent several years with a nurse, sometimes up to the five or six years that the eighteenth-century regulations mandated.[13] Nurses occasionally adopted the children they nurtured from infancy. Sometimes neighbors adopted children they had come to know within the community.[14] But the majority of surviving children returned to the foundling home. Thus wet-nursing intersected with child circulation in multiple ways: through the need to provide nourishment for abandoned infants, through the children's extended stay with their nurses, and through adoption.

For over a century little occurred to disrupt the established wet nurse regime, especially as stable community use of the foundling home held annual admissions so low. By the late 1870s, however, despite the steady rate of orphanage admissions, village nursing began to show signs of strain. For example, more women began nursing two or more babies, known as nursing *a media leche*. Some woman nursed three babies simultaneously and received the full wage for each.[15] Babies also moved more frequently between households, suggesting that women had to adjust economic strategies in response to shifting family demands on their labor. As Tacuba and Tlalnepantla became more closely integrated with the urban economy, women's domestic economic roles changed, influencing the dynamics of village nursing. By the early 1880s Tacuba fell within the jurisdiction of the expanding Federal District. Two railway lines converged on the village, linking it to commercial and migratory networks that extended throughout the republic. Tlalnepantla, numbering about a thousand inhabitants in early 1880s, remained relatively rural, ringed by haciendas cultivating corn and wheat.[16] But the arrival of a textile mill in the 1870s may have drawn laborers out of agriculture and into factory work, and thus made households more dependent on the cash economy.[17]

The nursing trajectory of María de Jesús of Tlalnepantla illustrates the kinds of strategies some families followed in the face of changing economic conditions. Between 1875 and 1881 María de Jesús nursed foundlings continuously, nineteen in all, usually several at a time.[18] Making wet-nursing a virtual career required a high tolerance for a houseful of children demanding her breast and strong defenses in the face of repeated child death. Eight children died in her care. In February 1879, with four children already in her charge, she received María Sabina and was paid the full monthly rate of four pesos for nursing her through July 1880, when the baby died of diarrhea. When a child died, the nurse followed established procedure and carried the corpse to the foundling home for examination and burial. Because María Sabina's death was recorded on the last day of July, the nurse received her full wages for the month. Administrators usually gave María de Jesús a replacement baby immediately, even though their record books showed that death tended to strike one of her charges soon after they gave her a new one.[19] With a new infant at her breast, the nurse may have been supplementing her milk with contaminated, inappropriate, or insufficient food and drink for the older babies: undernourished babies would have been more susceptible to infection and disease. As her capacity to nurse diminished, María de Jesús maintained her income level by taking more children at the half, or weaned, rate of two pesos a month.[20]

María de Jesús of Tlalnepantla was not the only woman who stretched the wet nurse system, but few women attempted to care for so many children or to extend their nursing for so long. Some nurses, like María of Tacuba, formed lasting relationships with their charges. She received María Francisca Nicasia in October 1878, weaned her in July 1880, but did not return her to the foundling home until February 1883. Her coparishioner Dolores received José Darío de Jesús Cresencio in December 1878, weaned him in May 1880, and cared for him until he left in adoption in July 1881.[21] Others who nursed several children at once did better at keeping them alive. Juana of Tacuba nursed eight children between 1881 and 1884 and not one died in her care.[22] The nursing career of María de Jesús of Tlalnepantla demonstrates one woman's strategic exploitation of her own reproductive capacities and suggests the potential for commercializing wet-nursing and its implication in foundling mortality. That orphanage staff overlooked the tendency of children to die in her household made them as complicit in the arrangement as she was strategic.

Yet the problems developing in the Mexico City foundling home's wet nurse system paled in contrast to the profound reconfiguration of the political economy of wet-nursing in Europe. Studies of eighteenth- and nineteenth-century European wet-nursing reveal dramatic increases in infant abandonment, provoked by the commercialization of agriculture, urban migration, and women's employment in domestic service and manufacturing. Together these factors expanded and commercialized the practice of wet-nursing and led to the rise of related services like nurse and infant transport.[23] In the area around London, for example, an underground market developed in foundlings and wet-nursing. Occasional exposure of conditions on the "baby farms" erupted into national scandals. In Russia, thousands of foundlings from the state homes and their passbooks, which recorded the nurslings' movement from one nurse to another, circulated at cash value in the Moscow and St. Petersburg regions, and thousands of foundlings died.[24] In France, especially Paris, wet-nursing was practiced on an industrial scale. As women left agriculture for paid labor, many moved into cities in search of domestic jobs. When they became pregnant far from home, they had little choice but to abandon their infants to orphanages and nurse for wages. Families of means routinely placed their infants out to nurse. Rampant mortality among nurslings and revelations about corrupt placement and oversight bureaus prompted the government to form a medical commission to investigate the industry. The resulting Roussel law of 1874 required registration and regular inspection of every nurse and nursling in France. But regulation reconfigured the practice once again: instead of sending their babies out of the home for nursing, families of means increasingly brought wet nurses into their homes, and only the working poor continued to place their infants out to nurse.[25]

Although the Mexico City area experienced trends like those in Europe, such as commercial agriculture displacing peasant producers, and young women moving to the city for domestic work and factory jobs, it never developed this kind of highly commercialized wet nurse economy. The Casa de Niños Expósitos was the largest single employer of wet nurses in the region, but for much of the nineteenth century its low annual admissions rate provided little temptation to develop related commercial services like foundling transport or passbook fosterage and nursing. By the time foundling home admissions surged between 1898 and 1903, public welfare administrators had brought wet-nursing inside the institution. Despite the number of wet nurses on the foundling home's payroll, most wet-nursing took place in private homes. There, the personal politics of paternalism may have tempered any trend toward commercialization, although private employment also made the practice more difficult to regulate. Given the mounting critique of wet-nursing in Mexico City's general and medical press, however, the lag in reforming the foundling home's infant-feeding arrangements indicates that most of the concern around the practice of wet-nursing pertained to elite reproduction.

Wet-Nursing and the Moral Foundations of Motherhood

The 1898 reform of the foundling home's infant-feeding regime did not spring from an investigation of the rural wet nurse system or from debates among policy makers about the role and direction of public welfare services for babies and young children. Rather, the reforms were a response to the chorus of journalists and physicians who for decades had inveighed against the dangers of hired wet nurses and advocated breast-feeding as the fundamental duty of motherhood. Indeed, one of the major voices in that chorus, Dr. Manuel Domínquez, claimed the credit for initiating changes in wet-nursing at the foundling home.[26]

In both the general and medical press, the literature on child hygiene combined medical advice on child care with moral strictures on women's prescribed social roles: exclusive devotion to motherhood and the home.[27] Wet-nursing epitomized the dereliction of maternal duty in two ways. Women who hired wet nurses evaded their maternal responsibilities, and women who worked as wet nurses deprived their own babies of the milk they sold for wages. But this criticism was not uniform: in the eyes of Porfirian moralists, women who employed others to breast-feed their babies were selfish, while wet nurses were morally corrupt and sexually deviant.

In early 1884 the influential journalist Enrique Chávarri, using the pen name "Juvenal," wrote one of the few sympathetic portrayals of wet nurses for the Mexico City newspaper *El Monitor Republicano*. But his sympathy was mostly a rhetorical strategy to paint a bitingly satirical portrait of frivolous upper-class mothers:

How irritating to hear the baby scream; how dreadful to be awake all night cooing to the creature that shrieks like a peacock. For this there's the wet nurse, sent to the far end of the house so one doesn't hear the little chap's cry, while the young mother sleeps soundly dreaming of the dress she'll wear tomorrow to the opera, and, the following day, when they bring her child, blue in the face and nearly suffocated from so much crying, she gives it a perfunctory kiss and quickly hands it back anew to the arms of the wet nurse.[28]

He argued that for "a relatively scant wage," wet nurses were "obliged to endure all the duties of motherhood . . . which are so much about abnegation and heroic sacrifice." He warned his privileged readers that "she who wishes to be mother in name only must pay dear for the substitute," implying that the price of such selfishness could be the life of her baby.[29]

Like most critiques of wet-nursing, Chávarri's represented a masculine perspective on the issue: there was a long Mexican literary tradition of men criticizing the use of wet nurses. Almost immediately, Concepción Gimeno de Flaquer, editor of *El Álbum de la Mujer*, published a spirited defense of the maternal virtues of her readership and deployed her feminine insights into maternal feeling and practice. She advised the journalist to "repent of his error." If he would only visit Mexican homes he would "always find the same altar and the same god: the cradle and the baby." She also admonished Juvenal to learn directly from the doctors of private patients. Those physicians, she claimed, battled daily "to prevent women of delicate complexion from nursing their children. Mexican mothers are offended by doctors who forbid breast-feeding."[30] Chávarri had been quite clear that he believed wet nurses did the hard work of infant care. But even as Gimeno de Flaquer defended bourgeois motherhood, she sidestepped the issue of whether mother or nurse performed motherhood's central obligation. She even suggested that the health of many privileged women prevented them from nursing their babies.

Later the same year, in an essay on infant development published in *El Álbum de la Mujer*, Dr. Manuel Domínguez wrote, "I do not wish to concern myself with those women who, out of deplorable insipidity, ignore the cry of their hungry children." Siding with Juvenal, Domínguez asserted that women who rejected breast feeding "are unworthy to bear the lovely title of mother." If their reasons were merely frivolous, Domínguez considered it a doctor's duty to apply scientific and moral arguments to persuade women to honor their maternal responsibilities.[31]

Chávarri and Domínguez reiterated well-established tropes for depicting women who failed to breast-feed: the journalist's satire echoed that of early nineteenth-century Mexican novelist Fernández de Lizardi.[32] These persistent representations cycled through both lay and medical writing on the subject. For example, in his 1888 thesis for the Escuela Nacional de Medicina (National School of Medicine), Ramón Estrada accused elite women of susceptibility to vanity and fashion: "Among the well-to-do nursing is frequently entrusted to wet nurses, because the mother who wishes to preserve the smooth contours of her breasts sees how few of the upper class nourish their children with their own blood."[33] The negative portrayals contrast strikingly with the fulsome praise of Mexican motherly virtue that appeared in the same publications, and suggest that the truth about infant-feeding practices lay somewhere between the extremes.[34] Indeed, Chávarri's description of nighttime dynamics in a privileged home does have the ring of familiarity. Likewise, Domínguez appears to be speaking from professional experience, perhaps with young, first-time mothers. And Gimeno de Flaquer's somewhat evasive rejoinder to Juvenal suggests that many middle- and upper-class Mexican mothers breast-fed for a while before supplementing their own capacities with those of a wet nurse. Thus, both the extremely negative and the idealized representations of elite motherhood should be read as hortatory exaggerations. But there is no doubt that the wet nurse always played the foil against which to measure privileged maternal practice and, by extension, feminine virtue.

For late nineteenth-century medical moralists, however, not even economic necessity excused mothers who refused to nurse their babies. While Estrada conceded that some mothers had to return to work soon after delivery, he equated that necessity with child abandonment: "Among the poor and even in the middle class, women who have scarcely passed a few days since giving birth, forty at the most, abandon their children to strangers' hands, no matter whose, to go to work in pursuit of the indispensable wages to support their needs."[35] Like other polemicists, Estrada leveled his harshest criticism against women who sold their breast milk for wages: "Wet nurses abandon their unfortunate children to sell to the highest bidder the food that nature has given them and of which they are merely the depositories, without the evil being repaired by the mercenary care they give to the new child, with whom they have no ties except the wage they

5. Masthead of *El Álbum de la Mujer* 1, no. 4 (30 September 1883). Secretaría de Hacienda y Crédito Público, Biblioteca Miguel Lerdo de Tejada, Fondo Reservado.

earn for nursing."[36] A Spanish writer, whose essays appeared in *La Familia*, concurred: "Not so much horror as compassion and repugnance do those unhappy ones cause who traffic in maternity, those who perhaps leave their own children to fate to hire themselves out to the children of another woman; to sell for money the fluid of their breasts."[37]

Earning a wage for performing motherhood's sacred obligation placed wet nurses in the same category as prostitutes. Because wet nurses sold the use of their bodies, they were considered deviant, like women who trafficked in sex.[38] A note published in 1883 in the *Boletín de Higiene*, journal of the Consejo Superior de Salubridad (Public Health Council) of the state of Mexico, explicitly linked wet-nursing with sexual deviance. The Mexican author described what he believed to be a newly identified pathology, "mastomania or sensuality of lactation." He considered the vice common among wet nurses, "whether single, widowed, [or] completely separated from their husbands"; he also believed that "neither are some mothers free from it." If a woman became sexually aroused from nursing, the author urged her supervising physician to intervene in a manner "wise, discreet, prudent, and strict."[39] These concerns reflect anxieties about female sexuality that were not limited to lower-class wet nurses. Estrada revived a time-worn theme when he warned that marital relations were harmful to the well-being of the newborn.[40] Maternal virtue required an exclusive bond with the nursing infant. In the case of a wet nurse, however, marriage testified to her morality, according to a French essay published in Mexico in 1895. But because few married women opted to nurse for private employers, "one must be content with a primipara, a servant, for example, who has allowed herself to be seduced by her suitor but who does not for that have dissolute habits."[41] Such strictures sprang from a profound suspicion of a wet nurse's intimate relationships—whether with the nursling, her own baby, or the father of her child.

"Wet nurses know well what takes place in the intimacy of the home," warned Enrique Chávarri, drawing uncomfortable attention to the central position of the nurse within the family's innermost circle.[42] Indeed, employers who entrusted their offspring to wet nurses harbored special fears about their noxious influences. The intimate position of the wet nurse in infant care and the physicality of her labor transgressed the boundaries, physical and emotional, between employers and their live-in servants. Contemporary writers warned employers to avoid familiarity with their servants, never to confide in them or allow their children to do so.[43] Some blamed wet nurses, along with other servants, for instilling superstitious beliefs in children and thus counteracting the role of the Mexican elite as modernizers.[44] An advertisement placed in the newspaper, *El Imparcial*, reflected one employer's hope to find a wet nurse who would be malleable to the family's wishes: "Seeking a wet nurse, young, poor, and with some manners, without being pretentious."[45]

Employers feared most of all that a wet nurse might cause the infant physical harm. Nurses were suspected of administering opiates to quiet their charges. And a diseased nurse could transmit a fatal infection to the nursling.[46] Newspapers fanned those fears with articles that attributed infants' symptoms of syphilis to infected nurses.[47] While such cases may indeed have occurred, babies could also have inherited the disease from their parents. In a context where the double sexual standard prevailed—and most anti-wet nurse diatribes were written by men—scapegoating the wet nurse deflected attention away from male promiscuity and the possibility that a father may have passed the infection to wife and thus to his own child. In any case, the accusation contrasted the wet nurse's deviant sexuality to the presumed morality of their employers.

As these critiques illustrate, wet-nursing posed disturbing questions. Behind the invectives and threats, however, lurked a question that challenged one of the foundations of class identity among the privileged: did the physical or the emotional relationship between mother and child define maternity? Anti–wet nurse rhetoric challenged constructions of bourgeois motherhood that emphasized the emotional bond with the child rather than the labor of child care, which in privileged households was often performed by wet nurses, nannies, and other domestics. At the same time, critics of wet-nursing had difficulty reconciling negative stereotypes of heartless and corrupt nurses with evidence of their maternal feelings. Authors who condemned wet nurses for abandoning their children simultaneously feared the consequences of nurses' attachment to their own babies. Critics and employers insisted on enforcing the separation of a nurse and her child lest she "be tempted to give it her breast, with harm to the child she has to nurse."[48] Of course, for decades foundling home administrators had no compunction about routinely assigning multiple nurslings to a single nurse: these warnings against nursing a media leche applied only to private, medically supervised nursing. But the orphanage's reorganization of wet-nursing would incorporate many of the elements that emerged in earlier literature.

The foundling home's reforms were centered on medical supervision of infant feeding. The role of physicians in critiquing wet-nursing reflected their growing influence in a cosmopolitan movement to modernize practices of reproduction and childrearing. Mexican specialists in obstetrics, like their colleagues throughout Europe and the Americas, considered wet-nursing outmoded, along with other dangerous and harmful "old wives'" practices.[49] Dr. Manuel Domínguez denounced as "detestable" the practices of popular Catholicism that were associated with midwife-assisted childbirth. These superstitions included "hermetically closing the doors and windows" of the birth chamber and "lighting various lamps as offerings to the saints and for extra measure burning odorous substances."[50] Under the new regime of hygienic infancy, the physician's knowledge and authority set the standard. Articles like Domínguez's five-part series, "Higiene," published in *El Álbum de la Mujer*, interpreted the latest medical understandings of infant development and techniques of infant care for privileged women readers.[51] Similarly, Domínguez warned that families should hire wet nurses only when medically necessary, for example, if a mother lacked sufficient milk.[52]

In situations where wet-nursing could not be avoided, medical vigilance could minimize its potential dangers. Domínguez's junior colleague, Dr. Ramón Estrada, advocated comprehensive medical screening of wet nurses to detect disease and alcoholism. Doctors should examine a prospective nurse for the formation of her breasts, her reproductive health, and the quality and quantity of milk.[53] They should also evaluate the health and age of her child to assess her capacity and suitability, because a mismatch between nurse and nursling could be fatal: "The newborn receives the milk of a woman who gave birth some months before," which "causes diarrhea, vomiting, colic, and even the death of many children."[54]

Above all, critics of wet-nursing invoked the specter of infant death, an all-too-frequent occurrence in the Mexican capital. Concern over the problem of mortality in infancy and early childhood extended well beyond specialist circles. Countless poems published in the Mexico City family press depicted innocent lives cut short, agonized mothers weeping over the cradle, and loving fathers, bereft and helpless.[55] In 1890, when a medical society sponsored an essay contest on the question of "what leading methods should be adopted to prevent the high rate of child mortality in Mexico," the government considered the topic so important that it committed to publishing the winning entry.[56]

Nationally, deaths in infancy—technically from birth to twelve months—ran around three hundred deaths per thousand live births from the mid-1890s through 1910. In 1895, of more than twelve thousand deaths of children under age ten in Mexico City, close to five thousand were of infants. The 1900 census recorded more than twenty-nine thousand births in the capital that year, and more than twelve thousand child deaths: 70 percent of them were infants.[57] Moreover, Mexican readers of European reports learned that in 1893 one in four Parisian newborns was placed out to nurse and as many as half those children died, while mortality among wet nurses' babies, fostered and fed by other nurses, reached 77 percent.[58] By the early

1900s statistics like these prompted the introduction in Mexico City of judicial investigations of infant death in wet nurse care.[59]

Throughout the Americas, concerns over infant mortality and falling native-born or elite birthrates, and anxiety about maintaining racial purity influenced the timing of wet-nursing regulation. Frequently framed in medical terms, such as fears of urban epidemics emanating from the hovels of the poor, anxieties about race suffused late nineteenth-century campaigns against wet-nursing elsewhere in Latin America and in the United States. Argentina began to regulate wet-nursing between 1880 and 1905, a period marked by rising and then declining European immigration. When European immigration slowed and more rural mestizos migrated into Buenos Aires, concerns about race brought wet-nursing into disfavor and artificial feeding preoccupied Porteños. In Brazil the end of slavery in 1888, combined with fears of urban epidemics, led to the introduction of wet nurse regulation and inspection in Rio de Janeiro in the 1890s. In New York, a primary destination for Mediterranean and Eastern European immigrants during the 1880s and 1890s, physicians began to call for wet nurse inspection at the turn of the century.[60]

Late nineteenth-century Mexican diatribes against wet-nursing evaded the question of race, but racial discourse infused the Mexican politics of infant feeding. By that time Mexican racial categories had become firmly attached to ideas of social class and permeated the social sciences like criminology and debates over the nation's potential for progress.[61] While Mexican critics of wet-nursing sidestepped the subject of race, foreign observers did not, and they brought up race when describing and critiquing Mexican child care practices. In the early 1840s, for example, Fanny Calderón de la Barca had described the village women who had nursed for the foundling home as Indian and mestiza.[62] A European lady-in-waiting in the court of Maximilian and Charlotte lamented that upper-class Mexicans entrusted their children to Indian girls rather than to trained nurses and governesses.[63] Thus, Indian and mixed-race women were identified with the same infant and child care practices that came under increasing attack as outmoded and dangerous.

In Porfirian anti–wet nurse rhetoric, fears based on race were embedded in the suspicion of lower-class women's sexuality and vice and in associations between the urban poor and disease. By the late decades of the nineteenth century, for example, the belief that nurses conveyed their racial attributes through their milk had been replaced by concerns about infectious disease, especially syphilis, closely associated with characterizations of urban lower-class immorality.[64] In 1880 geographer Manuel Rivera Cambas wrote that lower-class mothers who abandoned their children carried "the germ of death" and that they and their children suffered from diseases that originated "in inebriation and licentiousness."[65] Those vices were projected onto wet nurses, whom critics accused of abandoning their babies for material gain. Ramón Estrada linked infant mortality, wet-nursing, and race in the title of his 1888 medical thesis, "Some light considerations on the lack of child hygiene in Mexico, in relation to the degeneration of the race."[66] Such anxieties converged in fears that wet-nursing threatened elite reproduction, and reflected the politics of urban class formation founded on women's reproductive and domestic roles: the virtuous bourgeois mother versus the corrupt and deviant lower-class wet nurse. As the persistence of the foundling home's village nurse network demonstrated, moreover, until 1898 the practice raised no alarms for the well-being of state wards, children of the urban poor.

When welfare officials reorganized the foundling home's infant-feeding system, they were motivated not only by decades of anti–wet nurse rhetoric but also by an ongoing comprehensive overhaul of urban sanitation designed to eradicate sites of infection. Measures to modernize Mexico City's infrastructure included ambitious public works projects to improve drainage and sewer systems, demolish slums, and construct broad boulevards that connected the new residential districts for the well-to-do.[67] Infant-feeding reform and wet-nursing regulation at the foundling home can be seen in the context of the related public health and medical regulatory campaigns that gathered momentum starting in the 1890s and bore directly on infant care. These included the 1891 Código Sanitario (Sanitary Code) and its 1894 and 1902 revisions that, among other provisions, regulated the processing and distribution of milk. Separate legislation regulated the practice of midwifery. Midwife registration and limitations on medicines available to female practitioners extended the vigilance of male doctors beyond institutions like the Hospital de Maternidad e Infancia, over a historically female practice exercised in the home and encompassing far more than childbirth. The new regulations challenged women's authority and practice in the female sphere of reproductive health and maternity in general.[68] Two years after the foundling home reconfigured its wet-nursing system, the national school of medicine introduced a course on lactation. Following the European precedent of using charity hospitals as training grounds and laboratories for the development of reproductive medicine, the course included a rotation at the public maternity hospital.[69]

Although centered in the foundling home, wet-nurse regulation also extended into private homes through the inspection service. This combined public-private approach highlighted the class-based assumptions inherent in the practice. Despite years of harsh criticism leveled at wet-nursing, the inspection service supported the preferences of private employers. In this regard, the supervision of wet nurses resembled Mexico City's regulation of prostitution. Seen as a necessary evil, commercial sex had been legalized and regulated by public authorities since the 1860s. Prostitutes were required to register and undergo regular medical inspections as a public health measure.[70] Similar motives prompted the opening of the wet nurse inspection at the foundling home. Moreover, the inspection service procured the best nurses and made the practice safer for private employers but created a shortage of nurses for foundlings. One of the most contradictory outcomes of the new regimen was the enforced separation of wet nurses from their own babies in the interests of public hygiene. Meanwhile, physicians gained access to welfare wards to pursue experiments with artificial feeding. Thus the decades of criticism of wet-nursing had more than a symbolic result: the changes were structural and material. Polemicists may have directed their anti–wet nurse rhetoric largely at the classes with means to hire servants, but the reality was that only working-class women nursed for pay.

The New Regime

The foundling home's 1898 reorganization of the infant-feeding program instituted the measures that critics of wet-nursing had been urging for decades in the general and medical press. The project centered on medical oversight of all aspects of infant feeding. The new regime also enforced the discipline of wet nurses that most critiques had either implied or suggested outright. In initiating the reforms, physician-administrator Domínguez and his supervisors in the Secretaría de Gobernación hoped that the foundling home would become the model of modern, medical infant-feeding practice.

The reforms created a three-tiered system: a Departamento de Niños en Lactancia (Department of Nursing Children), later renamed the Departamento de Lactancia Artificial (Department of Artificial Feeding); a wet nurse inspection bureau; and village fostering for the children of nurses certified by the inspection service.[71] These measures provided medically certified nurses for the babies of private employers; medically supervised in-house nursing for infants in the foundling home; and village nursing for wet nurses' babies. The foundling home's in-house infant-feeding arrangements established another tiered system: for boarders, sole use of a wet nurse; for foundlings and amparados, shared use of a nurse supplemented by artificial feeding; for employees' babies, village nursing or artificial feeding. As the numbers admitted rose to unprecedented heights, peaking at 455 in 1903, they had a significant impact on all aspects of infant feeding.

Wet Nurse Inspection: Labor Clearing House

The Inspección de Nodrizas (Wet Nurse Inspection) opened in September 1898. Dr. Miguel M. Márquez, former inspector of the village wet nurses, directed the unit.[72] The regulations described a comprehensive employment bureau and medical service guaranteeing healthy nurses to the urban public of means; the inspection service put into practice virtually all the precautions guiding wet nurse selection that doctors had urged for decades. To attract health-minded applicants the foundling home attached a vaccination clinic to the inspection in June 1899.[73] And, they charged the applicants. Before they were examined, women had to pay a fee to the foundling home's matron, the *rectora*, who supervised the nurses and housekeeping staff. Without the receipt for that fee the inspector would not refer a nurse for employment even if she passed the physical exam. Paying the fee and passing the medical exam entitled the nurse to a signed certificate. The inspector also entered into a register the nurse's name and address, age, the date she gave birth, an analysis of her milk, and the name of her new employer. Inspector Márquez kept another register with the names of women disqualified by the exam so that he or employers could identify unsuitable applicants who were trying to circumvent the regulations.[74]

Prospective employers could apply to the service for referrals and specify the kind of nurse they sought, but there were limits to accommodating their preferences. The inspector would vouch only for the health of the nurse and the quality of her milk, not for her honor, character, or habits. Nor was the service required to send an employer a choice of nurses. The regulations stipulated that the servant who accompanied the nurse to her place of employment was not to be tipped, nor was he required to accompany the nurse to an employer's private doctor for a second opinion.[75]

To accommodate the perceived medical necessity and employers' preferences for wet nurses without children by their side, the inspection ran a rural fostering and wet nurse network for applicants' babies. If a woman had not already made arrangements for her baby, the foundling home required her or her employer to prepay the cost of sending the child to the country by rail and the monthly board of five pesos. The regulations further stipulated that the police would pursue any woman who failed to retrieve her child after she left employment. These rules were read aloud to any woman depositing her child before she signed a form agreeing to the terms.[76] Designed to prevent nurses from abandoning their babies, this policy consigned the babies to loosely monitored village care. Domínguez expressed some qualms about the arrangement. "It is not possible," he wrote, "to supervise effectively, under the rough power of the wet nurses."[77] Furthermore, the arrangements achieved exactly what critics decried: nurses neglected their own babies to earn money nursing. Medical necessity, however, now mandated separation of child and mother, whether she was destined for private or public employment. Nurses who worked for the foundling home also had to pay a pension to board their children in the country.[78] Village nurses, considered too brutish, mercenary, and corrupt to nurse other public wards, were good enough for the children of servants.[79]

The examinations that Dr. Márquez conducted to assess the nurses' health and to test their milk could easily offend women who came to the clinic seeking employment. The inspector examined and recorded the condition of all major body systems, including the urogenital organs. He extracted breast milk to analyze its abundance, density, and fat and sugar content. The only other women made to suffer such invasive exams to qualify for their work were prostitutes and the similarity clearly offended the nurses' sense of honor.[80] Women upset by the intrusive examination publicized their complaints. In October 1899 the newspaper *El Liberal* published accusations that Márquez abused his office, implying that his examinations were sexually inappropriate. The report pitted the nurses' honor against that of a medical professional. Welfare officials defended Márquez and protested that the doctor fulfilled his duties with "prudence and immaculate honor."[81] But over time information about how women were treated at the inspection probably influenced the declining numbers of applicants.

In-House Nursing: Factory Regimen

From the perspective of the wet nurses, working inside the foundling home differed in every way from village-based nursing. The new labor regime in the nursing ward combined the routine of a factory, the confinement of a hospital, and the lack of privacy that live-in domestics would experience in a private household. The establishment's regular reports listed wet nurses among the servidumbre, the lowest-ranking employees. Like cleaners and laundry workers, they received sixty-five centavos a day but they enjoyed far less mobility than their coworkers. They nursed around the clock and worked and lived under constant supervision in a routine of enforced sexual abstinence and regular physical examinations. Nurses were allowed to go out to visit their families and do errands but only if accompanied by another employee who supervised the outings to prevent them from getting drunk or contracting any diseases that might infect the babies.[82] At various times, foundling home administrators sought to enclose the wet nurses more securely by shutting off access to the roof terrace and blocking the street-level grates, where nurses chatted with passersby—or perhaps arranged other employment—during their breaks.[83]

The nurses had only a limited leverage over the terms of their work. Although their wages were among the lowest in the establishment, the pay was high by rural standards. Staff doctors realized that wet nurses required an ample diet; the women ate well and were permitted a ration of *pulque*, an alcoholic drink of fermented agave or maguey juice. The matron occasionally petitioned on their behalf for more food or for greater variety in their diet.[84] Some nurses also negotiated free board for their children.[85] Despite these concessions and a wage five times the pay of their village counterparts, most women chafed at the institutional regimen and walked off the job. Equally unpopular were provisions that allowed mothers who wished to nurse their own babies to live in the establishment as wet nurses without salary. These unpaid nurses received food and permission to wash their clothes but they were subject to all rules ordering the regimen of the paid nurses: they were required to nurse other infants and had to submit to monthly physical examinations and analysis of their milk. As of March 1899 not a single mother had opted to intern herself with her child on these terms.[86]

Given the requirements of live-in nursing, foundling home administrators and medical staff developed their ideal of the wet nurse: a homeless, first-time, single, widowed, or abandoned mother whose child had died in infancy. Few applicants conformed to the profile. At the high-water mark of inspections in 1903, over half the women examined and certified were twenty-five years old or older and had given birth more than once.[87] But administrators could not afford to hold out for ideal applicants as decreasing numbers of women submitted to inspections, even during a period of rising economic stress on the poor. From September through December 1903, the inspection made ninety-three examinations and referrals, but only twenty-six during the same period in 1907. And although the number of applicants rose in subsequent years, it never rebounded beyond half of the 1903 high.[88]

Under the new regime, wet-nursing for the foundling home resembled nursing in private employment and may have deflected potential applicants for similar reasons. In contrast, the new fostering arrangements for servants' babies, like the former village system, permitted some rural nurses to maintain their family and community relationships. That option became even more constricted in February 1904, when the Dirección General de la Beneficencia Pública ordered all weaned children still boarding in the country to be brought inside the institution. When the women arrived with their charges, the administrators tried to persuade them to stay and nurse in-house. Only one out of twenty-six agreed: eight others offered to return, but only if they received permission from their husbands.[89]

The administrators' surprise at this poor showing reflected their exclusive focus on wet-nursing as a moral and hygienic problem. They were oblivious to the structural constraints of extradomestic waged labor for women with family responsibilities. Yet they had ample evidence close at hand. Between May 1903 and July 1904, only one of the fifty-two in-house nurses was childless; thirty-two had different surnames from their children, indicating that they were married or that the children's fathers had recognized their offspring.[90] The high turnover among foundling home nurses suggests that the majority rejected paid confinement in favor of resuming to their normal lives and relationships.

Within the space of a few years, fewer and fewer women sought employment through the wet nurse inspection service or were willing to accept the foundling home's restrictive conditions. This pattern of avoidance represented the sum of countless individual preferences and also showed that social networks were circulating information about welfare policies and work conditions. In the otherwise complete absence of wet nurses' voices in surviving records, the high turnover among nurses and the lack of applicants for unpaid nursing offers some insight into the women's perspectives. Women who left the job—or simply never applied—rejected the assumptions embedded in the terms of regulated private employment and institutional confinement. Like their counterparts, the mothers who retrieved their children from the foundling home at their earliest opportunity, these nursing mothers either looked for work elsewhere or took their first chance to return to the mobility and relationships that the foundling home regimen denied them.

Good Mothers or Bad Workers?

In wet-nursing, welfare administrators and staff physicians confronted a conundrum: wet nurses were mothers but they were also workers, two categories that were deemed mutually exclusive in elite moral and medical discourses. Indeed, in their dealings with the nurses, welfare administrators made judgments and decisions that demonstrated time and again that they could not see the nurses in both lights.

Nor could they bring themselves to apply to the nurses the same medical diagnoses they made of private patients. For example, doctors like Domínguez and Estrada argued that only when a mother lacked sufficient milk should she hire a wet nurse. Some women who delivered their babies in the public maternity hospital for the poor claimed that they sent their infants to the foundling home because they lacked milk to feed them. Domínguez suspected that they used "lack of milk" as a cover for outright abandonment, in other words, for a lack of maternal feelings. He wrote to the hospital prefect for clarification: "Please inform this office in the present instance and in subsequent cases if the mothers of the children you send to this house really lack milk to feed them or if they have been abandoned or their mothers have died."[91] In one sense, Domínguez was correct that the claim of "lack of milk" conflated medical with economic motivations for abandonment. Poverty and a poor diet increased the likelihood of a difficult delivery and trouble producing milk. Yet these mothers may, in fact, have been demonstrating their awareness that only medical necessity excused the failure to breast-feed.

More importantly, from the perspective of poor mothers, breast-feeding complicated a woman's reentry into the workforce. Asserting that she lacked milk to feed him, María Vázquez sent her nineteen-day-old son Amado Vázquez from the maternity hospital to the foundling home in September 1900. Mother and son shared a surname, indicating that María bore her child outside of marriage, and it seems likely that she sent him to the foundling home so that she could resume work. Indeed, she had sufficient resources to pension her son to nurse in the country at four pesos a month and she retrieved him at age one and a half.[92] Mothers who claimed lack of milk as grounds for interning their children in the foundling home avoided the dishonor of being labeled bad mothers for refusing to nourish their infants. In claiming a medically defined problem, they took advantage of a loophole created in part by the critics of wet-nursing like Domínguez himself.

Many wet nurses were in fact good mothers and sought employment as wet nurses in the hope that they would be allowed to keep and nurse their babies. That they preferred their own children to assigned nurslings posed a perennial problem for welfare administrators and staff physicians. After an 1899 report on the St. Petersburg foundling home described how advertising had increased admissions and how admitting mothers to nurse their own children had reduced mortality by about 10 percent, Domínguez was inspired to introduce similar measures.[93] But the few mothers with children who were brought in to nurse without wages ignored their assigned nurslings in favor of their own babies. In February 1905 Domínguez wrote to his superiors: "In the past I was authorized to receive wet nurses with their respective offspring . . . believing that this way the servants in question would not cease to present themselves, but the result has been that the few who usually have responded to the call prefer their own child and hardly pay attention to the one entrusted to them, as naturally happens with all these substitute mothers commonly called de media leche."[94] The matron refused to hire nurses with children by their side, even those certified by Dr. Márquez. She echoed the director's complaint: when wet nurses were allowed to keep their own children with them, they "did not attend to the children whom one had entrusted to them in favor of their own." But it was so "difficult to acquire nurses without children" that pragmatism prevailed.[95] Domínguez accepted nurses de media leche, even though he was convinced that the "second parasite," as he called the nursling, received insufficient nourishment.[96]

These compromises illuminate the class-based contradictions infusing the arguments that breast-feeding was the moral foundation of motherhood. Although privileged mothers were harshly criticized for failing to breast-feed, the inspection service assured that the healthiest nurses available went to work for families of means. But a poor mother who rejected her maternal obligation and nursed for wages lost her status as a true mother and became *una madre postiza*, a false or substitute mother. At the same time, in the name of hygiene, foundling home policy separated wet nurses from their own children, reifying the class-based stereotype of the morally deficient working-class mother who abandoned her baby for gain. If a mother who nursed for wages preferred her own child to the nursling, she violated labor discipline and codes of hygiene. Once she sold her reproductive labor a woman traded her identity as mother for that of worker, two mutually exclusive categories in the eyes of welfare officials and their class peers. A woman's willingness to shift from the selfless labor of motherhood to performing the same work for pay allowed foundling home administrators and physicians to invoke a tacit code of labor obedience and to condemn wet nurses for preferring to nurse their own babies. In 1905, after nearly seven years of trying to discipline the wet nurses and, failing that, to replace them with artificial feeding, Domínguez wrote in obvious frustration: "Either we must establish a special [artificial-feeding] service, as perfect as possible and attended by people competent in the preparation and administration of the milk, or we must dispense for now with this philanthropic objective, leaving the children during their first year of life to the breast of the wet nurses, no matter how powerful and morally legitimate be the reasons militating against those mercenary substitute mothers, whom I am the first to declare plagued with ugly defects."[97]

Artificial Feeding: Fatal Regimen

Morality militated against wet-nursing but artificial feeding proved to be a fatal substitute. In February 1905 Domínguez reported to his superiors that the foundling home had seventy nursing infants and only forty-three wet nurses. In consequence, twenty-seven infants were "fed artificially with notorious calamity to their health; and . . . if matters keep on this way . . . the little things will end up in our necrological charts, and families will cease to confide their children to the Home once they hear that we feed them artificially."[98]

Families in crisis had no choice but to intern their children, but Domínguez also aspired to drawing a better class of families who would pay to board their children. To attract those clients, he had to retain a sufficient staff of wet nurses. Parents and guardians of boarders demanded not only that their children be breast-fed, but also that they have the sole use of a nurse, as they would if kept at home. When the families of boarders discovered that their children received artificial feeding, they insulted and threatened the staff. The majority of bottle-fed babies were therefore of lower status—amparados and foundlings, and all employees' children.[99] Thus, mothers with babies who sought employment at the foundling home as a way to secure shelter and wages faced the likelihood that their children would die from formula feeding.

The foundling home's program reflected the experimental nature of bottle and formula feeding, although the urban market already supported a range of imported and locally made products. Indeed, the foundling home's artificial-feeding program had begun under the supervision not of a medical doctor but of a socially prominent philanthropist who was later patron of Mexico's first national mothers' congress, Luz González Cosío de López.[100] She advocated the use of sterilized cows' milk, which had worked well for one of her own sons. During the twenty-five days of the experiment she came personally or sent a servant to prepare the milk, with, wrote the director, "the meticulous, painstaking care of a good mother toward a beloved child." Most of the thirty babies subjected to the experimental diet died of diarrhea or inanition, the inability to assimilate the food.[101]

After that initial episode, Dr. Rafael Carrillo, medical supervisor of the artificial-feeding ward, and his assistants conducted trials with both commercial and specially prepared medical mixtures but suspended their use as soon as it became evident "that the organism of the children had become intolerant, that they were observed to become colicky, or develop vomit or diarrhea."[102] Carrillo preferred to administer sterilized milk, but without refrigeration it spoiled in summer, and he turned to the commercial brands Mellin and Horlik, which he considered "the least harmful."[103] Least harmful was a relative measure: mortality almost doubled, to over half the babies under one year that were part of this experiment.[104]

Despite early evidence that artificial feeding was harmful, even fatal, officials at the Dirección General de la Beneficencia Pública insisted on continuing its use to offset the unpleasantness of dealing with the wet nurses. Domínguez, for his part, had come to consider wet nurses a necessary compromise as he observed firsthand the deaths of the infants on boiled milk or formula. Inmate mortality rose in tandem with the expansion of the artificial-feeding program: 34 percent of children admitted in 1904 died, compared to 54 percent of 1905 admissions.[105] Staff doctors found themselves mired in a contradiction: hygiene and morality demanded that they administer a harmful and frequently fatal regimen. In 1904 the director's request to the Dirección General for supplies emphasized moral imperatives: "With the object of carrying out your noble idea of using whatever means possible to feed the children artificially to save them from the wet nurses, whose rough and corrupt practices endanger and frequently result in the death of the infants entrusted to them, I beg that you will see fit to authorize the expense for . . . a gross of bottles to sterilize milk . . . and to buy a gross of rubber nipples."[106]

The foundling home's hygienic regimen also failed to eliminate the diseases and accidents that had killed babies in the homes of the village wet nurses: even under medical supervision inmates died from the same causes. One night in June 1904, for example, while a nurse slept a nursling died with her nipple in its mouth. The director determined that suffocation caused the baby's death and blamed the incident on the medical nurses for letting the wet nurse sleep in the same bed as the child.[107] Later, in 1906, when typhus swept through the confined orphanage population, Domínguez's successor, Francisco de Paulo Carral, asserted that the epidemic originated with one of the in-house nurses.[108]

These causes of infant death, however, were isolated incidents compared to the consistently dismal results of artificial feeding. In June 1905, when Domínguez reported on recent institutional mortality, he cited as principal causes a recent measles epidemic, lack of hygiene in the infirmary, and artificial feeding: "Artificial feeding, so many times attempted in this establishment, has always had a mournful result, perhaps owing to idiosyncrasies of our race, perhaps owing to climatic influences, but, without any doubt, owing to the manner in which it is practiced here."[109]

Staff doctors also blamed their subordinates for infant deaths caused by lapses in the medical regimen. Carral complained that the establishment was "an asylum for poor old women and young women inclined to laziness," who "seek employment as nannies [niñeras] to resolve their life problems."[110] Dr. Márquez and Dr. Carrillo had a history of small disputes with the matron, who represented the highest female authority in the house, and they succeeded in having her dismissed.[111] With the matron gone, Dr. Márquez petitioned to introduce a training program for the cleaners, nannies, and medical nurses. A handful of nursing students volunteered in the hope of securing permanent employment.[112] But the training program produced no noticeable improvements. Carral accused the nannies of failing to follow proper medical procedures for artificial feeding, and he complained that the institution would have to offer twice the going wage to attract adequate help.[113] Not until 1912, however, were the staff doctors required to be present in the ward during the hours of artificial feeding.[114]

As the blame for the death of artificially fed infants was passed down the institutional hierarchy, ultimately it lay with women who rejected the opportunity to work as wet nurses within the foundling home. Carral wrote repeatedly that infants were dying for lack of nurses. In 1907, when the number of wet nurses fell so low the foundling home had more than two infants per available nurse, Carral even proposed to raise the wage to make the work more attractive.[115] Failing that, the obvious answer was to increase the number of infants on artificial feeding: the babies died "inevitably."[116]

This impasse over infant feeding continued until 1912, when Dr. Manuel Márquez, formerly wet nurse inspector, became director.[117] During his tenure, Márquez attempted to reduce the artificial-feeding program and restore the centrality of wet-nursing, his own medical specialty. But the eruption of the revolution and the growing scarcity of staff and food thwarted his plans. Infants and older babies predominated among the surging admissions.[118] Month after month, hardly a single woman sought employment through the inspection service. The foundling home remained short of nurses and turnover among them stayed high.[119]

Outside the orphanage walls the revolution caused acute food shortages in the capital. Within the foundling home, the question of whether there would be enough food overrode the question of what kind. Although the public welfare system's centralized provisioning could command supplies even during the war, orphanage administrators were hard-pressed to feed employees and dependents by any means. Cows' milk supplied under contract arrived consistently diluted and adulterated. At various times, the institution supplemented its resources with goats and a *burra*, and once received the gift of a cow.[120] Finally in 1918, with the military phase of the Mexican Revolution coming to a close, the foundling home vacated its crumbling colonial compound in the city center and moved to suburban Tacuba, originally home to fully half the institution's wet nurses.

Infant Feeding and Family Entitlements

The attempted interventions into infant feeding failed consistently, both inside and outside the foundling home. In 1910 a prominent medical society sponsored an essay contest on alternatives to breast-feeding but received no entries the judges considered worthy of the prize.[121] Shortly afterward, when revolution disrupted the foundling home's protracted experiment, the attending physicians had resolved neither of the two central problems: maintaining and disciplining a sufficient corps of wet nurses, or administering an artificial-feeding program that kept infants alive. For a time the inspection service ensured healthy nurses for employers of means, but within a few years it became so unpopular among potential applicants that, if anything, private wet-nursing fell back into the shadows of the informal economy and beyond the reach of regulation. The failure of artificial feeding confirmed that breast milk was superior for nourishing infants and for their survival but nothing could mitigate doctors and administrators' disdain for the women they paid to provide it.

Meanwhile, the burden of the foundling home's reorganization of infant feeding fell on the wet nurses, their children, and their class peers. Closing down the village system deprived childbearing women in two communities of a source of household income that allowed them to maintain their family relationships. But the reorganization of the foundling home's infant-feeding regime reached far beyond the communities of Tacuba and Tlalnepantla. Just as the contradictory trends in adoption at the turn of the century represented a moment of transition between competing concepts of childhood—working and protected—the end of the village nursing system represented a transition in the moral and medical economies of motherhood and infancy that could be resolved only by a profound rethinking of attitudes toward working-class reproduction. The reformers' goal may have been to introduce new hygienic techniques of infant feeding and care, but that could not be done successfully without overcoming deeply held prejudices against poor working mothers. Although welfare administrators insisted that breast-feeding was the foundation of motherhood, they never acknowledged the maternity of the women who nursed for pay. In the name of hygiene, they separated nurses from their babies and then criticized them for abandoning their children in favor of wages. Indeed, the contradictions at the heart of the attempted reforms highlight how closely women's work was tied to child circulation. When wet nurses were allowed to keep their babies, foundling home staff defined their attachment to them as a sign of poor labor discipline. On orders from top welfare officials, doctors also persisted in administering a fatal regimen of artificial feeding: the majority of victims were foundlings or servants' babies. Paying patients would never have tolerated the experiments with artificial feeding that resulted in the death of welfare wards. Such dubious outcomes placed in stark relief the class-based, structural, and material foundations of anti–wet nurse politics and regulation in the Mexican capital.

At the center of this failed experiment stood a public institution ostensibly devoted to child welfare, one of the principal institutions through which representatives of the capital's upper classes interacted with families of the urban poor. The attempted reforms to the foundling home's infant-feeding regime illuminated yet another facet of Porfirian politics of the family. Mexico City's wet nurse regulation reinforced class-based valuations of women's reproductive labor and of their children and served as a potent

6. *Tres Madres con Sus Hijos: Décimas "La Miseria"* (*Three Mothers with Their Children: Décimas [about] "Poverty"*). José Gaudalupe Posada, zinc engraving, 8.9 x 13.9 cm, n.d. University of New Mexico, University Libraries, Center for Southwest Research, Gamboa Collection of Prints by José Guadalupe Posada.

tool for maintaining and reproducing class entitlements to family life. The protections and cultural capital that accrued to virtuous mothers would lose value if they were equally available to mothers of the lower social orders. Like the servants whose work supported their employers' domestic standards, wet nurses performed the central labor of motherhood, as Juvenal had observed. But because they were paid for that labor, wet nurses were rhetorically and structurally denied the status of maternity. By focusing on wet-nursing exclusively as a moral and medical problem, reformers were blind to the role of the nurses' husbands, their babies' fathers: this erasure affirmed elite prejudices that painted wet nurses as immoral single mothers, which in turn exposed class-based entitlements to family life. The multiple ways that working-class women rejected employment on those terms demonstrated that they recognized what was at stake.

The foundling home's role in wet nurse regulation and its innovations in infant feeding established a prototype for public health and welfare programs following the revolutionary conflict, but with crucial differences.

Revolutionary politics discredited the elite biases of the Porfiriato and mass mobilization placed a new value on Mexico's working classes. Loss of population during the war elevated the project of reducing infant mortality to a national priority. Public health programs initiated in the early 1920s reflected the influence of puericulture on Mexican child welfare. An international movement, puericulture offered a scientific approach to child health and development from conception through puberty that was closely integrated with attention to the health of the mother, to the hygienic environment of the home, and to the places where children were supposed be spending their time, such as schools. Revolution and puericulture combined to make reproductive health central to rebuilding the Mexican nation.[122]

Physicians who administered the foundling home infant-feeding program emerged after the war as leaders in Mexican puericulture. Their specialty was spectacularly well placed: foundling home veterans assumed key positions in public debates about children's health and in the rapidly proliferating federal bureaucracies created to lead campaigns to improve maternal-child health at all levels of society. Those agencies constituted the core of Mexico's expanding welfare state structure and placed the family, especially mothers and children, at the center of regenerative social policies inextricably linked to nationalistic state building during the 1920s and 1930s.[123]

 # REWORKING THE FAMILY

Family Relations and
Revolutionary Reform,
1913–1943

The Family in the Revolutionary Order

Conceptual Foundations

In December 1914, as Mexico's revolution entered a new cycle of violence, Constitutionalist First Chief Venustiano Carranza issued the first of a series of decrees legalizing definitive divorce. Other factions had been outlining their political and social agendas through proclamations for some time, but Carranza had only recently begun to articulate the Constitutionalist program for the social dimensions of the revolution: the divorce decree made a forceful statement about the significance of the family in the new order.[1] First, the decree's authors argued that legalizing divorce would eliminate a series of social abuses and thus endorsed the principle that the revolution should correct injustice even in private life. The reform laws of the mid-nineteenth century had established marriage as a civil contract, not a religious sacrament, but allowed couples only to separate and forbade remarriage. In contrast, the Constitutionalist decree asserted that couples should be able to terminate a contract they had made voluntarily and have the opportunity to seek happiness in a new marriage. Legalizing divorce and remarriage would also reduce the noxious influence on public morality of informal unions, so prevalent among the poor. In addition, definitive divorce would emancipate women of the middle classes, whose husbands' affairs held them in a "condition of slavery."[2] In these ways, the Constitutionalists' opening salvo on family reform proposed a secular definition of the Mexican family that was simultaneously founded on civil contract and love, was both anticlerical and moralizing, and was concerned with disciplining the lower classes and emancipating women.

Surely divorce was the least of Mexico's problems that winter: the violence of war and its indirect effects of hunger and displacement had torn apart thousands of families and caused acute suffering. After defeating General Victoriano Huerta's counterrevolutionary attempt to reinstate the Porfirian status quo, Carranza and Francisco "Pancho" Villa then turned against each other and plunged the country into a fresh round of conflict. The rift opened along old fault lines during the Convención (Convention) of Aguascalientes, held in the autumn of 1914 to bring together representatives of the three principal revolutionary factions to hammer out a joint political and social program. Immediately after the rivals split, Carranza relocated from Mexico City to the port city of Veracruz, as Villa closed in on the capital from the north and the peasant armies led by Emiliano Zapata arrived over the mountains that separated the city from their stronghold in the state of Morelos.[3] Given these circumstances, an opponent of divorce had a good point when he later objected that in 1914 Carranza had no authority to issue the decree because he was "merely the chief of one faction among many in the middle of a civil war." Critics of divorce also trivialized the importance of the decrees by asserting that they merely catered to the immediate needs of two of Carranza's close associates.[4]

But the first decree on divorce and those that followed had a clear political purpose. Making a strong statement on divorce reinforced the Constitutionalists' claim to legitimate national authority as inheritors of the midnineteenth-century liberals, who had separated church and state and had crafted the laws on the secular family. The Constitutionalists also timed their decrees strategically: they issued the first as Villa and Zapata occupied Mexico City and the second in January 1915 as Villa abandoned the capital and General Álvaro Obregón reoccupied it to reassert Constitutionalist authority.[5] Moreover, the divorce decrees were hardly trivial: they provoked a heated and revealing debate among revolutionaries about the nature of the Mexican family, understood to be the primary social unit, and the values that should organize the society that would emerge from the crucible of revolution.

Constitutionalists were not alone in considering the implications of the revolution for the future of the Mexican family. But the definition of the family expressed in the Constitutionalists' first divorce decree — contractual, affective, and moralizing — had both committed supporters and ardent opponents. With the old dictator Porfirio Díaz deposed and driven into exile and the military defeat of Huerta's counterrevolution, many Mexicans saw the demise of the old regime as an unprecedented opportunity for social renovation and placed the family at the center of their reform agendas. They drew inspiration from the founding principles of mid-nineteenth-century liberalism and also from the modernizing currents in medicine and public health of the late Porfiriato. Combining these elements, reformers from all walks of life constructed a vision of citizenship that was shaped by family relations.

The discredited Díaz regime symbolized a suite of abuses that the revolution would correct. For many, Díaz's accommodation to the Catholic Church had violated the secular principles of Mexican liberalism. The closed circle of power around Díaz made his government synonymous with cronyism and corruption. Favoritism toward foreign investment and enterprise gave rise to the saying based on a family metaphor, "Mexico — mother of foreigners, stepmother of Mexicans."[6] The Porfirian elite's conspicuous consumption and preference for European fashion and culture accentuated economic and social inequalities.

In contrast, many Mexicans would have agreed with Carranza that the revolution stood for secular values. They also supported economic initiatives that favored Mexicans, social and economic justice, workers' rights, and the opportunity to modernize Mexican society on terms that benefited all social classes. Intellectuals sought the affirmation of a national identity rooted in Mexican history and experience. The revolution gave fresh momentum to Mexican feminists, who argued that the principles of political inclusion extended to women and that women should play a central role in national reconstruction. Scientific rationality and medical hygiene, improved status for women within the family, and more inclusive attitudes toward Mexico's working classes would infuse civilian proposals for modernizing motherhood, fatherhood, and childhood in the new order.[7]

A substantial number of their compatriots disagreed. They continued to believe that Catholic sacraments defined the family and that state initiatives on family issues usurped paternal authority in the private realm. Conservatives predicted that economic independence and equality would prompt women to abandon their maternal and domestic responsibilities and would bring about moral collapse and social dissolution. But revolutionaries also had their doubts about women and working-class participation in national reconstruction. Opponents of the church remained convinced that women's religiosity and limited experience outside home and family disqualified them for participation in the public sphere. Reformers warned that vice, laziness, and disease rendered working-class men and women unfit as workers and, worse, as parents: if families were the primary building block of society, what did working-class vice portend for working-class citizenship? Physicians feared that mothers' ignorance and superstition would thwart efforts to introduce modern, hygienic childrearing methods and thus threatened the survival of Mexico's rising generations and possibly the nation itself.[8] In these ways the family, seen as a microcosm of the nation, became at once the foundation for a unifying social vision and a platform for contesting the meanings of Mexican modernity and identity.

Thus, although family relations might seem a far cry from the contentious questions of political authority, labor rights, and land reform that prompted thousands of Mexicans to take up arms, discussions about the rights and roles of fathers, mothers, and children in the revolutionary order touched on fundamental concepts of class, gender, and power and revealed the family as a locus of controversy. While the armies of the revolutionary factions engaged on the battlefield to determine who would win the political prize, the social revolution engaged the energies of a broad spectrum of Mexicans and brought new players such as radical labor advocates and feminists into the debate. In the years following the revolution's military phase, the project of defining and modernizing the Mexican family would give rise to a far-reaching program of social reform. Moreover, Mexicans of the next generation, too young to have fought or experienced the revolution's most turbulent years, would encounter the revolutionary state through the medium of family-oriented programs.

The Revolutionary Family: Private Foundations of Public Order

The Constitutionalists, as their name asserts, claimed political legitimacy as defenders of Mexico's liberal heritage. When mid-nineteenth-century liberals had established the separation of church and state in the Constitution of 1857, they removed the family and life cycles from the purview of the Catholic Church and repositioned the family as the cradle of the nation. The 1859 decree establishing civil marriage defined the couple's primary social responsibility: to reproduce and raise citizens.[9] Declaring themselves the guardians of the liberal hallmarks of anticlericalism and the secular family, the Constitutionalists decreed that definitive divorce and remarriage were legal. These measures and the debates they provoked merit close examination: they had far-reaching implications for defining parental responsibility to children and, more broadly, concepts of nation, class, and social responsibility. By exploring the implications of divorce for Mexican society, revolutionaries drew direct connections between the principles they fought for and the intimate relationships of the family.[10]

The Constitutionalists' decrees on divorce raised troubling concerns even among revolutionaries. If marriage was the sole legitimate foundation of the family and the family was the primary building block of society and represented the nation in miniature, what did the legal dissolution of marriage portend for Mexico? The decrees legalizing divorce and the ensuing debate over proposals for revising family-related statutes exposed strongly held and conflicting positions on how revolutionary principles might influence family morality, maternal and paternal responsibilities, children's rights, and the state's role in regulating family relations. The debates revealed a broad consensus about gender and power within the family: fathers were to have authority but also responsibility, and mothers, economic dependence and sexual purity. Indeed, the debates prefigured a body of law primarily intended to preserve masculine authority and sexual privilege but provide paternalistic protections for women and children. In this, they foreshadowed the influence that concepts of family would have on class relations in the revolutionary order, with fathers representing the paternalistic state, and mothers and children serving as a metaphor for the lower classes.

In contrast to Catholic doctrine that marriage was an indissoluble sacrament, the Constitutionalist divorce decrees defined a family founded on contract and affirmed a secular model of family morality, by simultaneously encouraging marriage and legalizing its termination. Liberal nineteenth-century Mexican law on divorce allowed couples to separate but did not dissolve the marriage, which ended only with the death of one partner.[11] The Constitutionalists argued that prohibiting remarriage contradicted the premise established by the laws of the reform: that marriage was a civil contract undertaken voluntarily. They reasoned that the option to divorce and remarry would improve lower-class morality by encouraging the poor to marry, thus reducing "to the minimum the illegitimate unions among the popular classes, who form the immense majority of the Mexican Nation."[12] After all, if the majority of Mexican families were not founded on law, what kinds of citizens would they produce?

The divorce decrees also defined the parental obligations that survived the dissolved marriage and tied the preservation of parental authority to sexual morality. The partner whose behavior occasioned the divorce lost parental authority but not the obligation to pay child support. A divorced mother who was the innocent party retained parental authority but lost it if she lived in an unsanctioned union or bore an illegitimate child.[13] To ensure children's well-being divorced parents were required to continue to support and educate their sons until the age of twenty-one and their daughters until marriage, "as long as they lived by honest means."[14] Likewise, an innocent wife who lived honestly had the right to support unless she remarried.[15] Nineteenth-century civil codes had contained similar provisions. Although the benefits of these financial measures were confined to the propertied classes, they nevertheless affirmed the principle that financial obligations, especially to children, survived the marriage itself. On the other hand, the decree also premised a divorced woman's parental rights and right to alimony on her sexual probity.

The Constitutionalists' divorce decrees prompted their opponents to respond. When adherents of the Convención, the uneasy alliance between Villa and Zapata, gathered to produce their revolutionary program of political and social reforms, one participant complained, "Just because Don Venustiano Carranza has introduced divorce, we feel we must adopt it in order to say that we, too, are revolutionaries."[16] The assembly delegates, largely middle-class professionals rather than rank-and-file Villistas or peasant Zapatistas, nevertheless undertook to draft recommendations for revising laws affecting unmarried parents and their children, as well as divorce.[17] Their debate turned on issues like paternal abandonment, single motherhood, and illegitimacy and exposed the deep-seated assumption that containing sexual relations within the legal family defined the respectability that distinguished the gente decente from the disorderly lower classes, marked by informal unions and promiscuity.

The assembly examined the issue of whether or not illegitimate children should be permitted to investigate their fathers' identity and weighed the rights of single mothers and their children against those of men who fathered children outside of marriage. Like their counterparts in revolutionary France over a century before, the delegates were well aware that fundamental issues were at stake: investigations of paternity opened the way for unmarried women to sue the fathers of their illegitimate children for support and for children born of informal unions to publicly identify their fathers.[18] Such cases would tarnish the honor of married men and could embarrass them before their legal wives and legitimate children. Men could also be held financially accountable for sex outside of marriage.

The debates exposed the masculine sexual privileges that shored up respectable families. One speaker proclaimed that the measure would destroy the home and be a constant menace to honorable women if their husbands were exposed as philanderers.[19] Another opponent asserted that illegitimate children would only choose the father who suited them best because there existed no scientific method to ascertain paternity. He indicated the prevalence of married men's promiscuity when he added that within twenty-four hours of passing such a law, "every Mexican home would be unhinged and one would witness injustices in 99 percent of the cases, which would bring an end to peace and tranquility in society." A speaker who suggested that public welfare establishments should protect illegitimate children received a "prolonged ovation from the galleries."[20] Hardly a revolutionary concept, that timeworn idea assigned to the state the role of substitute father and protector of the socially weak: predominantly single mothers and their children.

In support of legalizing paternity suits, however, one speaker received sustained applause when he linked family morality and revolutionary commitments to social and economic justice for the poor. "What the same revolution has done with the rich man, it should do with the wrongdoer," he proclaimed. Another proponent argued that investigating paternity was "an eminently moral principle that protected the weakness of women and children left destitute and abandoned by criminal fathers, who turn their children into waifs and beggars."[21] Revolutionary principles won the day when the assembly approved by more than three to one the measure to allow paternity suits.

Overlapping concepts of class, gender, and power surfaced in the convention's debate over family relations. Statements by some delegates revealed that they believed that the class distinctions supporting the social hierarchy rested on maintaining firm boundaries between legitimate and illegitimate unions.[22] An opponent of divorce argued that the revolution sought to uplift the people and divorce ran counter to that end. He compared marriage to the army, likely to be defeated if discipline were relaxed. He was convinced that divorce would first "demolish the conjugal order and then the social order."[23] A tangle of unstated issues underlay his assertion. First, the notion of discipline reflected the central role of the legitimate family in defining social status and class identities. Inflexible boundaries between legal and informal unions established women's sexual purity and morality, a prerequisite of bourgeois respectability. The gente decente viewed informal union (*amasiato*), common among the poor, as a mark of lower-class immorality. Divorce, some feared, would reduce middle-class families founded on legal marriage to the level of stereotypical plebian families.

For other delegates, the issues turned on state versus church authority over social institutions like the family. For them, the revolutionary precept of anticlericalism trumped threats of social dissolution; one speaker noted that the Catholic Church was the greatest enemy of divorce, implying that revolutionaries should de facto support divorce.[24] But some found the concept of divorce challenging because it threatened to undermine fundamental family bonds premised on secular civil authority. Given that politics and government were male preserves, such a threat could pose a challenge to masculine authority.

The discussions over family morality and parental—particularly paternal—responsibility revealed the delegates' gender biases. Some speakers expressed suspicion of unmarried mothers and their children and suggested they sought only financial gain. Some believed that men should not be held accountable financially or morally for sex outside marriage and that single mothers, and by extension their children, bore the blame for sexual transgression: this view had roots in the colonial period. But the majority saw mothers and children as dependent, vulnerable to economic abandonment and social prejudice, and in need of protection. One speaker saw divorce as a defense against such prejudices. He argued that divorce would not only free partners from a loveless marriage but also defend women from social prejudice.[25] This comment speaks to the belief in the power of law to overcome social biases.

But an opponent of divorce cited prejudices that, he clearly believed, stood beyond the reach of legal reform. He countered that a divorcée would be vulnerable to abuse because her loss of virginity threatened her status as a respectable woman: that is, men would see her as sexually available rather than a virtuous candidate for remarriage. In addition, he feared that without the protection of their biological father, a divorcée's children would also be vulnerable to abuse. A new husband would have little feeling for the sons of the first marriage and might prostitute his stepdaughters. He also feared that siblings who had different fathers would feel little affection for each other.[26] His concerns expose an assumption that fathers, not mothers, created and sustained the bonds of kinship among their offspring. These debating points illuminate deep-seated prejudices against second unions, legal or not.

That the assembly finally approved the measure on divorce by more than five to one speaks to the delegates' confidence in the legitimacy of the secular family and, by extension, of the secular state.[27] The victory of the proposals to legalize paternity suits reflected the prevailing opinion that fathers held equal moral responsibility toward all their children, whether born within or outside of marriage. With fathers a stand-in for the state and children representing Mexico's lower orders, this position on the family augured greater public commitments to the poor, frequently through the medium of family-oriented programs.

The Constitutionalist defeat of Villa and Zapata prevented these measures from becoming the law of the land. But the tacit model—state as father, women and children as dependent and in need of protection—pervaded civilian proposals for social reform, and was so widely held that it shaped subsequent law and policy.

Blueprint for a Revolutionary Society: The Constitutionalist Family Program

When the Constitutionalists, led by Carranza, triumphed over their rivals on the battlefield in 1915, they secured the opportunity to write the initial laws defining the family in the revolutionary order and to incorporate into statute the secular model of family and morality prefigured in their divorce decrees. Carranza promised the delegates assembled at the 1916 constitutional convention at Querétaro that he would soon issue a revised family code to establish "the family on a more rational and just basis."[28] Yet he cautiously limited debate over his revisions to family legislation by taking several precautions. Adherents to the Villa and Zapata factions were systematically excluded from the constitutional convention, as were women, who had no vote on the outcome.[29] Feminists held their own congress in 1916 in Mérida, Yucatán, to develop a slate of proposals for women's equality, including suffrage.[30] Some, like Hermila Galindo, sent messages to the delegates of the constitutional convention exhorting them to support full citizenship and the vote for women.[31] Not surprisingly, however, the Constitution of 1917 and the Ley sobre Relaciones Familiares (Law of Family Relations) issued by decree the same year enshrined predominantly middle-class male views on gender and the family and excluded women from the political sphere.

Nevertheless, the delegates assembled at Querétaro proved to be more nationalist, more anticlerical, and more committed to the redistribution of wealth than Carranza's inner circle. The Constitution they produced went considerably beyond his draft proposals.[32] The document issued in February 1917 mandated a far-reaching land reform, drastically curtailed the social and political influence of the Catholic Church, established universal secular public primary education, legitimated labor organizations, and introduced significant protections for working women and children.[33] Even so, the assembly withheld full citizenship and suffrage from women. Some, like Félix Palavicini, Carranza's education chief, advocated for including women in the political world. But radical anticlericalists, whose views prevailed, believed that women were overly influenced by the church and barred them from political participation.[34]

In the spirit of paternalism, the new Constitution mandated pertinent protections for women and children, part of Article 123, which elaborated a slate of workers' rights that was quite advanced for the day. Article 123 set a maximum workday of eight hours for all workers. It also instituted protection from hard physical labor for women in their last trimester of pregnancy and maternity leave of one month after delivery, with the guarantee of wages and job security. Nursing mothers were to be allowed two half-hour breaks each day to feed their babies. Dangerous or unhealthy employment, including work after ten o'clock at night, was prohibited for women in general and minors under sixteen. Minimum salaries, however, could vary by sector, region, and custom.[35] The Constitution also endorsed new sociopolitical formations, such as unions and cooperatives, and promised future social legislation that would aid working-class families, such as cooperative societies that would construct low-cost, hygienic workers' housing and a social security law that would cover health, life, and unemployment insurance and workers' compensation.[36]

The new Constitution improved on Porfirian child labor legislation and on reforms introduced in 1914. As of 1907 children over seven could work in textile factories with parental permission. The 1914 labor code had prohibited minors under nine from working. Those aged nine to twelve could only take on work that that allowed them to attend school and was appropriate to or compatible with their physical development.[37] Now, Article 123 of the 1917 Constitution banned employment for children under twelve and established a maximum workday of six hours for minors aged twelve to sixteen.[38]

A new law regulating the family was one of the first fully realized statutes of the revolutionary order. Like Article 123 of the Constitution, the Ley sobre Relaciones Familiares, issued by decree in April 1917, instituted significant improvements in the civil status of women and children.[39] The law's preamble stated that the legislation established the family on a strictly secular and "modern" basis, finally eradicating remnants of Roman and canon law. Except for legalizing divorce and remarriage, however, the law largely drew on prior legal constructions of the marital relationship.[40] Concepts of paternal and maternal roles, parental discipline, and filial obedience also remained much the same. Reflecting widespread concerns about the years between puberty and full physical maturity, the law raised the legal age for marriage from fourteen to sixteen for men and from twelve to fourteen for women.[41] Similarly, theories of social hygiene and public health influenced the prohibition against marriage by habitual drunkards, the insane, and people infected with incurable and inheritable diseases such as syphilis.[42]

Other provisions in the new family law promised greater gender equality. Mothers and fathers now had equal parental authority.[43] No longer did a woman relinquish her legal identity with marriage. Once she had reached her majority, she could administer her own property, conduct her own business, make contracts and enter into suits, although she still needed her husband's permission to enter into service or take a job.[44] But the document also legislated the sexual division of labor: specific articles outlined women's obligation to care for the home and children and men's obligation to sustain the family with work.[45] This provision had far-reaching implications. Not only did it perpetuate the separation of production from home and family, but it also reinforced concepts of women's dependence.

Carranza's family law established important improvements in children's legal and social status but did not elevate the rights of children above their fathers'. The law eliminated the category of spurious children—those born of adulterous liaisons—and raised their status to that of natural children, that is, children of unmarried parents. Nevertheless, the law prohibited investigating the paternity of a child born outside of marriage, allowing only a few exceptions. A natural child could seek recognition only from an unmarried parent, and the courts could declare paternity in cases where rape led to conception. The law also allowed parents to recognize their children born outside of marriage, but if they did, the child had the right only to use the parent's name and had no claim to financial support.[46]

The statute recognized prerevolutionary trends in family formation by legalizing adoption—Carranza proclaimed it "an innovation among us"—and by defining the adoptive relationship as equal to that of parents and children by birth.[47] The reinstatement of formal adoption, omitted from late nineteenth-century family codes, reinforced the concept of family bonds formed by civil contract. Like legal divorce and remarriage, formal adoption affirmed the nuclear family model over that of the extended patronage household that absorbed working minors as dependents, but on an informal basis.

For all its innovations the law preserved most masculine prerogatives. Prohibition of paternity suits and careful wording that defined the grounds for divorce left untouched the institution of the *casa chica*, the family on the side maintained by many married men. Indeed, the family law encouraged men to the use the legal contracts of divorce, remarriage, and adoption to regularize their informal family relationships and provided a variety of ways for a man to recognize his children born outside of marriage.[48] These measures enabled men to fulfill their responsibilities to their children without infringing on the core of masculine privilege in Mexican family and sexual practice.

Combining continuity with innovation and emerging as one of the first developed statutes of the initial revolutionary regime, the 1917 Ley sobre Relaciones Familiares indicated that the regime placed a priority on establishing state definitions of parents' and children's mutual obligations and sexual divisions of labor for reproducing normative family forms and productive citizens. Indeed, those concerns ranked with agrarian and labor reform and church-state relations as some of the highest priorities of Mexico's nascent revolutionary order.

Predictably, the law drew criticism from both conservatives and progressives. Jurist Eduardo Pallares opposed the law, describing it as "profoundly revolutionary, silently . . . destructive of the family nucleus," and contrary to the sentiment of a significant portion of the Mexican people.[49] Others complained that the secular, contractual emphasis of the law Americanized the Mexican family; they predicted that a "wave of immorality" would permeate Mexican society, "seize" the young and "pervert" women's hearts.[50]

Feminists, however, saw the family law as an advance for gender equality, particularly in the area of women's parental authority and control of property, although they were quick to identify gaps in the Constitutionalist legal program. Yet Mexican feminists were deeply divided between moderates who sought to improve women's status based on their roles as wives and mothers and others who sought to fundamentally restructure sex and gender relations.[51] In 1921 Sofía Villa de Buentello, a moderate feminist, published her treatise *La mujer y la ley*, arguing against divorce on the grounds that the new law favored men and made women more vulnerable legally, socially, and economically because it failed to provide the necessary protections.[52]

On the other hand, feminists of the radical left and those associated with the workers' movement considered the law's advances inadequate: they pushed for full sexual, political, and economic emancipation for women and advocated for birth control and sex education.[53] The diversity of these perspectives and the controversy they provoked highlighted the volatility of politics bearing on gender and the family. Indeed, they suggest why Carranza never submitted his family law to debate or formal ratification. They also suggest why, time and again, the reformers who most influenced subsequent family programs sidestepped such controversy and built social consensus by focusing on children.

Families and Revolutionary Disorder in Mexico City

While factional leaders deliberated on the future of the Mexican family, the violence and disruption of the revolution propelled thousands of Mexicans from their homes. Entire families uprooted themselves and marched with the armies. Women not only carried their children and household gear and cooked for the troops but also fought alongside the men. Some children became combatants or joined a floating population of orphans and runaways. Throughout the war and especially as the fighting subsided, displaced people headed for the cities, the capital in particular.[54]

Residents who weathered the revolution in Mexico City witnessed their share of violence and hardship. In early 1913 some were caught in the crossfire of the bloody and destructive counterrevolution that ended with the assassination of President Francisco Madero and the installation of the strong-armed General Victoriano Huerta. The political turbulence affected public institutions as well as private citizens. By the late winter of 1913, the foundling home lacked sufficient provisions to feed its own residents and staff but still distributed food to the poor who gathered at the gates every morning.[55]

Huerta's defeat brought no relief to Mexico City. After the rift between

7. Boys at the site of Madero's murder, Mexico City, 22 February 1913. Instituto Nacional de Antropología e Historia, Fototeca Nacional, Fondo Casasola.

the former allies Carranza and Villa, successive army occupations and retreats buffeted the capital. Military campaigns hundred of miles away devastated agriculture, and food remained scarce. Sabotage disrupted national commercial networks, forcing factories and construction to shut down for lack of supplies and putting thousands out of work.[56] The rising number of children deposited in the public orphanages by parents with no known address testified to the desperate conditions in Mexico City, to the hasty flight of frightened residents, or to their sudden departure with retreating armies.[57] By late 1915 the Hospicio de Niños held 1,295 children, far beyond its capacity.[58]

But hunger and joblessness also spurred many *capitalinos* to take action. During the revolution, the city's working class repeatedly mounted and participated in collective action and challenged authority. In doing so, they cemented strong and positive class identities. Some women, inspired by discussions of the rights of the working class, organized workers in textile and food production.[59] Others, responsible for feeding their families, protested against food scarcity and worthless currency. Merchants came to fear the bands of angry women who mobbed their stores, brandished empty market baskets, and demanded bread. When the armies of Villa and Zapata occupied the city, women stormed the floor of their congress and challenged the delegates to act on their stated principles of social justice and defense of the poor. Derided by critics as a rabble of loose women and domestic servants, the women's focus on defending their homes and feeding their families led them to question whether the supposedly "grandiose revolution" was living up to its promise to benefit "the humble people."[60] For these women, the revolution's promises were not abstract, but concrete, and could be measured by material improvements in the daily tasks of providing for their families.

Revolutionary currents of protest also reverberated within the walls of welfare institutions. Foundling home wet nurses staged a walkout in 1913.[61] Like the staff, the children themselves viewed administrators as representatives of the repressive old regime. In November 1915 a group of boys barricaded themselves into the Hospicio's basements, coerced younger boys to steal supplies for them, and held out under siege by the police.[62] Administrators responded with plans to convert the orphanage into an armed camp, with observation towers at the corners of the compound.[63]

Confrontations like these revealed the challenges facing the Constitutionalists. Having won the war, they now had to win the allegiance of a politicized, mobilized urban, working-class population. At first, their actions only further alienated wary urbanites. In the summer of 1915 Carranza ordered the Cruz Roja (Red Cross) to close its soup kitchens, only to be embarrassed by reports of deaths from starvation.[64] As part of a massive program in public relief and also to control the growing number of homeless minors, the Constitutionalists established a fleet of new shelters to house children displaced by war.[65] By October 1915 asylums bearing the Constitutionalist name had been set up in requisitioned properties to supplement the capacities of the Hospicio de Niños and the foundling home. A newly established Constitutionalist foundling home housed 550 children and 70 wet nurses. The Asilo Constitucional (Constitutional Shelter) for boys sheltered 400 in the building formerly belonging to the Asociación de Jovenes Cristianos. The Constitutionalist shelter for girls housed 300 in the old Lotería Nacional (National Lottery). When authorities learned that administrators at the girls' shelter would only admit *niñas* of the middle class, they dismissed them, with this command: "It is necessary to finish once and for all with

8. Venustiano Carranza and Félix Palavicini at a charity event, Mexico City, ca. 1916.
Instituto Nacional de Antropología e Historia, Fototeca Nacional, Fondo Casasola.

people who are repelled by contact with the humble class."[66] But scarcity continued to impose hardship on the urban poor. Acute food shortages and the currency crisis added to labor woes and provoked a general strike in the summer of 1916. As social conditions spiraled out of control, the Constitutionalists responded by imposing martial law on the city.[67]

If loyalty could not be won, they seemed to think that it could be enforced. Public institutions for minors were militarized. Welfare employees had their appointments confirmed only after they took loyalty oaths. The children housed in the orphanages participated in patriotic ceremonies. Even the little boys at the foundling home took drill classes.[68] In December of 1916 the director of the Hospicio wrote to Carranza reporting that the children did well in their exams because of the "powerful stimulus" of the first chief's attentions to the institution. The inmates had also grown, gained weight, and improved in health. Many passed the final exams and, overall, showed their "moral energy in spontaneous resolutions for pursuing ideals, gratitude, and improvement in conduct."[69]

Meanwhile, new arrivals flowed into the capital region from the countryside. They came as families or alone and often had no local relatives or other networks of social support.[70] Between 1910 and 1921 the population of Mexico City proper grew by over 30 percent and that of the Federal District by nearly 25 percent, putting an additional strain on the weak urban economy.[71] Moreover, the number of single women among the migrants highlighted the economic vulnerability of many new arrivals. The imbalance of women to men in the age groups likely to have young children became increasingly pronounced. The female population of the Federal District increased by 117,130, while the male population grew by only 68,180, with the greatest sex imbalances among those aged fifteen to twenty-four.[72] In that age cohort, many of the mothers were abandoned or widowed. By 1921, 14.6 percent of women between the ages of twenty and twenty-nine who had been married were widowed, divorced, or separated: among them, almost 82 percent had at least one child.[73] Such statistics, and the rising population of the foundling home, testify to the consequences of postwar dislocations. In June 1917 the foundling home housed 412 children; in October, 515, not counting the nursing babies. By the end of November the number had dropped, but only to 428.[74] Director Refugio M. Caniedo noted that many parents of pensioners lacked homes themselves.[75]

By 1918 Mexico City appeared to some observers to be populated with beggars and vagabonds: the most destitute survived by scavenging. Homelessness made poverty all the more visible. Crime had increased. Typhus and influenza decimated a population weakened by hunger.[76] Army occupations and demobilizations fostered a culture of sexual permissiveness.[77]

Francisco Bulnes, a former Porfirian insider and acerbic social commentator, viewed the urban scene with apprehension. The decorum and cosmopolitanism he and his class peers had enjoyed under Díaz lay in ruins. Bulnes noted that employers scarcely had the means to house their live-in servants. Workers lived "crowded in with some relative or compadre or packed into a miserable hovel with eight or ten others." Streets and parks teemed with the unemployed: "numerous youths, beggars of both sexes, pickpockets, delinquents and all kinds of wretches ... spend the night in public dormitories, in doorways, on benches in the public gardens." The military presence only added to the sense of chaos, as the women of "rootless military families" entered "the barracks at night to sleep with all their little children and are thrown out at reveille, passing the day wandering around the city."[78] Like others of his class, Bulnes feared the social and political forces unleashed by the revolution, in particular the potential threat of a highly mobilized populace in the wake of the profoundly divisive civil war. But where Bulnes saw impending social dissolution, reform-minded citizens saw opportunity.

Family Reform and Citizenship

While Carranza's initiatives on the family provided legal and institutional frameworks, Mexicans from all walks of life saw the revolution and the promise of a more democratic polity as an unprecedented opportunity for social renewal. Out of the ferment of the moment came a vast number of social projects focused on the family. Proposals aimed at the urban working classes often exposed their Porfirian roots in combining medicine with morality. Some revealed a keen awareness of international trends in urban hygiene and maternal-child health. All construed the family, which represented both continuity and the future, as the nation in microcosm.

As the Constitutionalists consolidated their political victories, optimistic men and women animated by revolutionary fervor peppered First Chief Carranza with suggestions for social reform directed at working-class families, especially at women and children. One correspondent submitted a proposal for reforming urban tenements.[79] Young middle-class women who passed the revolution from the safe distance of the United States believed their studies would help in constructing the new society soon to emerge from the conflict. Eloisa Espinosa wrote enthusiastically from Boston, Massachusetts, of the classes in "domestic science" she had observed in the schools there and proposed to implement similar programs adapted for Mexican women.[80] Micaela Pérez, working in a settlement house in Bridgewater, south of Boston, reported that she was close to obtaining her certificate as a kindergarten teacher and looked forward to applying her skills to help the poor on her return to Mexico.[81]

From Celaya, site of one of the Constitutionalists' decisive military victories, the itinerant photographer Miguel Camacho wrote to Carranza "with due respect" to suggest that the country needed a new marriage code and that Camacho was the person to produce it. The photographer and would-be freelance legislator had traversed the country, "working in the homes of my clients, and that is how I have spoken calmly with the majority of the inhabitants of the republic; I know them, their ideas, customs, defects, the cause and finally the way of remedying them." The document he envisioned would "instruct all . . . in the obligations that they bear toward the supreme government, toward their spouses, and toward all others; this work will form a good citizenry that knows how to support its governors." He offered his services free of charge to produce "the great work that will consolidate national peace."[82]

From a suburb of Mexico City, a group of middle-class women, describing themselves as "revolutionaries and zealous of the prestige of our cause," wished "to celebrate its triumph . . . by founding a national orphanage, to give orphans and especially the children of soldiers who died on campaign a home better appointed than that which they lost with the death of their fathers." They planned to teach fatherless children "to know their laws and respect them; to distinguish brave from ambitious men, so that in the hour of the homeland's call, all will rise up and without hesitation join the standard bearer of law and justice."[83]

Some proposals built on Porfirian foundations. From Guadalajara, Joaquín Baeza Alzaga, a specialist in infant feeding, sent the draft of a law to regulate wet-nursing. However, Baeza went farther than his prerevolu-

tionary predecessors and urged that public authorities should take direct responsibility for the health of all children under age two, regardless of class.
The doctor alerted Carranza to Mexico's alarming rate of infant mortality,
especially among the poor. To improve infant survival, he proposed that
women in their ninth month of pregnancy should stop working and not
return until thirty days after giving birth. Every city in the republic should
establish committees for the protection of infancy that would oversee clinics and orphanages, and the federal Secretaría de Gobernación (Ministry
of the Interior) should publish annual reports on child mortality statistics.
Among a government's principal obligations, Baeza wrote, "is that of as-
suring the improvement of the race, not only intellectually and morally but
physically. One must ensure that children grow strong, so that when they
are adults they have the necessary aptitudes and conditions to fulfill their
obligatory social functions."[84]

Alberto Pani, an engineer and Constitutionalist insider, struck a similar note. He founded his program for urban reform on his conviction that
"there exists a precise and direct proportion between the sum of civilization acquired by a country, and the degree of perfection reached in its
administration and stewardship of the public health."[85] Like Bulnes, Pani
was appalled by the living conditions of the urban poor, but unlike that
cantankerous critic, Pani looked to science to solve such social problems.
Mexico's future, Pani wrote, lay "in hygienizing the population, physically
and morally, and in endeavoring, by all available means, to improve the precarious economical situation of our proletariat."[86]

Like Baeza, Pani placed infant mortality among the most urgent issues
facing the state: "In the City of Mexico we have to record the awful fact that
eight thousand one hundred children less than five years old die annually."
Pani was among the many Mexican professionals who lacked confidence in
women, even in their traditional roles. Indeed, he saw mothers as the main
culprits in infant death: "In this frightful toll of human life, more than forty
per cent of the total, we must recognize surely, besides the physical causes
of contagion, of defective feeding, and unhealthful habitation, this other
vital cause of a moral order: *crass ignorance and lack of motherly care*."[87]

Despite his punitive tone, Pani elaborated an integrated model of maternal-child health and child care education based on the successes of Maria Montessori's Beni Stabilii Institute in Rome and Milan. In contrast to

Porfirian welfare policies that dictated the separation of mother and child, the Montessori method introduced child care and health facilities into individual tenements so that mothers could learn modern hygiene and child rearing from observing the methods of the trained staff of the Casa dei Bambini.[88] Pani's formula for social improvements applied international trends in public health and in understandings of child development to local conditions and priorities and, as such, prefigured the public health measures focused on women in children during the 1920s and 1930s.

These proposals expressed civilians' animated engagement in the project of rebuilding Mexico and the centrality of family in their visions of social renewal. Their agendas revealed a shared belief that the family was an institution of primary political importance. In writing to Carranza they conveyed their expectation that the revolutionary state would take a leading role in family-oriented reform. The proposal for tenement reform and the young women's offers to use their experience in teaching domestic hygiene and working with low-income communities prefigured the intensive focus of revolutionary social programs on the home environments and families of the urban poor. In depicting national unity based on marital harmony, the itinerant photographer expressed the widely held view that the family constituted the fundamental building block of the nation and that intimate relationships should reflect the principles of the society emerging from the political struggle.

Similarly, the suburbanites' orphanage prospectus illuminated the ways that concepts of citizenship linked family to the state and positioned children as intermediaries between state and family. The pediatrician's proposal that the state take direct responsibility for infant health foreshadowed reformers' preoccupation with infant mortality that prompted later federal commitments to maternal-child medicine. Pani's formula of didactic, scientific management of urban populations and their living conditions represented the extraordinary faith among reform-minded Mexican professionals that science could cure social ills.

Despite these commonalities, public opinion remained divided over which principles should define the dominant model of the Mexican family in the coming decades. Still, across the social spectrum, Mexican citizens agreed on one point: children represented the hope and future of Mexico reborn.

The Politics of the Family

While the war tore countless families apart, many Mexicans looked to the family as the means to implant revolutionary values and raise the next generations of citizens in the revolutionary mold. The family-oriented programs that emerged from the ferment of revolution constructed the foundation for a society that was substantially more child-centered than during the Porfirian era. Family, although a contested and controversial concept, would become the overriding metaphor for Mexico's modern national identity.

In revising legal definitions of family relations, Mexico's revolutionary leaders emulated the liberals of the mid-nineteenth-century reform in asserting that the state—not the church—controlled the life cycle. Revolutionary legal frameworks did not offer radical reconfigurations of family relations. Instead, law and policy endorsed existing structures and gender norms, but the new laws incorporated trends such as the concept of protected childhood and formal adoption that had emerged during the late nineteenth century. In the coming years, public policy and programs would also incorporate influences drawn from international child health and protection movements that gathered momentum in the interwar period throughout Europe and the Americas.[89] During the 1930s, and particularly during the presidential administration of Lázaro Cárdenas from 1934 to 1940, officials combined these elements with the political logics of populism and nationalism that drove the development of similar public assistance and health programs throughout Latin America.[90]

But state agencies and public officials would hold no monopoly on promoting family reform. Public services that intersected with family life expanded in part because activists from all social sectors urged the revolutionary state to endorse and implement innovations in education, children's medicine, and youth discipline. Pressure from private citizens and organizations accelerated the consolidation of the revolutionary state's family-oriented programs and the expansion of government services that intersected at multiple sites with the family cycle at all levels of Mexican society.[91] By the late 1930s, when the Mexican state fused with the dominant political party, those intersecting processes fostered a close association between state and family and made family a central component of national identity.

Family-oriented movements and government policies and programs that emerged from the ferment of social revolution expressed a combination of optimism and reservation about fundamental changes to family relations and had far-reaching results. The Constitution of 1917 provided workplace protections for mothers but withheld the vote from women. Revolutionary family law advanced women's equality but preserved men's sexual privilege. Child-centered initiatives rooted in traditional concepts of the family gave rise to public programs that extended medical and social services to working-class women and children. Denied full citizenship, relegated to the domestic sphere, and officially defined by their maternal roles and identities, women across the political spectrum made motherhood their vehicle of social inclusion and political empowerment. And families of the urban poor obtained new resources, both material and ideological, to address immediate crises and to assert their rights as citizens.[92]

From the first revolutionary innovations in family relations, the language of family was fused to that of class. Like the Convención's debates over divorce in mid-revolution that illuminated associations between marriage and bourgeois respectability and between informal unions and lower-class disorder, state-family relations focused on stabilizing class formation in a fluid social context. A defining aspect of the state's increasing involvement in family life was the perpetuation of established gender roles. Public programs and policies promoted a middle-class model of family and domesticity: responsible wage-earning fathers, virtuous housekeeping mothers, protected children defined by medical care and prolonged education, with bodily and domestic hygiene for all. The masses mobilized by revolution would be transformed and uplifted by services for family and children.

In the 1920s and 1930s Mexico City's proliferating agencies of public health and assistance, strategically located in working-class neighborhoods, became integral resources for sustaining the domestic economies of thousands of urban families. Active clients of public services, long-term urban residents and new arrivals alike drew on the legacies of revolutionary mobilization that fostered a heightened consciousness of citizenship and rights.[93] Nevertheless, appeals for assistance by families in need would continue to involve complex negotiation across lines of gender, class, and power. Women needing public services still had to make difficult choices between supporting their children and relinquishing them to the care of others. As the value of children and the status of motherhood rose in public discourse, the cost of such exchanges rose higher in the interlocking economies of public assistance and private households.

The Revolutionary Family

Children's Health and Collective Identities

In 1928, after a tumultuous administration, outgoing president Plutarco Elías Calles made a gesture of reconciliation: he proclaimed the end of revolutionary factionalism and announced the birth of the revolutionary family. This family would be inclusive, but its strong central authority would quell the violence and regional revolts that had marked the 1920s. Revolutionary *caudillos* (chiefs) Zapata, Carranza, Villa, and, most recently, Obregón, had all been assassinated. And in 1926 when Calles had enforced the anticlerical articles of the Constitution and closed Catholic schools, the ecclesiastical hierarchy had countered by closing the churches and rallying the faithful behind the banner of "Cristo Rey." The ensuing conflict cost thousands of lives.[1]

In this unstable context, the family offered Calles a model for the era of unity, law, and institutionalization that he called for in his speech.[2] Since the mid-nineteenth century, Mexican law had given the state authority over the family cycle. Hierarchies based on gender and age strengthened the resemblance of individual families to the state—and *vice versa*. Like the nation, families set boundaries of belonging and exclusion; like governments, families distributed resources and labor. Family lineages connected Mexico's historical past with its modern future; thus, the family metaphor lent the revolutionary state political legitimacy.[3] And children carried the family forward, representing optimism and regeneration. While Calles's model of the revolutionary family emphasized the consolidation of the revolutionary state's power, it also implied political continuity.

Speaking in Guadalajara in 1934, ex-president Calles turned again to the metaphor of the family to address the question of revolutionary continuity. This time he explicitly claimed the paternal role for the revolution and invested its future in Mexico's children: through education the revolution would enter and occupy the national consciousness and the minds of children and youth. And this time the political boss used the family metaphor to provoke his opponents instead of calling for unity. Calles rejected private concepts of the family and denounced reactionaries who claimed that the "child belongs to the home, youth to the family." To him, that was "individualistic doctrine, because children and youth belong to the community; they belong to the collectivity. . . . Childhood and youth must belong to the revolution."[4] Calles also insisted on state control of secular education, an issue that divided Mexicans. Raising the ante, he proposed that revolutionaries would win the hearts and minds of Mexico's youth through education that was not only secular but also socialist, and thereby snatch "youth from the claws of the clergy" and from their conservative allies.[5] Although the 1917 family law gave mothers and fathers equal authority over their children, women had a lesser role in Calles's imagined collectivity. Proposing a family model more militant than nurturing, Calles notably omitted mothers from his formulation of the revolutionary family: he highlighted its masculine nature and the obligations of the paternal state to educate its future citizens. In return, the revolution's children owed obedience, productivity, and loyalty.

That Calles drew on family imagery first to call for harmony among revolutionaries and later to attack the revolution's enemies points to the power of real and imagined families and children to represent simultaneously a space of consensus and a lightning rod for contention. When it came to children, Calles's notion of a collectivity had distinct class connotations. Decades earlier, Mexico City officials had called the children in the Hospicio "sons of society."[6] Most of the children who came under public authority did so because their parents failed to support or discipline them. Now Calles implied that Mexican parents were failing to educate their children in revolutionary principles. His scorn for the private family also used tacit understandings of gender roles to needle his—and the revolution's—adversaries. In rejecting the private family, Calles denigrated domesticity and mothers' influence over children, feminine roles in the private domain that were central components of middle-class ideology and identity. In effect, he implied that his enemies—and all Mexicans who believed in the sanctity of the private family—were effete. But Calles's politicized, class- and gender-inflected formulation of the revolutionary family also dodged a key question: who would perform the necessary reproductive labor in the revolutionary collectivity, and on whose terms?[7]

That question had preoccupied health reformers since the late 1910s, as they mounted a crusade to improve reproductive health and reduce infant morality. In the early 1920s health activists helped establish the family as a model for national identity by calling for national unity based on family relations and claiming children as the standard bearers of Mexico's future. In the aftermath of Mexico's long, destructive and divisive civil war, the issue of reproduction was especially urgent and would foster a widely accepted image of Mexican society as a family that took collective responsibility for the nation's children. The health reform project began with improving infant survival to make up for Mexico's population losses from war, disease, and emigration. Babies born in the postwar years belonged to an all-important replacement generation, the physical embodiment of Mexico's future.[8] As such, they were the focus of anxiety, especially in light of the nation's elevated rates of infant mortality. In Mexico City, that toll continued to be particularly high: on average, 28 percent of babies born in the capital died before their first birthday.[9] Reformers such as Alberto Pani blamed maternal ignorance for this staggering loss of human and national potential.[10]

But the babies of the new generation were also a source of hope: their birth reestablished continuity after the traumatic rupture of civil war. And in the early 1920s, during the presidential term of former revolutionary general Álvaro Obregón, children's health became a vortex of activism. While the controversy over secular versus religious education polarized public opinion, the cause of improving children's health provided a platform for unity. With the press as ally and sometimes as instigator, leading professionals and government officials—often the same people—mounted a high-profile campaign to reduce infant mortality and to enlist Mexicans of all social classes in the patriotic mission of safeguarding the health of the next generations. Like Calles's model of the revolutionary family, health reformers claimed children for the collectivity, but it was one devoted to reproduction: centered on health and children and governed by medical principles. Instead of excluding mothers, the model of family and childhood they promoted included them but also highlighted their problematic role: maternal labor was both necessary and suspect.

The national child health crusade of the 1920s and 1930s had its roots in the concerns about reproduction that had motivated the anti–wet nurse campaign of the late nineteenth century. It also shared many characteristics with that earlier effort: it combined medicine with morality; it was directed at both privileged and poor Mexicans, although in different ways; and it was intended to change private domestic practices while also influencing public cultures and concepts of childhood. Like the earlier reform efforts, the campaign promoted a concept of childhood founded on health that required significant changes in women's reproductive labor. And like their nineteenth-century predecessors, when health reformers of the 1920s talked about gender roles and children's health, they were also talking about class and race.

Indeed, the goals and methods of the child health campaign reinforced established social hierarchies: they were patriarchal in their technocratic, top-down directives and paternalistic in their tutelary role over social groups deemed weak or dependent—children, mothers, and by extension the poor. In this revolutionary family, physicians and public health officials assumed the paternal position based on their medical knowledge of children's development, especially infancy. Experts also claimed authority over mothers and warned even middle-class mothers that the consequences could be fatal if they did not replace traditional child care practices with a strict adherence to the precepts of scientific childrearing.

Thus, the national campaign for children's health both elevated the importance of motherhood and subordinated mothering to professional, especially medical, expertise. For the poor, the campaign brought invaluable benefits: thousands of families unable to afford private medical care now had access to public health services. But for the urban working class, whose family lives had long been more open to interventions by public authorities, those services also brought yet another form of close oversight of intimate relationships and domestic arrangements. At the same time, Mexico's crusade to improve children's health charged the reproduction of individual families and, more broadly, of the entire population with powerful political and cultural significance. For many Mexicans, the healthier children of the future represented the physical and ideological fusion of Mexico's European and indigenous heritages into a unified modern nation.[11]

In its initial stages, the child health crusade mounted a broad program of propaganda to create a public culture of childhood founded on health and to enlist mothers' cooperation in changing private childrearing practices. Given the high stakes for the nation, however, the spotlight ultimately turned on public institutions of child welfare, which had been left out of the reform mainstream for most of the 1920s. As state-run substitutes for private homes and families, they bore the obligation to set and meet the highest standards of medical success. But, by 1934, even as Calles claimed children for the revolutionary collectivity, a new generation of physician administrators at the Mexico City foundling home admitted that the strict regimen of scientific infant care that they advocated for mothers was failing the babies in their own care: the foundling home had a far higher rate of infant mortality than the general population. Daily, staff doctors confronted the tragic evidence that large public institutions, even those with the most advanced medical facilities, could not provide the same benefits to children as families living in poverty.[12]

In the late 1930s this realization prompted officials to reassess the value of women's reproductive labor, to reorganize child welfare services on a smaller, more intimate model, and to bring the emotional aspects of mothering into the services. In that process, and in contrast to Calles's irreconcilable opposites of the masculine collectivity and the feminine realm of the private family, the collective family model came to resemble the private more closely. This convergence only strengthened the power of the family metaphor to represent the relationship between the revolution and Mexican society.

An Army of Experts

In January 1921 Emilia Enríquez de Rivera, founder and editor of the women's magazine *El Hogar*, addressed Mexico's first Congreso del Niño (Congress on the Child) about a private organization that would provide milk to poor children. But Enríquez de Rivera, known to her readers as "Obdulia," also took the occasion to frame the assembly's mission more broadly. Together with the experts and officials gathered at the congress she sought nothing less than to "erase the enormous distance" between the health of "poor and rich children" and thereby improve the race so that Mexico could join the company of civilized nations.[13] Her themes resonated throughout the congress, where leading physicians, educators, and philanthropists, many of them also public officials, equated children's health with the nation and its future.[14]

Participants in the first congress formed the vanguard of an army of experts mobilizing a national campaign to improve and safeguard children's health. They convened in the capital at the invitation of Félix Palavicini, who currently directed the prominent Mexican City newspaper, *El Universal*, but formerly had served as director of the trade school under Díaz and later as chief of education under Carranza. Like Palavicini's career, the proposals that the congress delegates elaborated had roots in Porfirian concepts of protected childhood but now embraced revolutionary opportunities for renovating Mexican society in the name of the child.

The participants in the 1921 congress and the follow-up meeting in 1923 constituted the core Mexican cohort of two closely related international movements: child protection and eugenics. Both drew on the principles of puericulture, literally the cultivation of children's health and development. The child protection movement focused on guarding children from physical abuse and economic exploitation. Internationally influential works, such as *The Century of the Child* by Swedish feminist and children's advocate Ellen Key, indicted unenlightened parents as the main culprits in deforming children's health and spirit and called for closer government oversight of families. In some countries the child protection movement promoted laws to establish children's rights and give the state more power to protect children by intervening directly in family affairs.[15]

Many Mexican advocates and specialists in childhood also espoused the goals of eugenics, which promised racial improvement through the application of science and medicine. Like European and Anglo-American eugenicists, who sought to prevent people considered biologically and mentally unfit from reproducing, Mexico's family law of 1917 barred alcoholics, syphilitics, and the insane from marrying.[16] But most Mexican eugenicists and their Latin American colleagues, who dominated the various fields of puericulture, believed that improvements to parents' reproductive fitness would be passed along to their offspring. Following Dr. Isidro Espinosa de los Reyes, whose presentation on "Intrauterine Puericulture" initiated the session of the congress section on eugenics, Mexican puericulturists focused their attentions, framed predominantly in medical terms, on the physical relationship between mother and child.[17]

Their concerns also extended into every aspect of social life that affected children's material and moral environments from conception through adolescence. They advanced proposals for close medical oversight of marriage, reproduction, and infancy. They planned schools and playgrounds, created programs in physical education, and advocated incorporating lessons in personal hygiene into school curricula. The principles of puericulture informed proposals for protecting children from the corrupting influences of streets, markets, factories, and public entertainments. Deploying arguments based on children's physical and intellectual development, reformers pressed for the creation of juvenile courts and the enforcement of laws against child labor. Indeed, puericulture, closely allied with eugenics and child protection agendas, became the platform for a child-oriented program of social reform more far-reaching than anything the earlier generation had imagined.[18]

The proposals advanced by this phalanx of specialists showed that the revolution had made some difference in professionals' attitudes toward the lower classes. In contrast to Porfirian modernizers, who viewed poor and indigenous Mexicans as obstacles to national progress, the reformers of the 1920s were committed to their improvement so that all Mexicans could participate fully in national reconstruction. But those commitments did not imply an ideology of social equality: apprehension also drove the reform mission. Eugenicists believed that disease and vice among the lower classes threatened the progress of the Mexican race. The mass mobilizations of the revolution and the militant labor movement of the early 1920s made privileged Mexicans anxious about social instability. These perspectives infused Enríquez de Rivera's speech to the 1921 congress. She recalled the credo of the Catholic reform movement, which embraced the precepts of *Rerum Novarum*. In that 1891 papal encyclical, Leo XIII had urged Catholics the world over to help the working class by finding a middle way between the excessive exploitation of industrial capitalism and godless Marxism. Enríquez de Rivera believed that private charities like her proposed network of milk dispensaries would improve the health of working-class children, demonstrate the goodwill of her class, and teach unity—and thus promote social equilibrium.[19]

In the new political environment that discredited outright expressions of class antagonism many congress participants tempered their negative characterizations of workers and the poor. Some did not. Dr. Francisco L. Casian advocated protecting wet nurses' children, but he described wet nurses as members of "the vilest classes of our society" and labeled them "the most cruel tyrant that families tolerate in all the world."[20] His colleagues in the congress section on child hygiene, led by Dr. Rafael Carrillo, countered with policies that recognized the maternity of wet nurses. This acknowledgment had consistently eluded Porfirian reformers, but now the precepts of puericulture integrated the health of mother and child. Before the revolution, Carrillo had directed the department of artificial feeding at the foundling home and knew firsthand the fatal consequences of separating wet nurses from their babies. Since then, he had risen to become director of the Hospital General. Under his leadership, congress members of the child hygiene section argued that doctors should condone wet-nursing only if the interests of both the nurse and her child were protected. Further, they acknowledged that mothers could also be workers. Recognizing the obstacles to breast-feeding that working mothers faced, Carrillo and his colleagues urged factory owners to honor the stipulations of Article 123 of the 1917 Constitution and provide day care facilities so that employees could nurse their babies.[21]

When congress participants called for enforcing existing laws and for new legislation, they responded to the changed political climate at home and abroad: public authorities now bore the primary responsibility for children's health and well-being. Social progressives in the United States had won the establishment of a new federal agency, the Children's Bureau, founded in 1912, and the passage of the Sheppard-Towner Maternity and Infancy Protection Act in 1921.[22] In the aftermath of World War I, the London-based Save the Children Fund tied child protection to children's rights. In 1924 the League of Nations ratified the movement's goals by adopting the Geneva Declaration on the Rights of the Child. Similarly, beginning in 1916, the Pan-American Child Congresses called on Latin American governments to take the lead in implementing child-centered recommendations.[23] Many speakers at Mexico's congress envisioned a fleet of new government agencies dedicated to children's health and proposed legal reforms to implement and enforce their ambitious agenda.[24] Some years before, Alberto Pani had anticipated this approach when he defined the Mexican state's responsibility for and authority over public health and the role of professionals in carrying out that mandate: "The State protects the health of the individual in order to make possible the progressive development of society," through "works of sanitary engineering" and through "laws and regulations for whose strict observance a trained technical personnel" is "especially organized to police and supervise."[25]

Some congress participants remained wary of state initiatives and favored private philanthropy. Many were involved in elite private organizations such as the Sociedad Protectora del Niño (Child Protection Society), founded in 1918 by writer and reformer Teresa Farías de Isassi. The organization ran its own maternity hospital for single mothers, along with a milk dispensary, kindergartens, and elementary and vocational schools.[26] Others pointed to the inadequacies of public health and welfare institutions. Dr. Espinosa de los Reyes would write that the Mexico City foundling home had "not only failed" to protect abandoned children but had "helped increase infant mortality."[27]

A visit by congress delegates to the Hospicio confirmed their worst fears about the deficits of public services for children. When it opened in 1905 the Hospicio compound had been a model child welfare facility, but now conditions had deteriorated. The kitchen was dirty and the food of poor quality. In the dormitories the beds were too close, inviting sexual impropriety. Classrooms were crowded and dark. Congress participants accused President Obregón and his welfare officials of neglecting their duty to the children in the protection of the state.[28] Others echoed Porfirian divides when they compared public welfare unfavorably to the ideal of the private home. Lawyer Antonio Ramos Pedrueza, an advocate for reform of Mexico's juvenile justice system, expressed similar sentiments when he contrasted the sterility of public welfare to the warmth and love of private charity. These characterizations drew on long-standing assumptions that the spirit of religious charity lived on in private philanthropy. In particular, by playing prominent roles in private organizations, women supposedly infused them with the warmth of home and family.[29]

Congress organizer Félix Palavicini, however, cultivated an alliance between private and public initiatives. He invited public officials to the congress and featured them prominently on the program: President Obregón attended the opening ceremonies. In his closing remarks, the conference secretary, Dr. Francisco Castillo Najera, reflected this spirit of cooperation. He praised the integrity and motives of the president and his officials. Integrating the piety associated with private philanthropy with the new political values that inspired public initiatives, he invoked the spirit of a "revolutionary Christ" and the "highest ideals of altruism and universal love."[30]

The first Mexican Congreso del Niño marked a major step in defining the collective enterprise of social responsibility for Mexican children. Participants looked to medicine and science to heal the political rifts of revolution and to bridge social cleavages of class and race. Enríquez de Rivera called for a child health campaign that closed the gulf of class difference. At the second congress in 1923, Dr. Alfonso Pruneda, a prominent physician, eugenicist, and director of the Departamento de Salubridad Pública (Department of Public Health), spoke of his dream in which Mexican children of European and indigenous descent nominated him as their spokesperson.[31] He urged the government to carry out the congress's slate of proposals to achieve the "ideal of a vigorous and healthy childhood" that would unite both races into a single nation.[32] His imagery shows how closely concepts of children's health were linked to racial ideology: medicine would cure the physical traits associated with racial inferiority. Repeated calls for national unity in the name of children's health also constructed an ideology of childhood as a universal status that transcended inequality and created a platform for inclusive politics that could unite Mexicans in a common cause. In consecrating their professions to children's well-being and in urging the state to support their crusade, congress participants allied with their international counterparts in the puericulture movement even as they forged an initial configuration of the revolutionary family.

The movement mobilizing in the name of Mexico's children quickly produced institutional results within the state sector. In September 1921, in conjunction with the centennial celebrations of Mexico's independence, the Departamento de Salubridad Pública organized a Semana del Niño (Week of the Child).[33] Palavicini used *El Universal* to publicize the festival with daily features describing the program and took every opportunity to claim credit for initiating these measures. The public health department inaugurated the capital's first public maternal-child health clinic in October 1922 and named it after Dr. Eduardo Liceaga, long-time director of the Hospital de Maternidad e Infancia under Díaz. A second clinic opened in 1923 and was named in honor of Dr. Manuel Domínguez, former director of the foundling home. By the end of the decade a network of clinics operated in urban, working-class neighborhoods and outlying municipalities. Other government branches also opened pediatric clinics, such as the Inspecciones Sanitarias (Health Stations) and the clinics of public welfare.[34] By 1930 the government had realized many of the proposals advanced at the 1921 congress, including the establishment of a juvenile court and a new federal office, the Servicio de Higiene Infantil (Child Health Service), which coordinated the services of the urban maternal-child health clinics. Prominent congress participants directed those new agencies and other attendees assumed administrative positions in the child welfare system. Meanwhile, the rising generation of physicians pursued careers in public health. Women participated in many ways. Elite women joined the Asociación Nacional de Protección a la Infancia (National Association for the Protection of Childhood), founded in 1929 and headed by the president's wife. But many women sought paying careers as doctors, nurses, social workers, and public health and welfare administrators. The growing number of trained and professional women in state agencies would help weaken the gender distinction between public services and private philanthropy, and lend public institutions some of the feminine qualities formerly associated with private charity.

But to achieve the goals of the child health campaign, professional and philanthropic engagement and infrastructure would not suffice. To succeed, the children's health crusaders had to persuade Mexican mothers of all social classes to replace their familiar childrearing and domestic practices with medically approved techniques and to identify their efforts and their children's health with national progress.[35]

Babies: The Face of the Nation

To that end, in May 1922 *El Hogar* launched a contest to select the healthiest, most beautiful baby in Mexico. Published in the capital and dedicated to promoting a child-centered middle-class domestic culture, *El Hogar* devised a contest that combined two of the central features of Mexican women's magazines: articles on child health and domestic hygiene, and photographs of children. To enter the contest, readers were to submit photographs of children aged six months to five years. Each entry should include the child's name, place of birth, age and weight, method of feeding—formula or mother's milk—and information about the parents' health before the child's birth. A panel of prominent doctors would judge the entries based on those data and the traits portrayed in the photographs.[36]

The contest invitation read, "There is nothing more pleasing for a mother than to display her healthy and beautiful children," and elicited an enthusiastic response.[37] So many readers submitted photographs of their children that the editors had to extend the deadline. When the contest finally closed and the jury completed its meticulous, "rational and impartial" review of the entries, the magazine announced three winners: one breast-fed and two formula-fed. The verdict, illustrated with the winners' photographs, appeared in the issue that coincided with the September national holidays, linking the health and beauty of the readers' children to the birth of the nation itself.[38]

The contest testified to the many ways that concepts of childhood and child health fostered collective identities, although those identities were demonstrably selective. *El Hogar* invited women to participate in an issue of national importance, but strictly in their role as mothers. The terms of the contest, moreover, kept mothers behind the scenes while placing their children in the foreground: the healthy faces and bodies portrayed in the children's photographs proved the mothers were succeeding. The descrip-

NUESTRO CONCURSO DE NIÑOS

Doctores don Alfonso Pruneda, don Ismael Osorno y don Juan M. Gonzá-lez, distinguidos facultativos que nos dispensarán el honor de integrar el Jurado.

N UESTRO concurso de niños her-mosos y robustos está próximo a tocar a su fin. De acuerdo con las bases que hemos fijado y con el término de prórroga de que tienen conocimiento nuestros lectores, este concurso quedará cerrado el día último del mes en curso.

Al llegar esta fecha, reuniremos todas las fotografías que hemos recibido, sepa-rando aquellas que nos han llegado sin los datos necesarios, y las que están en regla serán trasmitidas a los res-petables profesionales que integran el Jurado Calificador.

Hoy nos es muy satisfactorio repro-ducir en esta página las fotografías de

el concurso el día último del presente mes, no daremos entrada a ninguna fo-tografía.

También recomendamos a las perso-nas que nos han enviado retratos sin los datos necesarios, que nos envíen a la mayor brevedad estos datos, por es-crito, a fin de que puedan sus niños fi-gurar en el concurso. Estos datos son los que expresan las condiciones de nuestro concurso, las que una vez más, reproducimos, como sigue:

Podrán participar en el concurso to-dos los niños de ambos sexos, de la Re-pública, comprendidos entre las edades de seis meses a cinco años.

Niños Rubén Orozco M., César Otilio Aguilar y Guillermo Guerra Verdejo. Estos tres graciosos niños forman par-te de los que se disputan el premio en nuestro concurso.

Las fotografías de los niños deberán ser enviadas a la Redacción de "El Ho-gar". Cada fotografía deberá venir acompañada de una hoja de papel en la que han de constar los siguientes da-tos: Nombre del niño y su edad; lu-gar de su nacimiento; nombres de sus padres; peso del niño en el día en que se tomó la fotografía; clase de alimen-tación que ha recibido en la época de la lactancia; noticias generales sobre su salud; noticia sobre la salud de sus padres antes del nacimiento del niño.

Un jurado compuesto por tres médi-cos de esta capital decidirá cuáles son los niños más robustos y más hermosos

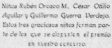

estos distinguidos facultativos. Al pro-pio tiempo, y siguiendo la costumbre establecida desde que iniciamos este concurso, reproducimos también algunas fotografías de niños de los muchos que para este certamen nos han llegado.

Poco tiempo queda ya para que las madres de familia que nos han envia-do fotografías, lo hagan. Las que de-seen remitirnos retratos, deben apre-surarse a ello, ya que una vez cerrado

entre los que muestren las fotografías que recibimos.

El Concurso quedará cerrado el día 31 del actual, y en nuestro número in-mediato daremos publicidad al fallo del Jurado.

Al publicarse el fallo se pondrán a disposición de las padres de los tres niños que el Jurado designe como más hermosos y más robustos, tres premios que daremos a conocer próximamente.

7

---

9. "Nuestro concurso de niños" (Our children's contest). Jury and instructions for *El Hogar*'s healthy baby contest. *El Hogar* 9, no. 151 (20 July 1922). Hemeroteca Nacional de México.

tion of the contest also suggested that all Mexicans were included, but in reality most of those sending photographs must have been of the middle class. And while the criteria for evaluating health may have seemed transparent, those for judging beauty favored European features. Judged by a panel of eminent doctors, the contest also pointed to the growing role of medicine in defining salient political and social issues and even family relations.

The terms of the contest reflected the extent to which the trend of medically mediated child care that originated in the late nineteenth century had become fully integrated into middle-class childrearing, domestic culture, and class-based identities. In addition to the sentimental model of virtuous motherhood that predominated during the Porfiriato, now mothers of all social classes had a heightened responsibility: to carry out doctors' instructions for raising healthy children. In 1914 a physician writing in the magazine had called the doctor "a friend of the family."[39] In 1922 another author in *El Hogar* observed that today, "It is not unusual to find in bedrooms, next to the baby's cradle of purest white, a treatise on domestic medicine."[40] The daily press and magazines for women and families barraged their readers with advice columns, especially on infant feeding and hygienic housekeeping.[41] Indeed, the contest criteria assumed that *El Hogar*'s readers were already conversant with the precepts and practices of modern infant and child care. The criteria also pointed to the influence of eugenics, through puericulture, on ideas about reproduction: the health of the child began with the health of the parents.[42] The photographs that readers submitted would have revealed symptoms of disease. Rashes or lesions, for example, might indicate congenital syphilis, a major concern among health reformers. A likeness of a healthy child presented evidence that parents had come to marriage virtuous and disease-free.[43]

Children's photographs also testified to a family's middle-class status and its participation in broader cultures of childhood. Like other illustrated magazines and newspaper supplements of the day, *El Hogar* regularly published photographic portraits of children. The illustrated press had featured similar pictures and photo-based beauty contests since the 1890s.[44] Since 1914 *El Hogar* had run a regular column entitled "The Pretty Tyrants of the Home," which reproduced studio portraits of children submitted by their readers. Newspapers ran similar columns: the Mexico City paper *Jueves*

Niño Alfredo Bejos

Nuestro Concurso
de Niños

El dictamen del Jurado
Calificador

Niña Maria del Socorro de la Peña.

Niña Angelina Galván y Santillán.

10. "Nuestro concurso de niños: Dictamen del jurado calificador" (Our children's contest: Judgment of the jury). Winners of *El Hogar*'s healthy baby contest. *El Hogar*, 10, no. 157 (20 September 1922). Hemeroteca Nacional de México.

de Excélsior called its gallery of child portraits "The Little Masters of the Home," and *El Universal* published children's studio portraits in its Sunday supplement.[45] They all publicized the names of studios, such as Foto Chic, where parents could have similar portraits taken.[46] The photographs themselves reflected patterns of consumption tied to middle-class cultures of childhood and domesticity: pictures of children showed that the home was child-centered and that the family could afford nonessentials.

These photographs further illuminated the elements that defined the middle-class culture of childhood. Newspaper and magazine articles often proclaimed the elements of protected childhood in terms of children's rights, such as the right to responsible parents, health, a loving home, play, and happiness.[47] In the photographic features of those publications, sentimental poses affirmed children's innocence, another central precept of the ethos of protected childhood. Historical and regional costumes spoke to the power of children to stand for continuity with the past and for national identity, as well as to represent middle-class aspirations to cosmopolitan

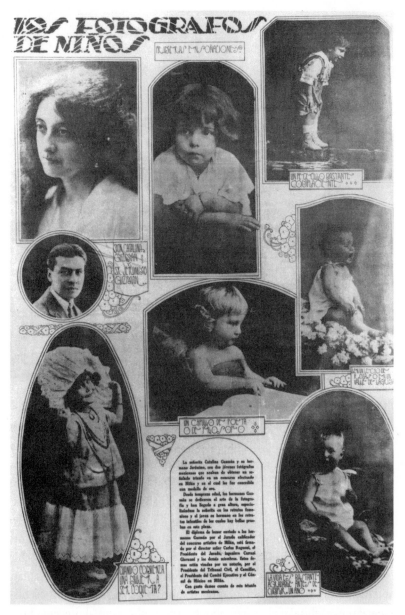

11. Photographs of children. From Catalina and Jerónimo Guzmán, *El Universal*, "Suplemento de Arte e Información" (Art and Information Supplement), 7 May 1922. Archivo General de la Nación, Hemeroteca.

sophistication. Chubby babies posed naked were the very picture of health. While the pictures reflected current photographic fashions, each portrait expressed liberal ideology by representing an individual child. The portraits of *El Hogar*'s contest winners affirmed those identities among the magazine's readers. Through pictorial features and photo contests for the healthiest baby, the press became both actor and arena for disseminating and reinforcing middle-class ideologies of family and childhood and tying them to national concerns.[48]

El Hogar's contest also reinforced the racial identities of the Mexican middle class. When the capital's newspapers and magazines ran beauty contests based on photographs, they revealed that in Mexico's fluid post-war society, whiteness and European features set the standard of mainstream beauty. For example, in 1921, when *El Universal* held a contest to select the prettiest Indian girl, the majority of the photographs submitted depicted not women who identified as indigenous but rather white, middle-class women dressed in regional costumes.[49] In early 1923 *Jueves de Excélsior* introduced a photographic feature on beautiful children; its editors stated their standards of beauty explicitly. The photographs would demonstrate to the nation and the world that "Hispanic beauty" predominated in the "physical features of our race." They also claimed that their efforts would promote national prestige abroad by counteracting the misperception among civilized Europeans "that we go around dressed in feathers" and that not a "trace of physical beauty" exists among the Mexican people. They inaugurated their journalistic gallery with photographic portraits of three girls from Mexico City, and asked their readers to admire "the delicacy of their features."[50] The judges of *El Hogar*'s contest for the healthiest, most beautiful Mexican baby selected winners whose appearance reflected the white, middle-class readership that the magazine's editors cultivated.

This preoccupation with race was closely tied to eugenicists' anxieties about the reproductive fitness of the Mexican people. Like their counterparts throughout Latin America, Mexican social theorists had struggled since the nineteenth century to reconcile European and Anglo-American theories of Caucasian physical and intellectual superiority with their own social reality of mixed indigenous, European, and African populations. In 1925 José Vasconcelos, head of public education during the Obregón administration, resolved this conflict with his concept of Mexico's "cosmic race," a stronger, more spiritual race forged from a fusion of the three, in which European—or Creole—characteristics predominated. This formulation would influence emerging conceptions of Mexico as a mestizo nation and culture.[51]

But some eugenicists took a different stance: they believed that race mixing exposed undesirable inherited characteristics, or atavisms. Moreover, they warned that the stresses and vices of modern life, especially those associated with the lower classes, like venereal disease, alcoholism, and women's fatigue from paid work, weakened Mexico's racial stock. In 1923 the film *Atavismo* confronted moviegoers with the gruesome effects of alcoholism, which eugenicists considered a primary cause of racial degeneration.[52] To counter these debilitating trends, eugenicists advocated the approaches of puericulture, which integrated parents' reproductive health with children's—and national—development.[53] These concerns had dominated the presentations at the first Congreso del Niño, where *El Hogar*'s editor was a participant. The terms of the magazine's healthy baby contest expressed the same preoccupations, and the portraits of the winning babies offered physical evidence of the vigor and the desirable racial characteristics of the next generation of middle-class Mexicans.

While *El Hogar*'s baby contest reflected the influence of discourses of race and reproductive health on middle-class identities and private life, it also measured the influence of the feminine domestic realm on public cultures of childhood. Like the frequent pictorial features of children in the mainstream press, the contest projected the sheltered realm of protected childhood into the public arena. In addition, the contest engaged women, as editors and mothers, in constructing collective identities and public cultures that included the feminine domain of home and family.

Indeed, the timing of the contest, first announced in May 1922, was neither coincidental nor politically neutral, but resonated with a heated debate over women's reproductive roles. Earlier that spring, *El Hogar*'s editors had opposed the distribution of contraception information in the socially progressive state of Yucatán.[54] The incident sparked a nationwide controversy that fed, in turn, off the growing debate about women's roles: should they remain at home, dedicated to bearing and rearing children, or should they play a greater role in production, the professions, and politics?[55] Access to contraception information went against widespread public opinion that motherhood was women's primary social responsibility. In opposing efforts to "avoid motherhood," *El Hogar*'s editors allied with the Asociación de las Damas Católicas (Association of Catholic Ladies) and with Rafael Alducin, the editor of the Mexico City newspaper *Excélsior*.[56]

Putting his editorializing into action, Alducin organized the first Mexican celebration of Mother's Day on May 10, 1922. In promoting the holiday, he affirmed that the Mexican family remained firmly rooted in tradition. Supporters of the holiday clearly understood those implications and also their religious connotations. Just before the first Mother's Day, a speaker to the Rotary Club declared, "In Mexico, the family is a sacred social unit."[57] The archbishop of Mexico endorsed the holiday and underscored these meanings.[58] Before long *Excélsior*'s Mother's Day graphics incorporated religious references to Madonna and child.[59] This imagery also stirred nationalistic sentiments: mothers were stand-ins for the Virgin Mary, especially Mexico's patron, the Virgin of Guadalupe. This symbolism constructed Mother's Day as a significant cultural challenge to the revolutionary secularism that restricted the power of the church. *El Hogar* endorsed Alducin's initiative to celebrate maternity.[60] Announcing its contest shortly after the first Mother's Day, it issued a call to arms to middle-class Mexican mothers to ratify their sacred reproductive role.[61]

El Hogar's healthy baby contest illuminated the powerful social and political currents that intersected in the crusade to protect and improve the health of Mexican children. Newspapers and magazines fostered national goals by spreading the message of hygienic childrearing to their middle-class readers. In doing so, the press circulated and reinforced representations of childhood and child health that affirmed the social status and identities of their readers and tied them to class-based cultures of domesticity and childhood. Health reformers stated repeatedly that their project would unite the nation across divides of race and class, but the terms of the *El Hogar* contest highlighted the ways that the child health campaign strengthened social distinctions.

The Other Faces of Health

Crusaders for children's health sought nothing less than national reconstruction and racial regeneration. Despite those universal goals, puericulturists aligned the categories of health and disease along axes of class difference – health and hygiene with privilege, and degeneration and disease with poverty. The anti–wet nurse discourse of the late nineteenth century had been based on a similar complementary relationship: the diseased, depraved working-class wet nurse served as the foil to the virtuous middle-class mother.[62] Like that earlier campaign, the methods for promoting the message of hygienic reproduction and modern child care practices were tailored to specific audiences. *El Hogar*'s contest illustrates the ways that puericulturists and their allies attached children's health to lofty ideals like patriotism and sentimental concepts of motherhood and childhood when they addressed middle-class audiences.

Health reformers dropped their sentimentality when they extended the concept of protected childhood to include working-class children, at least in terms of health. For curing the urban poor, health workers used hands-on, corrective, and sometimes intrusive methods to alter and discipline mothers' practices of personal and domestic hygiene and childrearing. Moreover, although the campaign to improve child health included all Mexicans, they were not included on equal terms: puericulturists trod carefully around sensitivities to social status and race difference when they addressed middle-class audiences.

In January 1923, shortly after the second Congreso del Niño, *El Universal* published a promotional piece about the "Eduardo Liceaga" Centro de Higiene Infantil, the first public clinic devoted to maternal-child health, named in honor of one of the founders of children's medicine in Mexico. The article exemplified the rhetorical interplay between concepts of health and patriotism and the subtexts of race and class that permeated publicity about the child health crusade. A banner headline rallied women to their patriotic duty: "Mexican Mothers, Give the Fatherland Healthy Children!" The headline was positioned over a photographic montage of studio portraits of healthy babies resembling those in *El Hogar*. While the headline's patriotic injunction ostensibly applied to all Mexican mothers and health to all children, journalist Rómulo Velasco Ceballos was careful to distinguish between his presumably middle-class readers and the working-class mothers and babies who were the primary objects of the urban infant health campaign.

Velasco Ceballos opened his article with a series of dire warnings drawn directly from the eugenics script: "Our race is degenerating. Our race is

12. "¡Madres mexicanas: Dad la patria niños sanos!" (Mexican mothers: Give the fatherland healthy children!). *El Universal*, 28 January 1923, sec. 4, pp. 4–5. Archivo General de la Nación, Hemeroteca.

sick." He then engaged his readers in a rhetorical dialogue that played on stereotypes of race and class. First, he supposed that they would associate racial degeneration with the lower classes and imagined them saying, "Poverty causes our children to be born weak and deformed. That is what kills them." He countered, on the contrary, "Poverty is not the cause. It is ignorance: an atrocious, frightening, punishable ignorance!"[63] This indictment applied to mothers regardless of social standing. He reinforced the universal goals of the child health movement by stating that the clinic drew no distinctions based on social class: rich and poor received the same attention, free of charge.[64]

But grouping all Mexican mothers and children together raised delicate issues. Newspapers would not win readers or their allegiance to the child health campaign by calling them degenerate, diseased, or atrociously ignorant. Velasco Ceballos avoided drawing derogatory connections between his readers and the clinic's patients. He mentioned the clinic's street address several times to emphasize that it was located in one of Mexico City's oldest "ramshackle and dirty" working-class neighborhoods. He anticipated his readers' disbelief that a "house of welfare" could exist "in the very heart" of this "archaic, wretched, and deplorable" environment.[65] Indeed, the first Centro de Higiene Infantil was deliberately located in a densely populated working-class neighborhood and was dedicated to modernizing the "archaic" and "punishable" practices of working-class mothers.[66]

The clinic's services targeted the factors that Mexican puericulturists saw as killing poor babies: disease and ignorance. From the start, the center was intended as a front line against venereal disease, which was prevalent among the entire population in the wake of the civil war. Doctors attributed the majority of miscarriages, premature and still births, and neonatal deaths to congenital syphilis. Although the law forbade syphilitics from marrying, many working-class couples lived in informal unions and did not have access to medical care, so their infections were undetected.[67] The clinic's prenatal program was meant to bring at-risk pregnancies to term: doctors tested pregnant women for syphilis, treated the infected ones, and then treated the affected babies.[68]

Velasco Ceballos mentioned the prenatal program, but did not offend his readers by naming the disease it treated. Similarly, in explaining why mothers should boil old clothes before using them to make diapers, he alluded only to the possibility of the baby contracting a shameful infection if the mother did not take precautions. His allusions would have been clear enough to his readers: syphilis was a shameful disease associated with loose morals, and it was also a secret disease, transmissible even when an infected person had no symptoms.[69] Yet even the journalist's discreet allusions highlighted the difference between the audience for *El Hogar*'s baby contest and the clinical program designed for the poor. That magazine never mentioned illness: the editors simply assumed their middle-class readers and their children were healthy, while the newspaper article was based on the assumption that their working-class counterparts were not. Moreover, the clinics' focus on venereal disease illustrated the way that health crusaders conflated medical with moral factors when treating the poor.

Velasco Ceballos also described in some detail the special methods devised for instructing poor and illiterate mothers in correct child care and housekeeping. In contrast to magazine and newspaper articles on childrearing and domestic hygiene directed at middle-class audiences, the clinic used posters to illustrate approved techniques, and the medical staff held daily sessions to explain the pictures to the mothers who attended the clinic. Every aspect of child care came under scrutiny: the newspaper article reproduced an image to illustrate the permanent damage mothers could inflict on their children if they carried them the wrong way. The warning pertained especially to working-class women who carried their babies slung over one hip or across their backs in their *rebozos* (shawls). Instructions in personal hygiene focused on the most basic principles: the center's staff demonstrated how to wash hands properly and used a mannequin to show how to bathe a baby. The staff also taught domestic techniques suitable for low-income households: they demonstrated, for example, how to construct a covered container for the baby's food and a baby's cot out of materials costing only a few pesos. Clinic administrators actively promoted the construction of baby's cots. Many poor families shared a single bed, a practice considered unhygienic and immoral. The article implied that improved infant care methods would raise the morals of the urban poor and transform their sickly children into the healthy babies depicted in the photographic centerpiece under the patriotic headline.[70]

A similar dichotomy between high-mindedness and hands-on instruction marked the celebrations of the Día del Niño (Day of the Child) in September 1923. The month of September was already punctuated by holidays marking the milestones of Mexico's history. Now the Departamento de Salubridad Pública tied health to patriotism by sponsoring a week of promotional events, including a festival in a downtown theater with patriotic performances by kindergartners and a speech by Dr. Alfonso Pruneda on "The importance of child care to the future of the Fatherland." The festival's themes reflected the idealistic rhetoric aimed at more privileged Mexicans.[71]

Meanwhile, in working-class barrios, the public health department celebrated by opening a second Centro de Higiene Infantil. And officials sponsored a healthy baby contest for the mothers who attended classes at the Liceaga clinic. There, the goals and methods were didactic. A journalist from *El Universal* reported that the mothers had learned their lessons well: they answered the journalist's questions about child care as a chorus. All breast-fed their babies at regular intervals. They bathed them every morn-

13. "Bellos exemplares de hombres fuertes y madres sanas de mañana" (Beautiful examples of strong men and healthy women of tomorrow). *El Universal*, 27 September 1923, sec. 2, front page. Archivo General de la Nación, Hemeroteca.

ing and then took them out for sun and fresh air. And none of them used pacifiers. As a result, their children were "beautiful examples of the strong men and healthy women of tomorrow."[72]

The awards for the clinic's healthiest babies revealed the social diversity of the mothers who frequented the clinic but highlighted the successes of the child health campaign among the poor. First prize went to a six-month-old boy whose parents lived in "extreme poverty," while second prize went to the son of a middle-class couple. The winning baby's mother told the reporter that she and her husband lived on a diet of tortillas and beans, although often they had nothing to eat. Despite the couple's deprivation, the reporter noted, the baby thrived because the mother followed the clinic's instructions to the letter.[73] The outcome of the contest appeared to demonstrate that poverty posed no obstacle to health and that the clinic's work could close the health gap between poor and privileged children. But focusing on the winning baby's glowing health slighted his parents' dire situation of frequent hunger.

This incongruity pointed to one of the central contradictions of the child health campaign. Reformers were convinced that health itself was social capital and that it also created wealth. But medical services to combat infant mortality and regenerate the Mexican race were never intended to correct economic inequality in the present: the benefits would accrue in the future as medicine cured the physical deficits of social backwardness. The babies treated today would become more productive adult workers. Individually they could improve their economic standing and collectively their labor would enrich the nation.[74] As the clinic's staff and their colleagues working in other neighborhoods quickly discovered, however, their patients' immediate economic plight influenced the reception and efficacy of the carefully planned medical services. In their efforts to attract mothers to the clinics, the medical staff, especially the corps of visiting nurses, would soon be drawn into the complexities of their patients' lives. In that process they gained a new appreciation of the social and community dimensions of children's health.

Curing Social Ills

El Universal's report on the 1922 healthy baby contest at the Centro de Higiene Infantil Eduardo Liceaga suggested that changing the infant care practices of the urban working classes would be a simple as opening a free clinic. The clinics' administrators and doctors and their target communities, however, acted on different understandings of the mother-child relationship and working-class family life. Clinic administrators and doctors believed that they were fighting with the weapons of modern medicine to save infant lives and thus the nation. They viewed working-class mothers through the twin lenses of ignorance and poverty and often did not distinguish between the two. They also viewed every aspect of family life from the perspective of children's health, to the exclusion of other concerns. These perspectives also shaped their understanding of the doctor-patient relationship: doctors would impart treatment and instruction; mothers would receive it and comply. Doctors and patients also held different understandings of babies' social environments. For doctors, their patients' homes, neighborhoods, and, indeed, the entire city held threats to infant survival. As critical as doctors were of mothers, they distrusted relatives and neighbors even more. So they instructed mothers to guard their babies from social interactions with others and to protect them from infection at all costs.[75]

In contrast, residents of the neighborhoods surrounding the clinics raised their children in the context of a daily struggle to meet basic needs on low wages. Many mothers who attended the clinics had factory jobs or worked as servants. They cared for their children around demanding work schedules and developed coping strategies that doctors considered hazardous to children, such as relying on support from neighbors and relatives. Mothers who sold goods or food in markets or on the street often took their babies with them, while they expected their older children to be independent and often to work. Living conditions allowed little privacy. Mothers who stayed at home did their laundry alongside their neighbors in the tenement courtyard, where all the residents' children played.[76]

As the urban child health campaign gathered momentum, however, the concerns of both doctors and working-class parents converged in their efforts to transform the city into a healthier environment. Health reformers saw this as a cumulative process, treating and curing one mother-child pair at a time; the way they kept statistics on appointments and treatments reflected this approach. Advice literature directed at parents showed that clinic administrators expected couples' relationships to be focused entirely on health and children. Mothers who received treatment and instruction at the clinics would convert their neighbors. In this way, the hygienic ideal would extend from individual bodies, to the families inhabiting single-room tenement apartments, to entire neighborhoods: "Clean homes and streets mean a healthy city."[77] Urban residents also wanted a healthier, safer city for their children. Their concerns often focused on conditions in their tenements, the safety of the surrounding streets, and the delivery of basic urban services like drinking water, sewers, and garbage removal. Instead of the model of individual responsibility—or culpability—fostered by clinic administrators, parents allied with neighbors, school administrators, and the visiting nurses to mobilize as communities to petition for services that improved the health of all residents.[78]

One of the first problems that doctors faced was enforcing infant care instructions beyond the confines of the clinic. Mothers of the working poor were thought to require close oversight to ensure that they adhered to a schedule of examinations and treatment and carried out an unwavering regimen of personal and domestic hygiene. The visiting nurses were charged with checking on their patients at home, and the clinics' monthly reports labeled as "disobedient" those mothers who missed appointments or failed to follow instructions.[79] In addition, a series of advice brochures distributed through the clinics gave detailed instructions that corroborated the methods taught in the clinics' classes. There is no way to know how many mothers—or fathers—actually read the advice literature. But the brochures convey a mixture of concrete health benefits with moralizing directives about family and community relations.

Without a doubt, the medical advice supported improved reproductive outcomes and infant survival. Women were urged to seek medical attention from the beginning of their pregnancies and to insist that certified midwives attend them during delivery. The brochures recommended a diet of fruits and vegetables, grains, and milk for pregnant women. Instructions for infant care focused on preventing illness, with breast-feeding the foundation of infant health. Doctors were particularly concerned that babies might be weaned too soon onto inappropriate diets and succumb to gastrointestinal diseases stemming from spoiled food. These factors took a higher toll in warm weather, leading doctors to warn that a child weaned in the summer months would be buried in the autumn.[80] Many housekeeping recommendations were eminently practical. A few simple measures made food safer and could prevent fly-borne disease and thus improve the health of the whole family. Census statistics showed that winter brought fatal respiratory infections associated with crowded and poorly ventilated living quarters. For that reason, mothers and babies should sleep with windows open and spend time outside every day.[81]

This child-centered regimen included fathers. Fathers were urged to guard their own health for the good of their offspring: brochures warned especially against venereal infection. Fathers should also fulfill their civic obligation by having their children vaccinated and registered. To encourage compliance, a civil registry was attached to the Liceaga clinic. Fathers were urged not only to take their role as protectors seriously but also to become active, involved parents. They should protect nursing mothers from arguments and worries and, along with mothers, be vigilant in guarding their babies from dust, dirt, and flies. Finally, while mothers and children remained safely at home, fathers should advocate for cleaner communities.[82]

Mothers appreciated the medical services that helped their children, and they seem to have spread news of those benefits by word of mouth: when a new clinic opened attendance started low but grew steadily. Still, to doctors' frustration, many mothers did not use the clinics as the administrators intended. They missed appointments because they worked during clinic hours. Too poor to afford private medical care, many were accustomed to waiting until they went into labor before calling a midwife or, as a last resort, going to one of the public hospitals. Only when their babies became sick did they seek professional help. Moreover, the best available medication for syphilis, derived from arsenic, required repeated injections and produced unpleasant side effects. No doubt both factors discouraged some women from completing the full treatment regimen.[83]

The advice literature reveals how little clinic administrators understood the poverty and multiple obligations of their patients. How were pregnant women to "abstain" from factory work for two months before giving birth, or ensure that their baby's day follow a strict schedule and still attend to other family members or go to work? For mothers who had domestics, some of the injunctions may have been easy enough to follow, but they were contradictory for women who did their own housework: on the one hand, new mothers should avoid heavy chores, while on the other, many of the instructions required considerable physical effort, especially in dwellings without running water. Other directions were overly exacting, such as measuring baby food to the cubic centimeter or bathing the baby in water of exactly 37 degrees centigrade.[84]

Still other instructions were simply impossible to follow for families on extremely limited incomes. Mothers who could afford only tortillas and beans certainly could not follow the recommended pregnancy diet. The baby was supposed to be given the exclusive use of the best ventilated room in the house, but many families shared a single, often windowless, room.[85] The stress of making ends meet could provoke domestic disputes and undermine the tranquility considered ideal for nursing mothers—and many nursing mothers worked. Among the clinics' patients, moreover, about 15 percent were single mothers, either widowed or abandoned: for them, the support of a protective and involved partner was simply wishful thinking.[86]

The brochures also offered advice that could strain relations between neighbors, especially in tenements where people lived at close quarters. Not only should mothers set an example of hygiene for their neighbors, they should also instruct them in the importance of following the same regimen. Meanwhile, under no circumstances should they take their neighbors' advice about childrearing: any advice except a doctor's could be harmful. Nor should mothers allow their neighbors to handle their babies.[87] It is difficult to imagine a first-time mother reprimanding a more experienced neighbor about childrearing methods or correcting the way her neighbors washed their clothes.

One woman's daily struggle to do what was best for her baby and her other children illustrates the predicament facing working mothers. Widowed while pregnant, this mother had four children ranging in age from six months to twelve years. She worked in a shoe factory to support them. They lived in a single tenement room, sleeping in a single bed. At night, they closed the apartment door, the only opening to the outside: this hardly met the strictures on ventilation. On her days off, she did the laundry and ironing, scrubbed the floor, and bathed her children. But on the days that she worked, her boys played in the street, her older daughter remained home alone, and a neighbor looked after the baby. So much for warnings against neighbors' interference: this mother depended on hers. She understood that breast-feeding was best for her baby, but her supervisors at the factory allowed her to leave only occasionally to nurse—certainly not at the recommended three-hour intervals.[88] The challenges this mother faced had nothing to do with ignorance: she had limited options and resources and she made the best of them, as did thousands of other working mothers throughout the city.[89]

Urban Encounters

Over time, doctors who had begun by focusing exclusively on disease and germs came to appreciate the ways that social and economic circumstances influenced their patients' health. Several years of work in the community of San Angel Inn taught Dr. Carlos Jiménez about the realities of his patients' lives. In 1925, after completing a vaccination campaign in that neighborhood, Jiménez began operating a pediatric clinic out of the Inspección Sanitaria there. He described the population he served as "purely working-class": several textile and paper factories were located in the area and employed about three thousand workers of both sexes.[90]

Jiménez was not prepared for the conditions he encountered. Like all doctors, he warned mothers against giving their babies inappropriate foods. But Jiménez was shocked at how many of his young patients were sick because they did not get enough to eat. Frustrated that mothers did not follow his instructions, he soon learned that they did not give their children the medicines he prescribed because they could not afford them. During their workday in the local factories, mothers were forced to leave their babies "unprotected or in the care of their older siblings or neighbors who cannot give them the necessary attention." And for the first year his clinic operated, it was clear that the mothers who brought their children represented only a small fraction of families in the area.[91]

Jiménez developed new strategies to address these local realities. He arranged with a nearby pharmacy to have medicines distributed for free. And he posted fliers and distributed leaflets promoting the clinic's services. By 1929, when Jiménez reported his progress to the newly created Servicio de Higiene Infantil, his clinic had reduced infant mortality among its patients by more than half.[92]

But Dr. Jiménez also realized that the medical program required complementary social services to meet local needs. To counteract malnutrition, he urged that a dispensary be established to distribute free milk to local families. He also recognized that babies were not the only children at risk. Like his colleagues in other working-class neighborhoods, he pressed for nursery schools so that preschoolers would be properly supervised and for factory nurseries so that workers could breast-feed their babies.[93] Working parents greatly appreciated such concrete benefits and petitioned the Departamento de Salubridad Pública to open clinics in their communities.[94]

The Servicio de Higiene Infantil, established in 1929, gave these efforts a fresh impetus. Under the direction of long-time child health advocate and eugenicist, Dr. Isidro Espinosa de los Reyes, the agency took over the administration of the Centros de Higiene Infantil and rapidly expanded their number in the city and its outskirts. Clinics like the one run by Dr. Jiménez now came under the umbrella of the service, as did the training of the visiting nurses. The expanded program took poverty into account: one new clinic had a supplemental food program for pregnant women.[95] But it was the visiting nurse program, ministering to the social dimensions of children's health, that made the clinics such an important resource for their surrounding communities. In exchange, however, families had to submit to close questioning about their personal lives and intervention into their family relationships.

Administrators viewed the visiting nurses as the feminine side of medicine. As described by Espinosa de los Reyes, they were to have all the virtues of motherhood. Theirs was the "noble and elevated task" of carrying the child health campaign into the "heart" of the home, not as a "sanitary police" but out of "true altruism."[96] Nurses should be motivated by a "collective love" for children, translated into a commitment to preserving children's health to safeguard and preserve the Mexican race.[97] Clinic administrators believed that working-class women avoided treatment because they were intimidated by the doctors and did not understand the benefits of modern medicine. The nurses had the job of winning their patients' trust so that they would keep bringing their children to the clinics. Their home visits to that purpose were called "reconquests."[98] But anywhere they found groups of women—on street corners, at corn mills, or washing clothes in tenement patios—the nurses were to preach the gospel of child health.[99]

The nurses also cultivated their patients' confidence to elicit information for a sanitary census. "Sanitary" was perhaps a misnomer, as much of the information that the nurses recorded about their patients' households concerned couples' relationships and parenting styles, or household income, debts, and amounts spent on necessities.[100] Administrators of the Servicio de Higiene Infantil and the nursing program considered these factors to be part of children's health environment. But they also saw this survey and the broader visiting nurse program as an opportunity to penetrate the "interior world" of their patients so as to understand their "way of thinking and being." Even so, nurses were reminded that their patients were not "laboratory cases" but "human beings who are suffering and waiting for an intelligent and effective intervention" to solve their problems. Despite these injunctions, administrators reiterated that "the ignorance of women in our humble classes is profound," not only in "domestic economy [and] moral education of their children," but also in their "complete lack of understanding" of "indispensable general knowledge of modern life."[101] The desire to understand the interior world of working-class mothers, the disparaging remarks about maternal ignorance, and the reminder to treat the poor humanely indicate the vast social distance that separated educated professionals and the urban working class. The visiting nurses were to bridge that gap.

In the first six months of 1930, the nurses dispersed throughout the city armed with questionnaires and visited more than a thousand homes. From a medical perspective their findings were encouraging. The census revealed a low incidence of disease associated with immorality. Most mothers were healthy: fewer than 8 percent had syphilis and fewer than 5 percent were alcoholics.[102] But the authors of the census questionnaire were as concerned about marital conformity and parental responsibility as they were about disease, and those findings appeared to confirm negative stereotypes of the urban lower classes. The nurses found that only 31 percent of their patients were legally married. Among the rest, 25 percent lived in amasiato (informal union) and another 30 percent had only a religious ceremony.[103] The high incidence of informal unions meant that 68 percent of the children were illegitimate and only 19 percent had been registered at birth. Some of these answers led to interventions: the nurses arranged for couples to marry and register their children.[104]

The nurses' questions also probed into intimate relations. They rated couples' interactions as affectionate, disaffected, or abusive. Likewise, they evaluated parents' treatment of their children: was their affection "instinctive" or "intelligent"; were they harsh or cruel?[105] Residents may not have known that the nurses were judging their family relations in this way. The nurses were instructed to take stock of the domestic situation while conducting conversations on other topics. They were not to take notes in front of their patients, lest they have "the least suspicion" that the conversation was in fact an inspection.[106]

Questions about marital relations, domestic violence, and parenting were important, but they led to some problematic interventions. Sometimes the nurses removed children from their families and placed them in public orphanages: did they take these actions because the parents were too poor to care for their children or because the nurses considered their affection "instinctive" rather than intelligent? On one occasion, the visiting nurse service received an anonymous denunciation of mothers who left their babies unattended. Many working mothers left their children in the care of neighbors or older siblings during the day, but the informer, who refused to leave his name, implied that these mothers effectively abandoned their babies. He also accused the women of loose conduct, implying that they did not deserve to be mothers. Even on the basis of such hearsay, the visiting nurse service, in concert with other welfare institutions, had the power to remove the children from their mothers' custody without consulting them.[107]

As their supervisor wrote in her own reports, some of the situations the visiting nurses encountered in their "moralizing and educational work" were so "intimate" that they eluded classification.[108] Administrators assigned the nurses this complex role: sometimes the nurses acted as a "judge" and sometimes as "a counselor, or to help resolve problems that are harming . . . the child, who is our concern."[109] With this mandate, the nurses made and acted upon moral judgments that were strongly biased against working-class family practice. Their charge to do so indicates how broadly their supervisors defined the scope of the health campaign: acting in children's best interests gave public health officials and employees unprecedented authority over thousands of families.

But the urban residents whose family lives were probed and recorded by the health workers had their own agenda and enlisted the nurses as allies to carry it out. In that process, the nurses, like Dr. Jiménez, came to appreciate the complex dimensions of working-class life and health. They often found, for example, that many of their patients' health problems stemmed not from lapses of personal or domestic hygiene but rather from the lack of clean drinking water and sewage removal. These factors "without a doubt" caused intestinal infections "that take the lives of many, especially in infancy."[110] To correct the problems, the nurses collaborated with community residents, who often took the initiative. The range of concerns that emerged from those interactions defined community and child health more broadly than the model of individual responsibility the experts emphasized.

The nurses played a crucial role as go-betweens, conveying their patients' concerns about housing and city services to their supervisors, who in turn had the ear of federal officials higher up.[111] Some health hazards were the fault of negligent landlords: in many tenements, up to twelve families shared a single latrine.[112] One nurse reported a tenement where uncovered wells in the courtyard posed a danger to the children who played there. Others reported tenement rooms without floors or with collapsing roofs.[113] Confronting landlords directly, the nurses used their "persuasive powers" to have the problems corrected: their supervisors and city officials believed their interventions were more effective than appealing to the law.[114]

Other health threats pointed to negligence among city officials, which could explain their reluctance to invoke city ordinances. Residents complained to the nurses about garbage dumps located next to schools. In one neighborhood, residents allied with the director of the local school and submitted a complaint about a dangerous intersection where two children had recently been struck and killed by cars.[115] In another neighborhood, residents complained that sewage spewed into an open railway cut and they petitioned to have new drainage pipes installed. They were willing to pay for the materials themselves but needed help from the municipality to connect the pipes to the main system.[116] Throughout the city residents acted collectively and strategically to convert the visiting nurses into advocates on their behalf and to use the high-priority child health campaign as political leverage. Perhaps they saw these demands as a fair exchange for letting the young nurses into their homes and divulging personal information.

The residents' petitions and nurses' interventions promised improvements in overall urban health, but economic conditions, already precarious, were deteriorating rapidly. By the summer of 1930, the global economic depression triggered by the Wall Street crash of October 1929 had reached the back alleys of the Mexican capital. In some of the poorer neighborhoods, nurses observed "a painful rise in poverty and unemployment." They reported that they could not demonstrate approved recipes because the "mothers had no way to buy the ingredients." Often they found "entire families" who had eaten nothing all day and little the day before.[117] As unemployment increased, the nurses began to bring their patients food and help them find work.[118]

Rising economic distress also exposed tensions between neighborhood residents and the clinic staff. Some mothers complained to the press that doctors would examine the truly poor only to meet minimum quotas. They said they were turned away from their local clinic with excuses that their clothes were dirty and that medicines had run out, while well-dressed patients were given preference. Rumors also circulated that doctors held other jobs that claimed their attention. Director Espinosa de los Reyes denied the charges. He responded dismissively that if the doctors examined only well-dressed patients, their attendance statistics would drop; everyone knew that most residents of the clinic's neighborhoods were poor. It was true, however, that patients were required to bathe and wear clean clothes for their appointments: this was to teach them the importance of personal hygiene. If they could not bathe at home, they could use the facilities provided at the clinics.[119] He also denied that the staff held other jobs, but they did. Dr. Federico Gómez Santos, for one, had served as doctor of puericulture at the foundling home since 1926 and as director of the Centro de Higiene Infantil "Francisco de Paulo Carral" since 1929.[120]

Both the nature of the mothers' complaints and Espinosa de los Reyes's dismissive rebuttal are revealing. They suggest that the condescending tone of the advice brochures and moral judgments embedded in the questions of the sanitary census also permeated doctors' attitudes toward their patients. Yet it is noteworthy that the mothers objected to being turned away from the clinics, not to the services they offered. Their complaints indicate that the Centros de Higiene Infantil had become important resources in the domestic economies of working-class families. Statistics affirm this: in 1930 the centers tallied more than ninety-two thousand visits of children under age two, and more than fifty-six thousand between January and May 1931.[121] Administrators concluded that high attendance demonstrated that "the public, especially mothers" had come to value the clinics that tried to "safeguard" their children's health.[122] The mothers' complaints also demonstrate a strong sense of class entitlement to the benefits of medical care for their children. Poor as they were, the women believed they and their children had as much right to treatment as their well-dressed neighbors. Just as urban residents organized collectively to improve community health and safety, these women spoke not only for themselves but also for their peers.

Thus, the Centros de Higiene Infantil may not have cured poverty, but their presence and broadly defined mission did reduce the unequal social distribution of medicine and urban hygiene and thus reduced poverty's impact on the health of thousands of families throughout the capital region. Although the clinics treated children only up to age two, the scope of the maternal-child health program fostered an unprecedented cross-class encounter focused on childhood and family life. While public health administrators celebrated the success of their campaign, working-class parents throughout the city could also have claimed some success in shaping the program to meet a greater range of their needs. Doctors like Carlos Jiménez in San Angel Inn and the corps of visiting nurses had recognized and responded to the social and economic challenges in their patients' lives and brought those concerns to the attention of influential officials. Families facing the immediate crises of job loss and hunger had received crucial assistance—all in the name of children's health.

At the outset, clinic administrators had envisioned a city transformed by the child health campaign, but they founded that vision on a view of their patients as obedient recipients of treatment and instruction. Instead, the more that the child health services addressed the social dimensions of health, the more urban residents actively seized opportunities to articulate community needs and to assert their collective right to a healthier environment and the benefits of medical attention.[123] Although those parents could not know the extent of their influence, the impact of their daily realities had also changed the way some prominent puericulturists thought about child health. Mexican delegates to the third Congreso Médico Panamericano (Pan-American Medical Congress) in 1931 included Dr. Espinosa de los Reyes, who would talk about the role of social work in public health. And Dr. Federico Gómez spoke on children's malnutrition and methods to combat it.[124]

Indeed, like his nineteenth-century predecessor Dr. Manuel Domínguez, the observant Dr. Gómez found that his young patients challenged his fundamental professional assumptions. The more he learned about their living conditions, the more he puzzled over the contrast between the babies he saw at the clinic he directed and those he treated at the foundling home. Director of one of the Centros de Higiene since 1929, Gómez observed that babies raised in crowded tenements were far healthier and more resistant to infection than the babies under his care at the clean and orderly foundling home, with its up-to-date medical equipment.[125]

Gómez's effort to understand this contradiction would launch a significant change in Mexican child welfare services, another important resource for urban families in economic distress. In the process, doctors and welfare administrators gained an appreciation of the labor of mothering that transcended rigid precepts of scientific child care. They also redefined the optimum environment for children: protecting babies from germs at all costs might not actually improve their health. Doctors came to realize that children thrived when their lives were fully integrated with family and community life. These realizations blurred the boundaries between clinic and community and reversed the hierarchy of doctor and patient.

Infant Mortality at the Foundling Home

Since his arrival in 1926 as a physician at the foundling home, Dr. Gómez had observed disturbingly high rates of morbidity and mortality among his infant patients. Indeed, the regimen of scientific infant care that the Servicio de Higiene Infantil promoted so aggressively among the urban poor produced contradictory results when it was fully enforced at the foundling home: it could not prevent a precipitous decline in the health of some babies and treatment only aggravated their symptoms. Gómez read widely in the foundling home's historical records and in current medical journals, and he recognized that those babies suffered from hospitalism, a debilitating and often fatal developmental syndrome afflicting infants in long-term institutional care. Only one treatment was effective: babies with hospitalism recovered on visits to their impoverished families. This seeming contradiction destabilized a fundamental distinction between doctors and their poor patients: doctors were supposed to be better at keeping babies alive than working-class mothers. Solving the problem of hospitalism at the foundling home gave Dr. Gómez a new appreciation for the mother-child relationship and the benefits of family life, even among the urban poor.

Since the eighteenth century, European foundling home administrators had observed that their infant charges suffered from a strange despondence: many died "of sadness." They believed that the malady stemmed "from lack of affection and home."[126] Administrators and doctors at the Mexico City foundling home, however, did not mention this malady, nor did they attribute infant deaths to the condition. Indeed, few foundlings spent their infancy in the Casa de Niños Expósitos because most were placed with wet nurses in nearby villages. On the occasions when wet nurses were not blamed for foundling mortality, ideological explanations predominated: nineteenth-century Mexican philanthropists attributed foundling deaths to a moral flaw inherited from their unmarried or poor mothers, whose sexual transgressions and incompetence justified the babies' internment and care by pious benefactors. In the late nineteenth century, staff physicians dressed those rationales in scientific terms to explain their failure to keep foundlings alive. When doctors could not attribute a foundling's death to a specific disease, they attributed it to "congenital weakness."[127]

After the revolution, in the context of Mexico's high-priority campaign to reduce infant mortality, the death of babies in state custody should have raised alarms. However, for most of the 1920s, even though it far outstripped the rate in the general population, the rate of infant mortality in the foundling home did not seem to require special explanations: 81.2 percent in 1926; 79.5 percent in 1928; and a lower but still problematic 61.3 percent in 1931.[128] Indeed, the orphanage was largely left out of child-centered reform although many of its medical personnel also served with the Servicio de Higiene Infantil. Located in the suburb of Tacuba from 1918 to 1932, the institution sank to a nadir of corruption and disease. Officials investigated allegations of mistreatment. Overcrowding required that two or three children share a bed. In 1931 admissions were suspended as epidemics of measles, rubella, diphtheria, and whooping cough swept through the wards. Only a few months later, with Mexico still feeling the impact of worldwide economic depression, a health inspector reported that the internal population had ballooned to 440 and that hygiene was deficient in every respect. In 1933, however, the foundling home moved to a new facility in suburban Coyoacán and started a new era. Inspectors found the technical and medical services in good order, placing the orphanage at a key juncture of public health and public welfare initiatives.[129]

The compound in Coyoacán was designed around medical criteria. Looking back, one of Dr. Gómez's colleagues wrote that the new facilities transformed the institution "from an asylum for abandoned children . . . into an establishment where children were studied meticulously from the point of view of integrated pediatrics."[130] The new plant boasted x-ray equipment, diagnostic laboratories to analyze the nutritional components and metabolic reactions of different diets, and a freezer bank for human milk. There were ample bathing facilities to maintain the requisite hygiene. Every ward had observation posts for the supervising nurses. A corps of uniformed wet nurses fed the babies on schedule. To prevent epidemics within the institution, new admissions spent ten days in quarantine, in "enclosed cells." Even when integrated into the general wards, each nursing baby occupied an individual cubicle and had a medical chart to indicate feeding schedules and diet.[131] In short, in its new facilities, the foundling home became a children's hospital.

Leaflets prepared in 1934 for distribution through the Centros de Higiene Infantil prescribed a similarly strict hygienic regimen for babies raised at home. Composed as a series of letters to a mother during her baby's first year, the leaflets instructed her to "habituate" her little one "to a schedule," and provided timetables for feedings, naps, baths, and daily fresh air. To keep the baby infection-free, mothers should minimize touching and social interaction: "Your child is growing quickly, . . . already he smiles, gurgles, and wants to grasp when you touch his little hands. It must make you want to pick him up in your arms and kiss him, but do not do it, nor let others do it. Kissing him may lead to catarrh or other illnesses." "Do not take him in your arms to put him to sleep, nor permit your friends or family to do so, or let them sing to him to soothe him: noises upset babies and make them nervous." "Accustom him to have fixed hours for play": the letters suggested one hour in the late afternoon.[132]

Only at the foundling home, however, could doctors enforce such a regimen to the letter, and then it produced unanticipated and counterintuitive results. The emphasis on medicine and hygiene isolated the infants. The more clinical the orphanage routine became, the more the babies were confined to their cribs. Like feedings, attention and handling were strictly

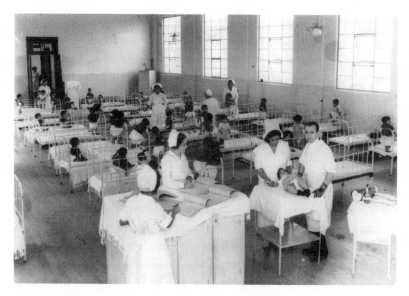

14. Doctors and nurses attending to older babies in the Casa de Cuna, Coyoacán, 1933–34. Archivo General de la Nación, Archivo Fotográfico Enrique Díaz, Sección Cronológica, 40/22.

scheduled. Confinement and feeding by the clock restricted the babies' social and physical contact with other children and with caregivers. Lack of stimulation and interaction with caregivers caused hospitalism.[133] In 1933 Dr. Gómez, now director of the foundling home, summarized his study of the syndrome in a paper, "The Problem of Prolonged Hospitalization in Infancy." Forwarding the paper the following year to the directorate of public welfare, he served notice that the tiny inmates of the foundling home confounded modern medicine and thwarted national public health initiatives of the highest priority.[134]

Gómez's study enumerated the symptoms of hospitalism, some of which doctors had only recently connected to the extended institutionalization of very young children. The affected babies became lethargic and indifferent to their surroundings and failed to develop physically and socially. Dr. Gómez observed that babies under a year old who acquired the syndrome seldom cried, not even to complain or demand attention. At ten or eleven months they could not sit unassisted. At a year they could not pull themselves up and remained immobile and expressionless. "They sit, propped up," he wrote, "And stay that way for hours on end without protesting of weariness; wet or dry, they never reveal by the least movement or demonstration any discontent; one never sees on their faces happiness or sadness; they give the impression of living sacks that vegetate in an untiring monotony."[135]

Still more troubling to Gómez, these babies became increasingly vulnerable to infection, and mortality among the affected group ran very high, despite the most assiduous medical attention, nutritious food, a sanitary environment, and hygienic handling. After four or five months, even babies who had entered the orphanage in good health became pale and anemic. Infections that in the general urban population had a highly benign prognosis, wrote Gómez, "in the wards" of the foundling home "kill with an astonishing rapidity."[136]

Hospitalism represented an ironic medical achievement, the fruits of scientific infant care. Although hospitalism had a history at least as long as foundling homes, it was only when doctors could identify individual infectious agents and by process of elimination clear the field of causation that they could grasp the peculiar etiology of the syndrome: melancholy, developmental deficits, heightened susceptibility to infection, and, frequently, death. Only when medicine could keep more of the interned babies alive could physicians observe the trajectory of the syndrome and its long-term, sometimes permanent effects. The prevalence of hospitalism among the foundling home babies and Gómez's astute observations of the syndrome marked the successful establishment of Mexican clinical pediatrics, a centerpiece of the revolutionary social program. Despite these advances, doctors could not cure hospitalism: indeed, in a sense, they caused it.

Babies who failed to thrive despite the doctors' vigilance recovered in the care of their families, even though their relatives "transgressed rules of hygiene" in ways that the foundling home medical staff "would not by any means excuse."[137] The children returned from their home visits with color, appetite, and resistance to disease, as if, wrote Gómez, they had received "an injection of life." Importantly, Gómez measured the children's improved health not only by their greater resistance to infection but also by their affect. They were "more active, more human, more aware of their environments. . . . They cry, respond, laugh, and, in a word, they are alive."[138] Children raised in the poorest homes—even homeless children rounded up in a campaign to eradicate begging—"were so different and so normal," although they did not "receive the daily medical attention" or the "careful diet given the inmates."[139]

In contrast, children raised in the foundling home lagged in all their vital functions, because, explained Gómez, they lacked the attention that even the poorest homes could provide but that the foundling home could not, despite the best intentions of the medical staff. This was an extraordinary admission from one of the child health campaign's foremost specialists. Most importantly, Gómez understood that children developed hospitalism because they lacked maternal attention and affection, interaction with older siblings, and an environment enlivened by new experiences.[140]

Gómez confessed that he had found only one cure for hospitalism: removing the afflicted children from the cold and monotonous orphanage environment and returning them to their homes. Gómez's prescription echoed the timeworn contrast between the warmth of the private home and sterile public institutions. Although critics of public welfare usually used that comparison to justify private philanthropy, in this instance it supported a complete reorganization of public welfare services for children. Gómez sought to integrate families with child welfare services and to recreate child welfare institutions on the model of the private home and family.

Gómez drew his recommendations from a range of sources. Child specialists in Europe and the United States were reaching similar conclusions: foreign medical journals suggested that orphanages create a home-like environment and that welfare services place more children in foster care. Gómez also advocated a program of "intense propaganda" through the welfare system's social workers to promote adoptions for orphans, "even promising free medical care" to adopting families. Parents who interned their children in the foundling home, moreover, should be required to take them out periodically. If the family were very poor, the foundling home should send food supplements for the period of the visit.[141]

Based on his new understanding of the requirements for healthy child development, Gomez wrote that the ideal foundling home would provide "all the social requirements of stimulation and entertainment that we find in homes." Instead of one large institution, he proposed a constellation of little "family houses" where "residents of different ages" would live with a caretaker: each unit would "reproduce a true home." He imagined those units surrounding an administrative and medical center that would exercise "close oversight."[142] Whenever possible, new foundling homes should be located in the country where children could play outside and receive personal attention, and older children could mix with the little ones.[143]

In a sense, this model already existed. Gómez had unwittingly described a neighborhood not unlike those surrounding the Centros de Higiene Infantil, where children lived with their families and had access to free medical care under the "close oversight" of clinic doctors and visiting nurses. There were, of course, significant differences between his utopian facility and urban realities. In the doctor's vision, caretakers were devoted exclusively to children and did not have to do factory or domestic work to support them. The orphanage would also be more spacious and better furnished than tenement apartments and have plenty of running water. Instead of a working mother struggling to keep her home and children clean, a staff of cleaners and laundry workers would maintain medical standards of hygiene. Finally, Gómez envisioned this idyllic scenario in the countryside, not the city. He had in mind the vacation camp in Cuernavaca that the foundling home had borrowed from the Asociación Cristiana Feminina.[144] Despite the differences, however, all of Gómez's recommendations were attempts to approximate the interactions between mothers and children in a family setting. True, he proposed highly mediated relationships: the substitute mothers of his "family houses" would be vetted state employees. But it is noteworthy that in the interests of children's health, Gómez encouraged the kinds of social environments and interactions that his medical colleagues had once considered threats to children's well-being.

Children and Family in the Revolutionary Collectivity

Gómez made his recommendations at a propitious time. Lázaro Cárdenas, president from 1934 to 1940, equated the secular family with the nation. Like Calles, Cárdenas asserted that the "revolution cannot tolerate that the clergy continue to use children and youth as a means to divide the Mexican family."[145] When Cárdenas became president, he threw off Calles's political control and sent him into exile in the United States, but he too constructed a model of family that validated his political goals. Indeed, Cárdenas went further than any of his predecessors to realize the revolutionary project outlined in the 1917 Constitution: not only land and labor reforms but also the ancillary social programs that supported the working classes. In that process, the president's solidarity with workers and peasants made children the symbol of the masses.

In his rhetoric, policies, and personal actions, Cárdenas cemented the symbolic ties between family and nation, between family and his administration, and between children and the working classes. In October 1935 Mexico hosted the seventh Pan-American Congress on the Child to showcase state programs for children.[146] A month later, in the celebrations of the revolution's twenty-fifth anniversary, boys marched under a banner that read, "The child is the most beautiful ornament in working-class homes."[147] The following year, events cultivating the administration's family orientation included a distribution of gifts by officials of the Secretaría de Hacienda (Finance Ministry); a children's festival sponsored by the Secretaría de Educación Pública and held at the Departamento de Trabajo (Department of Labor); a visit to the foundling home by the First Lady and another by firefighters; and ceremonies of the Semana de Higiene (Health Week) in October 1936.[148]

On his extensive travels throughout the country, Cárdenas also made a practice of bringing individual children under his personal protection. By 1938 ten of these children lived in the presidential residence in Mexico City, where Cárdenas oversaw their education "as if they were his own children." Each child represented one of the social and economic sectors that were the focus of the president's policies. One boy from Oaxaca was descended from Benito Juárez, the father of Mexican liberalism. Another came from the oil region of the Gulf coast, tying the president's fatherly benevolence to his expropriation and nationalization of foreign-owned oil companies. In an interview with reporters from the magazine *Hoy*, one boy of twelve said he wanted to grow up to be a doctor, and called Cárdenas "a very good man with a big heart, who is always concerned for the well-being of the poor."[149] These children validated the president's politics at their most militant and populist.

Yet the child-oriented policies of the Cárdenas administration were more than symbolic. Between 1934 and 1940 revolutionary ideals reinvigorated welfare services, which until then had been left out of the limelight accorded public health. The president's politics of solidarity with the working class recast assistance from the government as a right, not a handout, and a benefit to the nation, not merely to the needy individual. In 1935 a publicist for welfare argued that the new philosophy integrated national economic development with public well-being: assistance "forms the fatherland, receiving the proletarian human element from birth, bestowing health and physical strength, educating it . . . according to . . . the pure ideals of the Revolution . . . and incorporates it into society, converting it into a productive element, worthy and honest, that works together for the well-being of the collectivity."[150] The president himself featured prominently in publicity about public welfare. One article, whose headline proclaimed, "The Modern Concept of Assistance: In Brief, Social Solidarity as an Obligation of the State toward the People," described President Cárdenas as "instigator of modern Mexican public welfare and of its methods."[151] To reflect the new orientation and its congruence with "the revolutionary process," welfare administration was placed under a ministry first named Asistencia Pública (Public Assistance) and later renamed Asistencia Social (Social Assistance).[152]

The president's policies also fostered a positive and nationalistic model of motherhood. In contrast to his predecessors, Cárdenas was open to feminist demands to expand women's political, economic, and social rights. His support did not result in women's suffrage, but it did influence the tenor of family-oriented government programs. Feminists had long argued that work and motherhood should be compatible.[153] Welfare officials responded by expanding and multiplying existing programs specifically for working mothers. Some were already well established, such as the public soup kitchens, called Comedores Públicos, and kindergartens known as the Casas Amiga de la Obrera (Friend of the Woman Worker Houses). New services, such as mothers' clubs and additional day care centers, opened in working-class neighborhoods, including one day care especially for the children of domestics.[154]

Federal officials also reclaimed Mother's Day from social conservatives. They repudiated the sentimental and pious version of motherhood promoted by most rhetoric associated with Mother's Day celebrations. Instead, officials developed a secular, populist version of motherhood, with events such as the 1936 Homenaje a la Madre Proletaria (Homage to the Proletarian Mother). The Secretaría de Educación Pública organized ceremonies that honored working-class and agrarian mothers. Those events also

15. "Como la Casa de Cuna suple ahora el hogar" (How the Casa de Cuna now substitutes for the home). *Asistencia* 2 no. 9 (July 1936). Hemeroteca Nacional de México.

encouraged nationalism by promoting the works of Mexican authors, the president's political milestones, and, of course, medicine and hygiene.[155]

In 1939 welfare secretary Silvestre Guerrero distinguished between the Cárdenas government's concrete support for mothers and the sentimental and increasingly commercial Mother's Day celebrations: "The Mexican mother needs effective assistance to resolve her diverse problems and not empty words of praise with which she is often flattered." Such rhetoric only obscures the "reality of the situation in which she frequently finds herself," which negates "her authentic rights and value."[156]

These formulations linked family policies to the president's prolabor policies and programs of state-led industrialization, and like those policies they came under attack by his critics. In 1937 a journalist writing in a popular illustrated magazine took Cárdenas's personal welcome of hundreds of refugee children of Spanish Republicans as the occasion to lambaste his administration's left-leaning policies and their supposedly destructive effects on the family and the nation. The writer blamed Bolshevism, free love, and divorce for the degradation of childhood in the Soviet Union and, by implication, in Mexico under Cárdenas: "The State, the universal communist stepmother, can never replace the authentic mother."[157] Others lamented that the Spanish children were receiving celebrity treatment while thousands of Mexican children were hungry and homeless.[158] A broad range of policies that could be seen as supporting mothers and children came under fire. Writers critiqued the policy of allowing women prisoners to live with their babies in jail: "Why are these babies in prison?" asked one journalist. Another queried, "Can there be anything more immoral" than exposing young children to the vices of condemned criminals?[159] Much of this criticism was founded on the assumption that only the private family represented authentic Mexican values. To these critics, attempts to promote a public collective family that was tainted by *cardenista* politics not only fell short but also corrupted mothers and children living under the auspices of public agencies.

In this context, officials cultivated the image of child welfare institutions as true homes. The public welfare administration even published a magazine, *Asistencia*, aimed at a general audience to provide a forum promoting public agencies as true families.[160] Journalists sympathetic to the Cárdenas administration's politics lauded the substitute mothers and motherly feelings in the "collective" homes of public welfare, formerly considered cold and sterile environments. Writing for a weekly magazine, journalist Isabel Farfán Cano described the foundling home as clean and bright, like an authentic home. She chose an extraordinary example to illustrate motherly qualities among the staff: a wet nurse. The journalist described her encounter with a uniformed woman, weeping for a child who had left the home. Farfán Cano thought at first that the woman had been separated from her own child until she learned that she was speaking with a wet nurse. The woman told her that she had nursed the baby girl for a year, and "in all that time, I have seen her repeatedly at the doors of death. I cared for her as if she were my own daughter."[161] Although the nurse had children of her own, she told Farfán Cano that perhaps she loved this one more because the little girl did not have a mother. This uniquely sympathetic portrait of a wet nurse contrasted markedly not only with nineteenth-century characterizations but also with puericulturists' disparaging remarks about the foundling home at the outset of the child health campaign. The public, collective homes of child welfare could now supply the element that had formerly been missing: the warmth of feminine, motherly care.

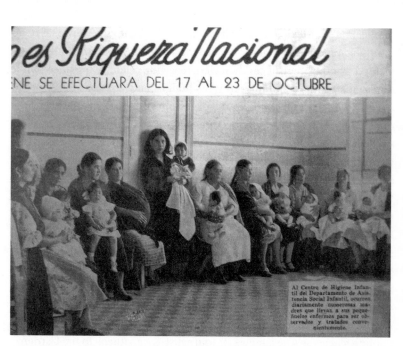

16. "Salud del pueblo es riqueza nacional" (The people's health is national wealth). *Hoy 34* (16 October 1937). Hemeroteca Nacional de México.

Gómez forwarded his observations on the causes and cure for hospitalism shortly before the Cárdenas administration rearticulated the place of mothers in the revolutionary family. His proposals were well received. Thanks to this convergence of social medicine with social policy, the doctor's recommendations reached far beyond the foundling home: they influenced a reorganization of child welfare services premised on the emotional benefits of the mother-child relationship. Guerrero, secretary of public welfare, launched the new initiative in 1939. Public welfare would reduce the number of children who were interned in large asylums by establishing a number of smaller facilities, especially for children just past the age of weaning. Guerrero noted that those children were prone to emotional problems of separation and neglect, and "almost always they become sick—some cases are fatal."[162]

The agency he directed would establish foster homes, where "substitute mothers" would nurture a maximum of five children. Officials predicted that the foster homes would provide a "cozier and more human" environment than the foundling home or the Casa del Niño, formerly the Hospicio, notorious for its overcrowding and lack of discipline. The state would pay a pension for each child and cover medical and maintenance costs. Women of any marital status who applied for the positions would, of course, undergo rigorous inspections of their health, conduct, cultural potential, and moral habits, because state-supported motherhood required conformity to state-approved criteria.[163]

Gómez's observations on hospitalism and his recommendations to combat it clearly influenced the new policy. Guerrero stated that the innovation of small group homes was based on the knowledge that "the asylum, in Mexico as in other countries, in reality does not permit the child, despite hygienic care ... a complete and easy development in the physical, the intellectual, or in the moral sense." Invoking but not naming hospitalism, Guerrero noted that "frequently the little ones sadden and become sick," but no one had found "the way to combat this strange malady successfully." In contrast, children flourished when placed in smaller settings, "where they encounter the warmth of the family" and "establish cordial and affectionate relations" with other children and caregivers. Within days of first publicizing the program, Guerrero announced that public welfare had opened twenty foster homes to "reduce to a minimum the collective internment of tiny tots" and "settle them in the heart of honorable families." Most of the 160 children selected for transfer to the smaller environments were from the foundling home.[164]

Bolstered from the outside by a growing international consensus on the benefits of home care and nationally by presidential support of policies that preserved "family integrity," the group home program continued to hold its place in federal child welfare policy through the administration of Manuel Ávila Camacho, the successor to Cárdenas. In 1941 Dr. Gustavo Baz, secretary of public welfare under Ávila Camacho, reinforced the program's rationales in a radio address: "Throughout the world large concentrations of children ... have been abolished, because they nullify their personality. Everywhere children are placed in small groups in homes, which return to them the affect they have lost."[165]

Although the medical value of the maternal-child relationship was now recognized, policy makers continued to be influenced by negative characterizations of poor mothers. They still thought infants were better off in professional hands than in the care of even closely supervised substitute mothers. In 1943, at the first Congreso Nacional de Asistencia Social (National Congress on Social Assistance), Dr. Luis Berlanga Berumen summarized the rationales behind the continuing policy of institutionalizing infants in clinical settings: because the general population did not understand the principles of puericulture, "the biological care that the nursing baby requires for the first year and a half of life is better achieved and at lower cost in technically constructed and well organized foundling homes than in substitute or foster homes." Once children were eighteen months old they could be transferred to the smaller group homes, because then internment in large asylums was considered "highly prejudicial" to their development.[166]

Berlanga Berumen's statements reflect some of the contradictory influences that puericulture had on concepts of motherhood and childhood, on concepts of collective responsibility for children, and on Mexican public policy. Just when mothers had gained the right to equal parental authority, puericulturists raised the stakes of childrearing, especially infant care, so high that specialists questioned mothers' capabilities to fulfill what many Mexicans believed was their fundamental social role. The puericulture movement and the health reforms it fostered promoted a concept of childhood so threatened and a regimen of child care so technical that they became the realm of the specialist. Dr. Federico Gómez began his career as a proponent of that approach. But Gómez was unusual among his colleagues in recognizing the limits of scientific childrearing and the nonquantifiable value of reproductive labor. Through his study of hospitalism he came to perceive that infant health and survival required the integration of family life with assistance for needy families. Gómez probably would not have had this epiphany without his experience working in the urban maternal-child clinics, where he was exposed to the social dimensions of children's health.

Countless commentators extolled the virtues of privileged mothering and disparaged working-class mothers. But by focusing on children's well-being, Gómez came to understand the value of mothering and family life among the poor. Although his proposals for integrating family life with social services did not result in a policy of outright grants or family pensions to help keep children with their own parents, his proposals did carve a space for mothering within welfare services. His insights influenced welfare policy in part because they came during a presidential administration that had appropriated and rearticulated the family metaphor to represent solidarity with Mexico's working classes.

Republic of Reproduction

Well before 1928, when Calles announced the dawn of an era of unity under the banner of a revolutionary family, or 1934, when he claimed children for the revolutionary collectivity, children had come to represent the relationship between society and the paternal state and between the state and the urban lower classes. Embodying the vanguard of modern Mexico, children became the real and metaphoric repositories for a wide range of aspirations and identities during a period of sometimes wrenching political, economic, and social transformation. As the government expanded its role in social life and culture through public education, health, and welfare, children of the working poor became prominent beneficiaries of those reform programs. Their health and well-being measured the state's delivery of the revolution's promise and strengthened its legitimacy.

The child health campaign and the public policies it fostered both forged and fed on the broader metaphor of the nation as a family. The puericulturists who initiated the child health movement extended the concept of protected childhood to include all Mexican children and encouraged Mexicans to invest in a collective responsibility for children's health. In tying children's health to the nation's future, puericulturists cultivated children and the family as powerful political metaphors. Political leaders drew on the resonant and flexible meanings of family to inflect Mexico's institutionalizing revolution with an array of meanings: unity and power, responsibility and continuity. Calles invoked the concept of family to overcome the factionalism that threatened the consolidation of the revolutionary state and attacked reactionaries by appropriating children for a militant revolutionary collectivity. Cárdenas cultivated the links between the concept of family and responsibility for children and a politicized collectivity. But rhetoric at the presidential level was not the only indication that social and political identities coalesced around concepts of family and childhood.

The concept of the revolutionary family drew on a spectrum of established identities and also generated new ones. It had roots in the liberal foundation of the secular family, but it also resonated with sentiments reminiscent of Porfirian pieties about family and motherhood. The revolutionary family was inclusive, but different social sectors and actors were included on different terms. At the outset of the child health campaign in the early 1920s, puericulturists associated health with the middle class and whiteness. Those associations infused the rhetoric of the child health campaign aimed at middle-class audiences, so that health became another difference that affirmed their social position and self-image and the privileges of child-centered domesticity. Puericulturists also linked disease and racial degeneration with the poor, while, at the same time, sincerely believing that medicine could cure traits and behaviors associated with racial inferiority. In these ways, the child health campaign provided a powerful opportunity for medical professionals to mark the vast social gulf between themselves and those they considered backward and socially inferior. But it also let them use medicine as a way to bridge that gulf.

For the urban working poor, who became primary targets of both the medical and moralizing strands of the child health campaign, the services of the urban clinics became important family and community resources. The ways that urban residents used the political leverage of the child health program to improve their housing and neighborhoods offer some insight into their collective concepts of community health and well-being. Although the services of the Centros de Higiene Infantil were confined to pregnant women and children up to age two, working-class communities lobbied through the visiting nurses for improvements that supported better health for all. In these ways, the child health campaign provided an arena for urban, working-class families to contest the identities of ignorance and irresponsibility projected onto them by medical professionals and public officials. And if health was part of belonging to the national collectivity, urban, working-class residents asserted their right to have access to medical care.

The clinics and improved urban infrastructure certainly brought material benefits to the poor. Then, during the Cárdenas administration, the policy focus on the working class supported a political and rhetorical shift: children became stand-ins for the working class and peasantry, social sectors favored by the president's politics. The child health campaign had laid the foundation for this by promoting the concept of collective responsibility for children. While the class inflections embedded in the national or revolutionary family may have bolstered the power of the concept to mobilize armies of professionals on the one hand and working-class communities on the other, the privileged place of children in that collectivity provided a basis for shared identity and purpose. This explains in part why attempts to appropriate children for one political faction or another were hotly contested.

In less than two decades, the concept of childhood founded on health and the notion of collective responsibility for children's health made Mexico a substantially more child-centered society. The child health movement also altered the meaning and changed the experience of childhood. But in subjecting domestic and childrearing practices to an ambitious reform program, the campaign also targeted the labor of social reproduction in ways that highlighted the problematic position of women in the revolutionary family and society more broadly. Extending the concept of protected childhood to all Mexican children, reformers placed the best interests of the child in tension with other family needs. In these ways, the campaign bolstered arguments against women's paid work, even as it fostered new career opportunities for women in medicine, nursing, social work, and public health administration.

Mexico's developing child-centered consciousness had far-reaching effects on the development and delivery of social services. Like their counterparts in public health, welfare officials overseeing legal adoptions pondered the characteristics that qualified a woman to be a state-approved mother. The concept of protected childhood militated against child labor, but women who applied to adopt would find that their own labor also came under official scrutiny. Officials of the juvenile court evaluated whether mothers and fathers met new standards of parenting to determine whether children should be placed in state care. Parents countered with their own definitions of acceptable family dynamics and expectations of their children. But often in the ensuing negotiations between families and officials, new concepts of childhood changed the terms of the argument and the outcome for the families in question.

Domestic Economies

Family Dynamics, Child Labor, and Child Circulation

In April 1930 thirteen-year-old Carlota Morales grew tired of cleaning, cooking, and minding her two small brothers while her mother, Carmen Romero, ran a clothing stall in Mexico City's La Lagunilla market. So she joined a group of girls, all neighbors in the same tenement, and ran away from home. After hiding for a few hours in a church not far from her home, Carlota emerged and went from house to house looking for work as a domestic servant. She quickly secured a position only a few blocks from her family's address by claiming to be a homeless orphan in search of shelter and wages.[1]

Carlota's story came to light because she stole money and clothing from her employer, whose complaint brought the girl before the Tribunal para Menores, Mexico City's juvenile court founded in 1926. To determine what had caused Carlota to go astray, the court sent an inspector to interview her mother. Carmen Romero's account of the family's history and domestic arrangements may not have given court officials much insight into the girl's motives for stealing, but her narrative did shed light on her family's strategies for survival and the ways they intersected with Mexico City's networks of child circulation and market for child labor. Like the majority of minors who came before the juvenile court during the 1920s and 1930s, Carlota came from a poor family. She had dropped out of primary school and moved in and out of a series of live-in jobs. Her early employment and residence away from home point to the widespread and persistent economic marginality that drove most child circulation and labor, even as specialists in child development increasingly condemned child labor and new laws prohibited it. Her responsibilities at home also point to well-established family labor practices: by having Carlota take care of the little boys, Carmen Romero could work for pay in the market.

Carlota's work and family histories resonated with those of her predecessors before the revolution but they unfolded in a new ideological and institutional landscape. Established in 1926, the juvenile court was a direct outgrowth of the child protection wing of Mexico's puericulture movement. Participants in Palavicini's 1921 Congreso del Niño were among the leading advocates of reforming Mexico's juvenile corrections.[2] The court was founded on the understanding that children and adolescents, owing to their intellectual, emotional, and physical development, were not fully responsible for their actions. Rather, reformers argued that children and youth broke the law because they were exposed to corrupting influences at home or at work. Although court officials were obviously interested in reducing youth crime, they sought primarily to rescue children and adolescents from those negative influences and set them back on the path to responsible and productive adulthood. To that end, the juvenile court had the power to remove them from their families, place them in detention, and take over the job of discipline, education, and job training.[3]

The court's mandate to reform and reeducate young offenders and reintegrate them into the social and economic mainstream placed the institution at the intersection of cross-currents of changing ideas of childhood, the family, and social responsibility for children. While the ideology of protected childhood—now extended to include adolescence—shaped the court's mandate, its founders and officials held contradictory attitudes toward both working-class families and underage labor. On the one hand, they believed that the family, as the primary social unit, was the foundation of social stability. On the other hand, they blamed parents for corrupting their children. They also believed that work corrupted minors. At the same time, they saw work as a moral force against crime and vice: vocational training and activities meant to instill a strong work ethic were central to the tribunal's reform program, and the court also used job placements as probation. But because they were committed to family stability, court officials often sent children home to work to help sustain their families. Thus the court simultaneously criticized and relied on the same social practices that perpetuated child circulation and labor. The court's inability to mitigate the conditions that kept Carlota and her class peers out of school and pushed them into work—and often out of their family homes—spoke to the limitations of public programs in the face of the complex social and economic dynamics that shaped working-class childhood and adolescence.

But the court, like the public maternal-child health services, fostered thousands of encounters between officials and working-class families. Despite the unequal power relations of these interactions, parents and children had opportunities to express their own ideas about their relationships and their labor. Their accounts reveal the strategies and values that held their families together. Confronted with the complex connections between subsistence and family relations among the urban poor, officials often compromised between ideal and practical interventions. As a result, the court was as much an instrument of continuity as it was of change in the construction of the capital's networks of circulation and market for underage labor; thus, it acted as a powerful agent constructing and perpetuating class-based family forms.

Carlota's Escapade: Child Circulation Revisited

When Carlota told her employer that she was a homeless orphan needing work, she fabricated her story from strands of her own family's very real predicament intertwined with her interpretations of social practice that linked labor and protection. Three years before, the girl's father had abandoned the family to join the army, or so he said. Left alone to support her five youngest children, Carmen Romero arranged a dishwashing job for Carlota in a restaurant belonging to a comadre; the girl also ate and slept at her workplace. Romero sent Carlota's younger sister to live with another comadre: that daughter worked with her benefactor during the day and attended school at night. Carlota, however, had a hard time settling into her new life and work. After two short stints at the restaurant, she worked for a month as a live-in domestic but quit because she did not like it. Thus, although she was not an orphan, Carlota had indeed lost her father and had been placed in service that required her to live apart from her family. But no free ride awaited the girl when she left paid work and returned home. In exchange for supporting her, Romero expected Carlota to do household chores and care for her preschool-aged brothers while she worked for income outside the house.[4]

Once her husband left her, the composition of Carmen Romero's family limited her resources for covering home and child care while she worked. She had three grown sons: two married and one still single, a clothing vendor like herself. Given their gender and life stage, none of them was available to undertake housework and child care. Her personal and economic challenges and the resources she mobilized to meet them reveal the structures that linked households like hers to the urban informal economy.[5] Child circulation and child labor were two of those links. Given men's high rates of un- and underemployment and women's limited employment options and low wages, families needed multiple incomes just to subsist.[6] Often their only option was to move their daughters into other households for live-in work or place their sons in low-paid jobs or unpaid apprenticeships. Sending her daughters to live and work with comadres solved two problems: the girls were supervised and she was relieved of their daily maintenance. But Carmen Romero still had little boys at home. Perhaps she took them with her to the market, or perhaps she left them with a neighbor while she worked, like many other mothers in similar situations. But when Carlota quit her first live-in domestic job, Carmen Romero solved her child care problem by bringing her daughter home. After all, her late nineteenth-century predecessors frequently withdrew their daughters from the Hospicio at about Carlota's age, probably to substitute for their mothers at home, just as Carlota was obliged to do. With Carlota in charge of the housework and child care, her mother could pursue work to support the whole family.

Many families like Carmen Romero's scraped out a precarious living in the city's informal market and service economies. Some vendors succeeded in establishing a fixed location in one of the bustling centralized markets and could rely on a small but steady income. But thousands of adults and children subsisted on minute wages or tiny profit margins as street vendors, market porters, and assistants, or as *papeleros* (newspaper vendors) and lottery ticket sellers. Or, they found low-end service jobs such as boleros (shoe shiners), errand runners, dishwashers, laundry workers, nannies, and domestics — the occupations generally available to their class before the revolution. Public and official opinion scarcely differentiated between the children in this fluid informal workforce and vagrants and delinquents.[7] Carlota's escapade only reinforced such views, especially as she stole from her employer. But the capital's informal economy absorbed children and adolescents who were expected to help support their families even though they had little schooling and few marketable skills. Their options, like their parents', were constrained by multiple factors, some explicit, such as laws regulating child labor, and some tacit, such as the gender and generational divisions of family labor and of the urban labor market.[8]

Carlota, like many other girls of her age and class, also faced a limited choice between housework and child care at home or similar but poorly paid work outside: washing dishes in a restaurant, child-minding, or performing domestic service. She had attended primary school but never finished third grade and had acquired only a few household skills from her work experience. When an older neighbor in the tenement suggested that the girls run away to find domestic jobs, she jumped at the chance to escape her family obligations.[9]

Carlota calculated well when she pretended to be an orphan seeking a domestic position. Her story and her employer's willingness to believe it — or at least to act as if she did — drew on enduring practices of child circulation and persistent associations between domestic service and protection. Like generations of Mexico City residents before her, Carlota's employer was prepared to consider domestic work the solution of first resort for a supposedly homeless orphan girl. Before the revolution similar assumptions had driven the foundling home and Hospicio's domestic placements under the rubric of informal adoption. Furthermore, the elision of protection within domestic work affirmed the employer's social status and sense of largesse but reinforced the domestic's dependence and subordination by blurring the boundaries between work and the supposed benefits of a family environment. Based on these assumptions, the woman gave Carlota a job instead of notifying the authorities.[10]

Carlota and her employer drew on social practice that stretched back decades — even centuries — but the girl soon found that a new government agency with considerable power determined her future. She was arrested for theft, detained by the court, and placed under observation until a panel of judges set the terms of her release. Although Carlota had made it clear that she did not want to return to her mother, the judges were persuaded that a family context was best for her: she needed close supervision, especially as she had reached puberty. Officials and moralists had long been concerned about guarding the virtue of young women and usually considered the home the safest place for them.[11] Indeed, her family had the same concerns. As soon as Carlota came home from her walkabout — and before her arrest — her mother and one of her brothers took her to the police station for a physical examination to determine whether or not she was still a virgin. At least physically, her virtue was intact. Given these preoccupations, it was clear that Carmen Romero's work in the market prevented her from overseeing her daughter properly. So the court remanded Carlota to the supervision of one of her married older brothers, and Romero lost control of her daughter's labor.[12] The paper trail stops at this point, but it is likely that Romero brought her younger daughter home to take up Carlota's former tasks of housework and child care.

The resolution of Carlota's case exemplifies the pivotal role of the Tribunal para Menores in the domestic economies of thousands of working families in Mexico City. But urban families like Carmen Romero's confronted systemic economic instability as well as periodic personal crises that public programs could not address. Indeed, the assumptions about gender, work, and family that shaped public services could reproduce the predicaments of the working poor. Carlota's employer was not alone in eliding domestic service with the protections of a family environment. After all, parents like Romero placed their young daughters in service. And the Mexico City juvenile court routinely released girls on probation to work as domestics for respectable families.[13]

As the late nineteenth-century patterns of use of Mexico City's welfare institutions amply demonstrate, the economic circumstances and strategies of families like Carlota's were not new, but the state's powers to intervene in family life had greatly expanded.[14] In the nineteenth and early twentieth century, welfare waited for parents to petition to have their children admitted to an orphanage or the trade school to assist with education and discipline. But during the 1920s and 1930s, as reformers and public officials took an unprecedented interest in children's health and education, the mission statements of the fleet of new public agencies mandated direct interventions into family dynamics in the best interests of the child. Moreover, the definitions of good and bad parenting and protected childhood and adolescence that informed official interventions shifted the ground and altered the meanings, if not necessarily the practice, of time-honored family strategies like child circulation and child labor, while remaining firmly rooted in well-established assumptions about gender roles at home and at work.

Family, Child Labor, and the Law

By the early twentieth century, child labor had become one of the salient differences between poor and privileged Mexican families. Lawmakers and reformers were acutely aware that regulating child labor would be key to forming a modern economy and society. The revolutionary Constitution of 1917, the Ley Federal del Trabajo (Federal Labor Law) of 1931, and institutions of social reform such as Mexico City's juvenile court created new legal frameworks reflecting those concerns. But the new slate of laws created tensions: between established labor practices and new ideas about childhood and adolescence as protected life states, and also between parental authority to allocate children's labor as part of an overall household strategy and the state's expanding roles in social reproduction. Public secular education and public medical services focusing on reproductive health and on modernizing domestic hygiene became cornerstones of Mexico's revolutionary reconstruction and vectors of the state's ideological and material involvement in family life. In these ways, parents' private decisions about their children's work intersected with high-priority public policies and programs.[15]

Yet other aspects of the law supported and perpetuated family practices that often entailed child labor, which in turn often moved children out of their homes. Thus, the law made contradictory statements about children's social and economic roles and about authority over them.

In some ways the law strengthened parents' authority over their children's labor. Granted equal authority with fathers in the 1917 family law, mothers potentially had a greater role in domestic decision making. The family law also extended the period of parents' authority over their children by raising the legal age for marriage from fourteen to sixteen for men and from twelve to fourteen for women.[16] Since marriage emancipated a minor from parental control, raising the legal age for matrimony made a statement that early adolescents were not ready for the responsibilities of forming and supporting a family. This change also reflected widespread medical concerns about the years between puberty and full physical maturity — the life stage that specialists now called "adolescence." Doctors considered early childbearing physically harmful to mothers and children alike.[17]

Legal definitions of parental discipline and filial obedience remained much the same as in earlier codes.[18] Included in those intergenerational relations were the obligations of support, called *alimentos*, inscribed in law since the colonial period.[19] Parents owed their children shelter, clothing, education, and medical assistance; in turn, children owed their parents respect, obedience, and support. The 1917 family law and the civil code that went into effect in 1932 reaffirmed these obligations and stated that they were "reciprocal. He who gives it has the right, in turn, to demand it."[20] But the law did limit the extent of support owed: it had to be within the means of the person supplying it, and the obligation to support ceased if the person simply lacked the means.[21] Within this system of reciprocity, children owed their parents support and older siblings were obliged to support their younger brothers and sisters until the latter reached age eighteen.[22] At the same time, the law defined a strict sexual division of labor: specific articles outlined women's obligation to care for the home and children and men's obligation to sustain the family with work.[23] In practice these gender roles also applied to children and shaped the kinds of work they were likely to perform.

The 1917 Constitution, however, made it clear that the revolutionary state had an interest in limiting child labor and went much further than earlier legislation in doing so. Only three years earlier the legal age for work had been raised from seven to nine.[24] When Article 123 raised the minimum age to twelve, the Constitution's framers defined the kind of childhood that was appropriate for Mexico's revolutionary society: it would be longer than under the old regime and protected from labor.[25]

During the 1920s and 1930s, Mexico's militant labor movement and its ties with the revolutionary state won important advances for workers in formal jobs, but fewer for informal workers.[26] In the mid-1920s, for example, the Confederación Regional Obrera Mexicana (Regional Confederation of Mexican Workers) actively organized workers in the urban informal sector and enabled some to win concessions from their employers.[27] Some unions—including some of newspaper vendors—had child members.[28] But unaffiliated unions of garment workers, market vendors, renters, and corn mill employees marched in the 1925 May Day parade to protest their exclusion from the mainstream labor movement.[29]

The Ley Federal del Trabajo of 1931 reflected the ambiguous status of informal labor. The code recognized informal work, offered new protections to young workers in informal occupations, and introduced valuable benefits.[30] But it also placed most informal work in separate categories from formal jobs and granted informal workers different rights. This pertained especially to the work available to children and adolescents. Employers could pay apprentices entirely in shelter, food, and clothing and could count room and board as 50 percent of domestic servants' pay.[31] The law also permitted the continued use of verbal contracts for casual and domestic labor. Many such workers found that the class, age, and gender differences between themselves and their employers put them at a disadvantage in negotiating the terms and conditions of their jobs.[32]

As migrants from all parts of Mexico poured into the capital, increasing the density of social life and extending the city boundaries, family economic strategies played out in a highly stratified and gender-segmented labor market.[33] Workers of all ages confronted familiar challenges, such as low wages for unskilled work. In addition, production was increasingly mechanized and many jobs required higher rates of literacy and training than before. Constitutionally mandated public education was supposed to prepare the workforce for Mexico's modernizing economy, although that preparation was different for boys and girls: a substantial part of girls' education focused on domesticity and preparation for motherhood.[34] And employers continued to discriminate against women, to the point that women dropped from a third of the industrial workforce in 1920 to less than a quarter by 1930.[35]

The progressive slate of labor rights outlined in the Constitution was meant to improve workers' bargaining power and protect women and children from exploitation. By law, primary education was mandatory, not optional.[36] But many families on the capital's economic margins could not afford to keep their children in school. And the same laws intended to protect women and children at work often pushed them into jobs beyond the reach of regulation or unions. Parents who put their young children into paid work out of need now violated the law. And despite legal protections and the evolution of concepts of childhood free from labor, child labor remained inextricable from urban, working-class family relationships.

In Mexico City the law and its loopholes had material consequences for thousands of working families. As before the revolution, these interrelated factors were especially relevant in women-headed households. The 1940 census of the capital counted more than 18,000 widows between twenty and thirty-nine years old, the age group most likely to have young children, and more than 34,700 female-headed families with at least two dependents. The same census counted 387,170 women in unpaid domestic work and 66,793 women categorized as paid servants.[37] With up to half their wages paid in room and board, adult domestics rarely earned enough to support a family. Moreover, adult live-in domestics had to leave their children in the care of others. As a result, many families chose to place their young daughters in service and their young sons in unpaid apprenticeships or low-paid jobs to save on their support. In these ways, Mexico's revised labor laws and modernizing formal economy perpetuated the working conditions of both adults and children on the margins of the capital's economy. Those margins were frequently located in the homes of more privileged families.

The Juvenile Court: Youth, Work, and the Family

Between 1926, the time of its foundation, and 1935, the Tribunal para Menores reviewed more than eleven thousand cases.[38] In that process, it became a significant forum for debate over the nature of the state's role in social responsibility for children and of working-class childhood. While family ideology in official circles became increasingly child-centered, many working-class families were hard-pressed to fit that mold. Their predicaments often challenged official theories about the working classes, their family morality, and children's social roles. Thus, despite the ethos of protection and reform that shaped the court's mandate and informed many of its decisions, it also became a primary player in Mexico City's system of child circulation, setting the terms and conditions under which children were removed from their families and placed in institutions or in other households to work.

In the early 1920s activists in Mexico's child protection movement spearheaded the foundation of the juvenile court, but the concept of a separate corrections system for minors had roots in the Porfiriato. In theory, youth corrections under Díaz favored education over punishment. In practice, boys and girls were tried as adults, the corrections facility for boys was little more than a jail, and no facilities existed for girls until 1906.[39] Reformers noted those deficiencies and recommended immediate reorganization emphasizing rehabilitation, but the onset of revolution postponed the task. After the fighting subsided, the rise of the Mexican puericulture movement provided the impetus for a major restructuring of laws and institutions for young delinquents. The new system drew on pioneering U.S. models and emphasized education and job training over punishment.[40] The court's mission to reform errant youth into responsible, productive adults also reflected the ideal that all Mexicans should contribute to national reconstruction. With these commitments Mexico City's juvenile court joined the constellation of public agencies carrying out high-priority federal programs in secular education, vocational training, hygienic domesticity, reproductive medicine, and child health, all targeting families of the urban poor.[41]

The tribunal's founders developed a sympathetic social analysis of juvenile delinquency. Reformers recognized that adolescence marked a distinct stage of intellectual and physical development and believed that the "psycho-physical perturbations" of puberty caused youth under the age of fifteen to commit "illicit acts" because they lacked "discernment."[42] They also believed that children and adolescents were susceptible to environmental influences and that most youth offenses stemmed from poverty and family problems. Many considered poverty a cause of youth crime: statistics appeared to support this theory. One early study found that fewer than

2 percent of the parents whose children came before the court could be considered professionals. The rest worked as laborers or market vendors, or had low-paid jobs in Mexico City's diverse commercial venues. While nearly 11 percent lived comfortably, more than 20 percent of tribunal clients were living in absolute destitution and nearly 50 percent "in very marked poverty on the brink of indigence."[43]

Like their counterparts in public health, legal reformers often conflated poverty with family pathologies. Authors of the 1928 Ley sobre Previsión Social de la Delincuencia Infantil (Law on the Prevention of Juvenile Delinquency) for the Federal District stated that "in our social context" young delinquents were "victims of legal or moral abandonment, of deplorable examples in an inadequate and unhealthy social environment, of a family context deficient or corrupted by their parents' neglect or perversion."[44] Despite this bleak depiction of family life among the urban poor, reformers were equally worried that 50 percent of the court's young clients did not live with their families, but with distant relatives or nonkin, employers, or on the street. These patterns prompted some social analysts to posit that family separation caused juvenile delinquency.[45]

Social analysts and court officials held contradictory views about the role of work in the family. Some saw work as the cause of family separation, while others saw work as the solution for keeping families together. Those who viewed work as a source of cohesion believed that it benefited both adults and minors by acting as a moral force against family dysfunction and youth crime. They saw work as normal and worried that nearly one third of the court's young clients did not work.[46] Ramón Beteta, author of a report on beggars in the capital, was hired to reorganize the public shelters for boys living on the street. He attributed children's begging rather than working to the dysfunction of their parents and disorganization of their households.[47] In 1935 another official argued that the best way to prevent youth crime was to "create a situation of steady work and sufficient remuneration for the classes of the lower layers of the population, which is the principal source of juvenile delinquency, thus eliminating the misery that forces the separation of family members."[48]

Those who saw work as the problem believed that family stability depended on maintaining the model of a male breadwinner and stay-at-home mother—the gender division of labor that provided the moral foundations of protected, nonworking childhood. At times they seemed to value this ideal more than family survival. Psychologist Matilde Rodríguez Cabo, who later directed the tribunal's network of institutions, conflated moral with economic factors in family stability when she attributed the extreme poverty of many delinquents' families to paternal abandonment. But she also blamed working mothers for youth crime: their absence from home during the workday left minors unsupervised and vulnerable to harmful influences.[49] Thus, fathers who rejected their family responsibilities pushed mothers out of the home where they belonged and into work, which in turn corrupted their children.

Taking a slightly different stance, Roberto Solís Quiroga argued that the kinds of family problems that gave rise to juvenile delinquency originated in work itself. A leader in the reform of juvenile corrections and a pioneer in Mexican psychology, Solís Quiroga also served as a judge in the juvenile court. Writing in 1937, he blamed work for exposing children and adolescents to exploitation because of the low wages they earned, but he focused particularly on the emotional experiences of young workers. He worried not only that the company of adult coworkers corrupted children and youth and that heavy labor hardened them, but also that these conditions turned them into insensitive, self-centered adults open to criminal influences.[50] Solís Quiroga was particularly concerned about children who worked as live-in servants, for it was in that context that working children confronted more privileged children at close quarters: "The minors observe the discrepancy that exists between their status and that of the other children in the family, with the result that it stimulates feelings of ill-will, of envy and even hate." This, he believed, opened young domestics to the temptation to steal or damage their employer's property.[51]

But it was not only children's labor that exposed them to corruption. Solís Quiroga believed that parents' work "disorganize[d] the home," particularly when mothers worked as servants or in restaurants, jobs that often demanded night work and left children unattended. He even argued that fathers who worked outside the home could not give their children due attention.[52] His critique implied that the children of families that needed such work to survive were destined to become delinquents.

Like the sanitary census conducted by the Servicio de Higiene Infantil, the home visits and family interviews conducted by the tribunal's corps of inspectors influenced the court's actions. Seeking both collective and individual explanations for youth crime, the inspectors investigated life histories, work and income, and spousal and intergenerational relations. Court officials based their interventions on evaluations of whether or not parents expressed and acted on concerns for their children's well-being and future that met new standards in health and education. They also measured family dynamics against new models of parenting that valued affection over harsh discipline.[53]

Always on the lookout for parental vices like alcoholism, court inspectors and officials were also inclined to blame stepparents for family dysfunction. Their concerns echoed those that arose during the debates over divorce during the revolution and revealed their negative view of serial unions. But when they analyzed the statistical profile of the families in question, they found that stepparents had a positive or neutral impact on family "organization" just as often as they had a negative impact.[54] Officials also judged parental morals by whether or not their children had become sexually active. Far more boys than girls came before the court and most boys were picked up for small infractions. In contrast, a significant number of girls' cases involved sex. Although early sexual initiation and activity were considered normal for boys, for girls they were equated with illegal underage prostitution and were often attributed to parental failings.[55] For these reasons, court officials were surprised when statistics revealed that few of the parents of young offenders exhibited the kinds of sexual promiscuity, particularly prostitution, they so often attributed to the urban poor.[56] Despite the statistics, however, these characterizations of the poor remained deeply engrained in official and public opinion.

To counteract negative influences of all kinds, officials ensured that many children and adolescents, even those originally arrested for petty theft, spent a few months to several years in correctional institutions, which provided a range of services. There they underwent psychological evaluations and received medical treatment. They also completed their primary education and were given gender-specific job training. Both boys and girls participated in team sports and group activities meant to socialize them into modern ideas of health, work, and citizenship.[57]

But not all children were removed from their families or their jobs. Often the judges merely admonished parents to supervise their children more closely or send them to night school and told children to obey their parents and work hard.[58] Indeed, although Solís Quiroga, among others, believed that work "disorganized" families, in practice court officials concluded that families whose members supported each other were "organized" and beneficial to children. They recognized, moreover, that the families whose children came before the court depended on child labor to sustain even a marginal subsistence and keep the household together. When those considerations prevailed, and when the tribunal released children and adolescents from detention into probation, boys were usually placed in apprenticeships with mechanics or artisans, while girls were placed in domestic service.[59] In this way, despite sometimes significant differences in the ways that court officials and families conceived of parents' and children's roles and relationships, their interventions frequently reinforced widespread practices of child circulation and child labor.

Reciprocity and Child Labor

Both child circulation and child labor contravened the principles of protected childhood, but they often stemmed from fundamental and long-standing legal definitions and social understandings of the labor obligations that flowed from and cemented family relationships. Parents and children owed each other support. These reciprocal obligations were inextricable from family bonds. Even when children left home to live and work in other households or on the street, their work and wages earned them the right to claim a place in the family.

Juvenile court officials recognized those obligations. Indeed, the law and the principle of family reciprocity applied not only to working-class families but to all Mexicans. True, middle-class families could afford to prolong their children's education, but children still owed their parents honor and respect, which would be expressed in material terms by support in later life. A tribunal inspector described one middle-class household composed of the parents and their grown sons, a daughter-in-law, and a grandchild as "an organized family of honest habits: they join together and help each other."[60]

So did families in more precarious circumstances. An inspector characterized one such family as "extremely poor but honest." One of the older sisters sold clothing, and a brother, fourteen years old, worked in a textile factory. They gave their wages to their mother, and their contributions helped keep three younger siblings in school.[61] Similarly, the children of Herlinda Gómez, a widow, contributed to the support of her household of six. An adolescent daughter brought home wages from her work sewing in a shirt factory while a son worked as a packer in a nail factory and gave half his wages to the household.[62]

The older brother of Carlota Morales, the young runaway whose story opened the chapter, also acted on his obligations when he offered to take his sister into his home. Writing to the court that "I am a married man and have a family independent of my mother," he promised to take charge of her education and prepare her for an appropriate occupation. He asserted, "I believe I can make her into a hardworking girl."[63]

Child labor was an integral part of this reciprocity. One court inspector outlined the role of child labor in maintaining the cohesion of a working-class family: "The family environment has been completely favorable for the minor's intellectual and moral development. He is part of an honorable family, which has the means to maintain themselves hygienically and without privation. Lately they have fallen on hard times, but even so have the means to live relatively well, although of course they had to put their children to work."[64]

As the inspector's comments suggested, children's labor obligations had both material and moral dimensions. Legally, children had control of their earnings from work.[65] But parent-child relationships were obviously more complex. The law stated that "children, whatever be their status, age, and condition, owe honor and respect to their parents."[66] Handing over part of their earnings expressed children's respect in material terms. Moreover, parents could claim that children who failed "to apply themselves to work" forfeited the right to support. So did children who flouted parents' authority by leaving home without permission.[67] Thus, although some court officials believed that work "disorganized" families, others believed that the reciprocal obligations of support were signs of a cohesive family based on strong intergenerational relationships.

Indeed, in the eyes of court inspectors and officials, this kind of family reciprocity could counterbalance factors that might seem to represent moral disorganization. For example, nine-year-old Ricardo Arrieta worked on the street selling newspapers with his mother, Dolores Uribe, and his two younger sisters. He had attended school only briefly and could not read or write. Uribe believed her son was lazy and inclined to vagrancy and wanted the court to help her discipline him. The boy's lack of education alone could have tilted the court's opinion against his mother. Even worse, after Ricardo's father died six years earlier, Dolores Uribe lived with a series of men and bore children with each one. Nevertheless, the inspector praised the family. Although they lived on a collective income of barely two pesos a day, they appeared "very humble . . . but hardworking." The stepfather fulfilled his paternal obligations by trying to teach the boy the trade of masonry. An older sister dutifully contributed to household support by taking in laundry and ironing. Moreover, the mother was "extremely affectionate and within her ability cares for the education of her children."[68] Uribe's understanding of her obligations, bolstered by appropriate maternal sentiments, persuaded the tribunal to endorse her efforts to discipline her son to work harder, even though the boy was below the legal age for work.

As this case suggests, the more closely a working-class family maintained the approved gender divisions of labor, the more orderly it appeared to be in the eyes of the court inspectors and judges. For instance, the father of Agustín Velasco, a bolero of fifteen, beat him for staying out late without permission. Yet except for "the father's extreme severity," the inspector described the family as "well-organized . . . moral and hardworking." The inspector's perceptions were shaped at least in part by the family's conventional structure. Agustín lived with his legally married parents and two older brothers in two small rooms, "perfectly clean and humbly decorated." The family conformed to the ideal of a male breadwinner and female homemaker: Agustín's father supported the entire household on his earnings as a jeweler. The father's fulfillment of his obligations influenced the tribunal to affirm his authority and expectations of respect, obedience, and work. The officials ruled that the boy should return to his family, finish school, and enter a workshop to learn the trade of his choice.[69]

When poverty and work separated families physically, the understandings of reciprocity could hold them together emotionally. For example, even though one twelve-year-old boy had been driven out of his home by an abusive stepfather and was forced to sleep in a public shelter, he worked and took some of his earnings to his mother every day.[70] Fourteen-year-old Enrico Robles had a similar story. When the death of his father and ensu-

17. Boys selling newspapers on the street, Mexico City, ca. 1920. Instituto Nacional de Antropología e Historia, Fototeca Nacional, Fondo Casasola.

ing poverty separated Enrico's family, he continued to fulfill his filial obligations. His younger sister had moved in with an aunt and uncle, and his mother worked in a restaurant. Enrico, meanwhile, lived on the street and worked a series of jobs in fireworks and ceramics factories, and as a bolero and papelero (newspaper vendor), among others. Enrico remained loyal to his mother and took her some of his earnings every week. The inspector who interviewed him noted that the boy "preserved intact the moral organization his parents provided."[71] Every time Enrico Robles took his mother some of his weekly earnings he also affirmed the survival of a meaningful relationship despite physical separation.

The court's inspectors often equated work with morality, but, as Enrico's actions showed, work was a way to express relationships. Children used the language of labor to express their feelings toward their parents and drew on those feelings to give meaning to their work. Miguel Rojas, at thirteen an apprentice shoemaker, stated that he did not love his father because he treated his mother so badly. He gave all his wages to his mother and further asserted that she was the one he would support; for her sake he would always try to get ahead in his work.[72]

Similarly, when Francisco Espinosa and his mother, Soledad Velázquez, reached an impasse in their relationship, they expressed their respective positions and emotions through the principles of reciprocity. Widowed in 1928, Soledad Velázquez sewed and washed laundry to support her family, until poverty forced her to place Francisco and his two sisters in the Hospicio. By 1933, when Francisco was released from the institution at age fifteen, he asserted that his internment had ruptured his relationship with his mother and therefore terminated his filial obligations. The boy refused either to recognize his mother's authority or to contribute work or wages to the household.[73] His contention did have a legal basis: because his mother had not been able to support him, he did not owe her work or wages. But his behavior also suggests that he experienced placement in the Hospicio as emotional abandonment.

Soledad Velázquez appealed to the juvenile court for help resolving the family crisis. Her account to the tribunal emphasized the ways that she had fulfilled her maternal obligations: she had struggled to raise Francisco to be an honorable adult and had sacrificed so that he could learn to work. After his release from the orphanage she found him a job in a metal workshop. But Francisco would not reciprocate. Dismissed for smoking at work, he refused to look for another position. He was disrespectful and disobedient, insolent and cruel, and stayed out late without her permission.[74] Certainly, Velázquez had sufficient reason to deny her son any further support, but that was not her intention: she had brought him home to be part of the family and that meant contributing to the household.

The tribunal attempted to work out a family reconciliation. Although no record of the interview with Francisco survives, it seems that court officials supported his mother's position. Francisco tearfully protested that he was a good son, acknowledged that he had been ungrateful, and promised to mend his ways.[75] There is no way to know whether Francisco and his mother overcame the deep rift caused by the boy's internment. But they shared the understanding that Francisco's work represented his commitment to the family.

Francisco Espinosa felt that his time in the Hospicio had ruptured his relationship with his mother, but work offered him the opportunity to rebuild it after years of painful separation. For many such families, children and adolescents made vital contributions to the household economy and understood that their working represented emotional as well as material reciprocity. Because of these meanings, when children left home to work, they had not necessarily broken family ties. Likewise, when poverty separated family members, the meanings they invested in their work helped them stay connected. Thus, labor gave families of the capital's working poor concrete and material ways to express their ideas of family and their roles and relationships as parents and children.

This significance explains in part why family violence often became entangled with work. Because Soledad Velázquez wanted her son to be part of the family, she expected him to work to contribute to the household. Parents invoked the same principle to justify evicting a child from the house: a child who did not work could not stay at home.[76] Many boys living on the street told similar stories. One thirteen-year-old boy left home and lived on the street because his stepfather forbade him to eat at home unless he worked and contributed wages to the household.[77] Another boy of fourteen told tribunal officials that he had run away from home because he lost his job and feared that his stepfather would beat him.[78] A child who abandoned the home without parental permission forfeited the right to support.[79] Violent abuse could achieve exactly that result. "A little more than a year ago," a court inspector wrote of another boy in 1929, he "left home owing to the bad treatment he received from his stepfather, who did not let him sleep in the bed nor eat at the table with the others."[80]

In the middle of the revolution, when the members of the Convención had debated the moral and practical implications of divorce, some had expressed fears that stepfathers would lack affection for the sons of a previous marriage and prostitute the daughters. Juvenile court officials were also suspicious of stepparents. Their concerns drew on deep-seated stereotypes, contradicted by stepparents who fulfilled their obligations. When one tribunal inspector observed that "this is a unified family despite the fact that the boy has a stepfather, who never has treated him badly," the "despite" reveals the underlying prejudices.[81] Another boy testified that his mother's *amasio* (unmarried partner) treated him well and "corrects him when it's necessary, but never treats him badly."[82] The concerns of the Convención delegates and the cautious approval of the tribunal inspectors, however, illuminate their distrust of family relations founded on serial unions.

Certainly, parents and other relatives could be just as abusive. Yet the court was often willing to overlook such violence if other "moral" factors were present, such as the conventional gender division of labor, as in the case of Agustín Velasco, discussed earlier. And while there is ample evidence that men considered violence a prerogative, mothers and stepmothers also resorted to violence to effectively terminate their obligations to support children.[83] One such mother evicted her fourteen-year-old son from the household when she initiated a new relationship. The boy, who had never known his father, told the investigating inspector that his mother's new amasio was worse than the last: he beat him and often drove him out of the house.[84] In this instance as in others, the boy's mother sided with her partner against her child. Her subordination to her partner highlights the gender dimensions of family violence.[85]

Juvenile court officials believed that these family dynamics caused youth crime. Certainly domestic violence contributed to the number of children and adolescents living on the city streets and, therefore, to that manifestation of child circulation. But not all boys who lived on the street had severed their family ties. When Enrico Robles took his wages to his mother, he drew on the same understandings of reciprocity to stay connected to her that other parents used to drive their children from home.

Family Strategies and Domestic Labor

Nineteenth-century admissions to the Hospicio showed that the children of single mothers who worked as domestics were highly susceptible to separation from their families. Informal adoptions of Hospicio inmates further illuminated the role of domestic service in child circulation. Juvenile court inspections shed more light on the gender dimensions of family subsistence that contributed to child circulation, but the court's cases also show that whether a mother or daughter worked as a domestic had very different outcomes for their families.

Within the framework of mutual obligation, mothers primarily owed housework and child care. These expectations were not merely tacit: they were inscribed in law. In return, daughters owed the same or related work. However, for families living barely above subsistence, both mothers and daughters were expected to contribute wages to household sustenance in addition to their unpaid work. Whether they worked at home or for wages depended on the stage in the family cycle, and mothers and daughters often exchanged roles. As the case of Carlota Morales shows, transitions and traumatic junctures in mothers' lives had a significant impact on their daughters' early work experiences and on their later employment opportunities, especially if the daughters had to shoulder the burden of housework and child care as adolescents. In addition, the limited range of occupations and the depressed wages available to mothers meant that their work in domestic service or related occupations affected the whole family: it could push girls into domestic service, or boys into welfare institutions, other households, or onto the street.

Because of the close reciprocity between mothers' and daughters' work, the latter were an invaluable resource for families in precarious economic and personal circumstances. Mothers without daughters faced difficult decisions. For Juana Granados, for example, live-in domestic service constrained her options and shaped the childhood experience of her son, Victor Acuña. When her husband died in 1920, Granados was left with four children, the oldest ten and the youngest still a baby. Her employers allowed her to bring only the baby to her live-in domestic job. As in Carmen Romero's family, the older children were boys. Social convention erected such high barriers between masculine and feminine spheres of labor that a boy who did housework, especially if he liked it, was marked as effeminate and potentially sexually deviant.[86] With no daughters of an appropriate age to take over her domestic responsibilities, Juana Granados was forced to find care outside her immediate family for her younger children.[87] When Victor, her second-to-youngest, was small he stayed with a neighbor in their tenement house while his mother worked. At age six he spent some time in the Hospicio but was expelled for bad behavior. Later he lived for six months with an aunt in Toluca. In 1927 his mother arranged an unpaid apprenticeship for ten-year-old Victor in the garage where his older brothers lived and worked.[88] These patterns of child circulation were sufficiently common that a tribunal inspector expressed surprise on discovering another fatherless boy who had never changed families.[89]

Juana Granados turned to neighbors before she resorted to placing Victor in a welfare institution. But as admissions to the foundling home in the mid-1920s illustrate, domestics with very young children often faced such difficulties. Recent migrants without family or community networks were at a special disadvantage. For example, a mother from Michoacán sought admission for her children, age two and five, both born before her migration, and gave her address as that of her employer. The cases of twenty-six other women like her, who lived with their employers, suggest they sought domestic positions because they were homeless, as nine additional mothers claimed specifically.[90] But solving one problem created another and they had to place their children in the orphanage.

Low pay for live-in domestic work created additional challenges for domestics with children. When Tomás Escobar was seven, poverty scattered his family. His unemployed father sold bread on the street. His mother took Tomás's half sister with her to a live-in domestic position. Tomás, twelve in 1929, worked as a bolero. He ate his meals at the house where his mother worked and she was also able to supply clothes for him, but she did not earn enough to keep the family under one roof.[91] Like Juana Granados, Tomás's mother had to make a difficult choice. She kept her daughter by her side, and the girl probably helped with her work. But Tomás had to fend for himself, homeless and vagrant in the eyes of the law.

In 1927 a mother's domestic work led tribunal officials to remove her twelve-year-old son from her care. After the boy's father abandoned the family, his mother moved in with her compadres and washed laundry for less than two pesos a day. Because of her occupation and dependence on others the court determined that she could not meet her obligation to support her son.[92] Instances like this one fulfilled the predictions of critics like Matilde Rodríguez Cabo, who blamed irresponsible fathers for family disorganization. They also illuminate the combination of family and economic constraints underlying child circulation.

To keep families together, parents might put their daughters in service. The strategies of fourteen-year-old Bertha Arratia's family provide an example. As unemployment rose during the autumn of 1930, a growing number of families like hers suffered hardship. Her father frequented the railroad station to hire out as a day laborer but rarely found work. Bertha's mother made a small income washing clothes and floors. Bertha's twelve-year-old brother also held a series of jobs, with a shoemaker and printer, among others. Bertha, meanwhile, was placed in a live-in domestic position earn-

18. Young domestic on a public street, Mexico City, ca. 1925. Instituto Nacional de Antropología e Historia, Fototeca Nacional, Fondo Casasola.

ing seven pesos a month.[93] Her steady wage, however small, was essential to the maintenance of four younger brothers and sisters. But a key factor from her parents' perspective may have been the savings on her support, which probably allowed her mother to spend more time at home with the five younger children.

Girls often entered domestic service when younger siblings were born. For example, Sofia Corral, fourteen in 1938, had worked as a domestic from age six and as a live-in servant from age ten in a series of positions that included housework and child care. Initially, her meager wages went largely to supplement her mother's scant income from washing laundry. After Sofia's father died and Sofia's mother took a new partner, the girl's wages helped support her two younger half brothers. Her early employment kept Sofia from going to school until she was nine years old, and then she attended only for six months.[94]

Sofia's work trajectory illuminates the ways that junctures in mothers' lives shaped patterns of girls' circulation and labor, especially in domestic service. Although the loss of her father precipitated the chain of events, Sofia's work was tied closely to the crises and turning points in her mother's reproductive life and work. Her mother's new relationship drew attention and resources away from Sofia.[95] Notably, the girl's six months in school predated the birth of her first half brother and her placement in a live-in position coincided roughly with his birth. Occupied with her two small sons, her mother had far less earning power, so that even Sofia's low pay as a servant made a valuable addition to the household economy. Placing the girl in live-in service also spared her parents the expense of her maintenance.[96]

Many girls began work as domestics for the same reasons as Sofia.[97] The father of Alicia Avalos, eleven in 1931, had abandoned the family years before. The girl remained at home until her mother gave birth to two additional daughters by her new partner, a laborer; then Alicia was placed in domestic service.[98] The father of Margarita Delgado died when she was a baby, but she remained at home until she was seven, when her mother, a *tortillera* (tortilla maker), formed a new relationship and had another baby. At that time, Margarita began a series of domestic positions, the first as a nanny. Eight years later, in 1930, when Margarita was fifteen, she was still working as a live-in domestic. Meanwhile, her married older sister took care of the house and watched her little half sister while their mother worked.[99]

Bringing daughters back into the home to take over housework and child care freed a mother to work outside for pay, as was the case for Carmen Romero and Carlota. But this transfer of responsibilities came at a cost to the daughter. For some girls it meant leaving school. Adolescents and young adults who replaced their mothers at home also forfeited income and independence. By running away, Carlota Morales made it clear that she did not accept those terms.

Unlike Carlota, Lucía Gómez returned home to substitute for her mother, but she attempted to set her own terms. When her mother brought an unwelcome man into the house, Lucía expressed her disdain for the arrangement by moving in with her boyfriend and his family. With that move, Lucía asserted that she was an independent adult, able to make her own decisions about her residence, her partner, and her power over her own labor.[100] Only when her mother's boyfriend left the home scene did Lucía return to fulfill her family labor obligations. She then assumed all the responsibilities of cleaning, cooking, and caring for her three younger siblings while her mother worked, and often slept, in a coffee stall in the center of the city.[101]

Lucía's new responsibilities enhanced her authority. In her mother's absence, she became the virtual head of household. But her new role brought constraints. With Lucía at home, her younger sister, María Paz, fourteen in 1928, was free to work in a box factory. María Paz's wages allowed her to attend movies and dances, while Lucía was confined to the house, losing earning power and the opportunity to develop marketable skills. Both sisters resented their situation. Lucía took on the role of family disciplinarian, and the sisters argued over María Paz's choice of company and entertainment.[102]

María Paz's access to spending money and her choice of entertainment help illustrate why critics considered work in factories, markets, and restaurants corrupting for girls and young women.[103] In contrast, domestic service in private homes supposedly provided girls with a safe and supervised work environment. Those benefits could be illusory.[104] Isolated young servants were highly vulnerable to abuse. One girl, who held a series of jobs as a nanny and servant, was robbed of her wages by one employer and raped by another.[105] Another girl came before the tribunal because she tried to set fire to her employer's house, "as vengeance against her boss for having mistreated her."[106]

Authors of the 1928 draft of the labor code went to considerable lengths to establish protections against such notorious abuses. They proposed, for example, that employers could not prevent live-in domestics from free communication with other workers or with people outside the workplace.[107] Domestics could leave a job if they experienced sexual harassment by employers or any member of the employer's family, or if the woman of the house should die, leaving the servant unprotected in an all-male environment.[108] But lawmakers seem to have balked at these provisions and the final version of the law omitted them.

Girls working at home or for relatives were equally vulnerable, and their attempts to escape abuse illuminate another aspect of child circulation. Alicia Ruiz left her mother's house to escape sexual abuse by her stepfather and found refuge in domestic service.[109] Ana María Juárez, an orphan raised by her aunt, fled from her aunt's beatings and the sexual advances of her cousin's husband, who lived in the house. A family friend gave the girl shelter and work as domestic without pay, but then beat her for doing the work badly. Once again Ana María escaped, this time to a family that she, and tribunal officials, believed would care for her; the family had "committed to become her guardians" and offered her the necessary "moral and economic guarantees."[110] In these instances, domestic service provided a safe haven. Ana María's experience also points to the convergence of popular practice and public officials' persistent use of domestic service as a substitute for immediate family.

As these examples show, domestic service played a significant and complex role in the family and economic lives of Mexico City's working poor and in the dynamics of child circulation and labor. Domestic service may have provided families with a flexible survival strategy, but it was always a compromised one. As critics observed, a mother's domestic service could "disorganize" her family: that is, it could leave her children unsupervised or, worse, separate her family. When homeless migrants or destitute widows turned to domestic service for shelter and wages, they often had to place their children with others or in welfare institutions. Some parents placed young daughters in service to fend off an economic crisis and separation.

Some mothers placed daughters in service when they initiated new relationships or had more children with a new partner. At times, those placements were the equivalent of driving a son onto the street: they effectively evicted the child from the new family circle. And girls also turned to domestic service as a refuge from abuse, only to encounter abuse anew.

Abuse of young domestics can be seen as an extreme expression of the degree to which the work itself was associated with dependence and subordination. Despite women's legal gains, domestic labor and child care were still considered women's primary work and thus linked to their dependent position in family relations and in society. In some cases, domestic service could represent a transition away from confinement and dependence at home and toward adult autonomy and a wage. For an adolescent like Carlota Morales, running away to find work as a domestic was her bid for independence from her mother. Few girls, however, controlled the decision to enter domestic service: most were placed there because of their mother's life transitions or family ruptures. Others who worked as domestics in childhood later returned home to perform the same labor without pay. Lucía's enhanced authority notwithstanding, such a move was hardly a bid for autonomy. The number of adult domestics and women with children employed in related occupations — laundry workers, cooks, and dishwashers — also suggests that the early experience of sporadic or truncated schooling limited opportunities to acquire other marketable skills and restricted employment options over a woman's life cycle. In these ways, the internal gender dynamics of working-class families intersected with the limited employment opportunities for women to reproduce Mexico City's reproductive labor force.

Child Labor and Protected Childhood

Juvenile court officials approached the issue of child labor with considerable flexibility. Often they based their rulings on well-established concepts of family reciprocity. In those instances, they evaluated parental expectations of children's work based on a combination of material factors, such as the family's economic circumstance and the child's sex. Officials also intervened when parents failed to deliver the legally defined elements of support: food, shelter, and education. And they advocated for children and adolescents when parents' expectations of labor seemed exploitative or excessive. Such rulings provide some insight into how officials set limits on children's labor obligations. They also point to ways that the tribunal's decisions turned on evolving concepts of childhood, which included biomedical understandings about children's physical development as well as the moral notion that childhood was a life stage rightfully protected from labor.

For example, the court judged that the grandmother of Teresa Trujillo expected too much work from the girl. Teresa had lived with her maternal grandmother, a fruit vendor, from a very young age because her mother "had an excessive number of children and could not support her." After only one year, however, the grandmother withdrew Teresa from school and assigned her all the housework. The court's inspector on the case considered the grandmother's expectations inappropriate. Not only was the work too heavy for a child of Teresa's age but also, as the inspector pointed out, there were other adult women in the household who should have done the housework rather than passing it to a child.[111]

Both old and new concepts of childhood underwrote the inspector's views. First, the old: law and custom had long since established that family labor should be reciprocal, and thus Teresa should contribute her labor to the household in return for support. But adults in the family should have done their share of work, rather than assign all of it to the child. Then, the new: recent labor law recognized that heavy work was detrimental to children's physical development.[112]

Education also played a role. Parents and guardians were required by law to educate children through primary school and to prepare them for "some honorable occupation, trade, or profession, adequate in view of . . . sex and personal circumstances," meaning class.[113] Educators argued, for example, that girls' schooling should prepare them for their future maternal and domestic roles.[114] Thus, a working-class parent might claim that placing a daughter in domestic service or keeping her at home to do housework and child care served the same purpose. Similarly, parents could construe boys' work as job training, which, if not schooling per se, did prepare them for adulthood.

But in the case of Esperanza Jiménez, the judges did not accept such an argument. Orphaned at eight, Esperanza lived with her grandparents until her grandmother died. Then her grandfather, who claimed that he had legally adopted the girl, removed Esperanza from school and put her into service as a domestic without salary. After moving to a second position, the girl was content. She felt well treated by her employers and her principal work of caring for a small child earned her six pesos a month. When her grandfather came to retrieve her, Esperanza refused to go. The family crisis brought Esperanza before the juvenile court. She claimed that her grandfather kept all her wages and that his new partner beat her. Concerned that the grandfather was exploiting the girl's labor, officials placed Esperanza in reform school. The child had broken no law; rather, court officials believed that she had a better chance of finishing primary school and acquiring job training in public custody than under her grandfather's authority.[115]

In the case of Benito Rendon, the court's ruling combined these factors. In 1928 Benito's mother brought the fourteen-year-old before the tribunal and accused him of disobedience, but court officials blamed her for the boy's lack of social adaptation. Until recently, when he had begun to socialize with a bad element, Benito had been apprenticed to a blacksmith to help support his mother and stepfather. Not only was he required to hand over all his earnings to his parents, but they also made him do all the housework. Moreover, according to the inspector, the mother and stepfather were "habitual drunks" and "lazy" and set a bad example. In the inspector's view, Benito had lost his motivation to work and become disobedient because his parents behaved badly and appropriated his earnings.[116] Benito's case affirmed official perceptions that parental vice bred youth crime. But it also illustrates the reciprocity in concepts of family labor obligations. The parents lost their right to the son's support and respect because they failed to fulfill their side of the compact.

When parents failed to express appropriate sentiments toward their children, court officials might side with the child. In the case of Daniel Maldonado, fourteen in 1927, the inspector doubted the sincerity of his widowed mother's feelings. Instead of attending school, Daniel had worked from a very young age, first assisting in a glass factory and then selling newspapers. His seven-year-old sister already worked as a nanny. Arrested for vagrancy and placed in the tribunal's observation center, Daniel missed his mother and sister and wanted to return home to help out. His mother, a tortillera, also wanted him home so that he could resume work, although she promised he would attend night school. The inspector, however, warned court officials that Daniel's mother seemed motivated less by affection than by her interest in what the boy earned.[117] In the eyes of the inspector, her lack of appropriate maternal feelings undermined her claim to his labor and his earnings.

The tribunal's decisions also turned on concepts of protected childhood rather than reciprocity, as in the case of Jesús Tovar. Although eight-year-old Jesús and his father lived in abject poverty, they had been better off in the past. Sr. Tovar had a clear grasp of the law concerning his paternal obligations. He explained to the inspector that "extreme poverty" made it "impossible" to educate his son. He added that the year before he had attempted "to comply with the obligation that all heads of families have to educate their children," but when he took his son to enroll in the nearest school the administrators refused to admit the boy because he was "dirty and unkempt." Jesús, for his part, was devoted to his father and understood that if he did not work he would not eat. Perhaps the boy's age prompted the inspector to remark that long hours of work had deprived the boy of free time "to play and enjoy himself, something he has a right to." Although father and son wanted to stay together, the inspector recommended that the boy enter the public welfare system.[118]

Like other parents confronted by tribunal officials, this father found himself in the awkward position: he had to justify decisions driven by need in other terms, such as concerns for education. But in this instance, the inspector introduced an unanticipated factor: a child's "right" to play and free time or, in other words, the right to a childhood without work. The father's knowledge of the law was no match for the inspector's authority, and a new concept of childhood became the official measure of family relations. When the court removed Jesús from his father's custody and placed him in the public orphanage, its intervention exposed the interplay of popular understandings of childhood, work, and family with new ideological models.

Similarly, when another father complained that his thirteen-year-old son spent all his earnings on "games, candies, and firecrackers, not giving him even one cent," the court's ruling ignored the legal framework and social understandings of intergenerational reciprocity, while honoring the boy's right to keep and spend his earnings as he pleased. For his part, the boy testified that his father left him alone in charge of his market stall and made him escort his sister to movies he did not like. If he did not comply his father beat him. The tribunal sided with the son and asserted that the father had expectations of work and responsibility far beyond the boy's years.[119] By law, the boy had control over his wages. But by endorsing his right to spend his money on games rather than contributing to family sustenance, the court was excusing him from participating in the system of family reciprocity, thus characterizing as a dependent a boy who was legally old enough to work.

The Court of Public Opinion

As these vignettes show, court officials worked from two competing concepts of working-class childhood. One they shared with many parents: children should contribute to family subsistence. But officials also construed childhood as a time that should be protected from adult concerns. Like the court's dual concept of working-class childhood, public opinion was also divided over the true character of the children and adolescents who worked and often slept on the city streets and passed through the corrections system: were they criminals or were they victims of criminal neglect? There was also disagreement over who ultimately bore responsibility for them: their parents, the state, or society at large? In seeking answers, the press judged all parties equally harshly. The chorus of criticism revealed that the concept of social responsibility for all children had gained qualified acceptance. Children represented the condition of society as a whole; their suffering or delinquency exposed society's failings—and the failure of the state's reform project. But at the same time, many critics feared the state's growing role in family relations.

The debate over social responsibility for children of the urban poor took place in a charged political atmosphere. The Cárdenas administration had expanded public services for poor families and children and identified those services with the fulfillment of revolutionary goals. But the president's support for socialist education, his alliance with Spanish Republicans, and his 1938 expropriation and nationalization of privately owned oil companies fueled opposition from business interests and social conservatives, while the rise of fascism in Europe nourished Mexico's extreme right wing. As Cárdenas began to moderate his stance and pull back from controversial positions, critics on the left accused him of failing to carry through on his commitments.[120]

A two-pronged attack against public programs for children played out in Mexico City's family-oriented illustrated press, where journalists deployed the concept of protected childhood to validate criticism of the government's shortcomings from all sides. To draw support from the middle classes, conservatives linked the administration's prolabor policies to communist sympathies.[121] In the 1938 Mothers' Day issue of the illustrated magazine *Todo*, a writer warned that if the government of the Soviet Union took children from their mothers, the same could happen in Mexico.[122] This article pointed to fears that the government had too much power to regulate or intervene in families. A similar magazine, *Hoy*, ran an article sympathetic to Mussolini's pronatal policies and another decrying women's lack of subordination and the decadence of the modern home and family.[123] Articles like these argued that any woman who did not devote herself exclusively to home and children was responsible for the corruption of youth. Other critics called on the state to be more attentive to its responsibilities toward children. *Todo*'s editors repeatedly wielded the concept of children's well-being to criticize the city and federal governments when they failed to provide adequate playgrounds in Mexico City's poor neighborhoods or sufficient funding for public schools.[124] This kind of criticism revealed that Mexicans considered responsibility for children a collective problem. It also implied that these government failures turned children into delinquents.

Reform projects such as the Tribunal para Menores that had begun with such optimism in the previous decade came in for harsh criticism. In the spring of 1938 *Hoy* launched a damning serial exposé on the capital's youth corrections system. Journalist Carmen Madrigal promised to reveal the causes of one of Mexico's "most terrifying" social problems and to explain how society created "criminal and vice-ridden" future adults by abandoning its children.[125] The first article focuses on the failings of delinquents' parents and communities. Illustrations accompanying the article show a child buying alcohol in a bar, a pregnant teenager, and boys sleeping on the street. To illustrate family dysfunction in the capital's tenements the magazine reused, but did not identify, a photograph taken in the courtyard of the adult women's prison and published the previous year.[126] The picture shows a mother reaching out to her crying toddler as other women and small children look on. The caption, however, describes the scene as a filthy tenement, where children learned from infancy that life is hard. The magazine's sensationalistic and misleading representation puts into question the source of the other images that it—and other publications—used to depict the family life of the urban poor as the cradle of youth crime. But rhetorically, the photograph equates the community life of urban tenements with prison and the mothers who gathered in tenement patios with convicted criminals.

Subsequent installments of *Hoy*'s series expose the deterioration of the tribunal's facilities: "like hamlets far removed from civilization, all is primitive." The writer concludes that the boys interned under the care of the state might as well be sleeping on the street.[127] Other journalists agree that the juvenile corrections system had produced only "disastrous results." Its institutions were "dens of vice" where the youth learned to be "the criminals of tomorrow."[128]

Less hostile articles paint a somewhat different picture. In June *Hoy* published an interview with Dr. Matilde Rodríguez Cabo, director of the tribunal. Although more sympathetic than earlier installments in the series, the article reveals the politics behind the exposé: Rodríguez Cabo was well-known as a Communist and feminist; an attack on the tribunal was, therefore, an attack on President Cárdenas's left-leaning politics.[129] But Rodríguez Cabo did not take the bait. She said that she believed that the exposé had raised social awareness of the plight of poor and delinquent youth. She also assumed personal responsibility for conditions in the network of institutions she directed, although she also explained that the system operated on an insufficient budget. Rodríguez Cabo's disarming approach may have tempered the reporter's characterizations of delinquent youths, because the article gives them a human face. The writer describes a scene in the facility's refectory, where the young men gathered around Rodríguez Cabo. One youth approached her to thank her for his training as a mechanic and for giving him hope: he considered her a true friend. Yet even this sympathetic portrayal depicts the inmates as a group in the most pejorative terms: they suffered from congenital syphilis, tuberculosis, or were "merely children," their souls "destroyed before they have even lived."[130]

Those well-worn characterizations point the blame at parents, poverty, and early labor, and echo the rationales in the court's founding documents, where reformers had proposed that youth crime arose from the dysfunction and vice of poor families. Now, however, commentators held up the failings of court administrators and of poor parents—along with the debility of their children—as reflecting society's failings, as exemplified in a quote from the secretary of the interior: "Society has the delinquents it deserves."[131]

In the ensuing months, the magazines repeatedly sounded the theme of neglected childhood. "Mexico is an uncivilized city," wrote one journalist, "not because of political or economic reasons but because it neglects its children, which is like neglecting itself."[132] "Just as poor as before!" ran the accusing title of a photo-essay on poverty in the capital.[133]

In that vein, Demetrio García, writing in *Todo* in 1939, proclaimed that Mexico "condemns" its children.[134] Only two years earlier, the same magazine had run an optimistic article praising the work at the girls' corrections facility. The inmates were described as healthy and happy and doing productive work.[135] Now this critic painted a portrait of despair. In particular, he cited the plight of an inmate who tried repeatedly to escape and then attempted suicide. While the state was to blame for conditions in the facility, the writer argued that the failure to provide effective reform also stemmed from public indifference. If only his readers would take a few minutes to compare the fate of those young men and women to that of their own children, then perhaps society could find a human solution.[136]

The problem of abandoned youth, García argued, extended beyond the confines of government institutions. No matter how many children were interned in reform schools or welfare institutions, there were more on the street. The government's campaigns to engage the public in assistance for needy children elicited sympathy but produced no lasting engagement. Every winter, the welfare administration mounted a poster campaign inviting the public to help unfortunate children, but children like those depicted on the posters were still everywhere in the city. Their presence mocked Mexico's pretensions to modernity and its revolutionary ideals. García described a scene at the monument to the revolution: "night falls on the great avenues," and "hungry boys . . . seek the refuge" of the stone "benches and arches." Likening that noble monument to a shelter for the homeless, he accused the government of failing to provide effective programs for those children, but he also accused his readers of passing on to the state most responsibility for abandoned children and youth. Until Mexican society addressed this problem as a whole, those children would work from an early age "to help support the household." But their work would accomplish nothing: "Poverty will not let them escape. It imposes work that prevents their physical, psychological, and moral development."[137] García implied that society conspired in robbing them of childhood.

García's article pointed to the gulf between children living on street and his readers' children. He implied that the poor had no family life. Yet his indictment of the government's shortcomings and society's indifference was based on his belief that all Mexican children deserved the protections that *Todo*'s readers could provide for theirs. If parents and the government had defaulted on their responsibilities, then Mexicans as a society should step in.

"Ser pobre sale caro": Being Poor Is Expensive

Among Mexico City's working poor, shared understandings of family relationships founded on labor cemented intergenerational bonds. Parents put children to work out of need but they expected their children to work because they were family. In turn, children understood that working was inseparable from their relationships with their parents. This reciprocity was especially important because poverty and work often separated families. Many mothers performed housework and child care for wages, rather than in their own homes and for their own children. Girls as young as six and seven left their families to work as nannies or domestics for little more than room and board. Daughters often became the primary caregivers of younger siblings and assumed the burden of housework so that mothers could take paid work outside the house. Boys' incomes as low as a few centavos a day made vital contributions to household economies.[138] But children who lived and worked away from home continued to contribute their wages to their families as a way to claim their place and to affirm their feelings toward their parents and siblings. Parents expected and accepted those contributions and viewed them as expressions of respect and affection. In these ways, parents and children's economic activities were constitutive of the family itself, of belonging, and of identities tied to intimacy and life stages.

Beyond debates about whether work caused or cured delinquency, critics of child labor were correct: the long-term social costs of child labor were rising. Child labor did not lift families out of poverty: it merely allowed them to subsist. Boys without schooling and skills would have difficulty securing better-paid factory work and the benefits of collective bargaining that often came with it. Girls cleaned houses for families who could afford to keep their own children in school. Some parents earned so little that poverty could scatter the children they struggled to support. Other families used separation as a strategy to keep the family together. Despite their challenging circumstances, parents and children on the capital's economic margins saw themselves as families.

Initially, the tribunal's sympathetic analysis of juvenile delinquents marked their families as deficient and dysfunctional. But throughout the 1920s and 1930s, the juvenile court usually affirmed working-class family practice founded on reciprocal obligations of support. Additionally, the court's probationary work placements were similar to the jobs that families found for their children. Like the public orphanages of the nineteenth century, the court also became a powerful agent in the capital's networks of child circulation. In this, the juvenile court as a state institution played an active role in class formation in the economic sense, and also in the sense of perpetuating class identities and family bonds founded on labor.

Yet the tribunal's interventions also exposed the interplay between popular understandings of childhood, work, and family and the new ideological models. Many of the court's decisions were child-centered, based on a concept of childhood and adolescence as life stages protected from physical exploitation and exposure to corrupting influences. Similarly, Roberto Solís Quiroga's critique of children's work environments implied that the family and the home should be child-centered, devoted to nurturing children, and not putting them to work. Solís Quiroga had even proposed that fathers' work deprived their children of due attention. His stance was based on a fundamental conceptual divide between the realms of work and family.

Although his analysis ignored the complex need- and family-based motivations for children's work, the diversity of contexts in which they worked, and the fluidity of family work and residence patterns among Mexico City's working poor, his conceptual separation of work and family did clarify the issue of child domestics. Solís Quiroga perceived that most children who worked as servants in private homes, "no matter whether the house has all the requirements of morality and culture," benefited little because the employers treated them merely as servants.[139]

When court officials used or endorsed domestic placements, they believed that they were acting in the child's best interests. Such understandings had also pervaded Mexican adoption practice. In 1917, however, adoption became a formal legal instrument for creating binding parent-child relationships. The law, when fully enforced, had the potential to strike at the foundations of widespread practice that had long blurred the boundaries between children's domestic labor and dependence.[140] At the least, the law on formal adoption reflected the growing consensus against child labor among policy makers and their class peers. It also reflected the growing conceptual divide between the spheres of home and work.

Even so, in contrast to welfare officials, who were charged with reviewing adoption applications closely to protect girls from exploitation, the juvenile court continued to use domestic service as probation. The justification for doing so seemingly rested on the distinction that those placements made no pretense of establishing family relationships but instead provided girls with moral supervision and honest work. In this, the court concurred with parents who put their daughters in service. They were not relinquishing their daughters but rather using a time-honored strategy to relieve economic pressures on the family. The advent and enforcement of legal adoption, however, inflected the fluid practices of child circulation with new meanings and transformed some of those placements into permanent and legal separation.

7 Breaking and Making Families

Adoption, Child Labor, and Women's Work

In his preamble to the 1917 Ley de Relaciones Familiares, Venustiano Carranza proclaimed that adoption was an innovation in Mexican society. Providing the adoptive relationship with the same rights and obligations as those between parent and child by birth was indeed a novelty, although one with colonial legal precedent.[1] But legal adoption posed a fundamental challenge to widespread adoption practices that embraced a spectrum of relationships, especially those around child labor. Such relationships equating dependence with labor also dated back to Mexico's colonial period. After 1917 Mexicans from all walks of life made slow and uneven adjustments to the law's requirements and their implications for family relationships and class identities.

221

Administrators who served as guardians of orphaned and abandoned welfare clients and were charged with enforcing the law also pondered the problem of identifying suitable environments to meet the new criteria. They had to determine what kinds of families they would endorse through legal instruments and what kinds of families to form to support broad national goals. In that process welfare officials grappled with questions about the meaning of family and the interrelationships of class, gender, and labor. As they became more familiar with the purpose of the law and the new meanings attached to the parent-child relationship that formal adoption created, officials favored adoptions that promised the adoptee a childhood protected from labor. The growing trend of expert opinion condemning child labor, especially children in domestic positions, helped welfare officials reach decisions about placing children with permanent families. But as the focus moved away from the question of child labor, the adoption review process increasingly turned on concepts of motherhood, domesticity, and women's paid work, offering another revealing example of how changing concepts of childhood influenced understandings of women's roles and labor.

Formal adoption was introduced and implemented in a context of intense public discussion of children's rights, health, and well-being, and a growing consensus that all of Mexican society shared responsibility for children. The process of assimilating formal adoption opens a window onto the ways that Mexicans across the social spectrum absorbed or responded to these new concepts of childhood—and their relationship to ideas about social class. For more privileged Mexicans, accepting a lower-class child into one's family was a magnanimous gesture, but historically it had not implied social equality with that child. Now adoption meant exactly that. Moreover, as the policies and interventions of the juvenile court revealed, the family proved to be a stronghold against attempts to regulate child labor. Middle-class Mexicans might condemn child labor in principle but still expect to be able to adopt a young servant. As time passed, officials rejected such adoption applications with more confidence. But in working-class families, parent-child relationships entailed reciprocal obligations of support based on child labor. Therefore, when welfare officials reviewed working-class applicants for adoption, they were more suspicious and critical of their motives than with more affluent petitioners.

Adoption practice at the turn of the twentieth century had exposed conflicting concepts of childhood. Adoption applications after the revolution showed that earlier expectations about adopting for labor persisted, although they declined over time. By the early 1940s adoption petitions illuminated the centrality of children to concepts of family and of motherhood to women's identities. Still, social adjustment to the implications of formal adoption exposed the underlying class relations based on family and echoed the nineteenth-century regulation of wet-nursing: the best interests of the working-class child took precedence over the interests of the working-class mother. Meanwhile, the state's role as gatekeeper to forming families through adoption reflected its growing role in formulating and regulating the terms of social responsibility for children.

Forming Families by Contract

The adoption contract created a parent-child relationship. As Carranza stated in 1917, formal adoption did "no more than recognize the freedom of affection and consecrate the freedom of contract."[2] The law made adoption available to married and single adults. A married woman could adopt independently of her husband with his consent. Catering to men who fathered children outside of marriage, the law allowed a married man to adopt without his wife's consent, but he could not bring the adoptee to live in the conjugal home. Adoptees age twelve or over had to consent to being adopted. Like civil marriage, adoptions could be terminated, except when the adoptee was a natural child of the adopting adult.[3] Although the law insisted that adoptive parents and children bore mutual obligations identical to those between parents and children by birth, provisions for termination perpetuated in law a widely held understanding that adoption was a temporary or limited relationship.

The legal definition of adoption as a means of forming a family should have eliminated the adoptions of older children for labor and the law often succeeded in doing so. But for decades the public orphanages of Mexico City had regulated adoptions on their own authority, calling the practice "administrative adoption," and had tolerated—or turned a blind eye—to the practice of adoption for labor. Directors of welfare institutions were in no hurry to comply with the law, as the history of one young woman illustrates. Admitted to the Hospicio de Niños in 1906 at age eight, she was adopted as a servant and returned to the Hospicio several times. Both administrators and adopters complained of her bad conduct, especially stealing. But adoption offered a tempting way to dispose of difficult inmates. In October 1918 the Hospicio drew up a new contract for the girl's adoption that omitted any reference to the law but did require that the adopter care for the adoptee "not as a servant but as one of the members of her family." The contract also provided for the girl's return—which occurred quickly. At this point the paper trail ends, but given her age she was probably released to support herself.[4]

It took a firmly worded 1919 presidential circular, reiterating that adoptions must adhere to the letter of the law and receive judicial authorization, to jolt orphanage administrators into compliance. The review process was also removed from their control and placed in the central welfare office, the Dirección General de la Beneficencia Pública. But orphanage directors, as the legal guardians of orphaned and abandoned children, still held responsibility for their wards' well-being. They were ordered to investigate every adoption applicant to evaluate his or her "honor, morality, and financial possibilities." Now, however, the inspectors making the investigations reported to the director of public welfare, who made the final decision. Moreover, the orphanages were periodically to inspect each adoptee's condition. Any adopter who "treated the adoptee with excessive severity, failed to educate the minor, did not attend to his or her support, or imposed immoral precepts or gave corrupt example or counsel" would lose parental authority and the minor would return to the custody of the welfare establishment.[5] In 1921 new Hospicio regulations specified that adoptions of the inmates were subject to the law.[6]

Still, legal loopholes remained. Indeed, a lawyer reviewing a 1921 draft of the new foundling home regulations identified and even defended some of them. Specifically, since federal law now regulated adoption, the lawyer argued that the foundling home could not establish its own requirements for eligibility to adopt. The orphanage regulations required the adopter always to keep the adoptee "at his side" (*a su lado*). The lawyer argued that this constituted "an attack on individual liberty and a serious obstacle to the education of the adoptee," who might have to leave the parent's home for instruction beyond primary school. The 1919 presidential circular on adoption, which had the status of law, had insisted only that the judge record the legal residences of the adopting adult and the adopted minor, if they differed.[7] The foundling home's requirement, which dated from the nineteenth century, had been intended to protect adoptees from exploitation, expulsion from the adopter's home, transfer to work in another household, or even into the underground market for children, although authorities rarely pursued violations. Revised regulations in June 1921 detailed the authority of federal law over the foundling home's internal regimen and adoption practices.[8]

The letter of the law imposed important protections for state wards. In addition, the 1917 Constitution raised the minimum age for contracted work, making it doubly illegal to adopt children for labor. Although a stroke of the pen could not eliminate the expectation among Mexicans that adoption provided domestic labor, the revolutionary statutes gave officials a way to deflect such requests.

Establishing the New Regime

Welfare administrators responsible for implementing formal adoptions entered uncharted social territory with only the law and a presidential circular to guide them. Before the revolution orphanage directors oversaw two distinct kinds of adoptions: adoptions of babies and young children usually for family formation and adoptions of older children and adolescents for labor. For both types, the social class of the applicant outweighed all other considerations for approval. Foundling home director Manuel Domínguez had described one adopter as "a person perfectly suited by his social position and sufficient resources to defray the expense of maintaining the little one."[9] The law and guidelines now necessitated more complex evaluations of applicants and their motives. Moreover, adoption petitioners expressed a wide spectrum of ideas of family and came from every social class. The women inspectors who conducted the background investigations and their male supervisors had to assess the interplay of honor, morality, and economic position. This required weighing material wealth against reputation and behavior. Moreover, both inspectors and administrators confronted the challenge of defining family based on intangible criteria such as prospects for affection and nurture. Applications also touched sensitivities about gender norms and divisions of labor. Was a woman less honorable if she worked for pay? Both inspectors and supervisors drew on their own social biases in assessing how social class might influence understandings of the mutual obligations for support between parent and child and possible expectations of child labor. Thus, during the 1920s their decisions were not always consistent: sometimes they prohibited and sometimes they allowed adoptions for labor.

Two adoption applications from the mid-1920s illustrate how inconsistent officials' reasoning could be when confronted with adoptions for labor. In December 1924 a widow petitioned to adopt two girls from the Hospicio de Niños as servants, *hijas de la casa*, and promised to care and provide for them. She submitted the three required letters of recommendation that described her as "honorable in every way," "a person of absolute morality and magnificent conduct," with "exemplary habits and honor." The inspector proceeded to the home of the applicant, who stated openly that she wanted the girls for domestic work and was prepared to feed and clothe them. The frank admission offended the inspector. "In my opinion," she reported, "that situation is much worse than that of a maid ... who sets her pay of her own will and knows that on her day off she can arrange her life however she wants." The inspector equated the proposed labor adoption with "slavery." When the director of public welfare notified the applicant that her request had been turned down, he avoided directly confronting the motives of someone of good social standing. Instead of citing the law, he explained that at present no girls wished to leave the Hospicio to work as domestics.[10]

A few months later, a similar request drew a different outcome and reveals how difficult it was for officials to draw clear boundaries based on the law's new requirements. A married woman applied to adopt girl of ten or twelve. She promised to receive her "as an adopted daughter" and agreed to "comply with all the legal dispositions." The inspector reported that the woman was a "person of known honor with a good moral education and has sufficient resources to live comfortably." During the interview, the applicant made it clear that the adopted girl would not form part of her family but would help with housework, but that she would receive good treatment and anything she might need. Even though the inspector reported the applicant's intentions, the director of public welfare seems to have been swayed by the applicant's social standing. He authorized her to select a girl and take her before a judge to complete the adoption.[11]

At about the same time, a married man petitioned to adopt and requested a girl of about eleven. When the same inspector interviewed the applicant in his home, he said he would educate the girl just as he planned to educate his infant daughter. The adoptee would also be his daughter's companion and help his wife around the house. In this instance the inspector noted that although the couple had limited means, the applicant had good intentions and the girl they selected would have a fairly good life with them. The welfare director denied the application because the petitioner wanted a servant but offered to reconsider if he promised to treat the adoptee like a true daughter. The applicant evidently refused to accept those terms, and the director cancelled his conditional approval.[12]

During the early 1920s applicants requesting girls freely admitted that they planned to put them to work as servants: they were apparently unaware that the law had changed. One married man explained that he needed a domestic and might also assign the girl office work in his business if she showed the aptitude.[13] Others couched their requests in the standard formulas of charity; one desired to "contribute to the extent of my means to the betterment of orphaned children" and characterized his intentions as "humanitarian."[14] When confronted with the new terms of adoption, they declined to accept the adoptee as a family member and the adoption process terminated.

The inspectors and officials overseeing adoptions also seemed ill at ease with the new requirements. The director found it hard to explain to applicants who may have been his social peers why he turned down their petitions, and he tended to leave an opening for reconsideration. In one instance he approved the adoption of two girls and a boy by a woman whose application omitted any mention of family and openly stated that she planned to "teach them to work, because one cannot live without work."[15] The inspector who conducted most of the interviews also wavered. At times she moralized against exploitative intentions. At other times she approved the proposed arrangements, albeit in qualified terms. Clearly, the personnel in charge of the adoption process were struggling to incorporate the full meaning of formal adoption into their own ideas about family and class.

When applicants' intentions were ambiguous, inspectors and administrators drew on a range of family and household models to reach their decisions. An older man, a tailor, applied to adopt a boy and a girl, ages seven and eight, and promised to "educate them and give them a modest future according to my circumstances." The inspector found him to be honest and hardworking. Having no family, the applicant explained, he would treat the children as his own and they would help him in his work. In the past he had taken in other children on an informal basis and taught them his trade, but they had moved on. Now he wished to form a family. He preferred children who were orphans or without known parents so they would see him as their true father. The inspector recommended against approval on the grounds that there was no woman in the house to oversee a girl. The welfare director, however, approved the adoption of a boy.[16] The arguments for and against this adoption turned on gender roles. A home without a woman was unsuitable for a girl, but teaching a boy a trade was one of a father's fundamental obligations.

Although administrators were willing to approve an adoption applicant who worked in a trade, they did not approve of manual labor. A couple that owned property worth the substantial amount of one thousand pesos was denied their request to adopt from the foundling home. The inspector noted that their land was broken into small, cultivated parcels. In short, they were farmers, and the inspector suspected that they wanted to adopt a child only as an unpaid servant; she also doubted that they would provide the child with an education.[17] In this instance the inspector used class as the determining factor. The applicants worked the soil: their livelihood suggested to a welfare employee that the adopted child would work with them rather than attend school.

In contrast to adoptions of older children where labor was always a question, adoptions of babies and young children seemed more straightforward. Young childless couples seeking to form families and single women who wanted to raise children made ideal applicants. In 1925 all eighteen recorded adoptions from the foundling home conformed to this model, as did ten out of twenty-two approved petitions the following year.[18]

Unsuccessful petitions, however, also illuminate the criteria influencing the outcomes. The inspectors were looking for appropriate parental sentiments, but social class and income continued to bias their decisions. Indeed, if the inspector had her way one poor and childless couple would not have adopted at all because of their scant income. They had applied to adopt three children and received permission for only two, a boy and a girl, aged four and five. Then the señor, invoking love, charity, paternal duty, and—for good measure—patriotism, wrote again to the director of public welfare to request the third: "Sir, that child stole my heart and the same for my wife, to see him so humble and so contrite [as] he stood looking at us sadly. . . . I beg very respectfully that you allow me to adopt this other child to complete my charitable work for the sake of the unfortunate children, who with work and sacrifice I will educate to be good and honorable citizens who serve God and their country. I vow to fulfill my duty as a good father and provide a good example for them, treating them with all the consideration required of a man of good conscience and education."[19]

The inspector made a second visit to the family. She observed that the couple was poor but "correct and serious." Although their rooms were sparsely furnished, they treated the two children already in their care with tenderness and consideration and gave them toys despite their modest means. The señora had made them new clothes. Still, given their limited income, she recommended against approval and their petition to adopt the third child was denied.[20]

In adoptions of babies and young children, when inspector and supervisor reached different conclusions, the process revealed an official preference for a nuclear family model. One young childless couple owned no property, lived on the husband's income as a tailor, and shared their house and expenses with relatives. Invoking the practice of informal kin adoption, the inspector suggested they adopt one of their six nieces or nephews "to satisfy their desire to have a child of their own." Despite the inspector's prejudices, the director approved the petition.[21]

As this last instance shows, couples with modest resources could receive approval, but the bar was higher for single women seeking to adopt babies and young children. They needed a substantial income and an impeccable reputation. A widow, who owned a hacienda in the state of Veracruz and impressed the inspector as a "good and unpretentious person," received permission to select a child from the foundling home. Another widow did not. She was not legally married to the man she lived with, her house was "fairly humble," and the inspector feared that her two grown sons might harm—that is, molest—an adopted child.[22] A young unmarried actress swore the inspector to secrecy so that the baby she hoped to adopt would appear to be her own: she failed to meet the morality standard. So did an applicant reputed to have run a brothel.[23]

At times, the inspectors seemed to grope as they weighed factors that might determine a woman's eligibility. One widowed schoolteacher applied to adopt two girls from the foundling home. She was over forty: was she too old to be eligible for state-approved motherhood? The law stated only that the adopter must be at least twenty-one. Did she have sufficient means? It was common knowledge that the public school system paid teachers low salaries, but the applicant owned property valued at close to five thousand pesos.[24] Was her conduct suspect? The woman supported herself in a profession that was not only honorable but a cornerstone of revolutionary policy. Did she meet tacit norms of femininity and domesticity? Neighbors and coworkers reported that she had a bad temper, which contradicted the maternal ideal of patience and self-sacrifice. The inspector expressed her reservations tentatively, writing that she feared the woman's temper might make a child unhappy. Moreover, with the applicant's work keeping her out of the house for long hours, who would tend to the girls? Ultimately, the inspector avoided recording judgments based on intangibles and recommended against approval on the grounds that the woman was too old and not financially secure.[25] But the case and its outcome prefigured the increasing focus on gender roles—particularly women's paid work—in the adoption review process.

Protected, Inclusive Childhood

Along with public education, restrictions on child labor, and expanded child health services, formal adoption law and policy demonstrated that the revolutionary state identified children and youth as vital national resources.[26] The implementation of legal adoption as a means of family formation dovetailed with a suite of policy initiatives tied to significant social and cultural changes in the meaning of childhood and the social value of children.[27] Adoption became an additional means for public agencies to reinforce specific family formations and practices centered on the concept of protected childhood.

Like the juvenile court system, adoption also served as an instrument for mediating parent-child relationships, but with some crucial differences. Juvenile court inspectors and officials scrutinized parents' expectations of their children's work. They were highly critical of family dynamics and morals. They often removed children from their families and placed them

19. Portrait of girls in the Hospicio de Niños, Mexico City, ca. 1932. Archivo General de la Nación, Archivo Fotográfico Enrique Díaz, Sección Cronológica, 42/7.

20. Portrait of boys in the Hospicio de Niños, Mexico City, ca. 1932. Archivo General de la Nación, Archivo Fotográfico Enrique Díaz, Sección Cronológica, 42/7.

in reform institutions. But court officials rarely recommended terminating a parent's legal authority or intervened to form new families. Adoption, in contrast, allowed the state not only to create families but also to encourage approved family forms.

In this spirit the Código Civil of 1928, which went into effect in 1932, strengthened the connection between legal adoption and the norms governing nuclear families by stating that only childless adults could adopt. The law now required adopters to be aged forty or older, perhaps to ensure their economic stability or perhaps so that women adopters would be unlikely to bear children who would compete with the adoptee for parental affection. Married partners could no longer adopt independently of one another, and all adopted children were to be considered family members. The new code, however, also reflected persistent anxieties about the permanence of the adoptive relationship and expressed a distrust of children brought into the home in this way. For example, the grounds for revoking an adoption could include the adoptees' failure to fulfill their side of the reciprocal obligations of support.[28] Yet by the late 1920s and early 1930s, there is also evidence of growing public awareness and acceptance of formal adoption. Critics of the new code considered the revised adoption requirements to be overly restrictive and called for lowering the age requirement and permitting people with children to adopt.[29] In response by 1938 the legal age to adopt was lowered to thirty.[30]

The growing public focus on motherhood and domesticity also increased incentives to adopt. The national press lavished coverage on the annual celebration of Mother's Day. Schools across the nation marked the day with special ceremonies, as it became a fixture in the Mexican secular holiday calendar.[31] A barrage of messages that women belonged in the home, which was not complete without children, came from all directions, from Catholic women's organizations to public programs such as the mothers' clubs that taught domestic hygiene and provided training in traditional women's work.[32] Social conservatives disparaged public programs for mothers and children and warned that the socialist sympathies of the Cárdenas administration would destroy the Mexican family.[33] With legal adoption, however, the government held an advantage over its ideological opponents: the state could create a mother.

When the Cárdenas administration reorganized the process of adopting children from state institutions, the revived program resonated with broad public discussion not only of motherhood and domesticity but also of national politics. Adoption fit within the context of the administration's expansion of family and children's assistance to reflect the renewed revolutionary commitment to labor rights and economic nationalism. In contrast to his predecessors who wanted to limit state commitment to public welfare, Cárdenas linked social welfare to broad social and economic national goals. Beginning in 1936 he stated that the federal government should strive to overcome the fundamental causes of social debility and incorporate every Mexican into the national economy. Revolutionary principles underwrote the state's obligation to promote full social integration through social assistance programs. The new ministry, Asistencia Pública, absorbed existing child welfare institutions and medical programs for mothers and children

UN LLAMADO A LA MUJER MEXICANA

Chiquillines actualmente internados en la Casa de Cuna, a quienes deben dirigir sus miradas las damitas que han manifestado interés por ser madrinas de estas criaturas.

¿QUIERE UD. SER MADRINA DE UN POBRE NIÑO?

También las pequeñitas que aquí aparecen reciben atención en la Casa de Cuna y esperan, a falta de familiares, el estímulo de una caricia, un consejo, un recuerdo...

21. "Un llamado a la mujer mexicana: ¿Quiere Ud. ser madrina de un pobre niño?"
(A call to Mexican women: Do you want to be the godmother of an unfortunate child?).
Asistencia 2, no. 11 (September 1936). Hemeroteca Nacional de México.

22. "Adopte Ud. un niño de la Casa de Cuna" (Adopt a child from the Casa de Cuna). *Asistencia* 2, no. 17 (March 1937). Hemeroteca Nacional de México.

to ensure that children would survive to participate in the national enterprise of production and consumption.[34]

In the wake of the economic depression of the early 1930s, the Cárdenas administration inherited severe overcrowding in Mexico City's principal orphanages. Welfare officials responded by publicizing adoption as well as fostering programs that paid foster families a stipend. To encourage public involvement women volunteers were encouraged to sponsor individual children; invoking the language of god-parenthood, they were called madrinas.[35] In October 1936 one social worker in the "proadoption campaign" reported that she had overseen fourteen adoptions and twenty-four foster care placements in recent months. Those placements required "extreme care" and close oversight to certify that the home conditions were favorable for the children in question.[36]

The staff also tried to persuade prospective adoptive and foster parents not to wait for blond, blue-eyed children but to accept available children housed in public institutions.[37] Yet the attitudes of welfare employees betrayed their own racial prejudices. In a 1935 interview by a popular weekly magazine, one staff member observed that there were so many adoptions that hardly any children remained in the foundling home: curiously, however, no one wanted to adopt the "ugly" ones. Those were the children destined to grow up in the network of public institutions.[38] Welfare's magazine, *Asistencia*, published photographs of children who had been combed and dressed to bring out their best features, as well as articles describing the personalities of individual children. To avoid overt racial designations such as white or mixed race, one such article used picturesque imagery to convey the children's coloring. A boy of two was described as a "delicate figure of wax," while the complexion of another boy looked "as if tanned by the caresses of a tropical sun."[39]

Adopters expressed their preferences in racial terms that revealed the influence of eugenics campaigns, as well as the persistent association between disease and the poor. One applicant wanted the child she adopted to be pretty and clear of any hereditary disease, "healthy in every sense."[40] Others feared the emergence of criminal "atavisms."[41] One couple explained that they had been advised to take a child on a temporary basis to observe whether she exhibited any "incorrigible atavisms."[42] Such concerns may have influenced adopters' preferences even more after 1938, when the policy shifted to promoting permanent adoptions.

Permanent adoptions were considered optimal for the child but also required even closer scrutiny of applicants. The Bufete de Terapia Social (Bureau of Social Therapy), an office within Asistencia Pública, centralized control and instituted rigorous background investigations of adoption applicants.[43] The emphasis on definitive adoption continued into the early 1940s under Cárdenas's successor, Manuel Ávila Camacho, when public welfare policy promoted legal measures to solidify family bonds. In the first two years of the Ávila Camacho administration, public welfare implemented 1,600 birth registrations, legitimized five thousand children born outside of marriage, reviewed 1,000 applications to adopt state wards, and approved 155 of them.[44]

Almost twenty years of social reform initiatives were consolidating into a full welfare-state structure that linked assistance to production and consumption and defined legalizing family relations as aid. In this context the adoption programs of the late 1930s and early 1940s highlighted women's roles in the national economic project and raised questions about the model of legal, state-sanctioned motherhood that emerged from the review and approval of adoption petitions. Adoption records reveal that all actors in the process contested constructions of motherhood, from the welfare officials and social workers, to would-be mothers and employers of domestic servants, to mothers seeking public assistance for themselves and their children. These cross-class interactions reflected the influence of nearly two decades of family-centered social reform that had focused on child health, childrearing, and domesticity; they also suggested that those programs had produced contradictory effects.

The actual negotiations over maternal qualifications for adoption revealed many of these conflicts. As state-employed social workers, adoption applicants, and mothers of children considered available for adoption interacted and officials made their decisions, the evolving constructions of maternity seemed to restate and perpetuate prerevolutionary ideas about entitlements to family life; these centered on gendered notions of dependence and reinforced a contradiction between motherhood and paid work. Approval for adoption favored women who depended on a husband's income and who could afford to employ domestic servants. The working-class couples most likely to win approval conformed to a traditional division of labor. Overall, the pattern of official endorsements reflected an enduring—often class-inflected—understanding of motherhood that separated the emotional maternal role from paid work; it especially devalued the motherhood of women who worked as domestic servants.[45]

Social workers played a pivotal role in these decisions. During the late 1930s and early 1940s, before most adoption petitions passed to the bureau's lawyers, applicants underwent the scrutiny of social workers' home visits and divulged their histories of infertility, ideas about family, and motives for adopting children. In turn, like the inspectors of the 1920s, the social workers, who came from a variety of backgrounds but largely harbored middle-class values, became the gatekeepers of state-conferred maternity.[46]

Since the 1920s proliferating public health and welfare agencies had relied on in-house training to staff new positions for visiting nurses and welfare inspectors, whose work was formerly undertaken by volunteer women's charitable groups. By the mid-1930s a social work training program based in the Secretaría de Educación Pública (SEP) combined secondary education with courses in domestic skills and attracted young, primarily working-class students. Meanwhile, a short-lived program under the Facultad de Derecho of the Universidad Nacional Autónoma (Faculty of Law of the National Autonomous University) offered a professional credential geared toward middle-class aspirants.[47]

A June 1937 directive mandated that graduates of the SEP program fill all social work positions in the Bufete de Terapia Social. Months later, however, when only eight out of forty staff members possessed the required credentials, a program administrator explained that unqualified employees had "entered anew . . . by mere favoritism" or by "special appointment": even some of the supervisors lacked qualifications.[48] In 1942 welfare officials, still concerned by the lack of training, encouraged social workers already on the staff to begin or complete the course at the Escuela para Trabajadoras Sociales (School for Social Workers) now at the university and sponsored internships and seminars for the students. While these measures soon produced "a notable improvement in the quality of work," their introduction in 1942 suggests that during the late 1930s social workers did not adhere to a single official standard for evaluating adoption applicants.[49]

Indeed, social workers in the Bufete de Terapia Social brought potentially conflicting attitudes to their dealings with women seeking to adopt through public welfare and with mothers seeking assistance. Social workers staffing community centers in working-class neighborhoods intervened in family crises. Emergency foster-care arrangements sometimes circumvented official procedures entirely. Instead of placing children in welfare institutions, the community-based social workers distributed the children of women who applied for aid to private households until the precipitating crisis could be resolved. The social workers referred to such placements as "temporary adoptions," but some foster families became attached to the children and formalized the arrangements through permanent adoption. The same social workers ran an informal employment service linking women needing paid work with employers seeking domestics.[50]

As so many juvenile court cases revealed, the low wages and live-in requirements of domestic service may actually have impeded the reunification of families separated by emergency measures. Moreover, legal adoption rendered separation permanent, gave legal weight to the informal transfer of children across class lines, and reinforced differentials in class entitlements to family. With the policy emphasis on children as future citizens and producers, and state endorsement of women's maternal identity, legal adoption also served to transfer valuable social capital to Mexico's middle class.

Seeking Motherhood

With society and political culture recognizing them primarily in their maternal roles, women needed children to participate in national life. By the late 1930s adoption petitions not only testified to a strong link between maternity and emotional fulfillment for women from all walks of life but also suggested that many women relied on motherhood to claim their adult status and participate in public arenas.

Except in permitting single women to adopt, neither the 1917 family law nor the 1928 civil code fully recognized the influence of women in changing Mexican adoption practice. By the late 1930s, in marked contrast to informal adoptions from public orphanages before 1917 and the applications of the mid-1920s, married men initiated few petitions and single men even fewer: officials screened such applications cautiously. Adoption practices now centered on fulfilling women's understandings of family and maternity, which did not necessarily include marriage. The desire for children among childless married and single women motivated the majority of the 160 adoption applications reviewed by the Bufete de Terapia Social from 1938 to 1942. Wives initiated most of the 105 applications from couples, and single, divorced, or widowed women submitted 45 petitions. Some of the women applicants lived in comfort; others supported themselves with marginal commercial ventures earning only a few pesos a day but still acted on a strong sense of entitlement to motherhood and family life. Overall, these adoption petitions testify to the centrality of maternity for Mexican women's identity and fulfillment across the social spectrum.

In their letters of inquiry women wrote of their yearning for children. The home, clearly defined as the female sphere, was incomplete without children. One applicant, who had lost her own three babies in infancy, confessed to being lonely and unhappy. Over the years she had taken in little children, but their mothers or grandmothers would reclaim them, leaving her alone again. Another woman wrote, "As we are a married couple without children and find that something is missing in our home, permit me to beg that you concede the great happiness" of allowing them to adopt.[51]

Most wife-initiated petitions from childless couples sought to adopt infants or toddlers, emphasizing a nurturing maternal role. One couple had the cradle and baby clothes ready, everything of the best quality, at the time of the social worker's home visit.[52] A couple from Coahuila wanted to adopt an infant "newborn so that they can feel more affection for it."[53] Another couple wanted "a baby, a little boy." The wife had been raised in a foundling home, which may explain her desire to adopt a child in infancy.[54]

Some petitioners also revealed the desire for the status that came from motherhood. An older married applicant traveled to the capital from Zacatecas to adopt orphan girls, two "little women," seven to fourteen years old. She saw adoption as a way to attain a reflected maternal identity: "When people see them all dressed up, it will seem like family."[55]

Single women applicants considered marriage irrelevant to their desire for maternal status and family life. One woman, a widow, applied to adopt on behalf of her daughter, who at twenty-two did not meet the age requirement. The mother told the disapproving social worker that her daughter had never been interested in marriage and planned never to marry.[56] Petitions also show that many single women had already brought children into their homes and sought only to formalize the arrangements. In 1939 a single woman applied to adopt a girl who had come to her four years earlier when the child's mother died. The girl's father was in the army and could not care for her. To enroll the girl in school the woman needed to present the birth certificate, but it was in the father's name, and she wanted "it to look like the girl is her own daughter."[57] An unmarried schoolteacher applied to adopt her brother's three orphaned, legitimate children. By 1939 she had taken care of the children for four years and, observed the social worker, they viewed her as their mother.[58] Another woman petitioned to adopt her two-year-old niece; the girl's mother relinquished her parental rights, stating that she lacked the financial resources to support the child.[59] These latter two instances reveal the long-established role of unmarried women adopting to keep relatives in the family network.[60]

Like their married counterparts, single women who petitioned to adopt also sought emotional fulfillment. After four years in the capital, an employee in a dentist's office was lonely. An orphan herself, she applied to adopt a girl.[61] An office worker in the property registry who was the only unmarried sibling in her family applied to adopt a seven-year-old girl.[62] Such applications offer some insight into ideas about family among women in Mexico's urban salaried middle class: in addition to emotional fulfillment, these would-be adoptive mothers sought the social inclusion they believed maternity would confer. In her petition to adopt a girl, one unmarried insurance company employee wrote, "My object is to use the money that I spend in amusements on the girl, and in this way support my country and benefit an orphan who lacks everything."[63] By invoking patriotism, this applicant underscored the ways that maternity represented public identity and offered access to participation in social and political life.

New Norms, Old Family Forms

Women applicants generally asked to adopt girls, pointing to a number of factors, including the divide between the social worlds of men and women. Girls were probably considered more docile than boys. But decades of informal adoption from public orphanages had also established a preference for girls and blurred the boundaries between adopting a family member and acquiring an unpaid domestic. Indeed, the persistent prerevolutionary ethos of protection and dependence that elided informal adoption with labor could still trump formal adoption, as one couple learned when they were told that the orphaned boy they wanted to adopt formally was unavailable. His sister had been released from the orphanage to work as a domestic. This arrangement affected the couple's adoption petition. The sister's employer assumed the role of the boy's godmother and sent him clothes, and his sister visited him weekly. The employer had the surname Lorenzana, indicating that she or a parent had been abandoned to the Mexico City foundling home.[64] Perhaps her own experience motivated her interest in the siblings. Although the sister, a minor, had no legal authority to prevent her brother's adoption, her employer's involvement established a claim to the boy that officials recognized.

Protective legislation against child labor and the legal definition of adoption as family formation did succeed in mitigating exploitation in an increasing number of cases. The situation of a fourteen-year-old girl illustrates both the expectations that adoptees perform domestic work and the state's role in enforcing legal protections. The girl had gone to live for a trial period with a brother and sister, proprietors of a fine yard-goods store. They explained that the girl behaved well, but that she was very serious and uncommunicative and cried whenever letters arrived from her friends in the orphanage. The prospective adopters told the social worker that they bought the girl clothes and let her go to the movies with one of their nieces, but she remained discontent and finally faked illness to return to the orphanage. The caseworker found the girl taciturn: she asserted only that she did not want to live with her prospective adopters because they made her do housework, which she considered a waste of time.[65]

To convince the girl to accept the arrangement, the social worker argued that formal adoption would oblige her adopters to protect her and treat her as a daughter and to put her interests before those of other relatives. The girl responded that she preferred to live with a friend whose mother had offered her a place to stay. She wanted to continue learning dressmaking and believed that adoption would confine her to housework. The social worker insisted that in her friend's home the girl would have no security, that her friend's mother would favor her own daughter, and that in the end the girl would find herself without home or family. Still she refused to return. Nor was she forced to do so. The store proprietors requested permission to inquire whether other girls would accept their proposal.[66]

Officials wielded the legal authority to deflect petitioners with blatantly exploitative agendas and now did so more consistently than their predecessors of the previous decade, but they still avoided directly criticizing petitioners who sought young workers. An applicant from Michoacán complained of the difficulty of finding domestics and sought to adopt a ten- or twelve-year-old girl, "no matter how ugly," to care for an infant. The confiding reference to the domestic's appearance may have been an allusion either to race or to the tendency for male employers to sexually exploit domestic servants. The lawyer of the bureau refrained from condemning the applicant's motives but, citing the law, denied the petition on the grounds that adopters had to be childless.[67] In other instances officials required assurances that the adopted child would receive a formal education. These measures reflected both legal intent and officials' optimism that adoption would confer middle-class status and opportunities rather than consign adoptees to domestic labor.

Thus, although legal adoption reinforced the trend away from child labor, it still proved difficult to eradicate expectations established by the long-standing practice of informally adopting girls as domestics. When a girl claimed she was being adopted to work as a domestic, the social worker ignored the evidence and argued that adoption promised her the protection of family relations and home. Nevertheless, for the gatekeepers of formal adoption, the relationship between motherhood and paid work proved far more problematic.

Labor and State-Approved Motherhood

Adoption petitioners had to meet requirements beyond those stated in the civil code. Explicit criteria included good health, economic stability, and, for couples, proof of civil marriage. Applicants needed to present three letters testifying that their economic, social, and educational conditions would improve the life and guarantee the future of the adopted child.[68] These ostensibly concrete qualifications were open to interpretation; qualitative criteria such as "correct behavior" or "honorable reputation" were even more so. Furthermore, only after the social worker interviewed the applicant and favorably evaluated the home environment could the case progress to the legal phase. Even more than the inspectors of the 1920s, social workers' home-visit reports consistently reflected middle-class biases, especially regarding gender roles. In general, the review process screened applications from single women by class, preferring professionals, and screened couples for their conformity to a traditional gendered division of labor.

Evaluations of women applicants also turned on race. The social workers never remarked on male applicants' appearance but made scrupulous note of women's, especially skin color: the darker the prospective mother, the more likely that the social worker would find fault.[69] This bias flew in the face of the official line encouraging adopters to accept mixed-race children. Like the descriptions of children that avoided racial terms, social workers found other ways to label the female applicants. One social worker described a thirty-two-year-old applicant, originally from the state of Michoacán, as "dark, like a farm woman." Moreover, she wrote, "She does not present the appearance of a well-dressed woman, despite the fact that she wears good things. . . . Her manner reveals little culture."[70]

In the homes of single, working-class women, prevalent attitudes toward women's paid labor predisposed social workers to perceive immorality or lack of approved domesticity. One such applicant, a widow, lived in a tenement and supported herself on the two pesos daily she made from her small shop. The social worker conceded that "this woman does not appear to be depraved" but disqualified her petition in part because the shop opened into the tenement, where she observed, with distaste, "an infinity of unkempt and half-dressed little ones." The applicant had already raised one foster son, now twenty-two years old, and all witnesses affirmed he was a respectable person with a steady job in a stocking factory, but that failed to counterbalance the negative impression created by the señora's neighbors.[71] Nor could the applicant's self-perception as a hard-working family provider counteract the social worker's preconceptions.

The approval process favored middle-class applicants, with taste in furniture and decor a measure of class and culture. The home-visit report condemned the application of a widow who earned her living making and selling sweets: "In addition to being of very poor quality, her furniture is ugly and uncared for."[72] By contrast, a caseworker exuded admiration for the tasteful acquisitions of a successful divorcée, a partner in a firm making children's clothes. The petitioner herself had been adopted informally at age three when her mother left her with the family that raised her. Married for thirteen years, during which time she had not worked, she divorced her husband in 1935 for living with and fathering children by another woman. In 1938 having reached the required age, she petitioned to adopt an eight-year-old girl whom she had fostered for a year. At the time of this girl's formal adoption, the woman was furnishing a newly purchased house, complete with garage and patio, in a fashionable neighborhood. Two years later she applied to adopt again. The first girl, the social worker observed, loved the applicant as if she were her true mother, had finished primary school, was studying dressmaking, and expressed enthusiasm about the prospect of a companion.[73] Although the applicant's divorce and career might seem to contradict approved models of dependent domesticity, her luxurious home and staff of servants instead represented the pinnacle of tasteful consumption and class-based concepts of modern maternity that distinguished emotional and nurturing mothering from domestic labor.

For couples lacking such means, social workers tended to recommend approval of petitions when the wife devoted herself to housework and maintained acceptable standards of domesticity. Evaluations largely reflected the criteria emphasized in the childrearing and domestic hygiene brochures distributed by public health agencies; the majority of the advice literature presumed a middle-class home and a homemaker without external distractions.[74] But rather than cite specific lapses of prescribed hygiene, such as inadequate ventilation or plumbing, social workers couched both positive and negative perceptions in qualitative terms that reflected the female applicant's moral character. For example, after visiting the home of a former hairdresser married to the proprietor of a clothing stall in La Lagunilla market, the social worker noted approvingly, "Within their means they live with sufficient comfort. . . . She does not have to work to help her husband." She described their small apartment, "furnished very modestly, but reflecting the activity of the señora as a good homemaker." The social worker concluded, "They seem to be very good people."[75] Another couple from Amecameca, in the state of Mexico, presented a marriage license describing them as "mixed race." The wife could not sign her name. The social worker described the applicants as members of the "peasant class," but she continued, "One sees that they are very decent people in their manners and dress; they show a neatness and cleanliness in their clothes and persons." This couple applied to adopt in the context of the Cárdenas administration's solidarity with peasants and workers: those policies seem to have influenced the social worker's perceptions.[76]

Even so, bias against married women working for pay remained strong. For working-class applicants, the wife's paid work presented the steepest obstacle to adoption approval. For example, both members of one working-class couple had completed primary school and finished their commercial course. He worked as a driver. She had a sewing business specializing in children's clothes. Although this couple employed a domestic, the wife's work probably prejudiced the social worker against their case. The infant girl they selected was denied them because "she had been requested by other people who were in a better economic position and had more time to attend to her."[77] Eventually, the señora's persistence prevailed, and the couple adopted a baby girl.[78] Immediate approval rewarded another couple living on less than four pesos a day, probably because the wife did not leave home to work and because the child they selected had not been "requested by people in a better economic condition." The social worker considered their apartment "a real home."[79]

When social workers chose to construe class as an obstacle, however, the wife's need to do her own housework justified denying the petition. Another applicant and her husband had both completed primary school. He made about four pesos daily working in a dairy store. One of the less judgmental social workers gave their home environment a negative evaluation: "It cannot be beneficial for the minor, since the petitioner has to dedicate herself exclusively to housework, because she lacks the money to pay a maid, and, although she appears to be an affable and kind person, she lacks a favorable education."[80] Their first petition was denied. When they applied again the wife had a sewing job outside the home and brought in an extra thirty pesos a month. Unfortunately, the most fastidious social worker performed the second home visit. Of their apartment house she wrote in obvious disgust: "So many people live here that one hears a loud murmur as in the markets." There were "many dirty children playing in the patio and in the corridors, offering a very disagreeable appearance." She told the couple that they would have to move to adopt, but her report recommended denying their application on the basis of their income.[81] Married or single, women who worked and/or could not afford a domestic became suspect in their capacity to care for a child. But the heaviest judgments fell on women who struggled to support their children.

Mothers and Domestics

Even as the state centralized the regulation of formal adoption, informal adoption networks continued to transfer children across class lines. Because formal, legal adoption was still a novelty, many adopters pursued both informal and formal means, especially when seeking infants. Although petitioners preferred infants and toddlers, often only older children were available through public welfare.[82] One couple seeking an infant withdrew their application after waiting over a year, and other files of couples requesting babies record no outcome, suggesting that they either let the matter drop or pursued other approaches.[83]

Couples who obtained infants through informal networks not only avoided the intensive scrutiny of the review process but also enjoyed the tacit approval of the social work staff. A college-educated couple sought to legalize the status of an infant girl they had acquired informally, meanwhile passing the baby off as their own. One person writing a testimonial for them noted that the señor "is enchanted since becoming a father; he is mad for the little daughter born a few months ago." The social worker noted coyly in her report that she refrained from comment.[84] She also refrained from investigating the child's history.

The intersection of official and unofficial routes to adoption exposes the networks that circulated children across class lines, often through the employment of domestics. A couple from Guerrero applied to adopt a six- or seven-year-old boy to be the companion of another boy they had raised; he had been born in their house to a Guatemalan domestic and "given" to the wife.[85] Officially, adoption required the consent of a surviving parent or relative.[86] But in relations between employers and domestic servants, the unequal positions of class and power put into question the nature of consent.

The experience of Sra. Flores de Trujillo, a recently widowed mother of six, illustrates the pressures on domestics to relinquish children to their employers—and the conflicts of interest that arose when social workers used domestic service as emergency aid. When Flores arrived in Mexico City from rural Michoacán, she was about to give birth to her seventh child. The Cruz Roja put her up in a hotel for the birth, but subsequently she lived in a construction site with her newborn and three-year-old daughter. When she approached the public welfare system for aid, she had not eaten since the day before and could not nurse the infant. A social worker took Flores, with her two youngest, to work as a servant in a private home in a fashionable neighborhood.[87]

A few weeks later Flores returned to the welfare office and reported that she had quit her job, was now living with a friend, and had given the baby to her employer's daughter. The social worker chastised Flores for giving her baby away, although she affirmed her right to do so.[88] Then together they proceeded to the employer's home to verify the story. The employer reported that Flores was not accustomed to serving and that she showed indifference to and refused to nurse her baby. In addition, the employer had offered to send Flores out of the city to stay with relatives, to pay for the journey, and to put all her older children in Catholic school. The social worker recorded that the family had fed the three-year-old at their own table, bathed her, and given her clothes and medical attention. Concerning the infant, the employer claimed that Flores had signed a paper consenting to the informal adoption, although out of Flores's hearing the social worker confided that the paper had no legal value. When the social worker visited the luxuriously furnished home of the employer's married daughter she found the baby asleep in her cradle and the daughter distraught that the baby might be taken from her. The social worker reassured her that she would do everything to facilitate the adoption process, in the interest of securing the future of "our special concern, the baby."[89]

Several factors combined to shift the social worker's focus from aiding Flores and her family to facilitating her baby's adoption. Since Flores had rejected domestic service as a solution to her needs, and the employer had offered to educate the older children, the social worker may have assumed that further efforts to improve her situation would prove fruitless. Meanwhile, Flores had found a place to live. Most importantly, having voluntarily relinquished her baby, she showed a lack of appropriate maternal sentiment, while the prospective adoptive mother not only was secure economically but also demonstrated her emotional attachment to the baby. From Flores's perspective, however, the employer's lavish attentions to her three-year-old and offers to educate her older children may have seemed like pressure to separate her from her children and her infant. This case and its outcome vividly illuminate the conflicting roles of public welfare in the politics of class and maternity.

In another instance dating from 1942, during the Ávila Camacho administration, the social worker also appeared to favor the interests of adopters over the interests of the mother receiving aid. Although the social worker evinced sympathy for a mother's duress and appreciated the strength of her maternal feelings, she offered no material assistance to the family. Poverty and depression made this mother contemplate giving up her seventh child, whose birth she awaited. The family, also migrants from Michoacán, lived in a tenement for the indigent; the husband had rheumatism and was unemployed. The couple learned about the welfare system's adoption program through an employee at the public cafeteria where their children ate breakfast. When the social worker visited the expectant mother in the hospital, she found her suffering physically and depressed over her dilemma. She had not discussed adoption with her husband; she stated that they understood their responsibility as parents. "She has the idea she is going to die," recorded the social worker. Still, the woman withheld her consent to adoption. The social worker was impressed by the woman's tenacious maternal sentiment, but she made no recommendation for aid that would help the mother keep her child. In effect, she encouraged her to relinquish it.[90]

The social worker's behavior seems at odds with other policy priorities in the welfare administration. From September 1941 through August 1942, public welfare officials processed 1,000 adoption applications from married couples and approved 155. This acceleration of the adoption program must be seen in the context of the policy shift, under the Ávila Camacho administration, that emphasized legalizing and normalizing families and promoting children's placement in a stable home and family environment for optimal development. To meet these goals the public welfare department expanded the number of group homes and revived programs facilitating temporary placements. Yet policy statements also explicitly asserted that "the indigence of the mother must not be reason to separate her completely from her children" and recommended grants or pensions to stabilize households in need.[91] These measures echoed Dr. Federico Gómez's recommendations for fighting hospitalism: infant welfare clients should be returned to their mothers. This trend in child welfare also reflected international policy developments that were moving away from the institutional internment of children and toward home-based assistance.[92]

In this context, the social worker should have immediately provided assistance to support the Michoacán couple to keep their family intact and provide for the awaited baby. That she failed to do so testifies not only to the critical ways that state agents mediated public policies but also to the persistence of biases that favored the transfer of children into families of means in the modernizing domestic economies of postrevolutionary Mexico.

Protected Childhood and Mothers' Work in the Revolutionary Family

Legal adoption, as an element of Mexico's revolutionary legislation, illuminates an important pathway of child circulation and exposes the tension between change and continuity in middle-class family practice. The law was a landmark in the nation's effort to institutionalize the concept of protected childhood, a childhood free from labor. By the late 1930s many applicants had embraced adoption as a way to form parent-child relationships. At the same time the more that legal adoption succeeded in protecting welfare wards from exploitation as workers, the more the approval process focused on mothers' work.

By the late 1930s proliferating community-based welfare programs and centralized oversight of legal adoption created multiple intersections where the paths of mothers and would-be mothers crossed, where women social workers assessed worthiness for motherhood, and where officials used law and public policy to arbitrate the movement of children out of their families of origin and into approved households. In this complex social economy, the choices about moving children followed class-based differentials in the value of women's reproductive labor and echoed the late nineteenth-century discourse and practice that surrounded wet-nursing. The ideal adoptive mother could afford to delegate domestic work to a domestic and devote herself to the emotional nurture of the child. Working-class women who held to traditional divisions of labor that kept them in the home and dependent on a husband's support also received approval for legal adoption. The very kinds of paid work that permitted women to keep their children with them during the day, whether in a shop opening into the tenement courtyard or next to a sewing machine in the living space, disqualified them for state-conferred motherhood. Women without even those options, who were forced to work as domestics, were perceived as doubly dependent—on state assistance and on their employers—and they remained vulnerable to temporary or permanent separation from their children. This continuity with nineteenth-century patterns of child circulation points to the limits of social reform in the face of deeply held concepts of family founded on class that persisted well into the twentieth century.

The social workers' judgments appeared to contradict policy established in other branches of the federal government—and when it came to race, their attitudes contradicted their own colleagues' efforts to place mixed-race children in permanent homes. At the upper levels of policy formations, Cárdenas tied public assistance to social and economic inclusion and to state solidarity with the working class. Reclaiming maternity from conservative Catholics, federal agencies under Cárdenas articulated and promoted a secular version of motherhood linked to national development. Under Ávila Camacho, public Mothers' Day rituals on a mass scale distributed labor-saving appliances, including pawned sewing machines, to working-class mothers.[93] During both administrations, proliferating neighborhood-based programs such as day care centers and factory crèches, mothers' clubs, and public cafeterias provided important resources that supported single working mothers in their efforts to keep their families together. But in the families depending on those resources, mothers worked and often their children did too, as the records of the juvenile court attest. The model of protected childhood that shaped federal adoption policy remained a largely middle-class privilege; in addition, federal officials used adoption to encourage and reinforce middle-class family formations.

The adoption cases of the late 1930s and early 1940s reveal enduring contradictions at the intersections of several key concepts: protected childhood, reproductive labor, paid work, and national goals. Formal adoption provided another instrument to protect children from labor exploitation. But the ideal of protected childhood—like the ideal of infant health—required full-time mothers. Whether policy priorities linked assistance to production or emphasized family legalization, two primary considerations qualified a woman for state-conferred motherhood: either she devoted herself to housework and did not work for wages, or she enjoyed the services of a domestic. To be entitled to the virtues of motherhood a woman had to be dependent on a male breadwinner or have access to the reproductive labor of women in a lower social and weaker economic position. The regulation of legal adoption through the welfare system separated emotional and nurturing motherhood from reproductive labor and affirmed class statuses based on divisions of labor. This process revealed the implicit hierarchies that ordered Mexico's "revolutionary family"—the family model that reflected the structure and priorities of state consolidation and economic development.[94]

Conclusion

Family, Work, and Welfare in Modern Mexico

When Mexico passed its first social security law in 1943, the legislation fulfilled a commitment to Mexico's workers that had been spelled out in the Constitution of 1917. That commitment emerged from the revolutionary struggle that overthrew the Díaz regime, but the ongoing conflicts in national politics postponed its fulfillment. When a political compromise had at last been reached and the law was finally issued, it established a pact of reciprocity between organized labor and the Mexican state.[1] Also reflected in the law was the influence of twenty-five years of social reform focused on the family and public debate over the state's relationship to the family.

Broadly conceived in terms of the state's moral responsibility to safeguard the "human patrimony" that represented the wealth of the nation, the law delineated the ideal characteristics of the modern working-class family: hardworking, healthy, stable, and prolifically reproductive.[2] Like the labor code of 1931, however, the social security code left informal workers in an ambiguous position. They were not included in the code's safety net and would have to wait until a future date for similar protections.[3] Thus, the law represented a landmark in the Mexican state's commitment to working families, and at the same time perpetuated the social marginality of those subsisting on the fringes of Mexico's formal economy. This legislation, therefore, provides an opportunity for a final reflection on continuity and change in Mexican concepts of family and work, children's social roles, and social responsibility for children over an arc of almost sixty years.

Forged through years of negotiations between leaders of organized labor and officials in the presidential administrations of Lázaro Cárdenas and Manuel Ávila Camacho, the social security code established the state's moral responsibility to support the well-being of the community, "of which the state is the representative synthesis."[4] Designed for workers in manufacturing, commerce, and transportation, the law focused on the economic sectors considered crucial for the development of a "modern industrialized democracy."[5] The code established a system whereby workers' contributions from their wages or salaries entitled them to health care and disability insurance, retirement pensions, pensions for widows — including unmarried partners — and support for orphans to age sixteen. The law's comprehensive maternity coverage tied national prosperity to children's health and population growth.[6]

In contrast to the bootstrap labor ethos of the Díaz regime, the provisions of the social security code were founded on concepts of reciprocity between the state and its working citizens that resembled the reciprocal obligations within families defined in Mexico's civil code. In the national collectivity, just as in working families, labor represented and cemented reciprocal relationships. As the law's authors explained in a preamble, workers' productivity contributed directly to national wealth: in return, the state owed them protection when accidents, illness, age, or death prevented them from working.[7] Through the reciprocity of workers' contributions and state benefits, the law also established that the state shared with working parents the responsibility to support and protect their dependents, because the social stability of the collectivity rested on the economic stability of those families.

Since the mid-nineteenth century, when Mexican liberals brought the family cycle under the authority of a secular state, statutes on the family had set forth the ideological terms structuring family relationships and the family's relationship to the state. During the revolution Mexicans engaged in an intense discussion about the values that should shape the family in the new order. Debates over the implications of divorce revealed a profound concern that sanctioning serial unions would destabilize the moral foundations of the family and society. The family law of 1917 granted some important new rights to married women, but it preserved the fundamental gender and generational order as the foundation of family morality.

The social security code also defined the ideal family and the ideal state-family relationship. Thus, its concessions on questions of gender and morality represented additional milestones. The code's authors acknowledged that many working-class couples did not get married: so unmarried partners and the children of those unions were included in the benefits system. Serial unions were not stigmatized, either, although the law did stipulate that couples had to live together for five years for the unmarried partner to receive benefits.[8]

The law's definition of the family also combined old and new views on women's roles. Women workers were included on an equal basis with men. But the code focused on women in their reproductive role: one of the law's fundamental rationales was to promote healthy and prolific childbearing. To that end, maternity coverage included pre-and postnatal care. Women workers would receive paid leave immediately before and after giving birth, as well as six months of support for breast-feeding after they returned to work.[9] These benefits were designed to reduce mortality in infancy and early childhood, and also to ensure that the birth of a child would not burden a worker's domestic economy.[10]

This official acceptance of working-class family practices contrasted markedly with earlier attitudes and policies and showed that some ideological contradictions had been resolved. As Mexico City's 1898 wet nurse regulations demonstrated, government officials had long been concerned about infant mortality, but they had also been prepared to sacrifice the babies of working-class wet nurses for the benefit of more privileged children.

Elite disdain for wet nurses and the terms of wet-nursing regulation had also shown how difficult it was for privileged Mexicans to accept women who worked for pay as mothers in their own right. In the 1920s administrators of the pioneering public programs in reproductive health still assumed that mothers remained at home and warned them that paid work endangered their babies. Thanks to the social security code, now women workers and workers' wives in the favored economic sectors would receive maternity benefits even more comprehensive than those offered by the Centros de Higiene Infantil. So would their children. Indeed, the code's authors placed great importance on children's health and argued that the future of the nation depended on it.

The social security code also marked an advance in the institutionalization of nonworking childhood. It included children in only one role: recipients of benefits. Parents were the workers; children were dependents. This definition of childhood highlights the dramatic changes in thinking about working-class children's economic roles that had taken place since the Porfiriato. In 1906 a lawyer in the Díaz government had stated that a child as young as seven could be self-supporting. Seven-year-olds could work legally in factories with parental permission. Welfare administrators, as the guardians of parentless children housed in Mexico City's public orphanages, routinely oversaw their adoption for work. These laws and policies were enacted in a society that valued children. Indeed, public welfare policies privileged them: beginning in 1884 admission to the Hospicio was restricted to children. But child labor was one of the defining differences between poor and privileged Mexican families.

When the 1917 Constitution raised the legal age for work to twelve and established special protections for young workers to age sixteen, two kinds of arguments supported that change. One stemmed from the labor movement: male workers were assumed to be sole supporters of their families and should earn a living wage. The other arose from changing concepts of childhood: children, like women, should be protected from exploitative and harmful work. From both perspectives Mexico's constitutional articles on labor were progressive for the day. But international support for the regulation of child labor gathered momentum quickly after World War I. In 1919 the International Labor Organization set a higher standard than Mexico's by establishing a minimum working age of fourteen.[11]

Over the next two decades the rulings and interventions of the juvenile court and welfare officials overseeing adoption showed how difficult it was to enforce legal standards on child labor within the realm of the family. Strong sentiments against child labor informed the mandate and programs of the juvenile court. The concepts of child and adolescent development that shaped the court's program reflected the influence of the medical and child protection wings of Mexico's puericulture movement. Juvenile court founder and judge Roberto Solís Quiroga saw work and family as diametrically opposed. But the circumstances of individual families often required court officials to compromise on those principles and to endorse both the moral and economic motives of parents who put their children to work. Meanwhile, welfare officials struggled with their own biases about the destinies of working-class children as they tried to enforce the new legal definition of adoption. Now that it was no longer legal to adopt children as servants, officials found it was difficult to determine the appropriate moral and economic characteristics of prospective parents, especially working-class applicants. Thus, the inner workings of those two government agencies reveal the complexity of negotiations over family practice, work, and concepts of childhood during a period of significant social transformation.

In 1937 international discussion of child labor was stimulated anew when the International Labor Organization issued a new convention that raised the minimum age for employment to fifteen. Mexico was among the nations favoring this change, a stance that reflected a consensus in official circles.[12] In 1943 an official in the labor ministry advanced the kinds of moral and economic arguments against child labor that informed the definition of children as dependents in the social security code. Paula Alegría, director of the Oficina de Investigaciones del Trabajo de la Mujer y del Niño (Investigative Office of the Labor of Women and Children) in the Secretaría del Trabajo y Previsión Social (Ministry of Labor and Social Security), agreed with the criticisms of child labor that shaped the mandate of the juvenile court in the 1920s. Work harmed children; it drew them out of school and stunted their intellectual and physical development. She accused parents who put their young children to work of being selfish: they should put their children's well-being before economic imperative. She also accused such parents of violating child labor laws.[13]

But Alegría's main argument was economic: Mexico could no longer afford child labor. Now that machines had replaced people in so many Mexican workplaces, there were not enough jobs. Working children drove down wages and deprived deserving adults of employment. In these ways child labor contributed to unemployment, threatened hard-won labor rights, exacerbated poverty, and produced subnormal adults, undermining the competitiveness of the Mexican economy and the viability of the Mexican population.[14] Her critique placed the values, laws, and interests of a modern society and industrializing economy against the outmoded and even criminal practices of child labor. Instead of the legal concept of reciprocity between parents and children—and the family morality founded on work that those relations entailed—she described children and adults in conflict in a competitive labor market.

Her arguments delineated a radically different model of children's social and economic roles from those informing the family strategies of Mexico City's working families. As critics of child labor shifted the debate from the sphere of family dynamics and subsistence to the plane of national modernization and development, they widened the ideological distance between work and family—and between work and childhood. By defining children as nonworking dependents, the social security code marked a milestone in erasing labor from concepts of childhood, at least in some social and economic sectors. Indeed, the social security code was part of a long history of laws and policies that maintained the material and symbolic distinction between working and nonworking childhoods. Mexico's professionals and bureaucrats now viewed the labor practices of working families as unmodern, immoral, and illegal. These characterizations marked the social gulf between Mexico's professional and middle classes—now joined by the labor elite—and the poor.

Indeed, from the late nineteenth to the mid-twentieth century, policies that advanced the concept of protected, nonworking childhood reinforced class-distinct family forms and within them, traditional gender roles. As adoption reviews show time and again, protected children required stay-at-home mothers, better yet if they employed domestics so they could devote themselves to the emotional aspects of childrearing. In Mexico City households, those domestics may have been mothers who sought assistance from public welfare or girls released on probation by the juvenile court. Thus, the ideal family was founded not only on traditional gender divisions of

23. Portrait of a family with servants, Mexico City, ca. 1930. Instituto Nacional de Antropología e Historia, Fototeca Nacional, Fondo Casasola.

labor but also on a class-based hierarchy of work within the household. Indeed, like the colonial censuses that counted orphans among the servants of the house, the 1950 and 1960 national censuses included live-in nonkin economic dependents in the definition of the family.[15] That kind of worker was excluded from the moral economy established by the social security code. When the low wages those workers earned forced their families to separate, the state offered welfare assistance.

The social security code may have marked the maturity of Mexico's welfare state, but the code had fundamentally different goals from those of public welfare, and the Instituto Mexicano del Seguro Social (Mexican Institute of Social Security) issued a statement to make sure the Mexican public understood the difference. Most importantly, the workers covered by social security contributed to their own benefits: recipients of welfare did not contribute to their own aid. Social security was designed to prevent crises; welfare could not prevent but only alleviate them. Ultimately, no matter how well meaning and generous public welfare programs were, they only "perpetuated the economic disadvantage of the poorest classes" and did nothing to diminish the social inequalities of poverty and wealth in society as a whole.[16]

Mexico's social security code, then, illustrates yet again that different social sectors and actors were included in the national family on different terms. The social security bureaucracy's distinctions between productive workers and welfare clients showed that the model of welfare advanced during the Cárdenas administration had been short-lived. Then, social assistance had been defined as a right and a benefit to the nation. One official wrote that assistance transformed "the proletarian element" into healthy members of society and productive workers who contributed to "the well-being of the collectivity."[17] By 1943 the labor of that element of the working class no longer counted in national development. Yet in the interlocking domestic economies of the family, it would be their labor that reproduced the next generation.

Notes

Introduction

1. AHSSA, BP, EA, CNE, box 10, folder 5, April 1906.
2. "Constituciones," *Boletín del Archivo General*; Secretaría de Gobernación, *Reglamento provisional*, chap. 1, art. 1, p. 3.
3. AHSSA, BP, EA, CNE, box 10, folder 5, April 1906.
4. See Gonzalbo Aizpuru, "Casa de Niños Expósitos." For comparison, see Fuchs, *Abandoned Children*; González and Premo, *Raising an Empire*; Kertzer, *Sacrificed for Honor*; Kuznesof, "Sexual Politics"; Marcilio, "Abandonados y expósitos"; McClure, *Coram's Children*; Ransel, *Mothers of Misery*; and Sherwood, *Poverty*.
5. Blum, "Public Welfare"; Milanich, "Casa de Huérfanos."
6. Blum, "Dying of Sadness."
7. For comparison, see, for example, Gager, *Blood Ties*; and M. Holt, *Orphan Trains*.
8. Abadiano, *Establecimientos de beneficencia*; Arrom, *Containing the Poor*, 11–42.

See also Arrom, "Vagos y mendigos." For comparison, see M. Rose, *English Poor Law*.

9. French, "Prostitutes and Guardian Angels."

10. Schmidt, *Civil Law*, bk. 1, "Of the Domestic Relations," title 2, "Of the Paternal Power," chap. 3, "Duties and Obligations of Parents and Children," arts. 88–89, 99–104, pp. 22–24; Taylor, *Civil Code*, bk. 1, "Of the Domestic Relations," title 8, "Of Paternal Control," chap. 1, "Of the Effects of the Paternal Control with Respect to the Persons of the Children," arts. 363–73, pp. 60–61. See also Lavrín, "Niñez en México."

11. Agostoni, "Popular Health Education"; Castillo Troncoso, *Conceptos, imágenes y representaciones*.

12. Agostoni, "Delicias de la limpieza."

13. Blum, "Public Welfare."

14. French, "Prostitutes and Guardian Angels."

15. Blum, "Conspicuous Benevolence."

16. Instituto Mexicano, *Código de Seguridad Social*.

17. Bliss, *Compromised Positions*; Piccato, *City of Suspects*.

18. French, *Peaceful and Working People*.

19. Blum, "Abandonment."

20. Blum, "Conspicuous Benevolence."

21. Tena Ramírez, *Leyes fundamentales*, título 6, "Del Trabajo y de la Previsión Social," art. 123, fraccs. 1–5, p. 870.

22. Estados Unidos Mexicanos, Gobierno Federal, *Ley sobre Relaciones Familiares*.

23. See Goldman, *Women*, 1–13; and Kirchenbaum, *Small Comrades*.

24. Guy, "Child Congresses." See also Besse, *Restructuring Patriarchy*, 89–109; Ehrick, "Affectionate Mothers"; and Fuller, *International Year Book*, 8, 198, 207, 269, 272. This compendium of Latin American children's programs was published by the London-based organization, Save the Children International Union, which drafted the "Declaration of the Rights of the Child," adopted in 1924 by the League of Nations.

25. Vaughan, "Modernizing Patriarchy."

26. Bliss, *Compromised Positions*; Lear, *Workers, Neighbors, and Citizens*; Porter, *Working Women*; Schell, *Church and State Education*.

27. Stern, "Responsible Mothers"; Blum, "Dying of Sadness."

28. Solís Quiroga, "Familia anti-social."

29. Instituto Mexicano, *Código de Seguridad Social*.

30. Most famously, outgoing president Plutarco Elias Calles invoked the metaphor of the "Revolutionary Family" in a 1928 speech in Guadalajara. See Benjamin, *Revolución*, 68–78.

31. See Stern, "Responsible Mothers."

32. As I completed this study, I was unable to obtain but would like to acknowledge a new book on Mexican childhood: Padilla and Soler, *Infancia*.

33. Kuznesof and Oppenheimer, "Family and Society," 220.

34. Rapp, Ross, and Bridenthall, "Examining Family History," 177.

35. See, for example, Arrom's pioneering study, *Women of Mexico City*.

36. Essays in two recent anthologies develop this point. See Mitchell and Schell, *Women's Revolution*; and Olcott, Vaughan, and Cano, *Sex in Revolution*.

37. Historians often cite Joan Scott, "Gender." For two excellent précis of the incorporation of gender analysis into Latin American history, see Caulfield, "History of Gender"; and Bliss and French, "Power in Latin America," 1–30. On the influence of gender history on family history, see Blum, "Bringing It Back Home"; and Milanich, "Whither Family History?"

38. See Bliss and French, "Power in Latin America," 6. For a critique of the ways that these "naturalizing" assumptions have shaped social science approaches to family in Latin America, see Durham, "Family and Human Reproduction."

39. Castillo Troncoso, *Conceptos, imágenes y representaciones*.

40. See, for example, Birn, "Child Well-Being."

41. See, for example, Benería and Roldán, *Crossroads of Class*; García and de Oliveira, *Trabajo feminino*; González de la Rocha, *Resources of Poverty*; and Jelin, *Gender Relations*.

42. Examples of historical analyses of Mexican family forms in a political-economic context include Arrom, *Women of Mexico City*; and Lomnitz and Pérez-Lizaur, *Mexican Elite Family*.

43. Kuznesof, "Global Society."

44. Twinam, *Public Lives*.

45. See Jelin, *Gender Relations*, 9–11; and Jelin, "Family and Household."

46. For comparisons to contemporary Mexico, see González de la Rocha, *Resources of Poverty*; and Lomnitz and Pérez-Lizaur, "Dynastic Growth."

47. Premo, "Minor Offenses."

48. See, for example, Caulfield, *Defense of Honor*; and Sloan, "Disobedient Daughters."

49. Fonseca, "Foster Mothers"; see also Cardoso, "Creating Kinship"; and Guy, "Marginal Children."

50. See, for example, Kuznesof, "Domestic Service"; and Milanich, "Historical Perspectives."

51. Boswell, *Kindness of Strangers*.

52. For the early modern roots of these practices, see the essays on child circulation and institutions for children in Iberia and colonial Latin America, in González and Premo, *Raising an Empire*.

53. Farriss, *Maya Society*, 171, 465n9; for the allocation of orphans' labor during the

transition to abolition in Brazil, see Meznar, "Orphans and the Transition," 499–515.

54. John Chance notes that the bishop of Oaxaca, founding a new college in 1776, permitted admission of legitimate mestizos of mixed Indian and Spanish descent but excluded "Negroes, mulattoes, lobos, coyotes, and people of other malignant mixtures" (Chance, *Colonial Oaxaca*, 180–81). See also Twinam, "Abandoned."

55. Gonzalbo Aizpuru, "Casa de Niños Expósitos"; Muriel, "Protección al niño."

56. A. Thompson, "Children in Family."

57. Calderón de la Barca, *Life in Mexico*, 519–20; García Cubas, *Republic of Mexico*, 18.

58. García Cubas, *Republic of Mexico*, 18.

59. For comparisons, see Bowie, *Cross-Cultural Approaches*.

60. For a review of the erasure of adoption from Mexican law, see Blum, "Children without Parents," 66–88.

61. Zelizer, *Priceless Child*.

62. See Ginsburg and Rapp, "Politics of Reproduction."

63. Rapp, Ross, and Bridenthall, "Examining Family History," 177.

64. Fortunati, *Arcane of Reproduction*; Rapp, "Family and Class," 202; Thorne, "Feminist Rethinking." See also Jelin, "Family and Household."

65. Nelson, "Two-Channel Welfare State."

66. See García Castro, "Bought and Sold."

67. Blum, "Breaking and Making Families."

68. For historical studies based in Mexico City, see Bliss, *Compromised Positions*; Lear, *Workers, Neighbors, and Citizens*; Porter, *Working Women*; and Tenorio-Trillo, "1910 Mexico City." For two recent anthologies that demonstrate both the variety and consistency of the impact of the Mexican Revolution on women and gender, see Mitchell and Schell, *Women's Revolution*; and Olcott, Vaughan, and Cano, *Sex in Revolution*.

69. Public health and welfare records are housed principally in the Archivo General de la Nación (AGN), the Archivo Histórico del Distrito Federal (AHDF; formerly the Archivo Histórico del Ex-Ayuntamiento), and the Archivo Histórico de la Secretaría de Salubridad y Asistencia (AHSSA).

70. See, for example, French, "Te Amo Muncho."

71. See, for example, Gordon, *Their Own Lives*, 12–20.

72. On welfare clients' self-representation, see Gordon, *Their Own Lives*, 7–12.

73. Arrom, *Containing the Poor*, 31; Lear, *Workers, Neighbors, and Citizens*, 75–77; Salazar, "Trabajadores"; Ramos Escandón, "Comentarios," 460.

74. See Powell, "Comentarios," 456–58. For pioneering work on the history of domestic service in Latin America, see Graham, *House and Street*;

and Kuznesof, "Domestic Service." On Mexico, see Blum, "Revolutionary Household"; Goldsmith, "Doméstica"; Pérez, "More Intimate Ways"; and Salazar, "Trabajadores."

75. For example, see Jelin, *Gender Relations*; Thorne and Yalom, *Rethinking the Family*; and Putnam, "Work, Sex, and Power."

1. Porfirian Patterns and Meanings of Child Circulation

1. AHSSA, CNE, REG 19, 1884–94; AHSSA, CNE, AD, bks. 83, 1902–3; 87, 1903–15.

2. AHSSA, CNE, REG 11, 1852–84; Calderón de la Barca, *Life in Mexico*, 519–20.

3. Lear, "Mexico City."

4. M. Morales, "Expansión," 77–78.

5. Arrom, *Containing the Poor*.

6. Arrom, *Containing the Poor*, 206.

7. AHDF, HP, vol. 2295, folder 58, February 1868.

8. Secretaría de Gobernación, "Circular," 310–12.

9. Secretaría de Estado y del Despacho de Gobernación, *Hospital General*, quoted in González Navarro, *Pobreza en México*, 84–85.

10. Alfaro, *Reseña histórico-descriptiva*, 9, 67. The training facility for the Guardias Presidenciales now occupies the site.

11. Romero, *Ciudad de México*, 154, quoted in Lear, "Mexico City"; González Navarro identifies these trends and describes the major components of public welfare and private charity in *Porfiriato*, 4:495–503; and *Pobreza en México*, 54–67. Total federal spending on welfare rose from more than 30,000 pesos in 1877–78 to around ten times that amount, 320,784 pesos in 1898–99. Nevertheless, federal spending increases on other social services indicate public welfare's comparatively lower priority. For example, appropriations for education, large to begin with compared to other social spending, almost tripled: 605,945 pesos in 1877–78, and 1,708,624 pesos in 1898–99. Another striking rise in appropriations during that period came in the funding for public health, from 13,700 pesos in 1881–82 (the first year an appropriation is recorded) to 444,442 pesos in 1898–99. Extensive building campaigns required even larger appropriations, more than 1.3 million pesos for fiscal year 1909–10 (Moisés González Navarro, *Estadísticas sociales*, 37–38, table 41). See also Blum, "Conspicuous Benevolence."

12. AHSSA, BP, EA, HP, file 10, folder 9, 1881. See also Arrom, *Containing the Poor*, 289–91, app. 1.

13. See Blum, "Conspicuous Benevolence."

14. "Escuela Industrial de Huérfanos," *Boletín de la Dirección de Beneficencia Pública* 1, no. 1 (January 1881): 28–32. AHSSA, BP, EE, Escuela Correccional para Varones, box 3, folder 4, 1886; box 3, folder 23, 1897.

15. On the history of the Hospicio to 1871, see Arrom, *Containing the Poor*. See also Blum, "Children without Parents"; and Vargas Olvera, "Escuela Correccional," 65–91.

16. Arrom, *Containing the Poor*, 171, 225–26; Blum, "Children without Parents," 213–17; Vargas Olvera, "Escuela Correccional."

17. González Navarro, *Estadísticas sociales*, 7, table 1; 68, table 4.

18. The greatest sex imbalance fell in the age group of sixteen- to twenty-year-olds: about 45 percent male to over 54 percent female (González Navarro, *Estadísticas sociales*, 109, table 18). See also Arrom, *Women of Mexico City*, 110–11. De Oliveira notes that women's lead in urban migration was a distinguishing feature of internal migration in Mexico ("Migration of Women").

19. McCaa, "Peopling," 622, table c7; 624, table c8, p. 625.

20. In 1895 there were 3,715 total births, 2,208 legitimate births, and 8,052 deaths; in 1900 there were 29,433 total births and 9,661 legitimate births (González Navarro, *Estadísticas sociales*, 20, table 15; 21, table 16; 28, table 28).

21. González Navarro, *Estadísticas sociales*, 7, table 1; 68, table 4; González Navarro, *Porfiriato*, 31, 86–87.

22. L. Thompson, "Structures and Vicissitudes," 412.

23. Porter, *Working Women*, 11.

24. Díaz Zermeño, "Escuela nacional primaria." For comparison, see also Kuznesof, "Puzzling Contradictions."

25. "Industrial Census, Federal District, 1879" in Porter, *Working Women*, 11–12.

26. Keremitsis, "Metate al molino."

27. Keremitsis, *Industria textil mexicana*; Porter, *Working Women*, 33–34.

28. Lear, *Workers, Neighbors, and Citizens*, 75–77; Arrom, *Women of Mexico City*, 162, table 16.

29. See Arrom, *Containing the Poor*.

30. AHDF, HP, vol. 2295, folder 58, February 1868.

31. Peza, "Distribución de premios," 44.

32. García Icazbalceta, *Informe*, translated by and quoted in Arrom, *Containing the Poor*, 231; Blum, "Children without Parents," chaps. 4–6.

33. Peza, *Beneficencia en México*, 19, 71; Monroy, "Letras."

34. AGN, BPDF, box 57, folder 14, 1896.

35. AGN, BPDF, box 68, folder 14, 1912.

36. Manilla, "Segunda parte," 195.

37. González Navarro, *Porfiriato*, 497.

38. AHSSA, BP, EA, HP, box 30, folder 22, October 1905.

39. There are no extant admissions registers for the Hospicio.

40. AHSSA, BP, EA, HP, box 13, folders 15, 18, April 1886.

41. AHSSA, BP, EA, HP, box 32, folder 10, December 1906.

42. AHSSA, BP, EA, HP, box 34, folder 14, September 1912.

43. AGN, BPDF, box 68, folder 36, 1890.

44. AGN, BPDF, box 67, folder 31, 1912.

45. Bk. 1, "De las personas," title 5, "Del matrimonio," chap. 4, "De los alimentos," art. 212 (Estados Unidos Mexicanos, Gobierno Federal, *Códigos civil*, 18).

46. Bk. 1, "De las personas," title 8, "De la patria potestad," chap 1, "De los efectos de la patria potestad respecto de las personas de los hijos," art. 371 (Estados Unidos Mexicanos, Gobierno Federal, *Códigos civil*, 30).

47. AGN, BPDF, box 67, folder 91, 1885–88.

48. AGN, BPDF, box 1, folder 42, 1918.

49. On the practice of the deposit of women under the legal regime of nondefinitive divorce, see García Peña, "Depósito de las esposas."

50. Luis Curiel to Secretario de Gobernación, AHSSA, BP, EA, HP, box 6, folder 28, 11 June 1878.

51. AHSSA, BP, EA, HP, box 6, folder 9, July 1878.

52. See Bliss, *Compromised Positions*, 32–46.

53. AHSSA, BP, EA, HP, box 17, folder 27, 1895.

54. Alfaro, *Reseña histórico-descriptiva*, 31–32, 57.

55. Arrom, "Changing Definition."

56. Chap. 4, Art. 2, Reglamento, AHDF, HP, vol. 2295, folder 50, 1868.

57. Alfaro, *Reseña histórico-descriptiva*, 57.

58. Alfaro, *Reseña histórico-descriptiva*, 41.

59. AHSSA, BP, EA, HP, box 27, folder 3, 1903.

60. AHSSA, BP, EA, HP, box 29, folder 3, 1904.

61. AGN, BPDF, box 111, folder 18, 1890–93.

62. AGN, BPDF, box 2, folder 1, 1910–11.

63. AGN, BPDF, box 68, folder 39, 1907.

64. AGN, BPDF, box 68, folder 58, 1880–85.

65. Alfaro, *Reseña histórico-descriptiva*, 59.

66. Domínguez to Secretario de Gobernación, AHSSA, CNE, AD, bk. 79, 25 March 1899.

67. *Bien Social*, published by the Sociedad Filantrópica Mexicana. For a summary of the various strands of Domínguez's career, see León, *Obstetricia en México*, 634–37.

68. AHSSA, CNE, REG 27, 1899–1901.

69. Blum, "Public Welfare."

70. AHSSA, CNE, REG 19, 1884–94.

71. Bk. 1, "De las personas," title 9, "De la tutela," chap. 6, "De la tutela de los hijos abandonados," arts. 455–57 (Estados Unidos Mexicanos, Gobierno Federal, *Códigos civil*, 36).

72. Secretaría de Gobernación, *Reglamento provisional*, chap. 1, arts. 2, 3, p. 4.

73. Secretaría de Gobernación, *Reglamento provisional*, chap. 1, art. 6, p. 5;
Secretaría de Gobernación, *Reglamento provisional*, chap. 1, art. 19, p. 8.

74. Secretaría de Gobernación, *Reglamento provisional*, chap. 1, art. 1, p. 3.

75. Peza, "Himno."

76. Rivera Cambas, *México pintoresco*, 2:174.

77. AHSSA, CNE, REG 27, 1899–1901.

78. González Navarro, *Porfiriato*, 86–87.

79. AHSSA, CNE, REG 27, 1899–1900.

80. AHSSA, CNE, REG 27, 1899–1900.

81. There were forty-four children with siblings, and seven pairs of twins.

82. García Icazbalceta, *Informe*, 17–18, 119.

83. For admissions from the Department of Concealed Childbirth, see AHSSA, CNE,
REG 11, 1860–63; for admissions from the Casa de Maternidad (Maternity
Hospital), see AHSSA, CNE, REG 16, 1877–80.

84. Twenty-six mothers out of thirty-five died in childbirth.

85. AHSSA, CNE, REG 27, 1899–1901.

86. AHSSA, CNE, AD, bk. 85, 1903–4.

87. AHSSA, CNE, REG 27, 1899–1901.

88. AHSSA, CNE, REG 19, 1884–94.

89. A total of 83 out of 260 children who lacked madrinas left the institution.

90. A total of six out of twenty-one children who had only a padrino left the
institution.

91. In contrast, some historians have concluded that the high number of children
legally recognized by neither parent pointed to widespread parental
indifference. See González Navarro, *Porfiriato*, 42.

92. AHSSA, CNE, REG 31, September 1901–June 1904.

93. AHSSA, CNE, AD, bk. 86, 1905.

94. AHSSA, CNE, REG 27, 1899–1901.

95. Domínguez to Secretario de Gobernación, AHSSA, CNE, AD, bk. 83, 23 March
1903.

96. "Registro de niños pensionados. 27 Noviembre 1902–22 Marzo 1904," AHSSA,
CNE, AD, bk. 84.

97. Domínguez to Dirección General de Beneficencia Pública, AHSSA, CNE, AD, bk.
86, 24 September 1904.

98. Domínguez to Dirección General de Beneficencia Pública, AHSSA, CNE, AD, bk.
86, 22 March 1905.

99. Domínguez to Dirección General de Beneficencia Pública, AHSSA, CNE, AD, bk.
86, 24 September 1904.

100. Domínguez to Dirección General de Beneficencia Pública, AHSSA, CNE, AD, bk. 86, 10 May 1905.

101. Domínguez to Dirección General de Beneficencia Pública, AHSSA, CNE, AD, bk. 86, 10 May 1905.

102. Domínguez to Dirección General de Beneficencia Pública, AHSSA, CNE, AD, bk. 86, 8 June 1905, 10 June 1905, 12 June 1905, 17 June 1905.

103. Domínguez to Dirección General de Beneficencia Pública, AHSSA, CNE, AD, bk. 86, 17 June 1905, 30 June 1905.

104. CNE Secretary Esther de la Rosa, AHSSA, CNE, AD, bk. 87, 21 August 1905.

105. Domínguez to Treasurer, Beneficencia Pública, AHSSA, CNE, AD, bk. 86, 7 June 1905; AHSSA, CNE, AD, bk. 84, 1904.

106. AHSSA, CNE, REG 31, 1901–4.

107. AHSSA, CNE, REG 35, 1904–10.

108. Carral to Dirección General de Beneficencia Pública, AHSSA, CNE, AD, bk. 90, 11 December 1905.

109. AHSSA, BP, EA, CNE, box 10, folder 5, April 1906.

110. Ojeda Verduzco, "Sepulcro de la Madre."

2. *Labor or Love*

1. Alfaro, *Reseña histórico-descriptiva*, 54–55.

2. Alfaro, *Reseña histórico-descriptiva*, 55.

3. AGN, BPDF, box 5, folder 2, 1912.

4. *Mexican Herald*, 26 November 1907, broadside reproduced in Tyler, *Posada's Mexico*, 228.

5. Manuel Domínguez to Juez 2 Correccional, AHSSA, CNE, AD, bk. 79, 9 January 1901. *El Imparcial*, a Mexico City daily newspaper illustrated with prints and photo engravings, sold for one centavo. Papers of the penny press accused *El Imparcial* of receiving subsidies from the Díaz regime to print articles favorable to the government and to sell the paper at a price that undercut independent competition (Tyler, *Posada's Mexico*, 222–23, 300).

6. Schmidt, *Civil Law*, bk. 1, "Of the Domestic Relations," title 1, "Of Matrimony," chap. 2, "Of Marriage," sec. 4, "Persons Incapable of Contracting Matrimony," art. 29, pp. 8–9.

7. Schmidt, *Civil Law*, bk. 1, "Of the Domestic Relations," title 2, "Of the Paternal Power," chap. 2, "Of the Mode of Acquiring the Paternal Power," sec. 3, "Of Adoption," art. 87; bk. 1, "Of the Domestic Relations," title 7, "Of Donations *Inter Vivos*, and of Testaments," chap. 4, "Of Irregular Successions," sec. 6, "Of the Right of Succession of Adopted Children," arts. 1260–61, pp. 21, 269.

8. Constit. XXIV, De las prohijaciones, "Constituciones," *Boletín del Archivo General*, 26.

9. AHSSA, CNE, AD, box 1, folder 9, 1793.

10. Arrom, *Women of Mexico City*, 126.

11. These patterns and interpretations of adoption were by no means unique to Mexico, or even to Latin America. On adoption for family formation and for labor, see Milanich, "Casa de Huérfanos." For a discussion of adoption for labor in nineteenth-century United States, see Zelizer, *Priceless Child*, 177–79; on late nineteenth-century programs distributing urban children to rural homes, largely for labor, see M. Holt, *Orphan Trains*.

12. Calderón de la Barca, *Life in Mexico*, 519–20.

13. Calderón de la Barca, *Life in Mexico*, 531.

14. AHSSA, BP, EA, HP, box 6, folder 16, 1878.

15. AHSSA, CNE, AD, bk. 87, 1904–15; and AGN, BPDF, box 198, among other sources, contain many examples.

16. The laws include the *Ley orgánica del Registro Civil*, 27 January 1857 (Dublán and Lozano, *Legislación mexicana*, 8:364–74); *Ley de sucesiones por testamentaría y ab-intestato*, 10 August 1857 (Dublán and Lozano, *Legislación mexicana*, 8:548–57); and *Ley orgánica del Registro Civil*, 28 July 1859 (Dublán and Lozano, *Legislación mexicana*, 8:696–702).

17. Sierra, *Proyecto*, iii.

18. See, for example, García Cubas, *Republic of Mexico*, 18; and A. Thompson, "Children in Family."

19. See Kaufman, "Patron-Client Concept."

20. "Quedan secularizados," *Legislación mexicana*; "Creación y planta de la Dirección de Beneficencia Pública," *Salubridad y asistencia*.

21. AHDF, HP, vol. 2295, folder 35, 1866.

22. AHDF, HP, vol. 2295, folder 35, 1866.

23. Blum, "Children without Parents," chap. 2.

24. Chap. 8, arts. 9, 11, Reglamento, AHDF, HP, vol. 2295, folder 50, 1868.

25. On the exercise of charity by elite men and women in the liberal era, see González Navarro, *Porfiriato*, 495–509.

26. "Constituciones," *Boletín del Archivo General*; "Proyecto de la nueva forma de gobierno política y económica del Hospicio de Pobres en esta capital," AHDF, HP, vol. 2295, folder 16, 1806; Reglamento, AHDF, HP, vol. 2295, folder 50, 1868; Reglamento, Hospicio de Pobres, AHSSA, BP, EA, HP, box 12, folder 11, 1884; Reglamento, Casa de Cuna, AHSSA, BP, EA, CNE, box 8, folder 27, 1898.

27. Estados Unidos Mexicanos, Gobierno de la Unión, *Exposición*, 39–40, quoted in González, "Cien años," 31–41, 41nn31–35.

28. "Se modifican los reglamentos del Registro Civil," in Dublán and Lozano, *Legislación mexicana*, 218.

29. See Twinam, "Illegitimacy"; Jack Goody traces a close association between

adoption and concubinage back to Roman law and practice (*Development of the Family*, 39).

30. Brinton, *French Revolutionary Legislation*, 22–41.

31. Código Civil, 1870, lib. 3, "De los contratos," título 13, "Del contrato de obras ó prestación de servicios," cap. 1, "Del servicio doméstico," art. 2570, fracc. 2, in Dublán and Lozano, *Legislación mexicana*, 11:362; Taylor, *Civil Code*, bk. 3, "Of Contracts," title 13, "Of Contracts for Labor," chap. 1, "Of Domestic Service," art. 2453, no. 2, p. 323.

32. Taylor, *Civil Code*, bk.1, "Of Persons," title 9 "Of Guardianship," chap. 6 "Of Legitimate Guardianship of Abandoned Children," arts. 455–57, p. 72.

33. For a discussion comparing Russian and other European societies' sex preference in adoption, see Ransel, *Mothers of Misery*, 134–42.

34. AHSSA, CNE, REG 16, 1877–80.

35. For other typologies of adoption and fostering, see E. Goody, *Parenthood and Social Reproduction*, 250–57; J. Goody, *Production and Reproduction*, 68.

36. Jens, "¡Pobre Ernestina!" pt. 1, p. 15.

37. Jens, "¡Pobre Ernestina!" pt. 3, pp. 52–53.

38. See also Guy, "Mothers Alive and Dead."

39. AGN, BPDF, box 198, folder 123, 1888.

40. Ángel Carpio to Secretario de Estado y del Despacho de Gobernación, AGN, BPDF, box 65, folder 10, February 1887.

41. Ángel Carpio to Secretario de Estado y del Despacho de Gobernación, AGN, BPDF, box 65, folder 10, February 1887.

42. Reglamento del Hospicio, chap. 2, Dirección, art. 3, AHSSA, BP, EA, HP, box 12, folder 11, 1884.

43. AGN, BPDF, box 57/65, folder 10, 1887.

44. Ángel Carpio, Director, CNE, to Director, Escuela Correccional, AHSSA, CNE, AD, bk. 65, 22 and 26 May 1886; Ángel Carpio, Director CNE to Secretaría de Gobernación, AHSSA, CNE, AD, bk. 65, 2 and 10 September 1886.

45. AHSSA, CNE, REG 19, 1884–94. Adoptions, like retrievals and deaths, were noted in the margin next to the original admissions record.

46. AHSSA, CNE, REG 25, 1896–98.

47. Gimeno de Flaquer, "Esposa y madre," 131. See French, "Prostitutes and Guardian Angels."

48. Fausto, "Mujer del hogar," 498.

49. The magazine serialized La Mujer, by the Spanish writer Francisco Alonso de Rubio ("Mujer considerada," 419).

50. Gimeno de Flaquer, "Crónica Mexicana," 108.

51. Catalina, "Maternidad," 3.

52. Taylor, *Civil Code*, bk. 1, "Of Persons," title 9, "Of Guardianship," chap. 6, "Of

the Legitimate Guardianship of Abandoned Children," arts. 455–57, p. 72; Secretaría de Gobernación, *Reglamento provisional*, art. 20, sec. A, pp. 8–9.

53. Arrom, "Mexican Family Law," 305–17; Secretaría de Gobernación, *Reglamento provisional*, art. 20, sec. A, p. 9.

54. Adoption contract, AHSSA, BP, EA, CNE, box 1, folder 23, 20 May 1899.

55. Adoption contract, AHSSA, BP, EA, CNE, box 1, folder 23, 5 December 1900.

56. "Libro de entradas, salidas y fallecimientos en este establecimiento," AHSSA, CNE, REG 25, 1896–98.

57. AHSSA, CNE, REG 27, April 1899–August 1900.

58. See, for example, AGN, BPDF, box 5, folder 2/217, 1910–12.

59. AHSSA, CNE, REG 27, 1899–1900.

60. Peniche Rivero, "Comunidad doméstica"; Várguez Pasos, " Élites e identidades."

61. AHSSA, CNE, REG 19, 1884–94; AHSSA, CNE, REG 27, 1899–1900.

62. Adoption contracts, 30 September 1890, 3 March 1890, AHSSA, BP, EA, CNE, box 1, folders 12, 16; 1891–96, AHSSA, BP, EA, CNE, box 1, folder 23.

63. Secretaría de Gobernación, *Reglamento provisional*, art. 20, sec. B, p. 9.

64. Adoption contract, 5 December 1900, AHSSA, BP, EA, CNE, box 1, folder 23, 1900.

65. AHSSA, CNE, REG 27, 1899–1900.

66. AHSSA, CNE, REG 19, 1884–94; AHSSA, CNE, REG 27, 1899–1900.

67. AHSSA, CNE, REG 27, 1899–1900.

68. AHSSA, CNE, REG 31, September 1901–June 1904.

69. Domínguez to Secretario de Gobernación, AHSSA, CNE, AD, bk. 83, folder 5, 10 August 1902.

70. Domínguez to Juez Correccional, AHSSA, CNE, AD, bk. 79, 9 January 1901.

71. Petitioner to Domínguez, AGN, BPDF, box 198, folder 42, 16 August 1905.

72. Petitioner to Domínguez, AGN, BPDF, box 198, folder 42, 16 August 1905; Domínguez to Juez Segundo de Instrucción, AHSSA, CNE, AD, bk. 90, 25 August 1905.

73. AHSSA, CNE, REG 19, 1884–94.

74. Domínguez, AHSSA, CNE, AD, bk. 87, 20 February 1904.

75. Knight, "Mexican Peonage"; Joseph, *Revolution from Without*, 72–73, 78; Peniche Rivero, "Comunidad doméstica"; Turner, *Barbarous Mexico*, 13, 70–72; Várguez Pasos, "Élites e identidades"; Wells, "Family Elites."

76. Alfaro, *Reseña histórico-descriptiva*, 55.

77. Domínguez, AHSSA, CNE, AD, bk. 87, 24 December 1904.

78. Francisco de Paulo Carral, Director, CNE, AHSSA, CNE, AD, bk. 87, 16 June 1906.

79. Domínguez, AHSSA, CNE, AD, bk. 87, 7 December 1904.

80. AHSSA, CNE, REG 35, 1904–10.

81. "Acuerdo: Octubre 17 de 1911," Secretaría de Gobernación to Dirección General de la Beneficencia Pública [attached to contract], AGN, BPDF, box 198, folder 92.

82. AHSSA, CNE, REG 41, 8 March 1913; AGN, BPDF, box 198, folder 92, 1913.

83. AHSSA, CNE, REG 41, 8 March 1913; AGN, BPDF, box 198, folder 92, 1913.

84. Miguel Márquez, Director, CNE, to Dirección General de Beneficencia Pública, AHSSA, CNE, AD, bk. 87, 8 April 1913; Márquez to Dirección General de Beneficencia Pública, AHSSA, CNE, AD, bk. 99, 19 December 1913.

85. Márquez to Dirección General de Beneficencia Pública, AHSSA, CNE, AD, bk. 99, p. 197, 30 October 1913.

86. "Acuerdo, Octubre 17 de 1911," [attached to adoption contract], AGN, BPDF, box 198, folder 92, 12 March 1913.

87. Director, Hospicio de Niños, to Dirección General de Beneficencia Pública, AGN, BPDF, box 198, folder 99, 16 April 1914,

88. AGN, BPDF, box 198, folder 80, 1914; AGN, BPDF, box 198, folder 99, 1914. On lack of recourse to rectify abuse, see Director, CNE, AHSSA, CNE, AD, bk. 87, p. 17, 20 February 1904; on prohibition of adoptions to the Gulf states, see Director, CNE, to Sr. Dr. Dn. Manuel Domínguez B., Orizaba, AHSSA, CNE, AD, bk. 87, p. 66, 24 December 1904.

89. AGN, BPDF, box 198, folder 92, 1914.

90. Méndez de Cuenca, *Hogar Mexicano*, 70.

3. Moral and Medical Economies of Motherhood

1. Secretaría de Gobernación, *Reglamento provisional*.

2. For earlier views on wet-nursing see Tuñón, *Siglo XIX*, 33. See also the satire of elite women's attitudes toward breast-feeding in Fernández de Lizardi, *Educación de las mujeres* (1818), excerpted in León, *Obstetricia en México*, 95.

3. See French, "Prostitutes and Guardian Angels."

4. See, for example, the five-part series, "Higiene," by Domínguez. See also, Castillo Troncoso, *Conceptos, imágenes y representaciones*, 59–84.

5. "Reglamento de la Inspección de Nodrizas de la Casa de Niños Expósitos," Secretaría de Gobernación, *Reglamento provisional*, 27–28.

6. See Porter, *Working Women*, 63–68.

7. See Porter, *Working Women*, 63–68.

8. AHSSA, CNE, NOD, bk. 1, 1853–56, to bk. 12, 1884–90; Calderón de la Barca, *Life in Mexico*, 520.

9. "Nómina de lo pagado a los empleados de la Casa de Niños Expósitos, Enero de 1877," AGN, GS, vol. 607, folder 2.

10. López Monjardín, "Jornales de artesanos."

11. Nurses from Tacuba came at mid-month and nurses from Tlalnepantla came at the end of the month, AHSSA, CNE, NOD, bk. 1, 1853–56, to vol. 15, 1908–15.

12. Constituciones XII–XIII, "Constituciones," *Boletín del Archivo General*, 23.

13. Constitución XVII, Archivo General de la Nación, "Real cédula," 17; AHSSA, CNE, NOD, bk. 1, 1853–56.

14. AHSSA, CNE, REG 11, 1852–84.

15. The same eighteenth-century regulations that in one paragraph forbade nursing a media leche set the wage for it in another paragraph (Constituciones XII–XIII, Núñez de Haro y Peralta, *Constituciones*, 23).

16. Rivera Cambas, *México pintoresco*, 2:341; 3:103–4.

17. Morgan, "Proletarians, Politicos, and Patriarchs."

18. "Nómina de lo pagado a los empleados de la Casa de Niños Expósitos," AGN, GS, vol. 607, folder 2, January–April 1877; AHSSA, CNE, NOD, bk. 8, 1876–81.

19. AHSSA, CNE, NOD, bk. 8, 1876–81.

20. AHSSA, CNE, NOD, bk. 8, 1876–81.

21. AHSSA, CNE, NOD, bk. 9, 1881–84.

22. AHSSA, CNE, NOD, bk. 9, 1881–84.

23. See, Fay-Sallois, *Nourrices a Paris*; David Kertzer, *Sacrificed for Honor*; Ransel, *Mothers of Misery*; and Sherwood, *Poverty*, 51–91.

24. L. Rose, *Massacre of the Innocents*, 93–107; Ransel, *Mothers of Misery*, 198–221.

25. Fay-Sallois, *Nourrices a Paris*, 86–96.

26. Domínguez, "Positivo beneficio a la sociedad mexicana," *Imparcial*, 20 October 1898, 1.

27. See Agostoni, "Discurso médico."

28. Chávarri, "Charla de los Domingos," *Monitor Republicano*, 20 January 1884, 1.

29. Chávarri, "Charla de los Domingos," *Monitor Republicano*, 20 January 1884, 1.

30. Gimeno de Flaquer, "Crónica Mexicana," 56.

31. Domínguez, "Higiene V," 7.

32. Fernández de Lizardi, *La educación de las mujeres o la Quijotita y su prima* (1818), quoted in León, *Obstetricia en México*, 95.

33. Estrada, *Algunas ligeras consideraciones*, quoted in León, *Obstetricia en México*, 160–62.

34. See, for example, Fausto, "Mujer del hogar."

35. Estrada, *Algunas ligeras consideraciones*, 160.

36. Estrada, *Algunas ligeras consideraciones*, 160–61.

37. Catalina, "Maternidad," 1–3 (quote on 3).

38. See Bliss, *Compromised Positions*, 30–32; French, "Prostitutes and Guardian Angels"; Ramos Escandón, "Señoritas porfirianas."

39. "Variedades," *Boletin de Higiene*, 34.

40. Estrada, *Algunas ligeras consideraciones*, quoted in León, *Obstetricia en México*, 163–64. See also Castillo Troncoso, *Conceptos, imágenes y representaciones*, 82.

41. "Acerca de la elección," *Boletín de Higiene*, 53.

42. Chávarri, "Charla de los Domingos," *Monitor Republicano*, 20 January 1884, 1.

43. Pascual de San Juan, "Guía de la mujer"; "Consejos a las mujeres," *Álbum de la Mujer*; Alonso y Rubio, "La Mujer. XXVII."

44. "La educación del niño," *Imparcial*, 6 June 1899.

45. Advertisement, *Imparcial*, 10 December 1899.

46. See a selection excerpted from *Journal de Clinique et de Therapeutique Infantile*, "Acerca de la elección," *Boletín de Higiene*.

47. See "La nodrizas y el Departamento de Inspección," *Imparcial*, 2 August 1898, 1.

48. Excerpt from *Journal de Clinique et de Therapeutique Infantile*, "Acerca de la elección," *Boletín de Higiene*, 53. For comparison, see Marko, "Wet Nurse."

49. See Agostoni, "Discurso médico"; Castillo Troncoso, *Conceptos, imágenes y representaciones*, 70–77; Apple, *Mothers and Medicine*; Fildes, *Breasts, Bottles, and Babies*; and Wolf, "Mercenary Hirelings."

50. Domínguez, "Higiene II," 70. León, in his 1910 review of the history of Mexican obstetrics, reproduced icons and religious tokens widely used in the birth chamber (*Obstetricia en México*, 145–58).

51. Domínguez, "Higiene III"; Domínguez, "Higiene IV."

52. Domínguez, "Higiene V." See also "Decálogo a la madre," *Periódico de las señoras*, 14.

53. Except from the Academy of Medicine, Paris (14 January 1896), "Mortalidad de los niños."

54. Estrada, *Algunas ligeras consideraciones*, quoted in León, *Obstetricia en México*, 162.

55. See, for example, Peza, "Amaneciendo"; Valle, "Madre y el niño."

56. León, *La obstetricia en México*, 507–9. See also Castillo Troncoso, *Conceptos, imágenes y representaciones*, 77–84.

57. González Navarro, *Estadísticas sociales*, 20–29; Centro de Estudios, *Dinámica de la población*, 24–25; Castillo Troncoso, *Conceptos, imágenes y representaciones*, 78–79.

58. "La mortalidad," *Boletín de Higiene*.

59. AHSSA, CNE, AD, bk. 86, pp. 115, 118–19, April 1904; AHSSA, CNE, AD, bk. 86, p. 140, June 1904.

60. Fildes, *Wet-Nursing*, 233; Fuchs, *Abandoned Children*, 57; Golden, *Wet-Nursing in America*, 128; Graham, *House and Street*, 108–36; Pagani and Alcaraz, *Nodrizas de Buenos Aires*.

61. Buffington, *Criminal and Citizen*.

62. Calderón de la Barca, *Life in Mexico*, 520

63. Kolonitz, *Viaje a México*, 105–6.

64. Bliss, *Compromised Positions*, 46–48.

65. Rivera Cambas, *México pintoresco*, 2:173–74.

66. Estrada, *Algunas ligeras consideraciones*.

67. Agostoni, *Monuments of Progress*; Lear, "Mexico City"; Perló-Cohen, *Paradigma porfiriano*.

68. "Reglamento del Consejo Superior de Salubridad," 29 February 1892, cap. 6, arts. 48–72, in Dublán and Lozano, *Legislación mexicana*, 22:36–45; "Reglamento de las parteras," 24 March 1892, in Dublán and Lozano, *Legislación mexicana*, 22:80–82; Dublán and Lozano, *Legislación mexicana*, 22:36–45, 80–82; "Código Sanitario" [Revision of the regulations of milk processing and sale], in Dublán and Lozano, *Legislación mexicana*, 24:277–99 . The maternity hospital in Toluca introduced a certification program for midwives in 1896; see Rocha, *Porfiriato y la Revolución*. See also Agostoni, "Médicos y parteras."

69. Before the establishment of a pediatric clinic at the Escuela Nacional de Medicina in 1904, a generation of physicians trained at the Hospital de Maternidad e Infancia. Álvarez Amézquita et al., *Salubridad y asistencia*, 3:537–44; AHSSA, CNE, AD, bk. 86, p. 89, 22 March 1904; "Programas que deben regir," in Dublán and Lozano, *Legislación mexicana*, 31:885–99.

70. Bliss, *Compromised Positions*, 27–29.

71. Secretaría de Gobernación, *Reglamento provisional*; and "Reglamento de la Inspección de Nodrizas de la Casa de Niños Expósitos," Secretaría de Gobernación, *Reglamento provisional*, 27–28.

72. Ángel Carpio, Director, CNE, to C. Secretario de Estado y del Despacho de Gobernación, AHSSA, CNE, AD, bk. 76, p. 23, 14 April 1897.

73. Domínguez to Secretario de Gobernación, AHSSA, CNE, AD, bk. 79, 9 June 1899.

74. "Reglamento de la Inspeccion de Nodrizas de la Casa de Niños Expósitos," Secretaría de Gobernación, *Reglamento provisional*, 27–28.

75. "Reglamento de la Inspeccion de Nodrizas de la Casa de Niños Expósitos," Secretaría de Gobernación, *Reglamento provisional*, 27–28.

76. Secretaría de Gobernación, *Reglamento provisional*, 29–30.

77. Domínguez to Secretario de Gobernación, AHSSA, CNE, AD, bk. 79, 25 March 1899.

78. Domínguez to Dirección General de la Beneficencia Pública, AHSSA, CNE, AD, bk. 86, p. 326, 10 February 1905.

79. Domínguez to Secretario de Gobernación, AHSSA, CNE, AD, bk. 79, 25 March 1899; Domínguez to Dirección General de la Beneficencia Pública, AHSSA, CNE, AD, bk. 86, p. 216, 22 October 1904. See also Golden, *Wet-Nursing in America*, 129.

80. On plebian honor, see Piccato, *City of Suspects*. For comparative perspectives on maternity and honor, see Ruggiero, "Disciplining of Women."

81. Director to Dirección General de Beneficencia Pública, AHSSA, CNE, AD, bk. 86, p. 195, 19 September 1904.

82. Márquez, AHSSA, CNE, AD, bk. 96, p. 92, February 1913.

83. Domínguez to Dirección General de Beneficencia Pública, AHSSA, CNE, AD, bk. 90, p. 27, 22 July 1905.

84. Interim Director to Dirección General de Beneficencia Pública, AHSSA, CNE, AD, bk. 95, p. 139, n.d.

85. Domínguez to Dirección General de Beneficencia Pública, AHSSA, CNE, AD, bk. 86, p. 270, 13 December 1904; Director to Dirección General de Beneficencia Pública, AHSSA, CNE, AD, bk. 86, p. 399, 7 April 1905.

86. Secretaría de Gobernación, *Reglamento provisional*, art. 5, p. 5; Domínguez to Dirección General de Beneficencia Pública, AHSSA, CNE, AD, bk. 79, 25 March 1899.

87. AHSSA, CNE, NOD, bk. 13, 1898–1901, to 15, 1908–15; AHSSA, CNE, NOD, bk. 14, 1902–7.

88. AHSSA, CNE, NOD, bk. 13, 1898–1901, to 15, 1908–15; AHSSA, CNE, NOD, bk. 14, 1902–7.

89. Rafael Carrillo to Dirección General de Beneficencia Pública, AHSSA, CNE, AD, bk. 86, p. 74, 27 February 1904.

90. AHSSA, CNE, AD, bk. 85, 24 May 1903–28 July 1904.

91. Domínguez to the C. Prefecto, Hospital de Maternidad, AHSSA, CNE, AD, bk. 79, 5 March 1898.

92. AHSSA, CNE, REG 27, 1899–1902.

93. Domínguez to Secretario de Gobernación, AHSSA, CNE, AD, bk. 79, 25 March 1899.

94. Domínguez to Dirección General de Beneficencia Pública, AHSSA, CNE, AD, bk. 86, p. 328, 10 February 1905.

95. Márquez to Dirección General de Beneficencia Pública, AHSSA, CNE, AD, bk. 86, p. 195, 19 September 1904.

96. Domínguez to Dirección General de Beneficencia Pública, AHSSA, CNE, AD, bk. 86, pp. 203–4, 4 October 1904.

97. Domínguez to Dirección General de Beneficencia Pública, AHSSA, CNE, AD, bk. 86, 19 June 1905.

98. Domínguez to Dirección General de Beneficencia Pública, AHSSA, CNE, AD, bk. 86, p. 326, 10 February 1905.

99. Carral to Dirección General de Beneficencia Pública, AHSSA, CNE, AD, bk. 90, p. 314, 1 June 1906; Márquez to Dirección General de Beneficencia Pública, AHSSA, CNE, AD, bk. 96, p. 209, 21 April 1913.

100. González Navarro, *Porfiriato*, 501.

101. Report on artificial feeding, AHSSA, CNE, AD, bk. 86, p. 64, 24 February 1904.

102. Report on artificial feeding, AHSSA, CNE, AD, bk. 86, p. 64, 24 February 1904.

103. Domínguez to Dirección General de Beneficencia Pública, AHSSA, CNE, AD, bk. 90, p. 74, 28 August 1905; Carrillo to Dirección General de Beneficencia Pública, AHSSA, CNE, AD, bk. 90, p. 301, 9 May 1906.

104. Carrillo, "Alimentación artificial, 158.

105. AHSSA, CNE, REG 35, 1904–10.

106. Domínguez to Dirección General de Beneficencia Pública, AHSSA, CNE, AD, bk. 86, p. 78, 29 February 1904.

107. Director Interino to 2a. Demarcación de Policía, AHSSA, CNE, AD, bk. 86, p. 134, 13 June 1904; Director to Dirección General de Beneficencia Pública, AHSSA, CNE, AD, bk. 86, p. 137, 15 June 1904.

108. Carral to Secretario del Consejo Superior de Salubridad, AHSSA, CNE, AD, bk. 90, p. 240, 16 February 1906.

109. Director to Dirección General de Beneficencia Pública, AHSSA, CNE, AD, bk. 86, pp. 471–73, 19 June 1905.

110. Carral to Dirección General de Beneficencia Pública, AHSSA, CNE, AD, bk. 91, p. 66, 15 June 1907.

111. Domínguez to Dirección General de Beneficencia Pública, AHSSA, CNE, AD, bk. 86, p. 271, 14 December 1904.

112. Domínguez to Dirección General de Beneficencia Pública, AHSSA, CNE, AD, bk. 86, p. 225, 29 October 1904.

113. Carral to Dirección General de Beneficencia Pública, AHSSA, CNE, AD, bk. 91, p. 66, 15 June 1907.

114. Márquez to Staff Doctors CNE, AHSSA, CNE, AD, bk. 95, p. 109, 27 April 1912.

115. Carral to Dirección General de Beneficencia Pública, AHSSA, CNE, AD, bk. 91, p. 77, 18 July 1907; bk. 92, pp. 139–40, January 1909.

116. Carral to Dirección General de Beneficencia Pública, AHSSA, CNE, AD, bk. 93, p. 489, 31 December 1910.

117. Márquez replaced Roque Macuset, who resigned officially in August, 1912. Director, CNE, to Dirección General de Beneficencia Pública, AHSSA, CNE, AD, bk. 95, p. 256, 2 August 1912. Márquez's appointment was confirmed by the Constitutionalists. Márquez to Dirección General de Beneficencia Pública, AHSSA, CNE, AD, bk. 102, p. 435, 5 June 1915.

118. AHSSA, CNE, REG 41, 1 June 1910–11 August 1915.

119. AHSSA, CNE, AD, bk. 100, pp. 129–32, 1914; AHSSA, CNE, AD, bk. 102, pp. 23, 205, 398, 430, 1914–15.

120. Director, CNE, to Director de la Escuela Nacional de Agricultura y Veterinaria, AHSSA, CNE, AD, bk. 95, p. 144, 22 May 1912; Director, CNE, to Dirección General de Beneficencia Pública, AHSSA, CNE, AD, bk. 96, p. 13, 29 December 1912.

121. León, *Obstetricia en México*, 509–10; Lara y Pardo, "Puericultura en México."

122. Stepan, *Hour of Eugenics*, 76–82.

123. See Vaughan, "Modernizing Patriarchy"; and Blum, "Dying of Sadness."

4. The Family in the Revolutionary Order

1. Knight, *Mexican Revolution*, 2:313–14.

2. "29 de diciembre," Lau and Ramos Escandón, *Mujeres y revolución*.

3. Knight, *Mexican Revolution*, 2:256–63; Lear, *Workers, Neighbors, and Citizens*, 262–69.

4. Sánchez Medal, *Grandes cambios*, 17–18.

5. Sánchez Medal, *Grandes cambios*, 17–18; Lear, *Workers, Neighbors, and Citizens*, 269–71.

6. See Brenner, *Wind That Swept Mexico*, 7–31, 24.

7. See Bliss, "Paternity Tests"; Lear, *Workers, Neighbors and Citizens*, 359–65; Quirk, *Mexican Revolution*; Schell, *Church and State Education*; Soto, *Modern Mexican Woman*; and Vaughan, *Social Class*.

8. A number of works examine these issues, among them are Bliss, *Compromised Positions*; Muñiz, *Cuerpo, representación, y poder*; Olcott, *Revolutionary Women*; Sherman, *Mexican Right*, 43–44; Soto, *Modern Mexican Woman*; and Stern, "Responsible Mothers."

9. "Ley de matrimonio civil," 23 July 1859, art. 15, in Dublán and Lozano, *Legislación mexicana*, 8:691–93.

10. See S. Smith, "If Love Enslaves."

11. Arrom, *Women of Mexico City*, 206–58; Arrom, "Mexican Family Law," 305–17.

12. "29 de diciembre," in Lau and Ramos Escandón, *Mujeres y revolución*, 311–14.

13. "29 de diciembre," in Lau and Ramos Escandón, *Mujeres y revolución*, arts. 247–48, 299, pp. 322, 324.

14. "29 de diciembre," in Lau and Ramos Escandón, *Mujeres y revolución*, art. 251, p. 323.

15. "29 de diciembre," in Lau and Ramos Escandón, *Mujeres y revolución*, art. 252, p. 323. See also, "14 de junio," in Lau and Ramos Escandón, *Mujeres y revolución*, 326.

16. Quoted in Knight, *Mexican Revolution*, 2:302.

17. "Crónica y debate," in Lau and Ramos Escandón, *Mujeres y revolución*, 273–310; Knight, *Mexican Revolution*, 2:256–60.

18. Brinton, *French Revolutionary Legislation*.

19. "Crónica y debate," in Lau and Ramos Escandón, *Mujeres y revolución*, 274.

20. "Crónica y debate," in Lau and Ramos Escandón, *Mujeres y revolución*, 281.

21. "Crónica y debate," in Lau and Ramos Escandón, *Mujeres y revolución*, 278.

22. See French, "Prostitutes and Guardian Angels."

23. "Crónica y debate," in Lau and Ramos Escandón, *Mujeres y revolución*, 302–5.

24. "Crónica y debate," in Lau and Ramos Escandón, *Mujeres y revolución*, 294.

25. "Crónica y debate," in Lau and Ramos Escandón, *Mujeres y revolución*, 298–99.

26. "Crónica y debate," in Lau and Ramos Escandón, *Mujeres y revolución*, 296–97. For a sense of the deep-seated nature of these concerns, see "El Divorcio," *La Mujer*.

27. "Crónica y debate," in Lau and Ramos Escandón, *Mujeres y revolución*, 310.

28. "Mensaje del Primer Jefe," in *Leyes fundamentales de México*, 755.

29. Knight, *Mexican Revolution*, 2:469–77; Quirk, *Mexican Revolution*, 81.

30. See Olcott, *Revolutionary Women*, 28–32.

31. Soto, *Modern Mexican Woman*, 54, 73–75; "Hermila Galindo," in Lau and Ramos Escandón, *Mujeres y revolución*, 248–69.

32. Quirk, *Mexican Revolution*, 84–98.

33. Quirk, *Mexican Revolution*, 98.

34. Soto, *Modern Mexican Woman*, 55; Olcott, *Revolutionary Women*, 34–36.

35. "Constitución política," título 6, "Del Trabajo y de la Previsión Social," art. 123, fraccs. 1–5, in Tena Ramírez, *Leyes fundamentales*, 870.

36. "Constitución política," título 6, "Del Trabajo y de la Previsión Social," art. 123, fracc. 29, in Tena Ramírez, *Leyes fundamentales*, 874.

37. "Laudo," *Historia documental de México*, 603.

38. See also Secretaría de Trabajo y Previsión Social, *Prontuario de legislación*, 369–70.

39. Estados Unidos Mexicanos, Gobierno Federal, *Ley sobre Relaciones Familiares*.

40. Estados Unidos Mexicanos, Gobierno Federal, *Ley sobre Relaciones Familiares*, cap. 2, art. 13, p. 24; cap. 6, art. 75, p. 37.

41. Estados Unidos Mexicanos, Gobierno Federal, *Ley sobre Relaciones Familiares*, cap. 2, art. 18, p. 26.

42. Estados Unidos Mexicanos, Gobierno Federal, *Ley sobre Relaciones Familiares*, cap. 2, art. 17, fracc. 7, p. 25.

43. Estados Unidos Mexicanos, Gobierno Federal, *Ley sobre Relaciones Familiares*, cap. 15, art. 241, p. 71.

44. Estados Unidos Mexicanos, Gobierno Federal, *Ley sobre Relaciones Familiares*, cap. 4, arts. 44–47, pp. 31–33; cap. 28, arts. 270–72, pp. 76–77.

45. Estados Unidos Mexicanos, Gobierno Federal, *Ley sobre Relaciones Familiares*, cap. 4, arts. 42, 44, p. 31.

46. Estados Unidos Mexicanos, Gobierno Federal, *Ley sobre Relaciones Familiares*, cap. 11, art. 187; cap. 12, arts. 197–211, pp. 62–66; cap. 12, art. 210, p. 66.

47. Estados Unidos Mexicanos, Gobierno Federal, Preámbulo, *Ley sobre Relaciones Familiares*, pp. 6–7; cap. 12, arts. 220–36, pp. 67–71.

48. Estados Unidos Mexicanos, Gobierno Federal, *Ley sobre Relaciones Familiares*, cap. 13, art. 222, p. 68.

49. Pallares, *Ley sobre Relaciones Familiares*, quoted in Sánchez Medal, *Grandes cambios*, 23.

50. Pallares, *Ley sobre Relaciones Familiares*, quoted in Sánchez Medal, *Grandes cambios*, 34.

51. See Olcott, *Revolutionary Women*, 28–32.

52. Villa de Buentello, *Mujer y la ley*, quoted in Macías, *Against All Odds*, 108–10, and discussed at length in Ramos Escandón, "Legal and Gender Constraints."

53. Macías, *Against All Odds*; Quirk, *Mexican Revolution*, 79–112; Buck, "Control de la natalidad."

54. A 1914 count of women and children attached to General Mercado's forces found 554 children and 1,256 *soldaderas* to 4,557 soldiers. See Salas, *Mexican Military*, 96. On child combatants, see Alcubierre and Carreño-King, *Los niños villistas*. During the period 1910 to 1921, the population growth of Mexico City accounted for 60 percent of the urban population growth for the entire country (González Navarro, *Dinámica de la población*, 123).

55. Miguel Márquez, Director, to Agustin Aponte, AHSSA, CNE, AD, bk. 96, 21 February 1913.

56. Knight, *Mexican Revolution*, 2:319; Lear, *Workers, Neighbors, and Citizens*, 271–72.

57. "Relación del personal de empleados, servidumbre y asilados," AHSSA, BP, EA, HP, file 36, folder 11, 1 December 1915.

58. Informe, AHSSA, BP, EA, HP, file 33, folder 20, 29 August 1912; "Relación del personal de empleados, servidumbre y asilados," AHSSA, BP, EA, HP, file 36, folder 11, 1 December 1915.

59. Lear, *Workers, Neighbors and Citizens*, 319–20.

60. Lear, *Workers, Neighbors and Citizens*, 309–11, 311.

61. AHSSA, CNE, AD, bk. 99, p. 73, 1913.

62. AGN, BPDF, box 1, file 27, 1915.

63. Sra. María V. de G. de la Cadena, Directora, Hospicio de Niños, to C. Jefe de la Sección Primera de la Secretaría de Gobernación, AHSSA, BP, EA, HP, file 35, folder 27, 12 November 1915.

64. Lear, *Workers, Neighbors and Citizens*, 312.

65. Lear, *Workers, Neighbors and Citizens*, 271–72.

66. CONDUMEX, collection 21, file 55, folder 6236. October 1915.

67. Lear, *Workers, Neighbors and Citizens*, 334–35, 303–13.

68. Loyalty oaths and confirmations of employment, AHSSA, CNE, AD, bk. 105, p. 189, 26 July 1916; p. 276, 22 August 1916; Military exercises, AHSSA, CNE, AD, bk. 108, p. 40, 20 June 1917; Patriotic ceremonies, AHSSA, CNE, AD, bk. 109, p. 176, 8 February 1918.

69. Em. Bustamante to Venustiano Carranza, CONDUMEX, collection 21, file 108/152, folder 12324, 23 December 1916.

70. For an account of a woman veteran who arrived penniless in Mexico City, see Poniatowska, *Jesús mío.*

71. Beteta, *Mendicidad en México*, 72, table 11.

72. Estados Unidos Mexicanos, Departamento de la Estadística Nacional, *Censo general de habitantes*, 15, table 1.

73. Derived from Estados Unidos Mexicanos, Departamento de la Estadística Nacional, *Censo general de habitantes*, 26, table 10.

74. Directora Refugio M. Caniedo, CNE, to Dirección General de Beneficencia Pública, AHSSA, CNE, AD, bk. 108, pp. 390, 473, 5 June 1917, 27 October 1917, 30 November 1917; Directora, CNE, to Dirección General de Beneficencia Pública, AHSSA, CNE, AD, bk. 108, pp. 390, 473, 5 June 1917, 27 October 1917, 30 November 1917.

75. AHSSA, CNE, AD, bk. 108, pp. 47–49, 1917.

76. See Agostoni, "Popular Health Education"; Knight, *Mexican Revolution*, 2:403–19.

77. Bliss, *Compromised Positions*, 63–94.

78. Bulnes, "Gran paso," 32–33.

79. Jesús H. Durán to Venustiano Carrranza, CONDUMEX, collection 21, file 28, folder 2965, 19 February 1915.

80. Eloísa Espinosa to Venustiano Carranza, CONDUMEX, collection 21, file 33, folder 3479, 25 March 1915.

81. Micaela Pérez to Venustiano Carranza, CONDUMEX, collection 21, file 38, folder 4113, 3 May 1915.

82. Miguel Camacho to Venustiano Carranza, CONDUMEX, collection 21, file 96/152, folder 10879, 22 December, 1916.

83. Petition, CONDUMEX, collection 21, file 65/152, folder 7161, 4 January 1916.

84. Joaquín Baeza Alzaga to Venustiano Carranza, CONDUMEX, collection 21, file 65/152, folder 7418, 14 February 1916.

85. Pani, *Hygiene in Mexico*, vi–vii.

86. Pani, *Hygiene in Mexico*, 171.

87. Pani, *Hygiene in Mexico*, 33. Italics in original.

88. Pani, *Hygiene in Mexico*, 104–10.

89. See, for example, Dwork, *War Is Good*; Guy, "Child Congresses"; Kirchenbaum, *Small Comrades*; and Pedersen, *Welfare State.*

90. For comparison, see Illanes, *En el nombre.*

91. Vaughan, "Modernizing Patriarchy." For comparison, see also Donzelot, *Policing of Families.*

92. Many of the contributions in two recent anthologies analyze the role of mothers

and maternalism in revolutionary culture. See Mitchell and Schell, *Women's Revolution*; and Olcott, Vaughan, and Cano, *Sex in Revolution*.

93. Lear, *Workers, Neighbors and Citizens*, 341–65.

5. The Revolutionary Family

1. J. Meyer, *Cristero Rebellion*, 59; Quirk, *Mexican Revolution*, 127.

2. See Benjamin, *Revolución*, 68–78; and Hirsch, *Family Photographs*, 32.

3. See Hareven, "What Difference?"

4. Quoted in Torres Septién, *Educación privada*, 126n69.

5. Quoted in Torres Septién, *Educación privada*, 126n69.

6. AHDF, HP, vol. 2295, folder 58, February 1868.

7. Franco, *Plotting Women*, 158.

8. For comparison, see Dwork, *War Is Good*.

9. Estadística, AHSSA, BP, SP, HI, box 11, folder 1; Espinosa de los Reyes, *Primera infancia*, 8–10; Cordero, "Subestimación," 205–27; and Alfonso Reyes, "La mortalidad," 22, table 5.

10. Pani, *Hygiene in Mexico*, 33.

11. Urías Horcasitas, *Historias secretas*, 103–23, 147–56; T. Holt, "First New Nations," vii–xiv; Wade, "Race and Nation," 263–81.

12. Blum, "Dying of Sadness."

13. Enríquez de Rivera (Obdulia), "Gota de leche," 349.

14. Stern, "Responsible Mothers."

15. Key, *Century of the Child*. See also Gordon, *Their Own Lives*; Guy, "Pan-American Cooperation"; Hawes, *Children's Rights Movement*; Rizzini, "Child-Saving Movement"; and Fildes, Marks, and Marland, *Women and Children First*.

16. Estados Unidos Mexicanos, Gobierno Federal, *Ley sobre Relaciones Familiares*, cap. 2, art. 17, fracc. 7, p. 25.

17. Castillo Nájera, "Informe del relator," 7. See also Birn, "Broken Pitcher"; Cooter, *Name of the Child*; Comacchio, *Built of Babies*; and Donzelot, *Policing of Families*.

18. See Stepan, *Hour of Eugenics*, 77–85; Stern, "Responsible Mothers"; and Departamento de Salubridad Pública, *Semana del Niño*.

19. Enríquez de Rivera, "Gota de leche."

20. Casián, "En pro del hijo," 377.

21. Sección de Higiene, [Recommendations], *Memoria del Primer Congreso Mexicano del Niño*, pp. 23–24.

22. Ladd-Taylor, "Agony and Grief."

23. See Koven and Michel, *New World*; and Guy, "Child Congresses."

24. Castillo Nájera, "Informe del relator"; Aréchiga Córdoba, "Dictadura sanitaria." See also Carreras, "Hay que salvar"; Clark, "Género, raza y nación," 219–56.

25. Pani, *Hygiene in Mexico*, vi.

26. D'Erzell, "Casa de Maternidad"; Enríquez de Rivera, "Gota de leche."

27. Espinosa de los Reyes, *Primera infancia*, 36.

28. *Universal*, 5 January 1921, 4, 8.

29. *Universal*, 3 January 1921, 4–5. See also Conto, "A las honorables damas que forman la directiva de la Asociación Nacional de Protección a la Infancia," AHSSA, SP, HI, box 6, folder 6, 24 November 1930.

30. Castillo Nájera, "Informe del relator," 26.

31. "El ideal de una niñez vigorosa y sana ha triunfado," *Universal*, 7 January 1923, 1–3.

32. "Niñez vigorosa," *Universal*, 7 January 1923, 1–3; see also Stern, "Responsible Mothers."

33. Departamento de Salubridad Pública, *Semana del Niño*.

34. AHSSA, SP, HI, box 5, file 4, 1929; "En la Colonia," *Boletín de la Beneficencia Pública*.

35. For comparison, see Illanes, "Aproximándose a los pobres."

36. "¿Cuál es el niño?" *Hogar*, pt. 1,

37. "¿Cuál es el niño?" *Hogar*, pts. 1, 2.

38. "Nuestro Concurso de Niños: El dictamen del jurado calificador," *Hogar*.

39. Marsan, "Médico como amigo," 12.

40. Manrique de Lara, "Siglo de los niños," 9, 38. See also Muñiz, *Cuerpo, representacion, y poder*; Agostoni, "Popular Health Education"; and Stern, "Responsible Mothers." For comparison, see Besse, *Restructuring Patriarchy*, 89–109.

41. Marsan, "Higiene y medicina," *Hogar*, 6; Estrellita, "Belleza y los trabajos," *Hogar*; "Página Femenil," *Universal*, 4 January 1920, 16; "La alimentación de los niños," *Universal*, 3 March 1920, 11; "Hay que hacer de nuestros hijos hombres útiles y fuertes: Brillante conferencia del Dr. don Rafael Carrillo; La alimentación del niño en el primer año de su vida," *Universal*, 14 September 1921, 1.

42. González Tejeda, "Llegad vigorosos al matrimonio," *Amigo de la Juventud*, April 1921, 1. See also Escalona, "Inconvenientes higiénicos y sociales de la lactancia mercenaria," *Amigo de la Juventud*, 1913, 1–3. See also Stern, "Responsible Mothers"; and Bliss, *Compromised Positions*, 95–125.

43. Bliss, "The Science of Redemption." See also Caldwell, "Congenital Syphilis."

44. Castillo Troncoso, *Conceptos, imágenes y representaciones*, 153–54.

45. "Los pequeñuelos amos del hogar," *Jueves de Excélsior*, 31 May 1923;

"Suplemento de arte e información," *Universal*, 7 May 1922; "Suplemento de arte," *Universal*, 21 January 1923.

46. See, for example, "Lindos tiranos del hogar," *Hogar* 9: 124 (15 September 1921): ix; "Lindos tiranos del hogar," *Hogar* 9: 134 (30 January 1922): 7. See also, Castillo Troncoso, *Conceptos, imágenes y representaciones*, 153–56.

47. See, for example, "Declaración de los niños acerca de sus derechos," *Universal* 12 March 1921, 1; and Manrique de Lara, "Siglo de los niños."

48. See Anderson, *Imagined Communities*, 36–40. On the construction of collective identities and public spheres in Latin America, see Eisenstadt, "Construction of Collective Identities." See also S. M. Smith, *American Archives*, 113–35.

49. López, "India Bonita Contest"; Poole, "Our Indian"; Zavala, "India bonita"; S. M. Smith, *American Archives*, 132–35.

50. "La belleza infantil mexicana," *Jueves de Excélsior*, 8 February 1923. See also Poole, *Vision, Race, and Modernity*.

51. Stern, "Mestizophilia to Biotypology."

52. Reyes, "Silent Cinema," 76.

53. Stepan, *Hour of Eugenics*, 76–95; Stern, "Responsible Mothers."

54. Enríquez de Rivera (Obdulia), "Sobre tendencies opuestas," 3; Enríquez de Rivera (Obdulia)," "Inicua propaganda." See also Schell, "Gender, Class, and Anxiety."

55. See Porter, *Working Women*; Olcott, *Revolutionary Women*; and Schell, "Gender, Class, and Anxiety."

56. Buck, "Control de la natalidad." See also Boylan, "Gendering the Faith."

57. "La celebración del Día de las Madres tiende a hacerse general en toda América Latina," *Excélsior*, 3 May 1922, secs. 2, 6.

58. "La celebración del Día de las Madres tiende a hacerse general en toda América Latina," *Excélsior*, 3 May 1922, secs. 2, 6; Sherman, *Mexican Right*, 44.

59. Acevedo, *10 de mayo*.

60. Enríquez de Rivera (Obdulia), "Corazón de madre."

61. See also Schell, "Gender, Class, and Anxiety."

62. See also French, "Prostitutes and Guardian Angels."

63. Velasco Ceballos, "Madres mexicanas, dad la patria niños sanos," *Universal*, 28 January 1923, sec. 4, pp. 4–5.

64. Velasco Ceballos, "Madres mexicanas," sec. 4, pp. 4–5.

65. Velasco Ceballos, "Madres mexicanas," sec. 4, pp. 4–5.

66. Departamento de Salubridad Pública, Servicio de Higiene Infantil, 12.

67. "Labor desarrolada por las enfermeras visitadoras," AHSSA, SP, HI, box 7, folder 36, 10 July 1930; Bliss, "Science of Redemption."

68. Velasco Ceballos, "Madres mexicanas"; Bliss, *Compromised Positions*, 100–102.

69. Bliss, "Science of Redemption."

70. Velasco Ceballos, "Madres mexicanas."

71. "Bellos exemplares de hombres fuertes y madres sanas de mañana, premiados en el concurso convocado por el Departamento de Salubridad, con motivo de la celebración del Día del Niño," *Universal*, 27 September 1923, sec., 2, p. 1.

72. "Bellos exemplares," *Universal*, sec., 2, p. 1.

73. "Bellos exemplares," *Universal*, sec., 2, p. 1.

74. Espinosa de los Reyes, *Primera infancia*, 39–41; "Texto y orden del formato que deberá llevar el folleto de propaganda de la protección de la infancia," AHSSA, SP, HI, box 1, folder 1.

75. "Texto y orden del formato que deberá llevar el folleto de propaganda de la protección de la infancia," AHSSA, SP, HI, box 1, folder 1.

76. "Informe técnico de post-natalidad en el Centro de Higiene Infantil de la Delegación de Mixcoac," AHSSA, SP, HI, box 6, folder 19, 1930 See also "El trabajo de las enfermeras visitadoras del Departamento de Higiene Infantil en la Ciudad de México," AHSSA, SP, HI, box 7, folder 5, 21 April 1930.

77. Espinosa de los Reyes, *Primera infancia*, 7.

78. See also Bliss, *Compromised Positions*, 67–69, 158–62.

79. See, for example, "Centro de Higiene Infantil adscrito a la Delegación S. de Tacubaya: Datos sobre mortalidad infantil en el mes de agosto de 1930," AHSSA, SP, HI, box 7, folder 16.

80. Departamento de Salubridad Pública, *Centro de Higiene y Salubridad Pública "Eduardo Liceaga*," 1.

81. Departamento de Salubridad Pública, *Centro de Higiene y Salubridad Pública "Eduardo Liceaga*," 5; Espinosa de los Reyes, *Primera infancia*, 6–21, 19.

82. Servicio de Propaganda y Educación Higiénicas, *Padres de familia*; Velasco Ceballos, "Madres mexicanas." See also Bliss, *Compromised Positions*, 134; Bliss, "Love Is the Problem."

83. Velasco Ceballos, "Madres mexicanas"; Departamento de Salubridad Pública, *Servicio de Higiene Infantil*, 36; Bliss, *Compromised Positions*, 100–102.

84. Departamento de Salubridad, *El niño*, 3–8; 23; "Propaganda de la protección nacional de la infancia," AHSSA, SP, HI, box 1, folder 1, p. 2.

85. See, for example, a home inspection report by the Mexico City juvenile court, Tribunal para Menores, "Estudio social," AHSSA, SP, HI, box 1, folder 10, 1929; "Cifras generales obtenidas de los trabajos de Censo realizados por el cuerpo de enfermeras visitadoras," AHSSA, SP, HI, box 6, folder 11, 4 June 1930.

86. "Propaganda de la protección nacional de la infancia," AHSSA, SP, HI, box 1, folder 1; "Cifras generales obtenidas de los trabajos de Censo realizados por el cuerpo de enfermeras visitadoras," AHSSA, SP, HI, box 6, folder 11.

87. "Propaganda de la protección nacional de la infancia," AHSSA, SP, HI, box 1, folder 1, p. 3.

88. Tribunal para Menores, "Estudio social," AHSSA, SP, HI, box 1, folder 10, 1929.

89. Dr. Manuel Cárdenas de la Vega, Jefe Interino del Servicio de Higiene Infantil, "Labor desarrollada por el Servicio de Higiene Infantil," AHSSA, SP, HI, box 7, folder 36, 10 July 1930.

90. "Datos estadísticos de la labor de Higiene Infantil, San Ángel," AHSSA, SP, HI, box 5, folder 4, 6 April 1929.

91. "Datos estadísticos de la labor de Higiene Infantil, San Ángel," AHSSA, SP, HI, box 5, folder 4, 6 April 1929.

92. "Datos estadísticos de la labor de Higiene Infantil, San Ángel," AHSSA, SP, HI, box 5, folder 4, 6 April 1929; Rodolfo Ayala González to C. Jefe del Servicio de Higiene Infantil, AHSSA, SP, HI, box 1, folder 30, 1 July 1929.

93. "Datos estadísticos de la labor de Higiene Infantil, San Ángel," AHSSA, SP, HI, box 5, file 4, 6 April 1929. See also Rodolfo Ayala González to C. Jefe del Servicio de Higiene Infantil, AHSSA, SP, HI, box 1, folder 30, 1 July 1929; Isidro Espinosa de los Reyes to José Millán, representative of the cigarette factory, "El Águila," AHSSA, SP, HI, box 7, folder 5, February 1930.

94. Ezequiel Padilla to Sr. Dr. Aquilino Villanueva, Jefe del Departamento de Salubridad Pública, AHSSA, SP, HI, box 6, folder 1, 11 June 1929.

95. Agostoni, "Mensajeras de la salud"; Espinosa de los Reyes, *Primera infancia.*

96. Isidro Espinosa de los Reyes, T. S., AHSSA, SP, HI, box 4, folder, 21, pp. 30–36; Departamento de Salubridad Pública, *Servicio de Higiene Infantil*, 67–68.

97. Isidro Espinosa de los Reyes, "Del cuerpo de trabajadores sociales del Servicio de Higiene Infantil," AHSSA, SP, HI, box 9, folder 10, January 1931.

98. Velasco Ceballos, "Madres mexicanas."

99. "El trabajo de las enfermeras visitadoras del Departamento de Higiene Infantil en la Ciudad de México," AHSSA, SP, HI, box 7, folder 5, 21 April 1930.

100. Departamento de Salubridad Pública, *Servicio de Higiene Infantil*, 71.

101. "El trabajo de las enfermeras visitadoras del Departamento de Higiene Infantil en la Ciudad de México," AHSSA, SP, HI, box 7, folder 5, 21 April 1930.

102. "Observaciones hechas en los Centros de Higiene Infantil, resultados del servicio post-natal," AHSSA, SP, HI, box 7, folder 36, 10 July 1930; "Labor desarrollada por las enfermeras visitadoras," AHSSA, SP, HI, box 7, folder 36, 10 July 1930.

103. "Cifras generales obtenidas de los trabajos de censo realizados por el cuerpo de enfermeras visitadoras," AHSSA, SP, HI, box 6, folder 11, 4 June 1930.

104. "Informe de los trabajos efectuados por las enfermeras visitadoras durante el mes de junio de 1930," AHSSA, SP, HI, box 10, folder 11; Elena Landázuri to C. Jefe del Servicio de Higiene Infantil, AHSSA, SP, HI, box 6, folder 11, 31 August 1930.

105. Departamento de Salubridad Pública, *Servicio de Higiene Infantil*, 79.

106. Espinosa de los Reyes, "Del cuerpo de trabajadores sociales," AHSSA, SP, HI, box 9, folder 10, 1931.

107. Elena Landázuri to Isidro Espinosa de los Reyes, Jefe del Servicio de Higiene Infantil, AHSSA, SP, HI, box 7, folder 5, 17 January 1930.

108. "Informe del trabajo de las enfermeras visitadoras en el mes de julio de 1930," AHSSA, SP, HI, box 6, folder 11.

109. "El trabajo de las enfermeras visitadoras del Departamento de Higiene Infantil en la Ciudad de México," AHSSA, SP, HI, box 7, folder 5, 21 April 1930.

110. "Informe del trabajos de las enfermeras visitadoras en el mes de julio de 1930," AHSSA, SP, HI, box 6, folder 11.

111. Elena Landázuri, Jefe de Enfermeras Visitadores to Espinosa de los Reyes, Jefe de Servicio de Higiene Infantil, AHSSA, SP, HI, box 7, folder 5, 17 January 1930 and 15 March 1930.

112. "Cifras generales obtenidas de los trabajos de Censo realizados por el cuerpo de enfermeras visitadoras," AHSSA, SP, HI, box 6, folder 11, 4 June 1930.

113. Elena Landázuri to Espinosa de los Reyes, AHSSA, SP, HI, box 7, folder 5, 17 January 1930.

114. "Informe de los trabajos realizados por las enfermeras visitadoras durante el mes de septiembre de 1929," AHSSA, SP, HI, box 5, folder 5, 7 October 1929.

115. Elena Landázuri to C. Dr. Manuel Cárdenas de la Vega, AHSSA, SP, HI, box 7, folder 5, 7 June 1930.

116. Espinosa de los Reyes to the Jefe de Servicios de Ingeniería Sanitaria, AHSSA, SP, HI, box 7, folder 5, 30 April 1930.

117. "Informe de los trabajos efectuados por las enfermeras visitadoras durante el mes de junio de 1930," AHSSA, SP, HI, box 6, folder 11.

118. "Informe d el trabajos de las enfermeras visitadoras en le mes de julio de 1930," AHSSA, SP, HI, box 6, folder 11.

119. "Irregularidades en delegaciones y centros de higiene," *Prensa*, 20 April 1931. AHSSA, SP, HI, box 9, folder 16; Espinosa de los Reyes, T. S., AHSSA, SP, HI, box 4, folder 21, p. 14.

120. Dr. Federico Gómez to Dr. Savador Bermúdez, Director de la Escuela de Salubridad, AHSSA, SP, HI, box 7, folder 11, 7 August 1930.

121. "Informe rendido a la Superioridad con los datos generales y comparativos del Servicio de Higiene Infantil durante el primer semestre de 1930 a 1931," AHSSA, SP, HI, box 10, folder 11.

122. Espinosa de los Reyes to Jefe del Servicio de Intercambio del Departamento de Salubridad Pública, AHSSA, SP, HI, box 9, folder 16, 25 June 1931.

123. "Informe de las labores del Servicio de Higiene Infantil en el año de 1930," AHSSA, SP, HI, box 7, folder 36, 22 January 1931.

124. Espinosa de los Reyes to Dr. Everardo Landa, Jefe del Servicio de Propaganda, Educación Higiénicas e Intercambio, AHSSA, SP, HI, box 8, folder 7, 2 May 1931.

125. Dr. Federico Gómez, "El problema de la hospitalización prolongada en la infancia," forwarded to the president of the Junta Directiva de la Beneficencia Pública, 7 May 1934, AHSSA, BP, EA, CNE, file 20, folder 5, 9 March 1933; Blum, "Dying of Sadness."

126. Spitz, "Hospitalism," 5; Gómez, "Problema de la hospitalización".

127. Rivera Cambas, *México pintoresco*, 2:173–74; AHSSA, CNE, REG 19, 1884–95; 27, 1899–1901.

128. Gómez, "Problema de la hospitalización".

129. AHSSA, BP, EA, CNE , box 17, folders 3, 6, 11, 19, 1928–29; box 19, folders 4, 6, 17, 19 (1931–33).

130. Toussaint Aragón, *Hospital infantil*, 8, 19–20.

131. Toussaint Aragón, *Hospital infantil*, 8, 19–20.

132. Cartas, números 1–12, Servicio de Higiene Infantil Post-Natal, Departamento de Salubridad, Mexico DF, AHSSA, SP, HI, box 10, folder 14, 1934.

133. Spitz, "Hospitalism."

134. Gómez, "Problema de la hospitalización."

135. Gómez, "Problema de la hospitalización," 6.

136. Gómez, "Problema de la hospitalización," 6–7.

137. Gómez, "Problema de la hospitalización," 7.

138. Dr. Federico Gómez, "Labor médica."

139. Gómez, "El problema de la hospitalización," 9; "Labor médica."

140. Gómez, "Labor médica."

141. Gómez, "El problema de la hospitalización."

142. Gómez, "Labor médica."

143. Gómez, "El problema de la hospitalización."

144. Gómez, "Labor médica."

145. Quoted in Torres Septién, *Educación privada*, 126n69.

146. See, for example, Editorial, *Todo* 112 (22 October 1935); Jorge Sandoval, "Los niños de América," *Todo* 112 (22 October 1935).

147. *Todo* 117 (26 November 1935).

148. *Todo* 123 (7 January 1936); *Todo* 127 (4 February 1936); *Todo* 139 (28 April 1936); *Todo* 158 (15 September 1936); *Todo* 162 (13 October 1936).

149. Hernández and Mendoza, "Los niños de la presidencia," *Hoy* 95 (17 December 1938), 34–35, 74.

150. "Editorial," *Asistencia* 1, no. 8 (May 1935): 5.

151. "Concepto moderno de la Asistencia: Se condensa en solidaridad social como una obligación del estado hacia el pueblo," *Nacional*, 23 October 1938, 8.

152. "Resumen de las labores," *Asistencia Social*, no. 1 (November–December 1939): 1.

153. Macías, *Against All Odds*, 128–31.

154. "En la 'Casa de la Madre Desamparada,'" *Nacional*, 22 October 1938, 8; "La campaña de la asistencia," *Nacional*, 20 February 1939, 8.

155. Tuñón Pablos, *Mujeres que se organizan*; Secretaría de la Asistencia Pública, *Asistencia social en México*, 51; "En favor de la madre y el niño," *Excélsior*, 25 April 1938, 10; "Nueva forma el 10 de mayo," *Nacional*, 9 May 1938, 8. Buck, "Control de la natalidad."

156. Secretaría de la Asistencia Pública, *Asistencia social en México*, 44–45.

157. Junco, "La infancia trágica," *Hoy* 22 (24 July 1937), 19.

158. "Drama, dolor, miseria . . . " *Todo* 196 (10 June 1937); Bertal, "Los miserables domingos en nuestros barrios," *Todo* 235 (10 March 1938).

159. Madrigal, "Las mujeres encarceladas: Una visita al Departamento Feminino de la Penitenciaria," *Hoy* 15 (5 June 1937), 12–13; de Villamil, "El infierno de 1937," *Hoy* 23 (31 July 1937), 29–33.

160. "Como la Casa de Cuna suple ahora el hogar," *Asistencia* 2, no. 9 (July 1936).

161. Farfán Cano, "Los niños expósitos," *Todo* 94 (18 June 1935).

162. "En favor de los expósitos," *Universal*, 17 April 1939, 9.

163. "Favor de los expósitos," *Universal*, 17 April 1939, 9.

164. "Constitución de 20 hogares substitutos," *Universal*, 21 April 1939, 9.

165. "El presidente recomienda medidas para proteger la integridad de la familia," *Prensa*, 10 November 1941, 10. See also Sanders, "Improving Mothers."

166. Secretaría de la Asistencia Pública, *Primer Congreso Nacional*, 276.

6. Domestic Economies

1. AGN, CTMI, box 7, file 3561, 1930. Documentation in this chapter is drawn principally from 247 case files sampled from these records and dating from 1927 through 1940. All names have been changed except those of public officials.

2. See Castillo Nájera, "Informe del relator," 17–18; Cruz, "Menores delincuentes"; Sandoval de Zarco, "Estudio"; Ramos Pedrueza, "Conclusiones formuladas"; and Torres Torija, "Escuelas Correccionales."

3. Marín Hernández, *Historia de las instituciones*, 21–24.

4. AGN, CTMI, box 7, file 3561.

5. For contemporary analyses of similar patterns, see Benería and Roldán, *Crossroads of Class*; García and de Oliveira, *Trabajo feminino*; Mercedes González de la Rocha, *Resources of Poverty*; and Katz and Correia, *Economics of Gender*.

6. On high rates of male unemployment in Mexico City in the early 1930s, see Secretaría de la Economía Nacional, *Anuario estadístico 1938*, 158, table 80, "Hombres sin trabajo."

7. See the inspector's report characterizing shoe shiners as "dedicated to theft and vagrancy," AGN, CTMI, box 1, file 1618, 1927.

8. Lear, *Workers, Neighbors, and Citizens*, 80–85, 224–25, 354; Porter, *Working Women*, 10–13, 16–18, 37–39.

9. AGN, CTMI, box 7, file 3561.

10. AGN, CTMI, box 7, file 3561.

11. Bliss and Blum, "Dangerous Driving."

12. AGN, CTMI, box 7, file 3561.

13. See, for example, a case of a girl who moved from one domestic position to the next and, after spending time in detention for theft, was released to work as a domestic in a respectable household, AGN, CTMI, box 7, file 3578, 1930.

14. See also González de la Rocha, *Resources of Poverty*.

15. Vaughan, "Modernizing Patriarchy." See also Bliss, "Paternity Tests."

16. Estados Unidos Mexicanos, Gobierno Federal, *Ley sobre Relaciones Familiares*, cap. 2, art. 18, p. 26.

17. See Bliss and Blum, "Dangerous Driving." See also Lemaitre, *La vie mentale*; Prescott, *Doctor of Their Own*.

18. Estados Unidos Mexicanos, Gobierno Federal, *Ley sobre Relaciones Familiares*, cap. 15, arts. 238–46, pp. 71–72.

19. Estados Unidos Mexicanos, Gobierno Federal, *Ley sobre Relaciones Familiares*, cap. 5, arts. 51–74, pp. 33–37.

20. Mexico, *Civil Code*, art. 301, p. 71.

21. Mexico, *Civil Code*, arts. 311, 320, pp. 73–74. For a case where the father had only occasional work and the oldest son supported a family of nine, see AGN, CTMI, box 7, file 3575, 1930.

22. Mexico, *Civil Code*, arts. 304, 305, pp. 71–72. See, for example, AGN, CTMI, box 2, file 2129, 1928; box 7, file 3620, 1930; box 14, file 5145, 1932; box 14, file 5306, 1932; box 14, file 5170, 1932.

23. Mexico, *Civil Code*, arts. 164, 168, pp. 42–43.

24. "Laudo," *Historia documental de México*, 603.

25. The Ley Federal de Trabajo (Federal Labor Law) of 1931 confirmed a minimum age of twelve for employment, and further required parental permission for employment of minors from twelve to sixteen; Secretaría de Trabajo y Previsión Social, *Prontuario de legislación*, 369–70.

26. See, for example, Haber, *Industry and Underdevelopment*; Hart, *Anarchism*; Lear, *Workers, Neighbors, and Citizens*; Middlebrook, *Paradox of Revolution*; Porter, *Working Women*; Seminario de Movimiento, *Vida social*.

27. See *Revista CROM*, 5; "Conflictos arreglados, *Revista CROM*. For domestic workers' organizations since 1931, see Goldsmith, "Politics and Programs."

28. See, AGN, CTMI, box 66, file 17892, 1936. The union of bakery workers petitioned

the tribunal for the release of a "young comrade" (AGN, CTMI, box 7, file 3617, 1930).

29. See Porter, *Working Women*, 113–17.

30. Mexico, *Federal Labor Law*, title 2, chap. 14, art. 130, nos. 3, 4, p. 13.

31. Mexico, *Federal Labor Law*, title 2, chap. 14, art. 130, 131, no. 2, p. 13; title 3, art. 224, no. 2, pp. 19.

32. Mexico, *Federal Labor Law*, title 2, chap. 1, art. 25, no. 2, p. 3. For discussion of the institutional and legal frameworks of domestic service, see Blum, "Revolutionary Household." For a discussion of Mexican labor legislation regarding domestic service since 1931, see Goldsmith, "Politics and Programs." See also Sosenski, "Niños y jóvenes."

33. For comparison, see Tilly, "Individual Lives," 137–52; Tilly and Scott, *Women, Work, and Family*; and Moch et al., "Family Strategy."

34. See Schell, *Church and State Education*.

35. Porter, *Working Women*, 115.

36. "Constitución política," título 1, cap. 1, art. 3, fracc. 6, in Tena Ramírez, *Leyes fundamentales*, 818–19.

37. Estados Unidos Mexicanos, Secretaría de la Economía Nacional, *Sexto Censo de Población*, 18, 24.

38. Marín Hernández, *Historia de las instituciones*; Navarro de Pérez C., "Legislación complementaria."

39. Marín Hernández, *Historia de las instituciones*, 36–38.

40. In 1920 a draft for a new Ley Orgánica de los Tribunales del Fuero Común (Organic Law of District Courts) of the Federal District included provisions for the creation of the Tribunal Protector del Hogar y de la Infancia (Court for the Protection of Home and Childhood), whose functions included enforcing the payment of support pensions for women with children and implementing procedural responsibility, with an emphasis on prevention, for crimes committed by minors under eighteen. The state of San Luis Potosí introduced Mexico's first juvenile courts in 1923. A year later the Junta Federal de Protección a la Infancia (Federal Committee for the Protection of Childhood) began operation in Mexico City, and the Tribunal Administrativo para Menores (Administrative Juvenile Court) began in 1926 ("Proyecto de reformas," *Delincuencia infantil*, 189).

41. Bliss, *Compromised Positions*; Schell, *Church and State Education*; Vaughan, *Social Class*.

42. Preamble, "Ley sobre previsión," in *Delincuencia infantil*.

43. Rodríguez Cabo, "Infancia abandonada," 24; Solís Quiroga, "La familia anti-social y la delincuenia infantil: Una de las múltiples manifestaciones de nuestro deficiente estado social," *Asistencia Social* (1 October 1937): 8–9.

44. Preamble, "Ley sobre previsión," in *Delincuencia infantil*, 257.

45. Solís Quiroga, "Familia anti-social."

46. Solís Quiroga, "Familia anti-social."

47. Beteta, *Mendicidad en México*, 69–75.

48. Navarro de Pérez C., "Legislación complementaria," 2:182.

49. Rodrígez Cabo, "Infancia abandonada."

50. Solís Quiroga, "Familia anti-social."

51. Solís Quiroga, "Familia anti-social," 9.

52. Solís Quiroga, "Familia anti-social," 8.

53. Bliss, "Paternity Tests."

54. Solís Quiroga, "Familia anti-social."

55. See Bliss, *Compromised Positions*. See also Bliss and Blum, "Dangerous Driving"; and AGN, CTMI, box 2, file 1700, 1928; box 2, file 1806, 1928; box 2, file 1825, 1928; box 2, file 1841, 1928; box 5, file 3018, 1929; box 93, file 21988, 1940.

56. Solís Quiroga, "Familia anti-social."

57. Synopsis of the internal regimen of the corrections program is derived from the files of the AGN, CTMI.

58. See, for example, AGN, CTMI, box 1, file 1596, 1928.

59. The Penal Code of 1929 introduced probation (*libertad vigilada*). The code's 1931 revision added to the extramural options, including residential detention (*reclusión a domicilio*) in an honorable home (García Ramírez, *Articulo 18 Constitucional*, 105–6). For examples of release to domestic service, see AGN, CTMI, box 1, file 467, 1927; box 1, file 1192, 1927.

60. AGN, CTMI, box 14, file 5197, 1932.

61. AGN, CTMI, box 1, file 1632, 1928.

62. AGN, CTMI, box 14, file 5170, 1932.

63. AGN, CTMI, box 7, file 3561, 1930.

64. AGN, CTMI, box 19, file 6168, 1933.

65. Mexico, *Civil Code*, art. 428, p. 96. This measure was introduced in the Civil Code of 1884.

66. Mexico, *Civil Code*, art. 411, p. 93.

67. Mexico, *Civil Code*, art. 320, p. 74.

68. AGN, CTMI, box 1, file 360, 1927.

69. AGN, CTMI, box 1, file 230, 1927.

70. AGN, CTMI, box 5, 2908, 1929. See also Hecht, *Home in the Street*, 80–89.

71. AGN, CTMI, box 1, file 228, 1927.

72. AGN, CTMI, box 11, file 4649, 1930.

73. AGN, CTMI, box 23, file 7126, 1933.

74. AGN, CTMI, box 23, file 7126, 1933.

75. AGN, CTMI, box 23, file 7126, 1933. See also AGN, CTMI, box 19, file 6137, 1932.

76. Pablo Piccato concludes that much family conflict and violence among Mexico City's popular classes turned on masculine control of wives' and daughters' labor power. Piccato cites an instance in which a fourteen-year-old girl accused her parents of keeping her "in complete slavery" (*City of Suspects*, 127–28).

77. AGN, CTMI, box 1, file 1138, 1927.

78. AGN, CTMI, box 1, file 1527, 1927.

79. Mexico, *Civil Code*, art. 320, p. 74.

80. AGN, CTMI, box 5, file 2908, 1929.

81. AGN, CTMI, box 5, file 2951, 1928.

82. AGN, CTMI, box 5, file, 3164, 1928.

83. See Gutmann, "Short Arm."

84. AGN, CTMI, box 1, file 229, 1927.

85. See also AGN, CTMI, box 1, file 1138, 1927.

86. See, for example, AGN, CTMI, box 1, file 308, 1927. On long-term change in men's participation in housework and child care, see Gutmann, *Meanings of Macho*.

87. AGN, CTMI, box 1, file 1482, 1928.

88. AGN, CTMI, box 11, file 4638, 1930.

89. AGN, CTMI, box 5, file 2984, 1929.

90. During the fourteen months from November 1924 through December 1925, admissions to the foundling home reached 333, comparable to the high numbers during the years of revolutionary conflict. Only about 1 in 3 children were retrieved (109), with 80 leaving with their mothers (AHSSA, CNE, REG 58, 1924–25).

91. AGN, CTMI, box 14, file 5195, 1929.

92. AGN, CTMI, box 1, file 284, 1927.

93. AGN, CTMI, box 11, file 4531, 1930. See also Sosenski, "Lejos del ojo público."

94. AGN, CTMI, box 66, file 17825, 1938.

95. See also AGN, CTMI, box 7, file 3621, 1930.

96. For further discussion of conflicts between adolescents and their parents, see Bliss and Blum, "Dangerous Driving."

97. AGN, CTMI, box 66, file 17825, 1938.

98. AGN, CTMI, box 11, file 4628, 1931.

99. AGN, CTMI, box 7, file 3542, 1930.

100. On young women's bids for autonomy from parental authority and sexual independence, see French, "Te Amo Muncho"; Piccato, *City of Suspects*, 130; Putman, "Work, Sex, and Power."

101. AGN, CTMI, box 1, file 1510, 1928.

102. AGN, CTMI, box 1, file 1510, 1928.

103. See Porter, *Working Women*, 62–63; Bliss and Blum, "Dangerous Driving."

104. Kuznesof, "Domestic Service."

105. AGN, CTMI, box 1, file 467, 1927; box 1, file 1634, 1928; box 5, file 2987, 1929.

106. AGN, CTMI, box 11, file 4495, 1931.

107. Estados Unidos Mexicanos, Secretaría de Gobernación, *Código federal del trabajo*, pt. 1, cap. 2, art. 16, p. 5.

108. Estados Unidos Mexicanos, Secretaría de Gobernación, *Código federal del trabajo*, pt. 1, cap. 5, art. 54, p. 12.

109. AGN, CTMI, box 23, file 7039, 1933. For a similar case, see AGN, CTMI, box 1, file 413, 1927. See also Bliss and Blum, "Dangerous Driving."

110. AGN, CTMI, box 23, file 7014, 1933.

111. AGN, CTMI, box 2, file 1884, 1928.

112. Secretaría de Trabajo y Previsión Social, *Prontuario de legislación*, 369–70.

113. Mexico, *Civil Code*, art. 308, p. 72.

114. Schell, *Church and State Education*; Vaughan, *Social Class*.

115. AGN, CTMI, box 2, 1739, 1928. See also AGN, CTMI, box 2, file 1841, 1928; box 7, file 3542, 1930; box 11, file 4595, 1931.

116. AGN, CTMI, box 1, file 1021, 1928.

117. AGN, CTMI, box 1, file 1029, 1927. See also AGN, CTMI, box 5, file 3018, 1929.

118. AGN, CTMI, box 7, file 3612, 1930.

119. AGN, CTMI, box 73, file 18974, 1938.

120. Sherman, *Mexican Right*, 59–61, 101–5.

121. Sherman, *Mexican Right*, 59–61, 101–5.

122. Alatriste, "En el Día de las Madres," *Todo* 244 (12 May 1938).

123. "Niños. Más niños," *Hoy* 63 (7 May 1938), 30; Baroja, "La crisis del hogar," *Hoy* 63 (7 May 1938), 31.

124. "Los niños de México no tienen donde jugar," *Todo* 198 (24 June 1937); "Del hambre a la delincuencia," *Todo* 204 (5 August 1937); Bretal, "Los miserables domingos en nuestros barrios," *Todo*, 235 (10 March 1938); Ariza, "En los jardines de los niños pobres," *Todo* 267 (20 October 1938); Ibarra de Anda, "¡Tan desvalido como antes!" *Todo* 276 (22 December 1938); García, "México condena a su infancia," *Todo* 283 (9 February 1930).

125. Madrigal, "Delincuencia infantil en México," *Hoy* 64 (14 May 1938), 31–35.

126. De Villamil, "El infierno de 1937," *Hoy* 23 (31 July 1937). See also Moreno, "Y ellos ¿qué delito cometieron?" *Todo* 215 (21 October 1937).

127. Madrigal, "La Casa Hogar para Varones," *Hoy* 70 (25 June 1938), 33–37.

128. "Dejad que los niños vengan aquí," *Todo* 235 (10 March 1938).

129. Olcott, *Revolutionary Women*, 163–64, 173.

130. Ortega, "Yo asumo la responsabilidad, dice la Dra. Rodríguez Cabo," *Hoy* 69 (18 June 1938), 28.

131. "La delincuencia infantil en México," *Hoy* 70 (2 July 1938), 21.

132. Ariza, "En los jardines de los niños pobres," *Todo* 267 (20 October 1938).

133. Ibarra de Anda, "¡Tan desvalido como antes!" *Todo* 276 (22 December 1938).
134. García, "México condena a su infancia," *Todo* 283 (9 February 1939), 26–27, 63.
135. Catalina, "La Casa de Orientación para Mujeres," *Todo* 211 (23 September 1927).
136. García, "México condena."
137. García, "México condena," 26–27.
138. See also Benería and Roldán, *Crossroads of Class*.
139. Solís Quiroga, "Familia anti-social," 9.
140. See Blum, "Revolutionary Household"; and Blum, "Breaking and Making Families."

7. Breaking and Making Families

1. Preamble, Estados Unidos Mexicanos, Gobierno Federal, *Ley sobre Relaciones Familiares*, 6–7.
2. Preamble, Estados Unidos Mexicanos, Gobierno Federal, *Ley sobre Relaciones Familiares*, 7.
3. Estados Unidos Mexicanos, Gobierno Federal, *Ley sobre Relaciones Familiares*, cap. 8, arts. 220–36, pp. 67–71.
4. AGN, BPDF, box 57/65, folder 90, 1906–18.
5. Estados Unidos Mexicanos, Gobierno Federal, *Ley sobre Relaciones Familiares*, cap. 13, arts. 220–36, pp. 67–71; "Acuerdo para que las adopciones de niños se reglamenten en la Ley de Relaciones Familiares, 1919," AHSSA, BP, EA, CNE, file 15, folder 4; "Acuerdo para adopciones tomadas de la Ley de Relaciones Familiares: Año de 1919," AHSSA, BP, EA, CNE, file 25, folder 1.
6. AHSSA, BP, EA, HP, file 45, folder 9.
7. Luis Jaso to Dirección General de Beneficencia Pública, AHSSA, BP, EA, CNE, file 15, folder 13, 28 May 1921.
8. "Proyecto de reglamento interior de la 'Casa de Niños Expósitos'," AHSSA, BP, EA, CNE, file 15, folder 14, 7 June 1921.
9. Domínguez to Secretario de Gobernación, AHSSA, CNE, AD, bk. 83, p. 5, 10 August 1902.
10. AHSSA, BP, EA, HP, file 55, folder 8, 1924.
11. AHSSA, BP, EA, HP, file 56, folder 3, 1924–25.
12. AHSSA, BP, EA, HP, file 56, folder 3, 1925–26.
13. AHSSA, BP, EA, HP, file 56, folder 3, 1926.
14. AHSSA, BP, EA, HP, file 56, folder 3, 1925.
15. AHSSA, BP, EA, HP, file 56, folder 9, 1926–27.
16. AHSSA, BP, EA, HP, file 56, folder 3, 1926.
17. AHSSA, BP, EA, CNE, file 26, folder 1, 1926.
18. AHSSA, CNE, REG 58, 1924–25; AHSSA, BP, EA, CNE, file 26, folder 2, 1926.
19. AHSSA, BP, EA, CNE, file 26, folder 2, 1926.

20. AHSSA, BP, EA, CNE, file 26, folder 2, 1926.

21. AHSSA, BP, EA, CNE, file 26, folder 2, 1926.

22. AHSSA, BP, EA, CNE, file 26, folder 1, 1926.

23. AHSSA, BP, EA, CNE, file 25, folder 14, 1924.

24. Schell, *Church and State Education*, 73, 144.

25. AHSSA, BP, EA, CNE, file 25, folder 14, 1924.

26. Blum, "Dying of Sadness"; Stern, "Responsible Mothers"; Vaughan, "Modernizing Patriarchy."

27. For comparison, see also Gordon, *Orphan Abduction*, 119–20; Jara Miranda, *Legitimación adoptiva*, 26–35; Weiner, *Child and the State* ; and Zelizer, *Priceless Child*.

28. Mexico, *Civil Code*, arts. 390–410, pp. 88–92.

29. Padilla, "Reformas legislativas."

30. See Mexico, *Civil Code*, art. 390, p. 88.

31. See "En favor de la madre y el niño," *Excélsior*, 25 April 1938, 10; "Con diversos actos se celebró el Día de la Madre en toda la república," *Excélsior*, 11 May 1939, 10.

32. On Catholic women's leagues, see Schell, *Church and State Education*, 59–61; and Soto, *Modern Mexican Woman*, 113–14.

33. Sherman, *Mexican Right*, 59–61, 101–5.

34. Secretaría de la Asistencia Pública, *Asistencia social en México*, 16–19.

35. "Un llamado a la mujer mexicana. ¿Quiere Ud. ser madrina de un pobre niño?" *Asistencia* 2, no. 11 (September 1936); Gutiérrez del Olmo "De la caridad."

36. "Cuáles han sido los resultados de la campaña pro-adopciones de niños," *Asistencia* 2, no. 10 (October 1936).

37. "Campaña pro-adopciones," *Asistencia* 2, no. 10 (October 1936).

38. "Las adopciones," *Todo* 94 (18 June 1935).

39. "Pétalos," *Asistencia* 2, no. 5 (March 1936).

40. AHSSA, BP, AS, AA, file 32, folder 1, 1942.

41. AHSSA, BP, AS, AA, file 32, folder 1, 1939.

42. AHSSA, BP, AS, AA, file 34, folder 13, 1939.

43. Analysis in this section is based on 160 adoption petitions (AHSSA, BP, AS, AA, file 32, folders 1–3; file 33; file 34, 1938–42).

44. The 1,000 applications and 155 adoptions were not archived with the adoption petitions analyzed for this paper (Secretaría de la Asistencia Pública, *Informe de labores*, 255, table 9).

45. Blum, "Revolutionary Household."

46. See also Gordon, *Their Own Lives*, 12–20.

47. Valero Chávez, *Trabajo social en México*, 50–58. See also Millan, *Mexico Reborn*, 162–66.

48. AHSSA, BP, DIR, OM, box 7, folder 11, 7 October 1937.

49. Secretaría de la Asistencia Pública, *Informe de labores*, 271.

50. AHSSA, BP, DIR, OM, box 7, folder 11.

51. AHSSA, BP, AS, AA, file 32, folder 1, 1940; folder 3, 1942. See also AHSSA, BP, AS, AA, file 34, folder 8, 1939.

52. AHSSA, BP, AS, AA, file 34, folder 12, 1940.

53. AHSSA, BP, AS, AA, file 32, folder 3, 1942.

54. AHSSA, BP, AS, AA, file 32, folder 3, 1940.

55. AHSSA, BP, AS, AA, file 32, folder 1, 1940.

56. AHSSA, BP, AS, AA, file 34, folder 7, 1938.

57. AHSSA, BP, AS, AA, file 32, folder 3, 1939.

58. AHSSA, BP, AS, AA, file 34, folder 6, 1939.

59. AHSSA, BP, AS, AA, file 34, folder 15, 1940.

60. On colonial practice, see Twinam, *Public Lives*. On twentieth-century practice, see Lomnitz and Pérez-Lizaur, *Mexican Elite Family*.

61. AHSSA, BP, AS, AA, file 32, folder 1, 1939.

62. AHSSA, BP, AS, AA, file 32, folder 1, 1941.

63. AHSSA, BP, AS, AA, file 32, folder 1, 1942.

64. AHSSA, BP, AS, AA, file 32, folder 1, 1941.

65. AHSSA, BP, AS, AA, file 32, folder 1, 1941.

66. AHSSA, BP, AS, AA, file 32, folder 1, 1941.

67. AHSSA, BP, AS, AA, file 32, folder 2, 1942.

68. Roberto García Formentí to Jefe del Departamento de Terapia Social, AHSSA, BP, AS, AA, file 32, folder 3, March 1940.

69. AHSSA, BP, AS, AA, file 32, folder 1, 1939; file 32, folder 3, 1939.

70. AHSSA, BP, AS, AA, file 32, folder 3, 1941.

71. AHSSA, BP, AS, AA, file 32, folder 1, 1939.

72. AHSSA, BP, AS, AA, file 32, folder 3, 1941.

73. AHSSA, BP, AS, AA, file 33, folder 11, 1938–43.

74. See Ochoa, *Niño*; Cartas (números 1-12), Servicio de Higiene Infantil Post-Natal, Departamento de Salubridad, DF, AHSSA, BP, SP, HI, box 10, folder 14, 1934.

75. AHSSA, BP, AS, AA, file 32, folder 1, 1941–42.

76. AHSSA, BP, AS, AA, file 33, folder 3, 1938.

77. AHSSA, BP, AS, AA, file 34, folder 1, 1939.

78. AHSSA, BP, AS, AA, file 34, folder 1, 1939.

79. AHSSA, BP, AS, AA, file 34, folder 14, 1940. See also AHSSA, BP, AS, AA, file 34, folder 9, 1940.

80. AHSSA, BP, AS, AA, file 32, folder 3, 1941–42.

81. AHSSA, BP, AS, AA, file 32, folder 3, 1941–42.

82. AHSSA, BP, AS, AA, file 32, folder 1, 1941.

83. AHSSA, BP, AS, AA, file 32, folder 1, 1941–42.

84. AHSSA, BP, AS, AA, file 34, folder 17, 1939.

85. AHSSA, BP, AS, AA, file 33, folder 2, 1939.

86. Mexico, *Civil Code*, art. 397, p. 89.

87. [The woman's name has been changed.] AHSSA, BP, AS, AA, file 32, folder 3, 1940.

88. AHSSA, BP, AS, AA, file 32, folder 3, 1940.

89. AHSSA, BP, AS, AA, file 32, folder 3, 1940.

90. AHSSA, BP, AS, AA, file 32, folder 3, 1942.

91. Secretaría de la Asistencia Pública, *Informe de labores*, 254–55, 285.

92. League of Nations, *Children in Families*.

93. Secretaría de la Asistencia Pública, *Informe de labores*, 51; "Nueva forma el 10 de Mayo," *Nacional*, 9 May 1938, 8. See also Buck, "Mothers' Day."

94. See García and de Oliveira, *Trabajo feminino*, 26; and Ginsburg and Rapp, "Politics of Reproduction."

Conclusion

1. Dion, "Political Origins." Abortive initiatives in 1921, 1929, and 1932 preceded this legislation (Instituto Mexicano, *Código de Seguridad Social*, 16).

2. Instituto Mexicano, *Código de Seguridad Social*, 10.

3. "Exposición de motivos," in Instituto Mexicano, *Código de Seguridad Social*, pp. 22, 45; cap. 1, art. 6, p. 56.

4. "Exposición de motivos," in Instituto Mexicano, *Código de Seguridad Social*, 39; Dion, "Political Origins."

5. Instituto Mexicano, *Código de Seguridad Social*, 10.

6. Instituto Mexicano, *Código de Seguridad Social*, 13–14, 36–37.

7. Instituto Mexicano, *Código de Seguridad Social*, 7–10.

8. Instituto Mexicano, *Código de Seguridad Social*, 32.

9. Instituto Mexicano, *Código de Seguridad Social*, 35–37.

10. Instituto Mexicano, *Código de Seguridad Social*, 13–14.

11. Abbott, *Child and the State*, 642.

12. Abbott, *Child and the State*, 639–48.

13. Alegría, "Trabajo infantil," 155–56.

14. Alegría, "Trabajo infantil," 155–56.

15. González Navarro, *Población y sociedad*, 1:79.

16. See "Diferencia entre el Seguro Social y los servicios de Asistencia Pública," *Gráfico*, 12 September 1943, 12; and Instituto Mexicano, *Código de Seguridad Social*, 9.

17. "Editorial," *Asistencia* 1, no. 8 (May 1935): 5.

Bibliography

Archives

Archivo General de la Nación (AGN)

Archivo Fotográfico Enrique Díaz (AFED)

Beneficencia Pública del Distrito Federal (BPDF)

Consejo Tutelar para Menores Infractores (CTMI)

Fondo Gobernación (FG)

Gobernación Secretaría (GS)

Secretaría de Salubridad y Asistencia (SSA)

Archivo Histórico del Distrito Federal (AHDF)

Beneficencia y Asilos (BA), vol. 416

Colegios de Educación y Corrección (CEC), vols. 517, 518

Consejo General de Beneficencia (CGB), vol. 420

Hospicio de Pobres (HP), vols. 2295, 2296

Archivo Histórico de la Secretaría de Salubridad y Asistencia (AHSSA)
Beneficencia Pública (BP)
Asistencia (AS)
Asilados y Alumnos (AA)
Dirección (DIR)
Dirección General (DG)
Oficialía Mayor (OM)
Establecimientos Asistenciales (EA)
Casa de Niños Expósitos (CNE)
Hospicio de Pobres (HP)
Establecimientos Educativos (EE)
Casa de Niños Expósitos (CNE)
Administración (AD)
Nodrizas (NOD)
Registros (REG)
Salubridad Pública (SP)
Higiene Infantil (HI)

Centro de Estudios de Historia de México (CONDUMEX)

Published Works

Abadiano, Juan. *Establecimientos de beneficencia, apuntes sobre su origen y relación de los actos de su junta directiva*. Mexico City: Imprenta de la Escuela de Artes y Oficios, 1878.

Abbott, Grace. *The Child and the State*. 2 vols. Chicago: University of Chicago Press, 1938.

"Acerca de la elección de una nodriza." *Boletín de Higiene* 2, no. 3 (15 November 1895): 53.

Acevedo, Marta. *El 10 de mayo*. Mexico City: Secretaría de Educación Pública, 1982.

Agostoni, Claudia. "Las delicias de la limpieza: La higiene en la Cuidad de México." In *Bienes y vivencias: El siglo XIX*, edited by Anne Staples, 563–97. Vol. 4, *Historia de la vida cotidiana en México*, edited by Pilar Gonzalbo Aizpuru. Mexico City: Colegio de México / Fondo de Cultura Económica, 2005.

———. "Discurso médico, cultura higiénica y la mujer en la Ciudad de México al cambio de siglos (XIX–XX)." *Mexican Studies/Estudios Mexicanos* 18, no. 1 (2002): 1–22.

———. "Médicos y parteras en la Ciudad de México durante el Porfiriato." In *Cuatro estudios de género en el México urbano del siglo XIX*, edited by Gabriela Cano and Georgette José Valenzuela, 71–95. Mexico City: Universidad Nacional Autonóma de Mexico, Programa Universitario de Estudios de Género, 2001.

———. "Las mensajeras de la salud: Enfermeras visitadoras en la Ciudad de México durante la década de los 1920." *Estudios de Historia Moderna y Contemporánea de México* 33 (2007): 89–120.

———. *Monuments of Progress: Modernization and Public Health in Mexico City, 1876–1910.* Calgary, Alberta: University of Calgary Press, 2003.

———. "Popular Health Education and Propaganda in Times of Peace and War in Mexico City, 1890s–1920s." *American Journal of Public Health* 96, no. 1 (2008): 52–62.

Agostoni, Claudia, and Elisa Speckman Guerra, eds. *De normas y transgresiones: Enfermedad y crimen en América Latina, 1850–1950.* Mexico City: Universidad Nacional Autónoma de México, Instituto de Investigaciones Históricas, 2005.

Alcubierre, Beatriz, and Tania Carreño-King. *Los niños villistas: Una Mirada a la historia de la infancia en México, 1900–1920.* Mexico City: Instituto Nacional de Estudios Históricos de la Revolución Mexicana, 1997.

Alegría, Paula. "El trabajo infantil: Estudio e investigación de los problemas de la protección a la infancia trabajadora." *Asistencia* 1, no. 10 (June 1942): 154–59.

Alfaro, Martiniano T. *Reseña histórico-descriptiva del antiguo Hospicio de México.* Mexico City: Imprenta del Gobierno Federal, 1906.

Almada Bay, Ignacio, ed. *La mortalidad en México, 1922–1975.* Mexico City: Instituto Mexicano de Seguro Social, 1982.

Alonso de Rubio, Francisco. "La Mujer. XXVII. Deberes de la mujer con sus domésticos." *La Familia* 4, no. 35 (6 June 1887): 494–95.

———. "La Mujer. XXXII. La mujer considerada con relación de la beneficencia pública." *La Familia* 4, no. 44 (24 June 1887): 518–19.

Álvarez Amézquita, José, Miguel E. Bustamante, Antonio López Picazos, and Francisco Fernández del Castillo, eds. *Historia de la salubridad y de la asistencia en México.* 4 vols. Mexico City: Secretaría de Salubridad y Asistencia, 1960.

Anderson, Benedict. *Imagined Communities: Reflections on the Origin and Spread of Nationalism.* London: Verso, 1983.

Apple, Rima D. *Mothers and Medicine: A Social History of Infant Feeding, 1890–1950.* Madison: University of Wisconsin Press, 1987.

Aréchiga Córdoba, Ernesto. "Educación, propaganda o 'dictadura sanitaria': Estrategias discursivas de higiene y salubridad públicas en el México posrevolucionario, 1917–1945." *Estudios de Historia Moderna y Contemporánea de México* 33 (2007): 57–88.

Armus, Diego, ed. *Disease in the History of Modern Latin America: From Malaria to AIDS.* Durham, NC: Duke University Press, 2003.

Arrom, Silvia M. "Changes in Mexican Family Law in the Nineteenth Century: The Civil Codes of 1870 and 1884." *Journal of Family History* 10, no. 3 (1985): 305–17.

———. "The Changing Definition of the Worthy Poor: Race, Age, and Gender in the Mexico City Poor House, 1774–1876." Paper presented at the Ninth Berkshire Conference on the History of Women, Vassar College, Poughkeepsie NY, 11–13 June 1993.

——. *Containing the Poor: The Mexico City Poor House, 1774–1871*. Durham, NC: Duke University Press, 2000.

——. "Vagos y mendigos en la legislación mexicana, 1745–1845." In *Memoria del IV Congreso del Derecho Mexicano (1986)*, edited by Beatriz Bernal, 71–87. Vol. 1, *Memoria del IV Congreso de Historia del Derecho Mexicano (1986)*. Mexico City: Universidad Nacional Autónoma de México, 1988.

——. *The Women of Mexico City, 1790–1857*. Stanford, CA: Stanford University Press, 1985.

Baitenmann, Helga, Victoria Chenaut, and Ann Varley, eds. *Decoding Gender: Law and Practice in Contemporary Mexico*. New Brunswick, NJ: Rutgers University Press, 2007.

Balderston, Daniel, and Donna J. Guy, eds. *Sex and Sexuality in Latin America*. New York: New York University Press, 1997.

Ball, Alan M. *And Now My Soul Is Hardened: Abandoned Children in Soviet Russia, 1918–1930*. Berkeley: University of California Press, 1994.

Barceló, Raquel. "Hegemonía y conflicto en la ideología porfiriana sobre el papel de la mujer y la familia." In *Familias y mujeres en México: Del modelo a la diversidad*, edited by Soledad González Montes and Julia Tuñón, 73–109. Mexico City: Colegio de México, 1997.

Beezley, William H. *Judas at the Jockey Club, and Other Episodes of Porfirian Mexico*. Lincoln: University of Nebraska Press, 1987.

——. "The Profirian Smart Set Anticipates Thorstein Veblen in Guadalajara." In *Rituals of Rule, Rituals of Resistance: Public Celebrations and Popular Culture in Mexico*, edited by William H. Beezley, Cheryl English Martin, and William E. French, 173–90. Wilmington, DE: Scholarly Resources, 1994.

Beezley, William H., Cheryl English Martin, and William E. French, eds. *Rituals of Rule, Rituals of Resistance: Public Celebrations and Popular Culture in Mexico*. Wilmington, DE: Scholarly Resources, 1994.

Benería, Lourdes, and Martha Roldán. *The Crossroads of Class and Gender: Industrial Homework, Subcontracting, and Household Dynamics in Mexico City*. Chicago: University of Chicago Press, 1987.

Benjamin, Thomas. *La Revolución: Mexico's Great Revolution as Memory, Myth and History*. Austin: University of Texas Press, 2000.

Bernal, Beatriz, ed. *Memoria del IV Congreso del Derecho Mexicano (1986)*. Mexico City: Universidad Nacional Autónoma de México, 1988.

Besse, Susan K. *Restructuring Patriarchy: The Modernization of Gender Inequality in Brazil, 1914–1940*. Chapel Hill: University of North Carolina Press, 1996.

Betanzos Cervantes, Irma. "Escuelas Casas Amigas de la Obrera: Una institución de asistencia para la infancia." In *La atención materno infantil: Apuntes para su historia*, edited by Secretaría de Salud, 147–67. Mexico City: Secretaría de Salud, 1993.

Beteta, Ramón. *La mendicidad en México*. Mexico City: Beneficencia Pública del Distrito Federal, Departamento de Acción Social, 1931.

Birn, Anne-Emanuelle. "Healers, Healing, and Child Well-Being: Ideologies, Institutions, and Health in Latin America and the Caribbean." *Latin American Research Review* 40, no. 2 (2005): 176–92.

———. "'No More Surprising Than a Broken Pitcher?' Maternal and Child Health in the Early Years of the Pan American Health Organization." *Canadian Bureau of Medical History* 19, no. 1 (2002): 17–46.

Bliss, Katherine Elaine. *Compromised Positions: Prostitution, Public Health, and Gender Politics in Revolutionary Mexico City*. University Park: Pennsylvania State University Press, 2001.

———. "'Love Is the Problem': Gender Politics, International Relations, and Family Planning in Mexico, 1925–1975." Paper presented to the Department of History at the University of Texas, Austin, January 2008.

———. "Paternity Tests: Fatherhood on Trial in Mexico's Revolution of the Family." *Journal of Family History* 24, no. 3 (1999): 330–50.

———. "The Science of Redemption: Syphilis, Sexual Promiscuity, and Reformism in Revolutionary Mexico City." *Hispanic American Historical Review* 79, no. 1 (1999): 1–40.

Bliss, Katherine Elaine, and Ann S. Blum. "Dangerous Driving: Adolescence, Sex, and the Gendered Experience of Public Space in Early-Twentieth-Century Mexico City." In *Gender, Sexuality and Power in Latin America since Independence*, edited by Katherine Elaine Bliss and William E. French, 163–86. Lanham, MD: Rowman and Littlefield, 2006.

Bliss, Katherine Elaine, and William E. French. *Gender, Sexuality and Power in Latin America since Independence*. Lanham, MD: Rowman and Littlefield, 2006.

———. Introduction to *Gender, Sexuality, and Power in Latin America since Independence*, edited by Katherine Elaine Bliss and William E. French, 1–30. Lanham, MD: Rowman and Littlefield, 2006.

Blum, Ann S. "Abandonment, Adoption and Reproductive Disruption: Transitions in Child Circulation in Mexico City, 1880–1910." *Childhood* 14, no. 3 (2007): 321–58.

———. "Breaking and Making Families: Adoption and Public Welfare, Mexico City, 1917–1940." In *Sex in Revolution: Gender, Politics, and Power in Modern Mexico*, edited by Jocelyn Olcott, Mary Kay Vaughan, and Gabriela Cano, 127–44. Durham, NC: Duke University Press, 2006.

———. "Bringing It Back Home: Perspectives on Gender and Family History in Modern Mexico." *History Compass* 4, no. 5 (2006): 906–26.

———. "Children without Parents: Law, Charity, and Social Practice, Mexico City, 1867–1940." PhD diss., University of California, Berkeley, 1998.

———. "Cleaning the Revolutionary Household: Domestic Servants and Public Welfare in Mexico City, 1900–1935." *Journal of Women's History* 15, no. 4 (2004): 67–90.

———. "Conspicuous Benevolence: Liberalism, Public Welfare, and Private Charity in Porfirian Mexico City, 1877–1910." *Americas* 58, no. 4 (2001): 7–38.

———. "Dying of Sadness: Hospitalism and Child Welfare in Mexico City, 1920–1940." In *Disease in History of Modern Latin America: From Malaria to* AIDS, edited by Diego Armus, 209–36. Durham, NC: Duke University Press, 2003.

———. "Public Welfare and Child Circulation, Mexico City, 1877–1925." *Journal of Family History* 23, no. 3 (July 1998): 240–71.

Boletín de la Beneficencia Pública del Distrito Federal 1, no. 1 (March 1922): 22–53.

Boswell, John. *The Kindness of Strangers: The Abandonment of Children in Western Europe from Late Antiquity to the Renaissance.* New York: Pantheon Books, 1988.

Bourdieu, Pierre. *Outline of a Theory of Practice.* Translated by Richard Nice. Cambridge: Cambridge University Press, 1977.

Bowie, Fiona, ed. *Cross-Cultural Approaches to Adoption.* London: Routledge, 2004.

Boylan, Kristina A. "Gendering the Faith and Altering the Nation." In *Sex in Revolution: Gender, Politics, and Power in Modern Mexico*, edited by Jocelyn Olcott, Mary Kay Vaughan, and Gabriela Cano, 199–222. Durham, NC: Duke University Press, 2007.

Brenner, Anita. *The Wind That Swept Mexico: The History of the Mexican Revolution, 1910–1942.* Austin: University of Texas Press, 1971.

Briggs, Laura. "Mother, Child, Race, Nation: The Visual Iconography of Rescue and the Politics of Transnational and Transracial Adoption." *Gender and History* 15, no. 2 (2003): 179–200.

Brinton, Crane. *French Revolutionary Legislation on Illegitimacy, 1789–1804.* Cambridge, MA: Harvard University Press, 1936.

Buck, Sarah A. "El control de la natalidad y el Día de la Madre: Política feminista y reaccionaria en México, 1922–1923." *Signos históricos* 5 (January–June 2000): 9–53.

———. "Mothers' Day, the State, and Feminist Action: Maternalist Welfare Initiatives in 1940s Mexico." Paper presented at the Twelfth Berkshire Conference on the History of Women, University of Connecticut, Storrs, CT, 6–9 June 2002.

Buffington, Robert M. *Criminal and Citizen in Modern Mexico.* Lincoln: University of Nebraska Press, 2000.

Bulnes, Francisco. "Un gran paso hacia el desastre. Algo peor que el comunismo."

In *Los grandes problemas de México*, 31–37. Mexico City: Universal, 1926.

Bunster, Ximena, and Elsa M. Chaney. *Sellers and Servants: Working Women in Lima, Peru*. New York: Praeger, 1985.

Calderón de la Barca, Fanny. *Life in Mexico: The Letters of Fanny Calderón de la Barca*. Edited and annotated by Howard T. Fisher and Marion Hall Fisher. New York: Doubleday, 1966.

Caldwell, Joseph G. "Congenital Syphilis: A Nonvenereal Disease." *American Journal of Nursing* 71, no. 9 (1971): 1768–72.

Cano, Gabriela, and Georgette José Valenzuela, eds. *Cuatro estudios de género en el México urbano del siglo XIX*. Mexico City: Universidad Nacional Autónoma de México, Programa Universitario de Estudios de Género, 2001.

Cardoso, Ruth C. L. "Creating Kinship: The Fostering of Children in *Favela* Families in Brazil." In *Kinship Ideology and Practice in Latin America*, edited by Raymond T. Smith, 196–203. Chapel Hill: University of North Carolina Press, 1984.

Carreras, Sandra. "'Hay que salvar en la cuna el porvenir de la patria en peligro . . .': Infancia y cuestión social en Argentina (1870–1920)." In *Entre la familia, la sociedad y el Estado: Niños y jóvenes en América Latina (siglos XIX–XX)*, edited by Barbara Potthast and Sandra Carreras, 143–72. Madrid: Iberoamericana, 2005.

Carrillo, Rafael. "El problema de la alimentación artificial." In *Memoria del Primer Congreso Mexicano del Niño*, 149–58. Mexico City: El Universal, 1921.

Casián, F. L. "En pro del hijo de la nodriza." In *Memoria del Primer Congreso Mexicano del Niño*, 374–81. Mexico City: El Universal, 1921.

Castillo Nájera, Francisco. "Informe del relator y conclusions de todas las secciones del congreso." In *Memoria del Primer Congreso Mexicano del Niño*, 7–26. Mexico City: El Universal, 1921.

Castillo Troncoso, Alberto del. *Conceptos, imágenes y representaciones de la niñez en la Ciudad de México, 1880–1920*. Mexico City: Colegio de México, Centro de Estudios Históricos and Instituto Mora, 2006.

———. "Médicos y pedagogos frente a la degeneración racial: La niñez en la Ciudad de México, 1876–1911." In *De normas y transgresiones: Enfermedad y crimen en América Latina, 1850–1950*, edited by Claudia Agostoni and Elisa Speckman Guerra, 83–107. Mexico City: Universidad Nacional Autónoma de México, 2005.

———. "Moral médica y secularización: El cuerpo infantil en el discurso médico del Porfiriato." *Política y Cultura* 16 (Fall 2001): 143–69.

———. "La visión médica del Porfiriato en torno a la infancia." Paper presented at the XXII International Congress of the Latin American Studies Association, Miami, FL, 16–18 March 2000.

Catalina, D. Severo. "La maternidad." *La Familia* 1, no. 9 (1 October 1883): 1–4.

Caulfield, Sueann. "The History of Gender in the Historiography of Latin America." *Hispanic American Historical Review* 81, no. 3-4 (2001): 451-90.

———. *In Defense of Honor: Sexual Morality, Modernity, and Nation in Early Twentieth-Century Brazil.* Durham, NC: Duke University Press, 2000.

Ceballos Ramírez, Manuel. *El catolicismo social: Un tercero en discordia; Rerum novarum, la "cuestión social" y la movilización de los católicos mexicanos (1891–1911).* Mexico City: Colegio de México, 1991.

Ceniceros, José Ángel, and Luis Garrido, eds. *La delincuencia infantil en México.* Mexico City: Botas, 1936.

Centro de Estudios Económicos y Demográficos, El Colegio de México. *Dinámica de la población de México.* Mexico City: Colegio de México, 1970.

Chance, John K. *Race and Class in Colonial Oaxaca.* Stanford, CA: Stanford University Press, 1978.

Chaney, Elsa M., and Mary García Castro, eds. *Muchachas No More: Household Workers in Latin America and the Caribbean.* Philadelphia: Temple University Press, 1989.

Clark, Kim. "Género, raza y nación: La protección a la infancia en el Ecuador, 1910–1945." In *Palabras del silencio: Las mujeres latinoamericanas y su historia,* edited by Martha Moscoso, 219-56. Quito, Ecuador: Abya-Yala / UNICEF / Embajada Real de los Países Bajos, 1995.

"Código Civil." In *Legislación mexicana o colección completa de las disposiciones legislativas expedidas desde la independencia de la República.* 33 vols. Edited by Manuel Dublán and José María Lozano, 11:362. Mexico City: Imprenta de Comercio, 1876-1903.

"Código Sanitario de los Estados Unidos Mexicanos." In *Legislación mexicana o colección completa de las disposiciones legislativas expedidas desde la independencia de la República.* 33 vols. Edited by Manuel Dublán and José María Lozano, 24:277-99. Mexico City: Imprenta de Comercio, 1876-1903.

Comacchio, Cynthia R. *Nations Are Built of Babies: Saving Ontario's Mothers and Children, 1900-1940.* Montreal, Quebec: McGill-Queen's University Press, 1993.

"Conflictos arreglados sin intervenir la Junta de Conciliación." *Revista CROM* 1, no. 15 (1 October 1925): 57-61.

Congreso Panamericano del Niño. *Memoria del VII Congreso Panamericano del Niño.* 2 vols. Mexico City: Talleres Gráficos de la Nación, 1937.

"Consejos á las mujeres." *Álbum de la Mujer* 5, no 24 (20 December 1885): 239-40.

"Constitución política de los Estados Unidos Mexicanos (1917)." In *Leyes fundamentales de México, 1808-1975,* 817-81. 6th ed. Mexico City: Porrúa, 1975.

"Constituciones para el mejor gobierno y dirección de la Real Casa del Señor San Joseph de Niños Expósitos." *Boletín del Archivo General de la Nación,* repr., 3rd ser., 5, no. 2 (April-June 1981): 20-34.

Cooter, Roger, ed. *In the Name of the Child: Health and Welfare, 1880–1940*. London: Routledge, 1992.

Cordero, Eduardo. "La subestimación de la mortalidad infantil en México." In *La mortalidad en México, 1922–1975*, edited by Ignacio Almada Bay, 205–27. Mexico City: Instituto Mexicano de Seguro Social, 1982.

Cosío Villegas, Daniel, ed. *Historia Moderna de México*. 7 vols. Mexico City: Hermes, 1955–57.

"Creación y planta de la dirección de beneficencia pública." In *Historia de la salubridad y de la asistencia en México*. 4 vols. Edited by José Álvarez Amézquita, Miguel E. Bustamante, Antonio López Picazos, and Francisco Fernández del Castillo, 3:430–34. Mexico City: Secretaría de Salubridad y Asistencia, 1960.

"Crónica y debate de las sesiones de la Soberana Convención Revolucionaria." In *Mujeres y revolución, 1900–1917*, edited by Ana Lau and Carmen Ramos Escandón, 273–310. Mexico City: Instituto Nacional de Estudios Históricos de la Revolución Mexicana, 1993.

Cruz, Manuel, "Los tribunales para los menores delincuentes." In *Memoria del Primer Congreso Mexicano del Niño*, 362–65. Mexico City: El Universal, 1921.

"¿Cuál es el niño más robusto y más hermoso?" *El Hogar* 9, no. 145 (20 May 1922).

———. *El Hogar* 9, no. 148 (20 June 1922): 13.

"Decálogo a la madre." In *El Porfiriato y la revolución*, 54–55. Vol. 4, *El Álbum de la Mujer: Antología ilustrada de las mexicanas*, edited by Martha Eva Rocha. Mexico City: Instituto Nacional de Antropología e Historia, 1991.

"Decreto de 14 de junio de 1916." In *Mujeres y revolución, 1900–1917*, edited by Ana Lau and Carmen Ramos Escandón, 311–14. Mexico City: Instituto Nacional de Estudios Históricos de la Revolución Mexicana, 1993.

"Decreto del 29 de diciembre de 1914." In *Mujeres y revolución, 1900–1917*, edited by Ana Lau and Carmen Ramos Escandón, 311–14. Mexico City: Instituto Nacional de Estudios Históricos de la Revolución Mexicana, 1993.

De la Torre Villar, Ernesto, Moisés González Navarro, and Stanley Ross, eds. *Historia documental de México*. 2 vols. Mexico City: Universidad Nacional Autónoma de México, Instituto de Investigaciones Históricas, 1964.

Departamento de Salubridad Pública. *Centro de Higiene y Salubridad Pública "Eduardo Liceaga."* Mexico City: Departamento de Salubridad Pública, 1922.

———. *Memoria de la Semana del Niño: Organizada por el Departamento de Salubridad Pública, con motivo de la celebración del primer centenario de la consumación de la independencia*. Mexico City: Departamento de Salubridad Pública, 1921.

———. *El niño: Editado y distribuido por el Departamento de Salubridad para el uso de las madres mexicanas*. Mexico City: Departamento de Salubridad, 1921.

———. *Servicio de Higiene Infantil, Colaboración al VI Congreso Panamericano del Niño, en la ciudad de Lima, Perú.* Mexico City: Departamento de Salubridad Pública, 1930.

Departamento de Salubridad Pública, Servicio de Propaganda y Educación Higiénica. *A los padres de familia.* 2nd ed. Mexico City: Departamento de Salubridad Pública, 1923.

D'Erzell, Catalina. "Cómo debe ser la Casa de Maternidad para que cumple debidamente su misión." In *Memoria del Primer Congreso Mexicano del Niño,* 183–84. Mexico City: El Universal, 1921.

Díaz Zermeño, Héctor. "La escuela nacional primaria en la Ciudad de México." *Historia Mexicana* 29 (1979): 59–90.

Dion, Michelle. "The Political Origins of Social Security in Mexico during the Cárdenas and Ávila Camacho Administrations." *Mexican Studies/Estudios Mexicanos* 21, no. 1 (2005): 59–95.

Distrito Federal, Junta de Beneficencia Privada. *Memoria que consigna la actuación de la Junta de Beneficencia Privada en el Distrito Federal.* Mexico City: Cultura, 1940.

Distrito Federal, Junta Directiva de la Beneficencia Pública. *Memoria de la labor realizada por la H. Junta Directiva de la Beneficencia Pública en el Distrito Federal, de septiembre de 1932 a agosto de 1934.* Mexico City: Cultura, 1934.

"El Divorcio." *La Mujer: Semanario de la Escuela de Artes y Oficios para Mujeres* 1, no. 6 (22 May 1880): 1–2.

Domínguez, Manuel. "Higiene I." *Álbum de la Mujer* 1, no. 3 (23 September 1883): 38.

———. "Higiene II." *Álbum de la Mujer* 1, no. 5 (7 October 1883): 70–71.

———. "Higiene III." *Álbum de la Mujer* 1, no. 7 (21 October 1883): 102–3.

———. "Higiene IV." *Álbum de la Mujer* no. 13 (2 December 1883): 197–98.

———. "Higiene V." *Álbum de la Mujer* no. 1 (6 January 1884): 6–7.

Donzelot, Jacques. *The Policing of Families.* Translated by Robert Hurley. New York: Pantheon Books, 1979.

Dore, Elizabeth, and Maxine Molyneux, eds. *Hidden Histories of Gender and the State in Latin America.* Durham, NC: Duke University Press, 2000.

Dublán, Manuel, and José María Lozano, eds. *Legislación mexicana o colección completa de las disposiciones legislativas expedidas desde la independencia de la República.* 33 vols. Mexico City: Imprenta de Comercio, 1876–1903.

Durham, Eunice R. "Family and Human Reproduction." In *Family Household and Gender Relations in Latin America,* edited by Elizabeth Jelin, 40–63. London: Kegan Paul International / UNESCO, 1991.

Dwork, Deborah. *War Is Good for Babies and Other Young Children: A History of the*

Infant and Child Welfare Movement in England, 1898–1918. London: Tavistock, 1987.

Ehrick, Christine. "Affectionate Mothers and the Colossal Machine: Feminism, Social Assistance and the State in Uruguay, 1910–1932." *Americas* 58, no. 1 (2001): 121–39.

Eisenstadt, Shmuel N. "The Construction of Collective Identities in Latin America: Beyond the European Nation State Model." In *Constructing Collective Identities and Shaping Public Spheres*, 245–63. Brighton, UK: Sussex Academic, 1998.

"En la Colonia de la Bolsa." *Boletín de la Beneficencia Pública del Distrito Federal* 12 (December 1921).

Enríquez de Rivera, Emilia (Obdulia). "Corazon de Madre." *El Hogar* 9, no. 143 (30 April 1922): 3.

———. "La gota de leche." In *Memoria del Primer Congreso Mexicano del Niño*, 349–53. Mexico City: El Universal, 1921.

———. "Inicua propaganda." *El Hogar* 9, no. 140 (30 March 1922): 3.

———. "Sobre tendencies opuestas." *El Hogar* 9, no. 136 (20 February 1922): 3

Escalona, Genaro. "Inconvenientes higiénicos y sociales de la lactancia mercenaria." *Amigo de la Juventud* (1913): 1–3.

"Escuela Industrial de Huérfanos." *Boletín de la Dirección de Beneficencia Pública* 1, no. 1 (January 1881): 28–32.

Espinosa de los Reyes, Isidro. *La mortalidad en la primera infancia en México: Sus causas y remedios.* Mexico City: León Sanchez, 1925.

Estados Unidos Mexicanos, Departamento de la Estadística Nacional. *Censo general de habitantes: 30 noviembre de 1921; Distrito Federal.* Mexico City: Talleres Gráficos de la Nación, 1925.

Estados Unidos Mexicanos, Gobierno de la Unión. *Exposición de los cuatro libros del Código Civil del Distrito Federal y Territorio de Baja California que hizo la comisión al presentar el proyecto al gobierno de la Unión.* Mexico City: Ancona y Peniche, 1871.

Estados Unidos Mexicanos, Gobierno Federal. *Códigos civil y de procedimientos civiles promulgados en 1884.* Mexico City: Díaz de León, 1891.

———. *Ley sobre Relaciones Familiares, expedida por el C. Venustiano Carranza, Primer Jefe del Ejército Constitucionalista, encargado del poder ejecutivo de la nación, 12 de abril de 1917.* Mexico City: Económica, 1917.

Estados Unidos Mexicanos, Secretaría de Fomento, Dirección General de Estádistica. *Censo general de la República Mexicana.* Mexico City: Secretaría de Fomento, 1900.

Estados Unidos Mexicanos, Secretaría de Gobernación. *Código federal del trabajo de los Estados Unidos Mexicanos.* Mexico City: Talleres Gráficos de la Unión, 1928.

Estados Unidos Mexicanos, Secretaría de la Economía Nacional. *Sexto censo de población, 1940*. Mexico City: Secretaría de la Economía Nacional, Dirección General de Estadística, 1943.

Estados Unidos Mexicanos, Tribunal Superior de Justicia del Distrito Federal. *Diario de los debates del Congreso Constituyente de 1916–1917*. 2 vols. Edited by Fernando Romero García. Mexico City: Tribunal Superior de Justicia del Distrito Federal, 1916–1917.

Estrada, Ramón. *Algunas ligeras consideraciones sobre la falta de higiene infantil en México, en sus relaciones con la degeneración de la raza*. Mexico City: Escuela Nacional de Medicina, 1888.

Estrellita. "La belleza y los trabajos domésticos." *El Hogar* 9, no. 134 (20 January 1922): 12.

"Estudio de la Srita. Hermila Galindo con motivo de los temas que ha de absolverse en el Segundo Congreso Feminista de Yucatán, Noviembre 20 de 1916." Mérida, Yucatán: Imprenta del Gobierno Constitucionalista, 1916.

"Exposición de motivos." In *Código de Seguridad Social*, 7–52. Mexico City: Instituto Mexicano del Seguro Social, 1945.

Farriss, Nancy M. *Maya Society under Colonial Rule: The Collective Enterprise of Survival*. Princeton, NJ: Princeton University Press, 1984.

Fausto. "La mujer del hogar." *La Familia* 5, no. 42 (8 June 1888): 498–99.

Fay-Sallois, Fanny. *Les nourrices a Paris au XXIe siècle*. Paris: Payot, 1980.

Fernández Aceves, María Teresa, Carmen Ramos Escandón, and Susie S. Porter, eds. *Orden social e identidad de género, México, siglos XIX y XX*. Mexico City: Centro de Investigaciones y Estudios Superiores en Antropología Social / Guadalajara: Universidad de Guadalajara, 2006.

Fildes, Valerie. *Breasts, Bottles, and Babies: A History of Infant Feeding*. Edinburgh, Scotland: Edinburgh University Press, 1986.

———. *Wet Nursing: A History from Antiquity to the Present*. Oxford, UK: Blackwell, 1988.

Fildes, Valerie, Lara Marks, and Hilary Marland, eds. *Women and Children First: International Maternal and Infant Welfare, 1870–1945*. Edited by William F. Bynum and Roy Porter. *The Wellcome Institute Series in the History of Medicine*. London: Routledge, 1992.

Fisher, Howard T., and Marion Hall Fisher, eds. *Life in Mexico: The Letters of Fanny Calderón de la Barca*. New York: Doubleday, 1966.

Folbre, Nancy. *Who Pays for the Kids? Gender and the Structures of Constraint*. London: Routledge, 1994.

Fonseca, Claudia. *Caminhos da Adopção*. 2nd ed. São Paulo, Brazil: Cortez, 2002.

———. "Orphanages, Foundlings, and Foster Mothers: The System of Child Circulation in a Brazilian Squatter Settlement." *Anthropological Quarterly* 59, no. 1 (1986): 15–27.

——. "Spouses, Siblings and Sex-Linked Bonding: A Look at Kinship Organization in a Brazilian Slum." In *Family, Household and Gender Relations in Latin America*, edited by Elizabeth Jelin, 133–60. London: Kegan Paul International / UNESCO, 1991.

Fortunati, Leopoldina. *The Arcane of Reproduction: Housework, Prostitution, Labor and Capital*. Brooklyn, NY: Autonomedia, 1995.

Fowler-Salamini, Heather, and Mary Kay Vaughan, eds. *Women of the Mexican Countryside, 1850–1990*. Tucson: University of Arizona Press, 1994.

Franco, Jean. *Plotting Women: Gender and Representation in Mexico*. New York: Columbia University Press, 1989.

French, William E. *A Peaceful and Working People: Manners, Morals, and Class Formation in Northern Mexico*. Albuquerque: University of New Mexico Press, 1996.

——. "Prostitutes and Guardian Angels: Women, Work, and the Family in Porfirian Mexico." *Hispanic American Historical Review* 70, no. 4 (1992): 529–54.

——. "'Te Amo Muncho': The Love Letters of Pedro and Enriqueta." In *The Human Tradition in Mexico*, edited by Jeffrey M. Pilcher, 123–35. Wilmington, DE: Scholarly Resources, 2003.

Frenk, Silvestre. "Historia reciente de la asistencia materno-infantil en México." *Salud Pública de México* 25 (1983): 513–17.

Frost, Elsa C., ed. *El trabajo y los trabajadores en la historia de México*. Mexico City: Colegio de México, 1979.

Fuchs, Rachel Ginnis. *Abandoned Children: Foundlings and Child Welfare in Nineteenth-Century France*. Albany: State University of New York Press, 1984.

——. *Poor and Pregnant in Paris: Strategies for Survival in the Nineteenth Century*. New Brunswick, NJ: Rutgers University Press, 1992.

Fuller, Edward, ed. *The International Year Book of Child Care and Protection*. London: Longmans, Green, 1925.

Gager, Kristin Elizabeth. *Blood Ties and Fictive Ties: Adoption and Family in Early Modern France*. Princeton, NJ: Princeton University Press, 1996.

García, Brígida, and Orlandina de Oliveira. *Trabajo femenino y vida familiar en México*. Mexico City: Colegio de México, 1994.

García Castro, Mary. "What Is Bought and Sold in Domestic Service? The Case of Bogotá: A Critical Review." In *Muchachas No More: Household Workers in Latin America*, edited by Elsa M. Chaney and Mary García Castro, 105–26. Philadelphia: Temple University Press, 1989.

García Cubas, Antonio. *The Republic of Mexico in 1876*. Translated by George F. Henderson. Mexico City: Enseñanza, 1876.

García Icazbalceta, Joaquín. *Informe sobre los establecimientos de beneficencia y corrección de esta capital; su estado actual; noticia de sus fondos; reformas que desde luego necesitan y plan general de su arreglo.* Mexico City: Moderna Libreria Religiosa, 1907.

García Peña, Ana Lidia. "El depósito de las esposas: Aproximaciones a una historia jurídico-social." In *Cuatro estudios de género en el México urbano del siglo XIX*, edited by Gabriela Cano and Georgette José Valenzuela, 27–69. Mexico City: Universidad Nacional Autónoma de México, Programa Universitario de Estudios de Género, 2001.

García Ramírez, Sergio. *El artículo 18 Constitucional: Presión preventiva, sistema penitenciario, menores infractores.* Mexico City: Universidad Nacional Autónoma de México, Coordinación de Humanidades, 1967.

Gauss, Susan M. "Working-Class Masculinity and the Rationalized Sex: Gender and Industrial Modernization in the Textile Industry in Postrevolutionary Puebla." In *Sex in Revolution: Gender, Politics, and Power in Modern Mexico*, edited by Jocelyn Olcott, Mary Kay Vaughan, and Gabriela Cano, 181–96. Durham, NC: Duke University Press, 2006.

Gill, Lesley. *Precarious Dependencies: Gender, Class, and Domestic Service in Bolivia.* New York: Columbia University Press, 1994.

Gimeno de Flaquer, Concepción. "Crónica Mexicana." *Álbum de la Mujer* 2, no. 4 (27 January 1884): 56–58.

———. "Esposa y madre." *Álbum de la Mujer* 1, no. 9 (4 November 1883): 130–31.

Ginsburg, Faye, and Rayna Rapp. "The Politics of Reproduction." *Annual Review of Anthropology* 20 (1991): 311–43.

Golden, Janet. *A Social History of Wet Nursing in America: From Breast to Bottle.* Cambridge: Cambridge University Press, 1996.

Goldman, Wendy. *Women, the State and Revolution: Soviet Family Policy and Social Life, 1917–1936.* New York: Cambridge University Press, 1993.

Goldsmith, Mary. "Doméstica, mujer o hija de familia: Indentidades en entredicho." *Debate Feminista*, no. 22 (2000): 16–26.

———. "Politics and Programs of Domestic Workers' Organizations in Mexico." In *Muchachas No More: Household Workers in Latin America and the Caribbean*, edited by Elsa M. Chaney and Mary García Castro, 221–43. Philadelphia: Temple University Press, 1989.

Gómez, Federico. "Labor médica y labor educacional." *Asistencia* 2, no. 3 (January 1936).

Gómez Robleda, José, ed. *Características biológicas de los escolares proletarios.* Mexico City: Secretaría de Educación Pública, Departamento de Psicopedagogía Médico Escolar, 1937.

Gonzalbo Aizpuru, Pilar. "La Casa de Niños Expósitos de la Ciudad de México:

Una fundación del siglo XVIII." *Historia mexicana* 31, no. 3 (January–March 1982): 409–20.

———, ed. *Familias novohispanas, siglos XVI al XIX*. Mexico City: Colegio de México, Centro de Estudios Históricos, 1991.

Gonzalbo Aizpuru, Pilar, and Cecilia Rabell, eds. *La familia en el mundo iberoamericano*. Mexico City: Universidad Nacional Autónoma de México, Instituto de Investigaciones Sociales, 1994.

González, María del Refugio. "¿Cien años de derecho civil?" In *Un siglo de derecho civil mexicano: Memoria del II Coloquio Nacional de Derecho Civil*, edited by Instituto de Investigaciones Jurídicas, 31–41. Mexico City: Universidad Nacional Autónoma de México, 1985.

González, Ondina E., and Bianca Premo, eds. *Raising an Empire: Children in Early Modern Iberia and Colonial Latin America*. Albuquerque: University of New Mexico Press, 2007.

González Ancira, Erasmo. "Cámaras de lactancia." In *Memoria del VII Congreso Panamericano del Niño*, 2:983–87. Mexico City: Talleres Gráficos de la Nación, 1937.

González de la Rocha, Mercedes. *Los recursos de la pobreza: Familias de bajos ingresos de Guadalajara*. Guadalajara, Mexico: Colegio de Jalisco, 1986.

———. *The Resources of Poverty: Women and Survival in a Mexican City*. Oxford, UK: Blackwell, 1994.

González Navarro, Moisés. *Dinámica de la población*. Mexico City: Colegio de México, Centro de Estudios Económicos y Demográficos, 1970.

———, ed. *Estadísticas sociales del Porfiriato, 1877–1910*. Mexico City: Secretaría de Economía, Dirección General de Estadística, 1956.

———. *Población y sociedad en México (1900–1970)*. 2 vols. Mexico City: Universidad Nacional Autónoma de México, Facultad de Ciencias Políticas y Sociales, Serie Estudios 42, 1974.

———. *La pobreza en México*. Mexico City: Colegio de México, 1985.

———, ed. *El Porfiriato: La vida social*. Edited by Daniel Cosío Villegas. Vol. 4, *Historia moderna de México*. Mexico City: Hermes, 1957.

González Tejada, Ernesto. "Llegad vigorosos al matrimonio." *Amigo de la Juventud* (April 1921): 1.

González y González, Luis, Emma Cosío Villegas, and Guadalupe Monroy, eds. *La República restaurada: La vida social*. Vol. 3, *Historia moderna de México*, edited by Daniel Cosío Villegas. Mexico City: Hermes, 1956.

Goody, Esther N. *Parenthood and Social Reproduction: Fostering and Occupational Roles in West Africa*. Cambridge: Cambridge University Press, 1982.

Goody, Jack. *The Development of the Family and Marriage in Europe*. Cambridge: Cambridge University Press, 1983.

———. *Production and Reproduction: A Comparative Study of the Domestic Domain.* Cambridge: Cambridge University Press, 1976.

Gordon, Linda. *The Great Arizona Orphan Abduction.* Cambridge, MA: Harvard University Press, 1999.

———. *Heroes of Their Own Lives: The Politics and History of Family Violence; Boston, 1880–1960.* New York: Penguin Books, 1988.

———. *The New Feminist Scholarship on the Welfare State.* Madison: University of Wisconsin / Institute for Research on Poverty, 1989.

———. *Women, the State and Welfare.* Madison: University of Wisconsin Press, 1990.

Gortari Rabiela, Hira de, and Regina Hernández Franyuti, eds. *Memoria y encuentros: La Ciudad de México y el Distrito Federal (1824–1928).* 2 vols. Mexico City: Departamento del Distrito Federal, Instituto de Investigaciones Dr. José María Luis Mora, 1984.

Graham, Sandra Lauderdale. *House and Street: The Domestic World of Servants and Masters in Nineteenth-Century Rio de Janeiro.* Austin: University of Texas Press, 1992.

Grant, Julia. *Raising Baby by the Book: The Education of American Mothers.* New Haven, CT: Yale University Press, 1998.

Gutiérrez del Olmo, José Félix Alonso. "De la caridad a la asistencia: Un enfoque de la pobreza y la marginación en México." In *La atención materno infantil: Apuntes para su historia,* edited by Secretaría de Salud, 9–51. Mexico City: Secretaría de Salud, 1993.

Gutmann, Matthew. *The Meanings of Macho: Being a Man in Mexico City.* Berkeley: University of California Press, 1996.

———. "The Short Arm of the Law: Naming Victims and Victimizers of Family Violence." Paper presented at the XXVI International Congress of the Latin American Studies Association, San Juan, Puerto Rico, 15–18 March 2006.

Guy, Donna J. "Mothers Alive and Dead: Multiple Concepts of Mothering in Buenos Aires." In *Sex and Sexuality in Latin America,* edited by Daniel Balderston and Donna J. Guy, 155–73. New York: New York University Press, 1997.

———. "The Pan American Child Congresses, 1916–1942: Pan Americanism, Child Reform, and the Welfare State in Latin America." *Journal of Family History* 23, no. 3 (1998): 272–91.

———. "The Politics of Pan-American Cooperation: Maternalist Feminism and the Child Rights Movement, 1913–1960." *Gender and History* 10, no. 3 (1998): 449–69.

———. "The State, Family, and Marginal Children in Latin America." In *Minor Omissions: Children in Latin American History and Society,* edited by Tobias Hecht, 139–64. Madison: University of Wisconsin Press, 2002.

———. *White Slavery and Mothers Alive and Dead*. Lincoln: University of Nebraska Press, 2000.

Haber, Stephen. *Industry and Underdevelopment: The Industrialization of Mexico, 1890–1940*. Stanford, CA: Stanford University Press, 1989.

Hale, Charles A. *The Transformation of Liberalism in Late Nineteenth-Century Mexico*. Princeton, NJ: Princeton University Press, 1989.

Hareven, Tamara. "What Difference Does It Make?" *Social Science History* 20, no. 3 (1996): 317–44.

Hart, John M. *Anarchism and the Mexican Working Class, 1860–1931*. Austin: University of Texas Press, 1985.

Hawes, Joseph M. *The Children's Rights Movement: A History of Advocacy and Protection*. Boston: Twayne, 1991.

Hecht, Tobias. *At Home in the Street: Street Children of Northeast Brazil*. New York: Cambridge University Press, 1998.

———, ed. *Minor Omissions: Children in Latin American History and Society*. Madison: University of Wisconsin Press, 2002.

Hirsch, Julia. *Family Photographs: Content, Meaning, and Effect*. New York: Oxford University Press, 1981.

Holt, Marilyn Irvin. *The Orphan Trains: Placing Out in America*. Lincoln: University of Nebraska Press, 1992.

Holt, Thomas C. "The First New Nations." In *Race and Nation in Modern Latin America*, edited by Nancy P. Appelbaum, Anne S. Macpherson, and Karin Alejandra Rosemblatt, vii–xiv. Chapel Hill: University of North Carolina Press, 2003.

Horn, Pamela. *Children's Work and Welfare, 1780–1890*. Cambridge: Cambridge University Press, 1997.

Hunefeldt, Christine. *Liberalism in the Bedroom: Quarreling Spouses in Nineteenth-Century Lima*. University Park: Pennsylvania State University Press, 2000.

Hutchison, Elizabeth Quay. *Labors Appropriate to Their Sex: Gender, Labor, and Politics in Urban Chile, 1900–1939*. Durham, NC: Duke University Press, 2001.

Illades, Carlos, and Ariel Rodríguez Kurí, eds. *Ciudad de México: Instituciones, actores sociales y conflicto político, 1774–1931*. Mexico City: Colegio de Michoacán / Universidad Autónoma de México, 1996.

Illanes, María Angélica. "Aproximándose a los pobres: Medicina y servicio social en Chile; El caso de una contrarrevolución inter-disciplinaria, 1924–1930." *Alamedas* 9 (2001): 18–28.

———. *"En el nombre del pueblo, del estado y de la ciencia . . .": Historia social de la salud pública en Chile, 1880–1973*. Santiago de Chile: Colectivo de Atención Primaria, 1993.

Instituto de Investigaciones Jurídicas, ed. *Derechos de la niñez*. Mexico City: Universidad Nacional Autónoma de México, 1990.

Instituto Interamericano del Niño. *Legislación atinente a menores de las Américas*. Montevideo, Uruguay: Instituto Interamericano del Niño, 1961.

Instituto Mexicano del Seguro Social. *Código de Seguridad Social*. Mexico City: Instituto Mexicano del Seguro Social, 1945.

Instituto Nacional de Estadística, Geografía e Informática. *Estadísticas históricas de México*. Vol. 2. Mexico City: Instituto Nacional de Estadística, Geografía e Informática, 1985.

Jara Miranda, Jaime. *La legitimación adoptiva*. Santiago: Jurídica de Chile, 1968.

Jelin, Elizabeth, ed. "Family and Household: Outside World and Private Life." In *Family, Household and Gender Relations in Latin America*, edited by Elizabeth Jelin, 12–39. London: Kegan Paul International / UNESCO, 1991.

———. *Family, Household and Gender Relations in Latin America*. London: Kegan Paul International / UNESCO, 1991.

———. Introduction to *Family, Household and Gender Relations in Latin America*, edited by Elizabeth Jelin, 9–11. London: Kegan Paul International / UNESCO, 1991.

———. "Social Relations of Consumption: The Urban Popular Household." In *Family, Household and Gender Relations in Latin America*, edited by Elizabeth Jelin, 165–96. London: Kegan Paul International / UNESCO, 1991.

Jens, Federico Carlos. "¡Pobre Ernestina! I." *La Familia* 4, no. 2 (8 August 1886): 15.

———. "¡Pobre Ernestina!" III." *La Familia* 4, no. 5 (1 September 1886): 52–53.

Joseph, Gilbert M. *Revolution from Without: Yucatán, Mexico, and the United States, 1880–1924*. New York: Cambridge University Press, 1982.

Joseph, Gilbert M., and Daniel Nugent, eds. *Everyday Forms of State Formation: Revolution and the Negotiation of Rule in Modern Mexico*. Durham, NC: Duke University Press, 1994.

Katz, Elizabeth G., and Maria C. Correia, eds. *The Economics of Gender in Mexico: Work, Family, State, and Market; Directions in Development*. Washington DC: World Bank, 2001.

Katz, Freidrich. "Mexico: Restored Republic and Porfiriato, 1867–1910." In *The Cambridge History of Latin America*, edited by Leslie Bethell, 3–78. Cambridge: Cambridge University Press, 1986.

Kaufman, Robert R. "The Patron-Client Concept and Macro-Politics: Prospects and Problems." *Comparative Studies in Society and History* 16, no. 3 (1974): 284–308.

Keesing, Donald B. "Employment and Lack of Employment in Mexico, 1900–70." In *Quantitative Latin American Studies: Methods and Findings*, edited by James W. Wilkie and Kenneth Ruddle, 3–21. Los Angeles: University of California, Latin American Center, 1977.

Keremitsis, Dawn. "Del metate al molino: La mujer mexicana de 1910 a 1940." *Historia mexicana* 23, no. 2 (1983): 285–302.

———. *La industria textil mexicana en el siglo XIX.* Mexico City: Secretaría de la Educación Pública, 1973.

Kertzer, David I. *Sacrificed for Honor: Italian Infant Abandonment and the Politics of Reproductive Control.* Boston: Beacon, 1993.

Key, Ellen. *The Century of the Child.* New York: Putnam, 1909.

Kirchenbaum, Lisa A. *Small Comrades: Revolutionary Childhood in Soviet Russia, 1917–1932.* New York: Routledge Falmer, 2001.

Klaus, Alisa. "Depopulation and Race Suicide: Maternalism and Pronatalist Ideologies in France and the United States." In *Mothers of a New World: Maternalist Politics and the Origins of Welfare States,* edited by Seth Koven and Sonya Michel, 188–212. New York: Routledge, 1993.

Knaul, Felicia Marie. "The Impact of Child Labor and School Dropout on Human Capital: Gender Differences in Mexico." In *The Economics of Gender in Mexico: Work, Family, State, and Market,* edited by Elizabeth G. Katz and Maria C. Correia, 46–84. Washington DC: World Bank, 2001.

Knight, Alan. "El liberalismo mexicano desde la Reforma hasta la revolución (una interpretación)." *Historia mexicana* 35, no. 1 (1985): 59–91.

———. "Mexican Peonage: What Was It and Why Was It." *Journal of Latin American Studies* 18, no. 1 (1986): 41–74.

———. *The Mexican Revolution.* 2 vols. Lincoln: University of Nebraska Press, 1990.

———. "Popular Culture and the Revolutionary State in Mexico, 1910–1940." *Hispanic American Historical Review* 74, no. 3 (1994): 393–444.

Kolonitz, Paula. *Un viaje a México en 1864.* Mexico City: Secretaría de Educación Pública, 1984.

Koven, Seth, and Sonya Michel, eds. *Mothers of a New World: Maternalist Politics and the Origins of Welfare States.* New York: Routledge, 1993.

Kuznesof, Elizabeth A. "Gender Ideologies, Sexuality and the Lives of Poor Women in Colonial Mexico." Third Carleton Conference on the History of the Family, Carleton University, Ottawa, Canada, 15–17 May 1997.

———. "A History of Domestic Service in Spanish America, 1492–1980." In *Muchachas No More: Household Workers in Latin America and the Caribbean,* edited by Elsa M. Chaney and Mary García Castro, 17–35. Philadelphia: Temple University Press, 1989.

———. "The House, the Street, Global Society: Latin American Families and Childhood in the Twenty-First Century." *Journal of Social History* 38, no. 4 (2005): 859–72.

———. "The Puzzling Contradictions of Child Labor, Unemployment, and Education in Brazil." *Journal of Family History* 23, no. 3 (1998): 225–39.

————. "Sexual Politics, Race, and Bastard-Bearing in Nineteenth-Century Brazil: A Question of Culture or Power?" *Journal of Family History* 16, no. 3 (1991): 241–60.

Kuznesof, Elizabeth A., and Robert Oppenheimer. "The Family and Society in Nineteenth-Century Latin America: A Historiographical Introduction." *Journal of Family History* 10, no. 3 (1985): 215–34.

Ladd-Taylor, Molly. "'My Work Came Out of Agony and Grief': Mothers and the Making of the Sheppard-Towner Act." In *Mothers of a New World: Maternalist Politics and the Origins of Welfare States*, edited by Seth Koven and Sonya Michel, 321–42. New York: Routledge, 1993.

Lara y Pardo, Luis. "La puericultura en México." *Gaceta Médica de México* 3, no. 19 (1 October 1903): 275–88.

Laslett, Barbara, and Johanna Brenner. "Gender and Social Reproduction: Historical Perspectives." *Annual Review of Sociology* 15, (August 1989): 381–404.

Lau, Ana, and Carmen Ramos Escandón, eds. *Mujeres y revolución, 1900–1917.* Mexico City: Instituto Nacional de Estudios Históricos de la Revolución Mexicana, 1993.

"Laudo del 4 de enero de 1907 dictado por Porfirio Díaz." In *Historia documental de México*, edited by Ernesto de la Torre Villar, Moisés González Navarro, and Stanley Ross, 2:603. Mexico City: Universidad Nacional Autónoma de México, Instituto de Investigaciones Históricas, 1964.

Lavrín, Asunción. "La niñez en México e Hispanoamérica: Rutas de exploración." In *La familia en el mundo iberoamericano*, edited by Pilar Gonzalbo Aizpuru and Cecilia Rabell, 41–69. Mexico City: Universidad Nacional Autónoma de México, Instituto de Investigaciones Sociales, 1994.

————, ed. *Sexuality and Marriage in Colonial Latin America*. Lincoln: University of Nebraska Press, 1992.

League of Nations. *The Placing of Children in Families*. 2 vols. Geneva, Switzerland: League of Nations, 1938.

Lear, John. "Mexico City: Space and Class in the Porfirian Capital, 1884–1910." *Journal of Urban History* 22, no. 4 (1996): 454–92.

————. *Workers, Neighbors, and Citizens: The Revolution in Mexico City*. Lincoln: University of Nebraska Press, 2001.

Lemaitre, Auguste. *La vie mentale de l'adolescent et ses anomalies, avec 30 figures dans le texte*. Saint-Blaise, France: Foyer Solidariste, 1910.

León, Nicolás. *La obstetricia en México*. Mexico City: Tipografía de la Viuda de Francisco Díaz de León, 1910.

LeVine, Sarah, and Clara Sunderland Correa. *Dolor y Alegría: Women and Social Change in Urban Mexico*. Madison: University of Wisconsin Press, 1993.

"Ley sobre prevision social de la delincuencia infantil en el Distrito Federal de 9 de junio de 1928." In *La delincuencia infantil en México*, edited by José Ángel Ceniceros and Luis Garrido, 257–63. Mexico City: Botas, 1936.

"Los lindos tiranos del hogar." *El Hogar* 8, no. 107 (I January 1921): ix.

"Un llamado a la mujer mexicana. ¿Quiere Ud. ser madrina de un pobre niño?" *Asistencia* 2, no. 11 (September 1936).

Lombardo de Ruiz, Sonia, ed. *Organización de la producción y relaciones de trabajo en el siglo XIX: Cuadernos de Trabajo del Departamento de Investigaciones Históricas*. Mexico City: Instituto Nacional de Antropología e Historia, 1979.

Lomnitz, Larissa Adler, and Marisol Pérez-Lizaur. "Dynastic Growth and Survival Strategies of Mexican Grand Families." In *Kinship Ideology and Practice in Latin America*, edited by Raymond T. Smith, 183–95. Chapel Hill: University of North Carolina Press, 1984

———. *A Mexican Elite Family, 1820–1980*. Princeton, NJ: Princeton University Press, 1987.

López, Rick A. "The India Bonita Contest of 1921 and the Ethnicization of Mexican National Culture." *Hispanic American Historical Review* 82, no. 2 (2002): 291–328.

López de Escalera, Juan. *Diccionario biográfico y de historia de México*. Mexico City: Editorial del Magisterio, 1964.

López Monjardín, Adriana. "Apuntes sobre los jornales de artesanos en 1850." In *Investigaciones sobre la historia de la Ciudad de México*, edited by Alejandra Moreno Toscano, 123–26. Vol. 2, *Cuadernos de trabajo del Departamento de Investigaciones Históricas, Instituto Nacional de Antropología e Historia*. Mexico City: Instituto Nacional de Antropología e Historia, Departamento de Investigaciones Históricas, 1976.

Macías, Anna. *Against All Odds: The Feminist Movement in Mexico to 1940*. Westport, CT: Greenwood, 1982.

Maldonado L., Celia. *Estadísticas vitales de la Ciudad de México, siglo XIX*. Mexico City: Instituto Nacional de Antropología e Historia, Departamento de Investigaciones Históricas, Seminario de Historia Urbana, 1976.

Manilla, Manuel. "Segunda parte del triste y muy doloroso llanto fúnebre." In *Posada's Mexico*, edited by Ron Tyler, 195. Washington DC: Library of Congress / Amon Carter Museum of Western Art, 1979.

Manrique de Lara, Juana. "El siglo de los niños." *El Hogar* 9, no. 149 (30 June 1922): 9, 38.

Marcilio, Maria Luiza. "Abandonados y expósitos en la historia de Brasil: Un proyecto interdisciplinario de investigación." In *La familia en el mundo iberoamericano*, edited by Pilar Gonzalbo Aizpuru and Cecilia Rabell, 311–23. Mexico City: Universidad Nacional Autónoma de México, Instituto de Investigaciones Sociales, 1994.

Marín Hernández, Genia. *Historia de las instituciones de tratamiento para menores infractores del D.F.* Mexico City: Comisión Nacional de Derechos Humanos, 1991.

Marko, Tamara. "A Wet Nurse, Her Masters, a Folkhealer, a Pediatrician, and Two Babies: Negotiation of a 'Raceless' Motherhood Ideal and Cultural Legacies of Slavery in 1880 Rio de Janeiro." In *Women, Ethnicity, and Medical Authority: Historical Perspectives on Reproductive Health in Latin America*, edited by Tamara Marko and Adam Warren, 49–78. San Diego: University of California, Center for Iberian and Latin American Studies, July 2004.

Marsan. "Higiene y medicina." *El Hogar* 2, no. 15 (31 October 1914): 6

——. "El médico como amigo en el hogar." *El Hogar* 2, no. 13 (30 September 1914): 12.

McCaa, Robert E. "Introduction." *Journal of Family History* 16, no. 3 (1991): 211–14.

——. "The Peopling of Nineteenth-Century Mexico: Critical Scrutiny of a Censured Century." In *Statistical Abstract of Latin America*, edited by James Wilkie, Carlos Alberto Contreras, and Cristof Anders Weber, 602–33. Los Angeles: University of California, Latin American Center, 1993.

McClure, Ruth K. *Coram's Children: The London Foundling Hospital in the 18th Century*. New Haven, CT: Yale University Press, 1981.

Memoria del Primer Congreso Mexicano del Niño. Mexico City: El Universal, 1921.

Méndez de Cuenca, Laura. *El hogar Mexicano: Nociones de economía doméstica*. 2 vols. Mexico City: Herrero Hermanos, 1910.

"Mensaje del Primer Jefe ante el Constituyente." In *Leyes fundamentales de México, 1808–1975*, 6th ed. Edited by Felipe Tena Ramirez, 745–64. Mexico City: Editorial Porrua, 1975.

Mexico. *The Federal Labor Law: United States of Mexico, Effective August 28, 1931*. Mexico City: American Chamber of Commerce of Mexico, 1931.

Mexico, Federal District. *The Civil Code for the Federal District and Territories of Mexico and the Mexican Laws on Alien Landownership*. Translated by Otto Schoenrich. New York: Baker, Voorhis, 1950.

Meyer, Jean A. *The Cristero Rebellion: The Mexican People between Church and State, 1926–1929*. Translated by Richard Southern. Cambridge: Cambridge University Press, 1976.

Meyer, Philippe. *The Child and the State: The Intervention of the State into Family Life*. Cambridge: Cambridge University Press, 1983.

Meznar, Joan. "Orphans and the Transition from Slave to Free Labor in Northeast Brazil: The Case of Campina Grande, 1850–1888." *Journal of Social History* 27, no. 3 (1994): 499–515.

Michel, Sonya. "The Limits of Maternalism: Policies toward American Wage-

Earning Mothers during the Progressive Era." In *Mothers of a New World: Maternalist Politics and the Origins of Welfare States*, edited by Seth Koven and Sonya Michel, 277–320. New York: Routledge, 1993.

Middlebrook, Kevin. *The Paradox of Revolution: Labor, the State, and Authoritarianism in Mexico*. Baltimore: Johns Hopkins University Press, 1995.

Milanich, Nara. "The Casa de Huérfanos and Child Circulation in Late Nineteenth-Century Chile." *Journal of Social History* 38, no. 2 (2004): 311–40.

———. "Historical Perspectives on Illegitimacy and Illegitimates in Latin America." In *Minor Omissions: Children in Latin American History and Society*, edited by Tobias Hecht, 72–101. Madison: University of Wisconsin Press, 2002.

———. "In the Shadow of the Law? Children in Latin American History and Society." Paper presented at the Facultad de Derecho, Universidad Diego Portales, Santiago, Chile, 22 June 2005.

———. "Whither Family History? A Road Map from Latin America." *American Historical Review* 112, no. 2 (2007): 439–58.

Millan, Verna Carleton. *Mexico Reborn*. Boston: Houghton Mifflin, 1939.

Miller, Francesca. *Latin American Women and the Search for Social Justice*. Hanover, NH: University Press of New England, 1991.

Mink, Gwendolyn. *The Wages of Motherhood: Inequality and the Welfare State, 1917–1942*. Ithaca, NY: Cornell University Press, 1995.

Miranda Guerrero, Roberto. "La vida de un obrero y la construcción de la masculinidad (1890–1940)." In *Orden social e identidad de género: México, siglos XIX y XX*, edited by María Teresa Fernández Aceves, Carmen Ramos Escandón, and Susie S. Porter, 299–321; Mexico City: Centro de Investigaciones y Estudios Superiores en Antropología Social / Guadalajara: Universidad de Guadalajara, 2006.

Mitchell, Stephanie, and Patience E. Schell, eds. *The Women's Revolution in Mexico, 1910–1953*. Lanham, MD: Rowman and Littlefield, 2007.

Moch, Leslie Page, Nancy Folbre, Daniel Scott Smith, Laurel L. Cornell, and Louise A. Tilly. "Family Strategy: A Dialogue." *Historical Methods* 20, no. 3 (1987): 113–25.

Monroy, Guadalupe. "Las letras." In *República restaurada: La vida social; Historia moderna de México*, edited by Daniel Cosío Villegas, 748–66. Vol. 3, *Historia Moderna de México*. Mexico City: Hermes, 1957.

Morales, María Dolores. "La expansión de la Ciudad de México en el siglo XIX: El caso de los fraccionamientos." In *Investigaciones sobre la historia de la Ciudad de México*. Vol. 1, *Cuadernos de trabajo del Departamento de Investigaciones Históricas, Instituto Nacional de Antropología e Historia*. Edited by Alejandra Moreno Toscano, 71–104. Mexico City: Instituto Nacional de Antropología e Historia, Departamento de Investigaciones Históricas, 1974.

Morelos Z., Rafael. "Grave prejuicio de la permanencia del niño en los mercados." In *Memoria del Primer Congreso Mexicano del Niño*, 205–6. Mexico City: El Universal, 1921.

Moreno Toscano, Alejandra, ed. *Investigaciones sobre la historia de la Ciudad de México*. Vol. 1, *Cuadernos de trabajo del Departamento de Investigaciones Históricas, Instituto Nacional de Antropología e Historia*. Mexico City: Instituto Nacional de Antropología e Historia, Departamento de Investigaciones Históricas, 1974.

Moreno Toscano, Alejandra, and Sonia Lombardo de Ruiz, eds. *Fuentes para la historia de la Ciudad de México*. 2 vols. Mexico City: Instituto Nacional de Antropología e Historia, 1984.

Morgan, Tony. "Proletarians, Politicos, and Patriarchs: The Use and Abuse of Cultural Customs in the Early Industrialization of Mexico City, 1880–1910." In *Rituals of Rule, Rituals of Resistance: Public Celebrations and Popular Culture in Mexico*, edited by William H. Beezley, Cheryl English Martin, and William E. French, 151–71. Wilmington, DE: Scholarly Resources, 1994.

"La mortalidad de los niños por descuido." *Boletín de Higiene* 2, no. 10 (15 June 1896): 184–85.

Moscoso, Martha, ed. *Palabras del silencio: Las mujeres latinoamericanas y su historia*. Quito, Ecuador: Abya-Yala / UNICEF / Embajada Real de los Países Bajos, 1995.

Muñiz, Elsa. *Cuerpo, representación, y poder: México en los albores de la reconstrucción nacional, 1920–1934*. Mexico City: Universidad Autónoma Metropolitana / Porrúa, 2002.

Murdoch, Lydia. *Imagined Orphans: Poor Families, Child Welfare, and Contested Citizenship in London*. New Brunswick, NJ: Rutgers University Press, 2006.

Muriel, Josefina. "La protección al niño en la Nueva España." In *Reunión Hispano-Mexicana de Historia: Universidad Hispanoamericana de Santa Ma. de la Rábida Huelva, España*, 39–63. Seville: Universidad de Sevilla, Instituto de Estudios y Documentos Históricos, 1980.

Navarro de Pérez C., Lucía. "Legislación complementaria de la prevención social de la delincuencia infantil." In *Memoria del VII Congreso Mexicano del Niño*, 2:179–83. Mexico City: Talleres Gráficos de la Nación, 1937.

Nelson, Barbara J. "The Origins of the Two-Channel Welfare State: Workmen's Compensation and Mother's Aid." In *Women, the State, and Welfare*, edited by Linda Gordon, 123–51. Madison: University of Wisconsin Press, 1990.

"Nuestro Concurso de Niños: El dictamen del jurado calificador." *El Hogar* 10, no. 157 (20 September 1922).

Núñez de Haro y Peralta, Alonso. *Constituciones para el mejor gobierno y dirección*

de la Real Casa del Señor S. Joseph de Niños Expósitos de esta Ciudad de México.
Mexico City: De Jauregui, 1774.

Ochoa, Alfonso R. *El niño*. Mexico City: Departamento de Salubridad, 1921.

Ojeda Verduzco, Ignacio. "Los huérfanos en el Sepulcro de la Madre." *Álbum de la Mujer* 2, no. 3–4 (27 July 1884): 47–50.

Olcott, Jocelyn. *Revolutionary Women in Postrevolutionary Mexico*. Durham, NC: Duke University Press, 2005.

———. "'Worthy Wives and Mothers': State-Sponsored Women's Organizations in Postrevolutionary Mexico." *Journal of Women's History* 13, no. 4 (2002): 106–31.

Olcott, Jocelyn, Mary Kay Vaughan, and Gabriela Cano, eds. *Sex in Revolution: Gender, Politics and Power in Modern Mexico*. Durham, NC: Duke University Press, 2006.

Oliveira, Orlandina de. "Migration of Women, Family Organization and Labour Markets in Mexico." In *Family Household and Gender Relations in Latin America*, edited by Elizabeth Jelin, 101–18. London: Kegan Paul International / UNESCO, 1991.

Ortega, Fernando. "Estado actual de la legislación sobre Tribunal para Menores en México." In *Memoria del VII Congreso Panamericano del Niño*, 2:162–69. Mexico City: Talleres Gráficos de la Nación, 1937.

Ortiz, Federico, and Pedro Pérez Grovas. "Sugestiones para la organización médica, educativa y social de la casa de cuna tipo." In *Memoria del VII Congreso Panamericano del Niño*, 2:959–67. Mexico City: Talleres Gráficos de la Nación, 1937.

Padilla, Antonio, and Alcira Soler, eds. *La infancia en los siglos XIX y XX*. Morelia, Mexico: Casa de Juan Pablo / Universidad Autónoma del Estado de Morelos, 2008.

Padilla, Florencio. "Reformas legislativas para facilitar y hacer más amplios los casos de adopción." In *Memoria del VII Congreso Panamericano del Niño*, 2:129–33. Mexico City: Talleres Gráficos de la Nación, 1937.

Pagani, Estela, and María Victoria Alcaraz. *Las nodrizas de Buenos Aires: Un estudio histórico, 1880–1940*. Buenos Aires, Argentina: Centro Editor de América Latina, 1988.

Palavicini, Félix F. *Problemas de la educación*. Valencia: Sempere y Cía, 1910.

Pallares, Eduardo. *Ley sobre Relaciones Familiares, comentada y concordada con el Código Civil vigente y leyes extranjeras*. 2nd. ed. Mexico City: Librería Bouret, 1923.

Pani, Alberto J. *Hygiene in Mexico: A Study of Sanitary and Educational Problems*. Translated by Ernest L. de Gorgoza. New York: Putnam's Sons, 1917.

Paranaguá, Paulo Antonio, ed. *Mexican Cinema*. London: British Film Institute / IMCINE, 1995.

Pascual de San Juan, Pilar. "Guía de la mujer." *La Familia* 1, no. 48 (24 July 1884): 1–3.

Pedersen, Susan. *Family, Dependence, and the Origins of the Welfare State: Britain and France, 1914–1945*. Cambridge: Cambridge University Press, 1993.

Peniche Rivero, Piedad. "La comunidad doméstica de la hacienda henequenera de Yucatán, México, 1870–1915." *Mexican Studies/Estudios Mexicanos* 15, no. 1 (1999): 1–33.

Penyak, Lee. "Obstetrics and the Emergence of Women in Mexico's Medical Establishment." *Americas* 59, no. 1 (2003): 59–85.

Pérez, Emma. "'She Has Served Others in More Intimate Ways': The Domestic Servant Reform in Yucatán, 1915–1918." *Aztlán* 20, no. 1–2 (1991): 11–38.

Perló-Cohen, Manuel. *El paradigma porfiriano: Historia del desagüe del Valle de México*. Mexico City: Universidad Nacional Autónoma de México, Instituto de Investigaciones Sociales, 1999.

Peza, Juan de Dios. "Amaneciendo." *La Familia* 4, no. 7 (16 September 1886): 77.

——. *La beneficencia en México*. Mexico City: Díaz de León, 1881.

——. "En la distribución de premios a los alumnos de la Escuela Industrial de Huérfanos." *Boletín de la Dirección de Beneficencia Pública* 1, no. 1 (1881): 41–44.

——. "Himno que dedican los hijos de la 'Casa de Expósitos' a la virtuosa Señora Da. Cármen Romero Rubio de Díaz. Letra de Juan de Dios Peza. Música de Julio Peimbert. Julio 16 de 1899." Pamphlet.

Piccato, Pablo. *City of Suspects: Crime in Mexico City, 1900–1931*. Durham, NC: Duke University Press, 2001.

Pilcher, Jeffrey M. *The Human Tradition in Mexico*. Wilmington, DE: Scholarly Resources, 2003.

Poniatowska, Elena. *Hasta no verte Jesús mío*. Mexico City: Era, 1969.

Poole, Deborah. "An Image of 'Our Indian': Type Photographs and Racial Sentiments in Oaxaca, 1920–1940." *Hispanic American Historical Review* 84, no. 1 (2004): 37–84.

——. *Vision, Race, and Modernity: A Visual Economy of the Andean Image World*. Princeton, NJ: Princeton University Press, 1997.

Porter, Susie S. *Working Women in Mexico City: Public Discourses and Material Conditions, 1879–1931*. Tucson: University of Arizona Press, 2003.

Potthast, Barbara, and Sandra Carreras, eds. *Entre la familia, la sociedad y el Estado: Niños y jóvenes en América Latina (siglos XIX–XX)*. Madrid: Iberoamericana, 2005.

Powell, Thomas G. "Comentarios." In *El trabajo y los trabajadores en la historia de México*, edited by Elsa C. Frost, 456–58. Mexico City: Colegio de México, 1979.

Premo, Bianca. *Children of the Father King: Youth, Authority, and Legal Minority in Colonial Lima*. Chapel Hill: University of North Carolina Press, 2005.

———. "Minor Offenses: Youth, Crime, and Law in Eighteenth-Century Lima." In *Minor Omissions: Children in Latin American History and Society*, edited by Tobias Hecht, 114–38. Madison: University of Wisconsin Press, 2002.

Prescott, Heather Munro. *A Doctor of Their Own: The History of Adolescent Medicine*. Cambridge, MA: Harvard University Press, 1998.

Primer Congreso Mexicano del Niño. *Memoria del Primer Congreso Mexicano del Niño*. Mexico City: El Universal, 1921.

"Programas que deben regir en la Escuela Nacional de Medicina, año 1900." In *Legislación mexicana o colección completa de las disposiciones legislativas expedidas desde la independencia de la República*. 33 vols. Edited by Manuel Dublán and José María Lozano, 31:885–99. Mexico City: Imprenta de Comercio, 1876–1903.

"Proyecto de reformas a la ley orgánica de los tribunales del fuero común, proponiendo la creación de un tribunal protector del hogar y de la infancia." In *La delincuencia infantil en México*, edited by José Ángel Ceniceros and Luis Garrido, 263–67. Mexico City: Botas, 1936.

Putnam, Lara. "Work, Sex, and Power in a Central American Export Economy at the Turn of the Twentieth Century." In *Gender, Sexuality, and Power in Latin America since Independence*, edited by Katherine Elaine Bliss and William E. French, 133–62. Lanham, MD: Rowman and Littlefield, 2006.

"Quedan secularizados los hospitales y establecimientos de beneficencia." In *Legislación mexicana o colección completa de las disposiciones legislativas expedidas desde la independencia de la República*. 33 vols. Edited by Manuel Dublán and José María Lozano, 9:32–33. Mexico City: Imprenta de Comercio, 1876–1903.

Quirk, Robert E. *The Mexican Revolution and the Catholic Church, 1910–1929*. Bloomington: Indiana University Press, 1973.

Ramos Escandón, Carmen. "Challenging Legal and Gender Constraints in Mexico: Sofía Villa de Buentello's Criticism of Family Legislation, 1917–1927." In *The Women's Revolution in Mexico, 1910–1953*, edited by Stephanie Mitchell and Patience E. Schell, 53–71. Lanham, MD: Rowman and Littlefield, 2007.

———. "Comentarios." In *El trabajo y los trabajadores en la historia de México*, edited by Elsa C. Frost, 460. Mexico City: Colegio de México, 1979.

———. "Entre la ley y el cariño. Normatividad jurídica y disputas familiares sobre la patria potestad en México, 1873–1896." In *Entre la familia, la sociedad y el Estado*, edited by Barbara Potthast and Sandra Carreras, 115–41. Madrid: Iberoamericana, 2005.

———, ed. *Presencia y transparencia: La mujer en la historia de México*. Mexico City: Colegio de México, 1987.

———. "Señoritas porfirianas: Mujer e ideología en el México progresista." In *Presencia y transparencia: La mujer en la historia de México*, edited by Carmen Ramos, 143–61. Mexico City: Colegio de México, 1987.

Ramos Pedrueza, Antonio. "Conclusiones formuladas por el Lic. Antonio Ramos Pedrueza." In *Memoria del Primer Congreso Mexicano del Niño*, 368. Mexico City: El Universal, 1921.

Ransel, David L. *Mothers of Misery: Child Abandonment in Russia*. Princeton, NJ: Princeton University Press, 1988.

Rapp, Rayna. "Family and Class in Contemporary America: Notes towards an Understanding of Ideology." In *Family, Household and Gender Relations in Latin America*, edited by Elizabeth Jelin, 197–215. London: Kegan Paul International / UNESCO, 1991.

Rapp, Rayna, Ellen Ross, and Renate Bridenthall. "Examining Family History." *Feminist Studies* 5, no. 1 (1979): 174–200.

———. "Examining Family History." In *Sex and Class in Women's History*, edited by Judith L. Newton, Mary P. Ryan, and Judith R. Walkowitz, 232–58. New York: Routledge / Kegan Paul, 1983.

"Real cédula de 3 de mayo de 1797 sobre las normas que deben observarse en las casas de expósitos." *Boletín del Archivo General de la Nación*, 3rd ser., 5, no. 2 (April–June 1981): 15–19.

"Resumen de las labores desarrolladas por la Secretaría de la Asistencia Pública hasta noviembre de 1939: Bajo la gestión del Secretario de Estado Lic. Silvestre Guerrero." *Asistencia Social*, no. 1 (November and December 1939): 1.

Revista CROM 1, no. 6 (15 May 1925).

Reyes, Alfonso. "La mortalidad." In *La mortalidad en México, 1922–1975*, edited by Ignacio Almada Bay, 11–32. Mexico City: Instituto Mexicano de Seguro Social, 1982.

Reyes, Aurelio de los. "The Silent Cinema." In *Mexican Cinema*, edited by Paulo Antonio Paranaguá, 63–78. London: British Film Institute /IMCINE, 1995.

Rivera Cambas, Manuel. *México pintoresco, artístico y monumental*. 3 vols. Mexico City: Editora Nacional, 1957.

Rizzini, Irene. "The Child-Saving Movement in Brazil: Ideology in the Late Nineteenth and Early Twentieth Centuries." In *Minor Omissions: Children in Latin American History and Society*, edited by Tobias Hecht, 165–80. Madison: University of Wisconsin Press, 2002.

Rocha, Martha Eva, ed. *El Porfiriato y la Revolución*. Vol. 4 of *El álbum de la mujer; Antología ilustrada de las mexicanas*. 4 vols. Mexico City: Instituto Nacional de Antropología e Historia, 1991.

Rodríguez Cabo, Matilde. *Estudios sobre delincuencia e infancia abandonada*. Mexico City: Razón, 1931.

————. "La infancia abandonada: Estudio leido ante el Congreso de Obreros y Campesinos." In *Estudios sobre delincuencia e infancia abandonada*, 23–30. Mexico City: Razón, 1931).

Romero, José. *Guía de la Ciudad de México*. Mexico City: Porrúa, 1910.

Roniger, Luis. "Human Rights Violations and the Reshaping of Collective Identities in the Redemocratized Southern Cone." In *Constructing Collective Identities and Shaping Public Spheres*, edited by Luis Roniger and Mario Sznajder, 168–95. Brighton, UK: Sussex Academic, 1998.

Roniger, Luis, and Mario Sznajder, eds. *Constructing Collective Identities and Shaping Public Spheres*. Brighton, UK: Sussex Academic, 1998.

Rose, Lionel. *The Massacre of the Innocents: Infanticide in Britain, 1800–1939*. London: Routledge / Kegan Paul, 1986.

Rose, Michael E. *The English Poor Law 1780–1930*. Plymouth, UK: David and Charles, 1971.

Ruggiero, Kristin. "Honor, Maternity, and the Disciplining of Women: Infanticide in Late Nineteenth-Century Buenos Aires." *Hispanic American Historical Review* 72, no. 3 (1992): 335–73.

Ruiz Gaytán F., Beatriz. "Un grupo trabajador importante no incluido en la historia laboral mexicana (trabajadoras domésticas)." In *V Reunión de Historiadores Mexicanos y Norteamericanos*, edited by Elsa Frost, Michael C. Meyer, and Josefina Zoraida Vázquez, 419–55. Mexico City: Colegio de México, 1977.

Salas, Elizabeth. "The Soldadera in the Mexican Revolution: War and Men's Illusions." In *Women of the Mexican Countryside, 1850–1990*, edited by Heather Fowler-Salamini and Mary Kay Vaughan, 93–105. Tucson: University of Arizona Press, 1994.

————. *Soldaderas in the Mexican Military: Myth and History*. Austin: University of Texas Press, 1990.

Salazar, Flora. "Los trabajadores del 'servicio doméstico' en la Ciudad de México en el siglo XIX." In *Organización de la producción y relaciones de trabajo en el siglo XIX en México*, edited by Sonia Lombardo de Ruiz, 184–94. Mexico City: Instituto Nacional de Antropología e Historia, 1979.

Salinas Meza, René. "Orphans and Family Disintegration in Chile: The Mortality of Abandoned Children, 1750–1930." *Journal of Family History* 16, no. 3 (1991): 315–29.

Sánchez-Cordero Dávila, Jorge A., ed. *Libro del cincuentenario del Código Civil*. Mexico City: Universidad Nacional Autónoma de México, Instituto de Investigaciones Jurídicas, 1978.

Sánchez Medal, Ramón. *Los grandes cambios en el derecho de la familia en México*. Mexico City: Porrúa, 1979.

Sanders, Nichole. "Improving Mothers: Poverty, the Family, and 'Modern' Social

Assistance in Mexico, 1937–1950." In *The Woman's Revolution in Mexico, 1910–1953*, edited by Stephanie Mitchell and Patience A. Schell, 187–203. Lanham, MD: Rowman and Littlefield, 2007.

Sandoval de Zarco, María A. "Estudio de la Sra. Lic. María Sandoval de Zarco." In *Memoria del Primer Congreso Mexicano del Niño*, 366–68. Mexico City: Universal, 1921.

Santamarina, Rafael. "Legislación complementaria de la prevención social de la delincuencia infantil para la adaptación y redención de los menores delincuentes." In *Memoria del VII Congreso Panamericano del Niño*, 2:171–78. Mexico City: Talleres Gráficos de la Nación, 1937.

Schell, Patience A. *Church and State Education in Revolutionary Mexico City*. Tucson: University of Arizona Press, 2003.

——. "Gender, Class, and Anxiety at the Gabriela Mistral Vocational School, Revolutionary Mexico City." In *Sex in Revolution: Gender, Politics, and Power in Modern Mexico*, edited by Jocelyn Olcott, Mary Kay Vaughan, and Gabriela Cano, 112–26. Durham, NC: Duke University Press, 2007.

——. "Nationalizing Children through Schools and Hygiene: Porfirian and Revolutionary Mexico City." *Americas* 60, no. 4 (2004): 559–87.

Schmidt, Gustavus. *The Civil Law of Spain and Mexico*. New Orleans: Rea, 1851.

Scott, Joan W. "Gender: A Useful Category of Historical Analysis." In *Gender and the Politics of History*, 28–60. New York: Columbia University Press, 1988.

Secretaría de Estado y del Despacho de Gobernación, Beneficencia Pública. *Hospital General*. Mexico City: Secretaría de Estado, 1905.

Secretaría de Gobernación. "Circular de 10 de septiembre de 1885." *Legislación mexicana o colección completa de las disposiciones legislativas expedidas desde la independencia de la República*. 33 vols. Edited by Manuel Dublán and José María Lozano, 17:310–12. Mexico City: Imprenta de Comercio, 1876–1903.

Secretaría de Gobernación. *Reglamento provisional de la Casa de Niños Expósitos, titulada "La Cuna." Aprobado por la Secretaría de Gobernación*. Mexico City: Secretaría de Fomento, 1898.

Secretaría de Gobernación, Beneficencia Pública del Distrito Federal. *Reglamento para el Hospicio de Niños*. Mexico City: Talleres Linotipográficos del "Diario Oficial," 1924.

Secretaría de la Asistencia Pública. *La asistencia social en México: Sexenio 1934–1940*. Mexico City: Secretaría de la Asistencia Pública, 1940.

——. *Informe de labores presentado al H. Ejecutivo de la Unión*. Mexico City: Secretaría de Asistencia Pública, 1942.

——. *Memoria del Primer Congreso Nacional de Asistencia*. Mexico City: Secretaría de la Asistencia Pública, 1946.

Secretaría de la Economía Nacional, Dirección General de Estadística. *Anuario estadístico, 1938*. Mexico City: Secretaría de la Economía Nacional, 1939.

Secretaría de Salud. *La atención materno infantil: Apuntes para su historia*. Mexico City: Secretaría de Salud, 1993.

Secretaría de Trabajo y Previsión Social. *Prontuario de legislación sobre menores*. Mexico City: Instituto Nacional de Estudios del Trabajo, Secretaría de Trabajo y Previsión Social, 1981.

Seminario de Movimiento Obrero y Revolución Mexicana, ed. *Comunidad, cultura y vida social: Ensayos sobre le formación de la clase obrera*. Mexico City: Instituto Nacional de Antropología e Historia, 1991.

"Se modifican los reglamentos del Registro Civil." In *Legislación mexicana o colección completa de las disposiciones legislativas expedidas desde la independencia de la República*. 33 vols. Edited by Manuel Dublán and José María Lozano, 12:215–19. Mexico City: Imprenta de Comercio, 1876–1903.

Servicio de Propaganda y Educación Higiénicas. *A los padres de familia*. 2nd ed. Mexico City: Departamento de Salubridad Pública, 1923.

Sherman, John W. "For Family, God, and Country: The Mexican Right and the Political Culture of the Revolutionary State, 1929–1940." PhD diss., University of Arizona, 1994.

———. *The Mexican Right: The End of Revolutionary Reform, 1929–1940*. Westport, CT: Praeger, 1997.

Sherwood, Joan. *Poverty in Eighteenth-Century Spain: The Women and Children of the Inclusa*. Toronto, Ontario: University of Toronto Press, 1988.

Sierra, Justo. *Proyecto de un código civil formado por orden del Supremo Gobierno*. Mexico City: Torres, 1859.

Sloan, Kathryn. "Disobedient Daughters and the Liberal State: Generational Conflicts over Marriage Choice in Working Class Families in Nineteenth-Century Oaxaca, Mexico." *Americas* 63, no. 4 (2007): 615–48.

Smart, Carol, and Selma Sevenhuijsen. *Child Custody and the Politics of Gender*. London: Routledge, 1989.

Smith, Raymond T. *Kinship Ideology and Practice in Latin America*. Chapel Hill: University of North Carolina Press, 1984.

Smith, Shawn Michelle. *American Archives: Gender, Race, and Class in Visual Culture*. Princeton, NJ: Princeton University Press, 1999.

Smith, Stephanie. "'If Love Enslaves . . . Love Be Damned!' Divorce and Revolutionary State Formation in Yucatán." In *Sex in Revolution: Gender, Politics and Power in Modern Mexico*, edited by Jocelyn Olcott, Mary Kay Vaughan, and Gabriela Cano, 99–126. Durham, NC: Duke University Press, 2006.

Solana, Fernando, Raúl Cardiel Reyes, and Raúl Bolaños Martínez, eds. *Historia de la educación pública en México*. 2 vols. *Ediciones Conmemorativas del LX Aniversario de la Creación de la Secretaría de Educación Pública*. Mexico City: Secretaría de Educación Pública, 1982.

Solís Quiroga, Roberto. "La familia anti-social y la delincuencia infantil: Una de las multiples manifestaciones de nuestro deficiente estado social." *Asistencia Social*, 1 October 1937, 8–9.

Sosenski, Susana. "Lejos del ojo público: Las servidoras domésticas infantiles en la Ciudad de México, (1917–1934)." Paper presented at the IV Coloquio de Historia de Mujeres y Género en México, Zamora, Mexico, 14–16 March 2007.

———. "Niños y jóvenes aprendices: Representaciones en la literatura mexicana del siglo XIX." *Estudios de Historia Moderna y Contemporánea de México* 26 (2003): 45–79.

Soto, Shirlene. *Emergence of the Modern Mexican Woman: Her Participation in Revolution and Struggle for Equality, 1910–1940*. Denver, CO: Arden, 1990.

Spitz, René A. "Hospitalism: An Inquiry into the Genesis of Psychiatric Conditions in Early Childhood." In *René A. Spitz: Dialogues from Infancy*, edited by Robert N. Emde, 5–22. New York: International Universities Press, 1983.

Stepan, Nancy Leys. *Hour of Eugenics: Race, Gender, and Nation in Latin America*. Ithaca, NY: Cornell University Press, 1991.

Stern, Alexandra Minna. "From Mestizophilia to Biotypology: Racialization and Science in Mexico, 1920–1960." In *Race and Nation in Modern Latin America*, edited by Nancy P. Appelbaum, Anne S. Macpherson, and Karin Alejandra Rosemblatt, 187–210. Chapel Hill: University of North Carolina Press, 2003.

———. "Responsible Mothers and Normal Children: Eugenics and Nationalism in Post-Revolutionary Mexico City, 1920–1940." *Journal of Historical Sociology* 12, no. 4 (1999): 369–97.

Szuchman, Mark. *Order, Family, and Community in Buenos Aires, 1810–1860*. Stanford, CA: Stanford University Press, 1988.

Taylor, J. P. *The Civil Code of the Mexican Federal District and Territories*. San Francisco: American Book and Printing, 1904.

Tena Ramírez, Felipe. *Leyes fundamentales de México, 1808–1975*. 6th ed. Mexico City: Porrúa, 1975.

Tenorio-Trillo, Mauricio. "1910 Mexico City: Space and Nation in the City of the Centenario." *Journal of Latin American Studies* 28, no. 1 (1996): 75–104.

Thompson, Angela Tucker. "Children in Family and Society, Guanajuato, Mexico 1780–1840." PhD diss., University of Texas, Austin, 1990.

Thompson, Lanny. "The Structures and Vicissitudes of Reproduction: Households in Mexico, 1876–1970." *Review* 14, no. 3 (1991): 403–36.

Thorne, Barrie. "Rethinking the Family: An Overview." In *Rethinking the Family: Some Feminist Questions*, edited by Barrie Thorne and Marilyn Yalom, 1–24. New York: Longman, 1982.

Thorne, Barrie, and Marilyn Yalom, eds. *Rethinking the Family: Some Feminist Questions*. New York: Longman, 1982.

Tilly, Louise A. "Beyond Family Strategies, What?" *Historical Methods* 20, no. 3 (1987): 123–25.

———. "Individual Lives and Family Strategies in the French Proletariat." *Journal of Family History* 4 (1979): 137–52.

Tilly, Louse A., Rachel G. Fuchs, David I. Kertzer, and David L. Ransel. "Child Abandonment in European History: A Symposium." *Journal of Family History* 17, no. 1 (1992): 1–23.

Tilly, Louise A., and Joan W. Scott. *Women, Work, and Family.* New York: Holt, Rinehart, and Winston, 1978.

Torres Septién, Valentina. *La educación privada en México, 1903–1976.* Mexico City: Colegio de México / Universidad Iberoamericana, 1997.

Torres Torija, José. "Necesidad de establecer sobre nuevas bases nuestras mal llamadas Escuelas Correccionales." In *Memoria del VII Congreso Panamericano del Niño*, 2:369–72. Mexico City: Talleres Gráficos de la Nación, 1937.

Toussaint Aragón, Eugenio. *Hospital infantil de México "Dr. Federico Gómez": 1943–1983.* Mexico City, 1983.

Tuñón, Julia, ed. *El siglo XIX (1821–1880).* 4 vols. Vol. 3, *El álbum de la mujer: Antología ilustrada de las mexicanas.* Mexico City: Instituto Nacional de Antropología e Historia, 1991.

Tuñón Pablos, Esperanza. *Mujeres que se organizan: El Frente Único por Derechos de la Mujer, 1935–1938.* Mexico City: Universidad Nacional Autónoma de Mexico, 1992.

Turner, John Kenneth. *Barbarous Mexico: An Indictment of a Cruel and Corrupt System.* 1st ed. London: Cassell, 1911.

Twinam, Ann. "The Church, the State, and the Abandoned." In *Raising an Empire: Children in Early Modern Iberia and Colonial Latin America*, edited by Ondina E. González and Bianca Premo, 163–86. Albuquerque: University of New Mexico Press, 2007.

———. "Honor, Sexuality, and Illegitimacy in Colonial Spanish America." In *Sexuality and Marriage in Colonial Latin America*, edited by Asunción Lavrín, 118–55. Lincoln: University of Nebraska Press, 1992.

———. *Public Lives, Private Secrets: Gender, Honor, Sexuality, and Illegitimacy in Colonial Spanish America.* Stanford, CA: Stanford University Press, 1999.

Tyler, Ron, ed. *Posada's Mexico.* Washington DC: Library of Congress / Amon Carter Museum of Western Art, 1979.

Urías Horcasitas, Beatriz. *Historias secretas del racismo en México (1920–1950).* Mexico City: Tusquets Editores México, 2007.

Valero Chávez, Aída. *El trabajo social en México: Desarrollo y perspectivas.* Mexico City: Universidad Nacional Autónoma de México, Escuela Nacional de Trabajo Social, 1994.

Valle, Ramon. "La madre y el niño." *La Familia* 4, no. 15 (16 November 1886): 172.

Vallens, Vivian M. *Working Women in Mexico during the Porfiriato, 1880–1910*. San Francisco: R & E Research Associates, 1978.

Vargas Olvera, Rogelio. "De la Escuela Correccional a la Escuela Industrial." In *La atención materno infantil: Apuntes para su historia*, edited by Secretaría de Salud, 65–91. Mexico City: Secretaría de Salud, 1993.

Várguez Pasos, Luis A. "Elites e identidades: Una visión de la sociedad meridana de la segunda mitad del siglo XIX." *Historia Mexicana* 51, no. 4 (2002): 829–65.

"Variedades." *Boletin de Higiene* 1, no. 3 (15 November 1883): 34.

Vaughan, Mary Kay. "Modernizing Patriarchy: State Policies, Rural Households, and Women in Mexico, 1930–1940." In *Hidden Histories of Gender and the State in Latin America*, edited by Elizabeth Dore and Maxine Molyneux, 194–214. Durham, NC: Duke University Press, 2000.

———. *The State, Education, and Social Class in Mexico, 1880–1928*. DeKalb: Northern Illinois University, 1982.

Vestina, "Crónica Mexicana." *Álbum de la Mujer* 1, no. 7 (21 October 1883): 108–10.

Villa de Buentello, G. Sofía. *La mujer y la ley*. Mexico City: Franco-Americana, 1921.

Wade, Peter. "Race and Nation in Latin America: An Anthropological View." In *Race and Nation in Modern Latin America*, edited by Nancy P. Appelbaum, Anne S. Macpherson, and Karin Alejandra Rosemblatt, 263–81. Chapel Hill: University of North Carolina Press, 2003.

Weiner, Myron. *The Child and the State in India: Child Labor and Education Policy in Comparative Perspective*. Princeton, NJ: Princeton University Press, 1991.

Wells, Allen. "Family Elites in a Boom-Bust Economy: The Molinas and the Peóns of Porfirian Yucatán." *Hispanic American Historical Review* 62, no. 2 (1982): 224–53.

Wilkie, James, Carlos Alberto Contreras, and Cristof Anders Weber, eds. *Statistical Abstract of Latin America*. Los Angeles: University of California, Latin American Center, 1993.

Wolf, Jacqueline H. "'Mercenary Hirelings' or 'A Great Blessing'? Doctors' and Mothers' Conflicted Perceptions of Wet Nurses and the Ramifications for Infant Feeding in Chicago, 1871–1961." *Journal of Social History* 33, no. 1 (1999): 97–120.

Zavala, Adriana. "De *Santa* a india bonita: Género, raza y modernidad en la Ciudad de México, 1921." In *Orden social e identidad de género: México, siglos XIX y XX*, edited by María Teresa Fernández Aceves, Carmen Ramos Escandón, and Susie S. Porter, 149–87. Mexico City: Centro de Investigaciones y Estudios Superiores en Antropología Social / Guadalajara: Universidad de Guadalajara, 2006.

Zelizer, Viviana A. *Pricing the Priceless Child: The Changing Social Value of Children*. Princeton, NJ: Princeton University Press, 1994.

Index

xxi; criticisms of women who failed to breast feed, 80–81; as fundamental duty of motherhood, 74, 79, 95; by poor women benefiting middle-class families, xxxvi; preventing return to workforce, 94. *See also* wet nurses and wet nursing

brokers, adoption, 62–63, 68

Bufete de Terapia Social (Bureau of Social Therapy), 235, 237

Bulnes, Francisco, 123

Calderón de la Barca, Fanny, 45–46, 86

Calles, Plutarcho Elías, 129–30, 260n30

Camacho, Miguel, 124

Campos, Pastor, 68

Cárdenas administration: politics of family, 127–28, 171–72; public welfare and economic nationalism, 232; social responsibility for children of urban poor, 214–15; solidarity with working class, 249

Carpio, Angel, 24, 53–54, 59, 65, 74

Carral, Francisco de Paulo, 32, 36, 65, 98

Carranza, Venustiano, *121*; on adoption, 221; assassination of, 129; on divorce, 105, 111; revised family code of, 114; social reforms of, 120–21, 123–24

Carrillo, Rafael, 97, 98, 136

Casa de Cuna, *168, 176, 234. See also* Casa de Niños Expósitos (Foundling Home)

Casa de Niños Expósitos (Foundling Home): education for domestic service, xix, 10, 15, 211; education for labor, xviii, 53–54; effects of revolution on, 120; history, 5–8; infant feeding reform, 84; infant mortality at, 165–71; as last resort for stressed families, 8,

31–32; in Porfiriato, 22–28; questionable adoptions from, 66–67; records for, xxxviii; regulations governing adoption, 45, 58; as resource for domestics with very young children, 204–5; retrieval of children from, xxii, 24, 31, 35; social geography of, 6; and village nursing system, xvii, 71–72. *See also* welfare institutions

Casa del Niño, 177. *See also* Hospicio de Niños (Children's Hospice)

Casian, Francisco L., 136

Castellanos, Luis, 18

Castellanos, Roberto, 16

Casteñada, Felicitas, 17

Castillo, Alfonso, 21

Castillo, Arturo del, 22

Castillo Najera, Francisco, 138

Catholic Church: and definition of family, 108; as enemy of divorce, 112–13; and midwife-assisted childbirth, 84; and Mother's Day celebrations, 147; removing influence of, xxiii, 109, 114; violator of principles of Mexican liberalism, 107. *See also* anticlericalism

Ceja, Teodora, 17

Centros de Higiene Infantil: condescending attitude of doctors in, 163; effect on community, 180; and "family houses" model, 171; medical inequality, 148–49, 151, 164; recommended regimen for infants, 167. *See also* maternal-child clinics

charity: preferable to state initiatives, 137–38; role of in Porfiriato, xxiii, 9; use of domestic service as, xxxv, 45, 48, 50, 61

Chávarri, Enrique (Juvenal), 79–80, 81, 83, 101

child abandonment: gulf between welfare officials and families, xvi; honor abandonment, xv, xxxi, 30, 68; as strategy in family crisis, xxii, 24–25, 31–32, 35, 184, 185; using lack of milk as reason for, 93–94

child circulation: across class lines, xxxii–xxxiii; definition, 4; and households without paternal presence, xxxii; and juvenile court, 219; in Porfiriato, 10–12; and wet nursing, xvii, 76. *See also* child labor; orphans

child development: changing understandings of, 11–12; and education of mothers, 126; influence of puericulture movement, 255; in juvenile court decisions, 211; in popular magazines, 85

child health crusade: and class differences, 138–39, 148; and collective responsibility for children, 131–34, 180–81

child labor: and adoption, xxxiv, 44, 221, 222; as cause of juvenile crime, 195, 216–17; changes in minimum age for employment, 191, 255, 289n25; and child-centered consciousness, 181; class distinctions in, 69, 189; as competition for adults, 255–56; as construction of childhood, xvi, xviii, 3; as contribution to household, 14, 186, 192, 198; criticisms of, xxvi; group adoptions as source of labor, 59, 60, 65; in Porfiriato, 14; and protected childhood, 210–14; in puericulture movement, 135; in reform period, xxiii, xxv, 190–91; social costs of, 219. *See also* adoption for labor

child labor legislation in 1917 Constitution, 115

child protection movement, 134–35. *See also* protected childhood

child support after divorce, 110

child welfare institutions. *See* welfare institutions

child-centered society, Mexico as, xxvi, 181, 193

childhood, concepts of: change in 1917 Constitution, 254; children as laborers, xvi, xviii, 3–4, 11, 17, 37, 254; dual construction of, 65; founded on health, 132, 181; in juvenile court decisions, 211; as realm of specialist, 178; under social security code, 254; and understanding of women's roles and labor, 222

childless adults and adoption, 231

children: community responsibility for, 130; as nonworking dependents, 256; obligations of support owed to family, 190; as representing relationship between society and the paternal state, 179; as social capital for middle class, 238; as stand-ins for working class, 180–81; as symbol of the masses, 172. *See also* family as model for national unity; obligations of support owed between parents and children

children's rights: to childhood without work in juvenile court decisions, 213; and formal adoption, 222; health equated with the nation and its future, xix, 132, 134; in revolutionary family law, 116; and state commitment to children, 26–27

church and state, separation of, xxiii, 106, 109, 127

Cículo de Amigos de Porfirio Díaz, 5

citizenship shaped by family relations, 107, 123–26, 128

Díaz Vda. de Cámara, Natalia, 60
Dirección de Beneficencia Pública (Directorate of Public Welfare), 9, 34–35
Dirección General de Beneficencia Pública, 224–25
disciplinary role of foundling home: gender differences in, 18–19; and placement in trade schools, 11; placement of problem inmates in domestic service, 53–54, 65; and younger children, 55
disease: associations with poverty, 86–87, 135–36, 148, 150; and criticism of wet-nursing, 72, 83–84, 85, 86–87. *See also* syphilis and venereal disease
divorce: favoring men, 118; implications for family, 109–10, 112–13; law governing, xxiii, 105–6; and negative view of serial unions, 196, 253
domestic labor, unpaid, as benefit to male workers, xxxv
domestic service by girls: dangers of for young girls, 195; as education for girls, xvii, 10, 15, 53–54, 211; and informal adoption, xviii; by older daughters, xxxvi, 186, 203–5, 207–10, 218, 220; as probation for juvenile offenders, xxxv, 197, 220; as safe and supervised work, 187–89, 208. *See also* adoption for labor; sexual abuse of domestic servants
domestic service by mothers: difficulties with very young children, 204–5; and emotional requirements of motherhood, 256–57; as family strategy, 203–10; pressure to relinquish children to employers, 246–47; role in social reproduction, xxvii, xli; and separation of families, 209–10, 237–38;

and use of welfare institutions, xxxiv; wages for, 15
domestic violence, 160–61, 202–3, 292n76. *See also* abuse of adoptees
domesticity: and adoption, 222; adoption petitions from women, 243–44; divide between spheres of home and work, 73, 220; as role for women, 232
Domínguez, Manuel: appointment as director of foundling home, 25–28; attempts to enforce adoption for creating heirs, 69; background, 22–23; on class of adoption applicant, 225; contradictory attitudes of, 65; on increased rates of admission, 34–35; on infant development, 85; on infant feeding, 80, 81, 96, 97, 98; and infant-feeding system, 74, 79, 88–89; on loss of poor parents' rights over children, 66; patterns of adoption under, 57–58, 61; social role of institution, 32; on village fostering for children of wet nurses, 90; on wet nursing, 84, 94–95
Domínguez Peón, José and Alfredo, 60, 61, 62, 64
double standard in application of medical diagnoses, 93–94
Duarte García, Leocadio, 61

economic pressures and admissions to foundling home, 32–33. *See also* family: strategies for holding together
education: children placed in Hospicio for, xviii; effect of child labor on school attendance, 14; gender differences in, 191–92; in hygiene in puericulture movement, 135; obligation of parents to provide, 211; state control of, xxiii, 114, 130, 189, 191; training for labor in welfare institutions, xviii, xxi, 53–54

education for boys, xvii, xviii, 10–11, 22, 191–92

education for girls: as domestics, xix, 10, 15, 53–54, 191–92, 211; training in professions not available to, 22

elites: and challenges to worldview, xxxviii–xxxix; and charitable practice, 6, 23, 45, 46, 48, 56, 137, 139; and contradictory ideals of childhood, xxii; and entitlement to family life, 39; and class prejudice, 27; influence of European culture on, xxxvi; and sympathy for motherless children, 37; and understanding of *compadrazgo*, 51. *See also* class; class differences; middle class

emotional bond of mother and child. *See* mother-child relationships

Enríquez de Rivera, Emilia, 134, 136, 138

entitlement to family life: and infant feeding, 99–102; in Porfiriato, 69; in press reports, 218; and public welfare policies, xxii, xxxv; and role of *compadres*, 31–32; for upper classes, 39, 74, 101, 250; for working classes, 31, 39

entitlement to medical care, 164, 180

entitlement to motherhood, 238–39

entitlement to social assistance, 258

Escuel Industrial de Huérfanos (Foundling Home), 10–11

Espinosa de los Reyes, Isidro, 135, 137, 159–63, 164

Espinoza, Eloisa, 124

Estrada, Ramón, 81, 85, 87

eugenics movement, 134–35, 142, 145–46, 235

Excélsior newspaper, 147

expósitos (foundlings): definitions of, xv–xvi, 25, 36–37; returned to parents, xxii, 24, 31–35, 66; role of *compadres* in retrieval of children, 29, 35–36

factionalism and concept of the family, 179

factory nurseries/day care, 91–93, 159

La Familia magazine, 51, 56, 82

family: centrality of children to in adoption petitions, 223; as contractual, affective, and moralizing, 107; determining suitable one for adoptions, 222; and honor abandonments, xv, xxxi, 30, 68; importance of family bonds, 117; modernization of, 108–9, 131; pathologies in conflated with poverty, 194; representing Mexican values, 175; role of work in, 194; strategies for holding together, xxii, 24, 31, 35, 184, 185, 203–10; threatened by divorce, 112–13

family as model for national unity, 126, 130, 131–34, 185

family formation: creation of by adoption, 52–53; founded on labor of girls and women, xix–xx; history of in Latin America, xxxi–xxxvii; as privilege of middle class, 39, 74, 101, 250. *See also* adoption for family formation

family houses. *See* group homes program

family law studies, xxix

family life: among the poor, 178–79; state interventions in, 189; and treatment of hospitalism, 165–66

family reform, 106–7, 123, 124, 128

family reunification, xxii, 24, 31–35, 66

family separation: as cause of juvenile delinquency, 194; children of single mothers, 17, 203; and domestic service by mothers, 209–10, 237–38; and wet nurses, 75–76, 88; women-headed households, 10, 192

family structure, 10, 12, 25, 194–95

heirs. *See* adoption for the creation of heirs

Higareda, Francisco, 23–24

El Hogar magazine, 140, 142, 145, 146–47

homeless children in press reports, 217–18

honor abandonments, xv, xxxi, 30, 68

Hospicio de Niños (Children's Hospice): adoption for domestic service, 47–48, 50, 54; adoptions to Yucatán, 64–65; and child as laborer, 4; and children as special social category, xxi; deficits of, 137–38; education for labor, xviii; effects of revolution on, 119–20; placement perceived by child as abandonment, 201–2; social geography of, 6. *See also* Casa del Niño; welfare institutions

Hospicio de Pobres (Poorhouse), 3–4, 8–10. *See also* Hospicio de Niños (Children's Hospice)

Hospital de Maternidad e Infancia, 30, 87

hospitalism, 168–69

Hoy magazine, 215–16

Huerta administration, 66–67, 106, 118

husbands of wet nurses, separation from, 75–76, 101

hygienic child rearing, xix, 147

illegitimate births: and abandonment of children, 57; and encouragement of marriage in lower classes, 110; and honor abandonments, xv, xxxi, 30, 68; outside legal protection of families, xxxi; rights to paternity suits, 111–12, 113, 116

El Imparcial newspaper, 42, 62, 83, 267n5

industrialization policy, 174, 252

infant feeding in foundling home, 73, 87, 88–89

infant feeding reform, 73–74

infant mortality: and artificial feeding, 74, 96–99, 100; attributed to moral flaws in parents, 150, 166; concerns about, 85–86; and development of children's medicine, xix; and family reform, xxv, 125; and hospitalism, 165–71; and regulation of wet nursing, 72–73, 86; and society's collective responsibility for children, 131

infants, adoption of. *See* adoption for family formation

infants' social environments and health officials, 154

infertility as reason for adoption, 45. *See also* adoption for family formation

informal economy: under federal labor laws, 190–92; marginality of, 252; role of children in, 187

informal unions (*amasiato*), 106, 111–12, 150, 160. *See also* marriage

inheritance. *See* adoption for the creation of heirs

insanity as bar to marriage, 135

Inspecciones Sanitarias (Health Stations), 139

international trends: child labor, 254; child protection and eugenics, 134; family codes in, xxiii–xxiv; government agencies for children, 137; infant mortality, 85–86; in public health and child development, 126, 127; wet nursing, 78–79, 86

interventions by public authorities, xxxii

interventions by social workers, 237

interventions by state, 189

interventions by visiting nurses, 160, 161–62

intimate relationships and parenting styles, 159

intimate relationships of families: interventions in, 133, 160–61; and parenting styles, 159. *See also* informal unions (*amasiato*); marriage

Jens, Federico Carlos, 51
Jiménez, Carlos, 158–59, 164
Juárez, Benito, 8–9
Jueves de Excélsior newspaper, 142–43, 145
justice for the poor and family morality, 112
Juvenal (Enrique Chávarri), 79–80, 81, 83, 101
juvenile court: in child circulation, 192–97; and child health crusade, 139; criticisms of, 215–17; difficulty of enforcing standards on child labor, 255; intervention in poor families, xxv, 183–84, 188, 230–31; and need for child labor in poor families, xxv–xxvi; and puericulture movement, 135; records of, xxxix–xl; support for poor families, xxxii, 219. *See also* Tribunal para Menores
juvenile delinquency, 27, 193–94, 215–16, 219

Key, Ellen, 134
kidnapping rings, 42, *43,* 44, 63, 64
kindergartens, 173

labor: and Cárdenas policy on children, 174; and meaning of family, 222; as reciprocal relationship, 252. *See also* adoption for labor
labor movement, 114, 191–92, 252
land reform, 114

legal codes as source of information, xxxix
Leo XIII, Pope, 136
Ley Federal del Trabajo (Federal Labor Law) (1931), 189, 191–92
Ley sobre Relaciones Familiares (Law of Family Relations), 114, 115–16, 221
liberal reforms: and changes in adoption law, 46–47; and Constitutionalists, 107, 109; family cycle under authority of secular state, 253; and Hospicio de Pobres, 8–9; and the individual, 145; and responsibility for the poor, xxiii; roots of revolutionary family, 180; and weakening of claims of illegitimate children, 49
Liceaga, Eduardo, 139
Lorenzana, Librardo, 55, 57
[Lorenzana], María Francisca Nicasia, 77
Lorenzana, María de Jesús Benita, 52–53
Lorenzana, Ricardo A., 42, 50, 65
Lorenzana as surname for foundlings, 25, 68, 240
Lorenzana y Buitrón, Francisco Antonio, 4
lower class. *See* working class

Madero administration, 66, 118, *119*
Madrigal, Carmen, 215
madrinas. See compadres and comadres (godparents)
magazines: on child development, 85; on class differences, 51; on entitlement to family life, 218; on hygienic child rearing, 140–47; on motherhood, 55–56; as source for views on family, xxxviii–xxxix. *See also* press reports and public opinion
male authority and sexual privilege: in

136, 146; and protected childhood, 179; and revolution, 102

single women as adopters, 223, 229–30, 238, 239–40, 242–43

social renewal, vision of family in, 126

social reproduction: role in shaping class identities, xxx; role of welfare institutions in providing labor force, xxxv; wet nursing as, xxvii

social responsibility for children: under Cárdenas, 214–15; and child health crusade, 131–34, 180–81; collective responsibility, 138; debates over, xxiv, 214–15; and formal adoption, 222; for foundlings, xvi. *See also* social security law

social security law (1943), xxi, xxvi, 251–52

social services: under Cárdenas, as right of people, 172–73; and child-centered consciousness, 181; need for, 158–59; role of in public health, 164–65. *See also* public welfare

social work training programs, 236–37

social workers: biases in, xl, 242–43, 246–47, 249; as gatekeepers, 236–37

Sociedad Protectora del Niño (Child Protection Society), 137–38

Solís Quiroga, Roberto, 195, 197, 219–20, 255

spiritual kin. See *compadrazgo* (godparenthood)

state paternalism: children as model for, 179; criticism of, 214; in divorce debates, 109–10; and expectation of work, 17; and ideal of protective father, xxvii; of national child health crusade, xxvi, 132–33, 137; and predominance of girls in Hospicio, 10, 20; protections for working women and children, 115; and revolutionary

continuity, 130. *See also* state role in family life

state responsibility to support the well-being of the community, 252

state role in family life: debates over, xxiv; as gatekeeper in adoptions, 223; powers to intervene in family life, 189; in social security code, 253. *See also* state paternalism

state-led social change in Constitution of 1917, xxiii

stepfathers, 113, 202–3, 209. *See also* fathers; paternal authority and responsibility

stepparents as cause of family dysfunction, 196

support networks for poor people: *compadres* as, 28–29, 32; difficulty of following medical advice, 157; information about wet nursing conditions, 93; neighbors in, 204–5; resources, xxxii; use of by mothers, 154; use of visiting nurses for community services, 161–62. See also *compadres and comadres* (godparents)

syphilis and venereal disease: as bar to marriage in family law of 1917, 135; as cause of infant mortality, 150; difficulty of treating, 156; fears of transmission by wet nurses, 83–84, 87; forbidding of marriage for people with, 116; not evident in baby contest winners, 142; as weakening Mexico's racial stock, 146; unexpectedly low incidence of among poor, 160

Tacuba as center of village nursing system, 75, 76

Tacuba as new location of foundling home, 99

Tagle, Francisco de P., 52
termination of adoptions, 60–62, 223, 231–32
Tlalnepantla as center of village nursing system, 75, 76
training for labor. *See* education
Tribunal para Menores: criticisms of, 215–17; role in child circulation, 192–97; role in domestic economies of working families, 188. *See also* juvenile court
Turner, John Kenneth, 64

El Universal newspaper, 139, 143, 148, 151
unmarried partners in social security code, 253

value of children: conflicting conceptions of, 44; and patterns of admission and retrieval from foundling home, 25
Vasconcelos, José, 145–46
Vázquez, María, 94
Velasco Ceballos, Rómulo, 148–51
venereal disease. *See* syphilis and venereal disease
Villa, Francisco "Pancho," 106–7, 110, 114, 119, 129
Villa de Buentello, Sofia, 118
village nursing system, 74–79; for children of wet nurses, 89, 90, 92; deaths of children in, 97–98; elimination of, 71–72, 87, 100; for wards of foundling homes, xvii, 87; as women's participation in economy, 75, 76. *See also* wet nurses and wet nursing
visiting nurses, 155, 159, 164, 180

water purification projects, 162
welfare assistance. *See* public welfare

welfare institutions: biases in enforcing adoption code, 255; centralization of, 72; children of working mothers in, xix; contrasted to private homes, 138; and development of citizenship, xvii–xviii; domestic servants as core clientele of, xxxiv; education for domestic service, xix, 53–54, 211; employees of as mothers with children, 31; expulsion from as factor in child circulation, 21–22; influence of maternal-child clinics on, 178–79; paternal role of, 18, 37; regulation of adoption by, 26, 49, 54–55; reorganization of, 133–34; as support for poor families, xxxii; as true homes under Cárdenas, 175. *See also* Casa de Niños Expósitos (Foundling Home); Hospicio de Niños (Children's Hospice)
wet nurse inspection service, 73, 74, 88, 89–91
wet nurses and wet nursing: attachment to their own children discouraged, 84; bonding with charges, 175; and boundaries between motherhood and paid work, 73, 95, 253–54; challenge to emotional relationship of mother and child, 84; commericalization of, 77, 79; controversy over, xxi; in family reform, 124–25; international trends, 78–79; as labor of social reproduction, xxvii; and media leche nursing, 76, 84, 95, 272n15; as mercenary for abandoning their own children, 72, 79; nursing their own children, 92, 94–95; performing central labor of motherhood, 101; in puericulture movement, 136; role in child circulation, xvii; separation from their own children, 73, 75–76, 81–82, 88, 95; sources of

wet nurses and wet nursing (*continued*)
information on, xli; vilification of, 72,
79–88, 136, 148; village fostering for
children of wet nurses, 89, 90, 92;
walk out during revolution, 120; wet
nurses participation in economy, 75;
as women's work, 71–72. *See also* village nursing system
woman suffrage, 114, 128
women: in child health crusade, 139;
debates over participation in public life during revolution, 108, 114;
defense of family during revolution,
119–20; emancipation of and divorce
law, 106; influence on public cultures
of childhood, 146; as overinfluenced
by church, 115; in private organizations, 138; in revolutionary army, 118,
279n54. *See also* mothers; women's
reproductive and domestic roles;
working women
women, dependence of: and divorce
debate, 106, 109–10, 113; and domestic
service, 210; evolving constructions of
maternal qualifications for adoption,
236; and foundling home policies, 39;
and predominance of girls in Hospicio, 10; in revolutionary family law, 116
women-headed households and likelihood of family separation, 10, 192
women's history studies, xxviii–xxix
women's reproductive and domestic
roles: and breast-feeding, 74, 79, 95;
challenged by male doctors, 87–88;
and class divisions, 87–88; contradictions in, 236; debate on, 146–47; in
revolutionary family law, 116; in social
security code, 253. *See also* domesticity; motherhood
women's sexuality: and boundaries

between legal and informal unions,
112; in divorce debates, 109–10; and
foundling homes, xvi, 19; and juvenile
court system, 188; and wet nursing,
82–83, 86–87
women's wages, declines in, 14–15
women's work: and changing nature of
childhood, 222; and child circulation,
100; and children's health campaign,
181; maternal qualifications for adoption, 236; protections for in 1917
Constitution, 115; and single women
as adopters, 242–43; as weakening
Mexico's racial stock, 146. *See also*
working women
workers' rights in 1917 Constitution, 115
working children. *See* child labor
working class: attitudes of professionals
toward, 135–36; bias against in adoption applications, 228–28, 244–45;
children as stand-ins for, 180–81; development of class identity, 119; fluid
patterns in family life, xxxi–xxxii;
interventions into intimate family relationships, 133, 160–61; marriage practices in, 110, 111–12; morality of, 146;
paternalistic relation of state to, 179;
public health officials understandings
of family life of, 154; reciprocal obligations and adoption, 222; reproductive
practices, 100; in revolution, 108; role
of welfare institutions in, 22. *See also*
poverty and poor people
working mothers: and attempt to protect
children, xix, 248–50; blamed for
youth crime, 195; both necessary and
suspect, in early 1920s, 132; contradictions between, 93–96; and daughters'
work, xxxvi, 186, 203–5, 207–10, 218,
220; difficulty of following medical

advice, 156–57; and disorganized homes, 195; equated with abandonment of babies, 81; and keeping her own children in village nursing system, 75–76; prejudices against, 100; programs for under Cárdenas, 173; protections for in constitution of 1917, 128; in puericulture movement, 136. *See also* working women

§ § §

To order or obtain more
information on these or other
University of Nebraska Press titles,
visit www.nebraskapress.unl.edu.